Lightwaves:
A Film Critic's Odyssey

Bill Thompson

Contents

Dedication	5
Foreword	7
Introduction	9
The Interviews	12
Theatrical Reviews	
a) English Language films	86
b) International films	204
Film Histories and the Oscars	242
Columns and Assorted Rants	306
Documentary reviews	332
Acknowledgements	354
Closing Notes	356

Copyright © 2023 by Bill Thompson
All rights reserved
ISBN: 978-1-7361264-2-4 (print)
ISBN: 978-1-7361264-3-1 (ebook)
Jacket and book design by Jules Bond

Dedicated to the memory of pioneering French filmmakers Louis (1864-1948) and Antoine (1862-1954) Lumière, inventors of the Cinématographe, and to Georges Méliès (1861–1938), French magician and visionary – who started it all.

Foreword

By Cara White

As a film publicist moving from New York City to Charleston almost 30 years ago, one of the most delightful surprises was meeting Bill Thompson, a film critic and writer for The Post & Courier. He not only reviewed films but wrote a weekly column of film news and interviews. If that wasn't enough, he was the book editor.

Little did I know then that we would become friends over the decades. Always debonaire, witty, and keenly observant, Bill, ever the journalist, asked probing questions. Having served as a sportswriter, film critic, book editor, and travel writer, he was well-read and well-traveled, with opinions backed by deep knowledge and experience.

Why read a book of reviews and interviews from the past? Because Bill Thompson wrote them. Reading this book is like having a trusted guide take you inside the world of each film, the vision of the director, or the mind of the interview subject. I saw many of the same movies as Bill, but not with his eyes. Bill's insights offer a new understanding and appreciation for the films and the director's achievement — or lack thereof. His curiosity and observation skills bring the movies to life for the reader. And now, even better, many of these titles are available for streaming, which wasn't possible when these reviews were written.

Working with Bill was a pleasure. He took his work seriously, did his homework, and was always fully prepared. And even more impressive, Bill wrote these reviews and interviews on deadline week after week after week as a professional and consummate newspaperman.

The period of time covered in this book — 1985-2010 — was a kind of Golden Age of cinema when independent and foreign-language films flourished in art houses across the country. Sadly, many of those theaters — and film critics — are now gone, depriving communities of vital local voices and places to share the experience of movies.

Like those arthouse theaters, Bill Thompson's film criticism is missed, but lucky for us, he has published this collection of his best work to re-read and savor.

Photo by Bill Thompson

Introduction

Movies are and always have been a snapshot of their age, a Cliff's Notes version of the life of an era with all its wonders and outrages, fads, fancies, and tragedies – all the things that compel our gaze.

As avid filmgoers, we love to talk about it. It was my privilege to have been a part of that conversation for two decades.

All in all, I reviewed close to 2,000 movies during 25 years as a film critic, 19 of them fulltime. I also enjoyed the good fortune of conducting hundreds of stimulating interviews with actors, directors, screenwriters, cinematographers, historians, and fellow writers on motion pictures while producing a regular weekly column of movie news, previews and commentary.

I also spent my fair share of time as an observer on movie sets.

The films represented here are but a small fraction of those I covered, though hopefully this collection does represent the best writing on film I had to offer.

Although much has been written and said about the dynamic, innovative energies of the 1960s and 1970s in film, the 25-year period between 1985-2010 – my years as a critic – was no less fertile, and perhaps more so.

The mid-'90s, in particular, saw the flowering of the American independent cinema and dramatic growth in the number of U.S. art house theaters. In turn, these developments heightened American appreciation of international filmmaking to a degree not seen since the heady days of Italian Neo-Realism, the French New Wave, German Expressionism and the post-war Japanese cinema.

North American audiences were introduced to extraordinary productions emerging from Canada, China, Spain, Russia, Cuba, India, the Czech Republic, Mexico and such South American hotspots as Argentina and Brazil.

Documentaries of great power and influence also flourished as never before, examining pressing issues in every corner of the planet.

The independent cinema did what its mainstream counterpart so often fails to do, make films of depth. As indy director David Veloz put it so succinctly, "The broader the audience you try to reach, the more diluted and homogenized the message."

Happily, the first decade of the 2000s produced at least 15 motion pictures of an extraordinary caliber, with independent features again showing the way. This quarter-century at the movies was a remarkable time.

Today, even as the standards for movies as art *and* cinema as entertainment have declined, the indies keep holding on by their fingernails.

Of course, as a journalist I was obliged to pay equal attention to mainstream movies, but enjoyed the freedom to focus on those I thought most accomplished or significant, not just the blockbusters.

Like any open-minded observer, I believe my tastes and expertise deepened and broadened over time, my skills became honed, and the work underscored the value of analyzing films and filmmakers from a point of view that evolved, and continues to do so.

Considering how often the movie industry turns to literature for fodder, I had the advantage of also being a book review editor and book critic during the same years I covered movies. I've always felt that a competent reviewer, whatever the arena, relates his or her field to the other arts and to the world from which they are drawn. Truth be told, making those connections was always part of the fun.

In 2000, roughly halfway through my tenure as the newspaper's film critic and columnist, I wrote the following: "Few things are as rewarding as writing about something for which you feel passion. Any critic worth his salt (or spleen) first must love the movies. Critics want movies to be the best they can be. We're disappointed when they're not. And it's our job to hold films to a higher standard. For without standards, there is no excellence."

While this might strike some as elitist, the reality is that the mass audience has never been a good barometer of quality; usually it's the reverse. And for all the talk about the appeal of the democratization of art, there is nothing "democratic" about art except the opportunity to produce it. Art cannot be democratized. Works of art – and artists – are invariably not equal.

But almost as bad as "reviewers" who never met a movie they didn't like is the self-consciously cerebral critic whose lofty tastes lead to disparaging everything but obtuse, justifiably obscure art pictures.

Traditionally, the role of a critic is not to reflect the popular taste, nor to hold it in contempt. Many, perhaps most, audiences go to movies just to be entertained. Nothing wrong with that. It's the same reason I go to baseball games, that and a love of the sport. But there are as many types of motion pictures with as many intents as there are categories and subjects.

Personally, even as a general audience member, I prefer films that entertain and enlighten. Or provoke.

How did I judge moves? Boil it all down, and it comes to this: Was there a genuine attempt at excellence? Even the most modest movie is worthy of craftsmanship. It can be made with care, with intelligence, with a certain interior logic, with wit and with feeling. If filmmakers are ambitious but happen to fall short, I tried to demonstrate how or why (in my view) they failed. Yet I also wanted to praise the attempt.

By contrast, it was when a director with all the resources at his or her disposal – hefty budget, good actors, skilled crew – got lazy and served up junk that I got rankled. It's a slap in the face to audiences. It says, in essence, "You're too stupid or undiscerning to know the difference."

I did my best never to get personal in a review, a reviewer's failing that's all too easy to succumb to. It should be about the work. But there are times when a skewering is both necessary and cathartic. I tried to avoid the cheap shot, no matter how tempting. The more I could rhapsodize about superb talents turning out memorable films and give empty $200-million heaps of garbage the dismissal they deserved, the longer I maintained my equanimity, and evaded the assumption that all critics are cynical clods.

Of course, critics of whatever stripe appear to be a dying breed. I lament that so few full-time newspaper critics are left: film, book, art or theater.

But enough carping.

Did I make mistakes? Heavens, yes. And sometimes, upon reflection, I didn't even agree with what I had written on deadline, with little opportunity to digest what I'd watched before having to review it. In daily journalism, that was the nature of the beast.

Repeat viewings almost always rendered additional or modifying impressions, things that one may have missed while feverishly taking notes. Sadly, there was no time to catch those, except at leisure.

I like to think that most of the time I managed to cut through and expose the hype, though sometimes I got caught up in it, too. Enthusiasm can be a double-edged sword.

I didn't mind when a reader called me to task. Difference of opinion is what makes for horse races. And I never, ever considered myself the Oracle. My goal was to take what I did seriously without taking myself too seriously in the process of doing it.

But I had a seriously good time. I hope you enjoy this look back as much as I did revisiting it.

Leslie Caron, courtesy of Plume/Penguin Books

— The Interviews —

The Interviews

I'll admit to having been a bit daunted when I first started doing interviews with famous movie and TV stars, despite the fact that as a sportswriter for 10 years I'd interviewed many of the great sports figures of the 1970s and 1980s, then later some of the most accomplished and celebrated literary lights of the day as a book critic.

Somehow the movie folk were different, not just because they tended to be more experienced and didn't always have scripted answers to questions (like far too many athletes), but because they seemed to be more diverse in background, style, temperament, worldliness, and sense of humor than the godlings of sports.

Most exemplified the sort of professionalism one respects and admires. Some were even appreciative of the fact that I'd done my homework and had come prepared. Others opened up to an almost embarrassing degree, trusting that you were courteous and principled enough not to print everything they said.

While I generally enjoyed the privilege of talking to the Big Stars, some of the most rewarding conversations were with gifted, versatile character actors free to be less concerned with image and fame than with their craft.

Happily in this movie age, some character actors ascend to character leads, at least now and then (Paul Giamatti and the late Philip Seymour Hoffman come to mind), not limited by beauty or handsomeness or screen presence. On the other hand, numerous one-time leading men and women segue to character parts because of age or diminishing box office or changing tastes, once their days of getting top billing are over. Often, they give more relaxed performances in support.

At Oscar time we see a slew of skilled supporting players fighting for a very few nominations, while the Best Actor and Best Actress categories often struggle to come up with five worthy nominees each. The supporting roles constitute the tightest and most competitive of all Academy Award categories. It's not just flavor they add to a film but depth and breadth, even if their roles seldom are as well-drawn as the leads.

What these roles may lack in being three-dimensional and well-rounded they compensate for with flavor, distinctiveness, verve, or the freedom to let it rip. As Janet Maslin wrote, "Good supporting roles command attention for their own merits and for placing leading characters in sharp relief." Many supporting roles serve a crucial, even defining, purpose in the narrative. Others allow an actor to steal the show (and some are expert at it) right out from under the titular star.

But let's not forget that, today, such talented character actors often have the starring roles in smaller, often more adventurous, films and television.

We lead with some of the bigger names in this chapter, but a sharp-eyed reader will be able to detect where, and with whom, my admiration lay.

John Travolta: 'Staying Alive' after all these years
November 4, 2001

ATLANTA – John Travolta slides onto a narrow couch and hugs a pillow to his belly. Trim and casually dressed, he looks a decade younger than his 47 years. His smile radiates the same inviting embrace he projects on screen.

Is he in character?

The manner is genial, forthcoming, as befits the man's off-screen reputation, even in an interview environment conducive to the softball question and scripted reply.

It's not always easy to tell when an actor is being himself, unalloyed, or when he is wearing a practiced public face, a protective armor that enables him to deal effectively with a not always sympathetic media, that shields him against unwanted intrusion but offends no one.

Cast a vote for genuine. Especially when it comes to the subject of his kids. Travolta, the father of a son, 9, and an 18-month-old daughter, is happy to report that the pressure's off his first born.

"She's getting along surprisingly well with her older brother," he beams. "The attention is off of him and onto this new scene-stealer, which is what she is."

But the pressure's never off a parent. Travolta & Co. deal with one of life's more painful quandaries in the thriller "Domestic Disturbance," about a divorced dad whose son, with great reluctance, is about to inherit a stepfather. A stepfather who also happens to be a killer.

The very idea of suffering the fate of the movie's protagonist, Frank Morrison, of the prospect of a stepfather raising his children, gives Travolta the quakes. The film may be a matter of amplified reality, but it's a potentially worst-case scenario that resonates with any parent.

"I think that's one vote for staying married, the fear of what would happen. It's your No. 1 anxiety. You don't even know that until you actually have your own children and experience the trials and tribulations. You wonder, `How would someone else deal with this?' `Do I trust someone else to deal with it?' You don't want anyone to even approach it."

Since his cinematic "rebirth" in Quentin Tarantino's "Pulp Fiction," Travolta's once faltering career has experienced a dramatic - and endlessly recounted - surge. Since 1994 he has savored the fruits of artistic and material success to such a degree that one wonders, does he ever have difficulty identifying with a character like Frank Morrison, someone just eking out a living?

"No, I'm proud to say, and I'll tell you why. I have a jones for the fellow. I really love people. I'm not an elitist. I will talk to anybody, anywhere, at any level. And I treat people with equal importance. Not equal value, but equal importance. A pilot in a plane is more valuable at that moment than the passengers. But he's not more important.

"I believe in that. I believe that everybody is equally important. But you have times where you're more valuable."

Audiences clearly have a love affair with Travolta as the hero, the figure they value most. Unlike many leading men, they've been almost as happy to accept him in darker roles ("Face/Off," "Broken Arrow"). If Travolta is willing to let people dislike a character of his, perhaps it's because he knows how much they like him.

But he was never concerned that people wouldn't accept him as a villain.

"My first film role, in Brian DePalma's `Carrie,' was as a villain. I was already a TV star on `Welcome Back Kotter,' and I was already what you might call a toy hoodlum. So I went from a toy hoodlum who was basically a good guy to suddenly playing a very wicked, misdirected kid. I thought, `I can do both.'

"I've got this wonderful gift of being able to perform in these various genres and various characters, and not only have the audiences accepted it, but the studios have bought into it. So they have offered me (roles as) the president, or as an angel, or a heroin addict, or a military officer. I have the luxury of doing everything they can imagine me doing. All I have to do is deliver the goods."

Travolta, eager to do another film with Tarantino, says he hears an insistent voice in the back of his mind — a nudge — to keep trying something different.

But one plum part Travolta passed on was the lead in James L. Brooks' "As Good As It Gets," which won an Oscar for Jack Nicholson as a misanthropic writer.

"I did not identify with the character. I didn't have a clue how to play that guy. I said, `Let someone else do it, because I can't figure it out. Jack did a great job, but even after I saw it, I was glad he did it and not me."

Following the explosive success of "Pulp Fiction" and "Get Shorty," vivid characterizations in small pictures such as "White Man's Burden" have been interspersed with largely conventional fare ("Michael," "Phenomenon"). There were accolades for Travolta's performances in the more demanding films "Primary Colors" and "A Civil Action," but of late his work has slowed to a profitable canter in such projects as "The General's Daughter" and "Lucky Numbers."

His pet project as an actor — producer, last year's "Battlefield Earth," may have been a critical and box office dud, but Travolta is philosophical - and can afford to be. As for having to take negative reviews with the positive, his is a practical approach.

"I hate to admit this, but I'm much more of a businessman about reviews. I ask, `What have we got as quotes?' And those are the ones I use (to promote). It's a survival activity. The ones that are negative I can't use to my advantage. I can only put time into the positive ones, the ones that are assets. I am a very highly paid actor, and the survival of my movies is important to me. Whether I'm producing or not, it's my duty to make sure they're marketing and promoting a film well."

The response is not yet in on "Domestic Disturbance," whose pacing reminds Travolta of the 1948 chiller "Sorry, Wrong Number," featuring one of his idols, Barbara Stanwyck. It was Stanwyck who chose newcomer Travolta to present her Oscar for career achievement in 1981.

"I love Barbara Stanwyck. She reminds me of my mother, a wonderful actress whose style was a cross between Stanwyck's and Joan Crawford's. I was surfing channels recently at 2 a.m. and caught the movie by accident. A thriller really takes you on a trip when it's done well, and this one was.

"Like that movie, `Domestic Disturbance' has a director (Harold Becker) who knows what he's doing and a strong cast."

Concerns that his previous film, the terrorist drama "Swordfish," might offend audiences sensitized after the events of Sept. 11, did not materialize. But studios remain jittery.

"That's true," says Travolta, who soon may be reunited with "Pulp Fiction" co-star Samuel L. Jackson in the feature "Basic."

"That's always been a wonderful thing about Hollywood that they get sensitive to social mores, and they need to. How long it lasts this time, I don't know. It all boils down to taste and discretion anyway. If you put `Goodfellas' in different hands than Scorsese's, or `Pulp Fiction' in different hands than Tarantino's, you have a different product. That's always the bottom line."

Since the destruction of the World Trade Center, there has been no end of entertainers and pro athletes who have declared how the tragedy has helped them put their careers in perspective. Travolta strikes one as somebody who managed a balance some time ago.

"I think I have. But (Sept. 11) has changed me personally, if not so much professionally. I feel very proud to be an American, very protective of our country and my family and friends. I feel appreciative of the freedoms and opportunities I have. I think I give it more value now than I did before."

Not one to revisit his movies, Travolta nonetheless reflects happily on individual scenes.

"The scene in `Pulp Fiction' with Uma (Thurman), I love it. It has a modern art feeling to it. The bench scene from `Saturday Night Fever.' Scenes from `Urban Cowboy.' The initial scene from `Michael.' There are scenes from each movie that are my favorites. I enjoy the memory of what it was like to do it and the memory of watching an audience respond to it.

"I get a kick out of myself on screen. Last week in California I had a 2-hour briefing, or debriefing, from former President Clinton on the terrorist bombings.

"But the first 20-30 minutes I was watching him and all I could think about was `God, I was good in "Primary Colors!"' It was overwhelming to me that I had captured him that well."

Yet, like any filmgoer, he wants to get lost in story and character.

"You forget that you're playing it, and you're just watching an actor in character doing their thing. If I can do that, if I can lose myself to the extent that I'm watching `another' actor that just happens to be me, I know it's working. I've nailed it. And that's exhilarating."

....

Jodie Foster: On child acting and staying true to a vision
May 21, 2000

Jodie Foster says that at least every six to eight weeks she has a career crisis. Minor tremors, compared to the real crises she's survived.

"I run through different things I could do. Like, I can do cappuccinos really well. Or, I speak French and I could be a French teacher somewhere. I run through my skills and I think, `Well, maybe it's not too late.' I think we all have this secret fantasy of doing something that's really meaningful and isn't about someone else's idea of what that meaningful is."

Meaning was irrelevant when Foster began her career at age 3 in a Coppertone ad, or when she became a sensation as a child actor in the mid-'70s with "Alice Doesn't Live Here Anymore" (1975) and "Taxi Driver" (1976).

But she probably knows more about the demands, and perils, of being a child star as anyone now working.

"The biggest moment in a child actor's life is when he or she realizes they no longer can play themselves. It hit me on `Taxi Driver' – like a bolt of lightning. I thought, `Oh my God, this is what my job is?' I had thought the job was kind of stupid. You know, be yourself and say the lines and when someone told you to do something, you'd do it.

"I'd played complicated characters before, but without any kind of consciousness at all. It was the first time anyone asked me to play someone that wasn't myself."

Foster is gratified that conditions have improved for child and teen actors over the past 15 years. She remembers only too well the ages 14-17, which Foster calls the worst years of her life.

"I think that now, if I had to go through it all over again, I don't think I would have gotten through it. I don't think I could go through that pain again. I don't feel that I have the strength to go through it. The only thing that got me through it before was how unconscious I was. You just took one step in front of the other without knowing where you're heading.

"From my perspective I think things are a lot better now, because our culture is better. I do remember some of the horror stories, like being in a commercial and being 4 or 5 years old and having the actor go, `Get that kid away from me!' Having directors blaming you for things you didn't do because it was easier to blame the kid. Or being constantly yelled at or just never feeling like you had the option to say no. Our culture's come a long way since then and we're not like that anymore."

Foster believes her new film "The Dangerous Lives of Altar Boys" will appeal greatly to today's kids — especially 14- or 15-year-old boys — who should find it refreshing to see a movie "that shows their lives in turmoil on the screen."

Arsenal of mischief

Subversion. It's a vital part of the adolescent boy's arsenal of mischief, as genetically ordained as awkwardness and confusion.

An indispensable quality, it is at the heart of "The Dangerous Lives of Altar Boys," an adaptation of the 1994 autobiographical novel by the late Chris Fuhrman about growing up Catholic in Savannah. Produced by Foster's Egg Pictures, the film is being shot now in Charleston and Wilmington, N.C., by British director Peter Care.

This darkly comic story, described as capturing "the anarchic joy and sublime intensity" of adolescence, follows the adventures — or misadventures — of eighth-graders Tim Sullivan (Kieran Culkin), Francis Doyle (Emile Hirsch) and their close-knit circle, all altar boys at a parish school, and all alike in various disrespects.

Such as for authority. Not least the forbidding Sister Assumpta (Foster), who confiscates an illicit comic strip drawn by the boys that showcases their heroic alter egos. They retaliate with an elaborate heist.

"Altar Boys" blends live-action footage with animation by the hugely popular Todd McFarlane of "Spawn" fame. The script is by Jeff Stockwell. Also starring are Vincent D'Onofrio (as Father Casey), Jena Malone as the troubled girl drawn to Doyle, and Saluda's own Tyler Long (as Joey).

Foster and her partner, Peabody Award-winning producer Meg LeFauve, are known for selecting their projects with great care. This one is no different.

"In all the films we make what guides our vision, in some ways, is that we look to do things that are kind of hard, that require a really personal touch," says Foster. "So that means we do less than most people. And I think the films we do usually have a lot to do with our own lives."

Egg Pictures was founded in 1992. It has generated such films as "Nell" (1994), "Home for the Holidays" (1995, with Foster directing), "The Baby Dance" (1997) and this year's "Waking the Dead." On "Altar Boys" Foster and LeFauve are working in association with producer and Fuhrman family friend Jay Shapiro of Cinema Go-Go, who has shepherded the project for three years.

"The studios are out there scouring all the books that are written with being movies in mind," adds LeFauve. "For an independent producer to schlep around a project for three years, as we have, is one thing. But some do it for six years. For 10 years. It really has to have something in there, for that person to emotionally have connected so deeply with it."

And that something may be truth, says Foster.

"So many things drew me to the story. But there's really only one answer for me and that is that it's really true. If you start from something you know is true and that you know is emotionally compelling — sort of a very connected place in your own life — then you can extrapolate from there."

Culkin, for one, is happy just to be playing a character that's not an appendage.

"It's a relief to do something this good," says the former child actor, now charting a transition to meatier roles in pictures like "Music of the Heart" and "The Cider House Rules." "For someone my age there's not much that comes around that's really this good. A lot of parts for our age are usually very small or very supportive. This movie is more about the kids."

Poignant tone

As with John Kennedy Toole, who died before seeing the publication of the Pulitzer Prize-winning "A Confederacy of Dunces," there is something inherently poignant about Fuhrman and his posthumously published novel. The writer was doing a final revision of "The Dangerous Lives of Altar Boys" when he died of cancer in 1991.

"I do feel a sense of it (Fuhrman's presence), without really having known him," says Care, whom Shapiro originally approached to direct. "We changed a lot from the book but I think that the spirit of Chris Fuhrman will come through. What I found most compelling about the book is its mixture of honesty and poetry. It's got this great feeling of humanity about it. The story is quite dark and some of it is satirical, sort of sick humor. But it also has this lyricism that I thought offered a great balance."

Care, taking his maiden voyage as a feature film director on the strength of success in documentaries, commercials and music videos, says he was drawn to the idea that the kids are trying not to conform but to find their own way in life.

Care also was drawn to the scale of the project, a modest production in feature terms, but a substantial increase for a man accustomed to pinch-penny budgets and skeleton crews.

Everyone knows video directors can do images, but can they do story?

Foster knew right away.

"Most videos are pretty to look at but don't mean anything," she says. "Peter has an amazing ability not just visually but in terms of character. There's no question that he and Jay picked Egg, not the other way around. They stuck it out. They had a consistent vision.

"To an extent you do movies for selfish reasons, to explore yourself. Then the best part is collaborating with a whole bunch of people who bring in new perspectives."

After all the fitful starts involved in getting a movie made, Foster says it's only on the second day of shooting that cast and crew realize "we're actually making this movie."

"It's a sense of finally having achieved something you've been dreaming about for a long time."

Southern comforts

Apart from the good-naturedly malicious chuckles one hears about Charleston doubling for Savannah, a competition of which the filmmakers were unaware, no concerted attempt is being made to render an intrinsically "Southern" movie.

"I always loved novels about the South that were much more inclusive about what the South is and yet show how it's very much part of the fabric of America," Foster adds. "What's great about Chris' novel is that it's also universal."

LeFauve suggests that the film is a conglomeration.

"There are parts of it that are autobiographical, but it is not actually supposed to be Chris Fuhrman's life. We're accenting the '70s, not necessarily trying to define a place or region. There was this very big debate about whether or not the characters should speak with distinct Southern accents."

Shapiro says there is a distinction between the film's animated realm and its real-world sequences. The live-action characters are focused and true. The confusion of adolescence is integral to the story.

"It's a tricky thing going from live action to animation," he says. "How do you translate the emotional content? For this film the animation is written independently of the script, which is much more real and in touch with what kids are really feeling."

Class act

Later this year, Foster will produce and direct "Flora Plum" (starring Russell Crowe and Claire Danes) for Touchstone Pictures. Egg has several other films in development, among them "Investigation," written by David Mamet and Paul Schrader, and a screen adaptation of the Margaret Atwood novel "Alias Grace."

Try as she might to project her young co-stars into the foreground, and to downplay her supporting role, the gravity brought to bear by Foster is unmistakable. Her reputation is that of being the classiest of class acts, a woman who radiates integrity and conviction on screen and off, but who occasionally makes for difficult casting.

"Jodie carries with her a level of quality but also a sensibility that is authentic and unafraid, yet responsible," says LeFauve.

Few filmmakers demonstrate such a sense of purpose or such devotion to the collaborative aspects of film. Not to suggest Foster is this oppressively serious person. Her hair-trigger wit and 10-candlepower smile make the actress almost instantly appealing. Steel in a velvet glove? Perhaps. But the steel seems eminently flexible.

And she surrounds herself with talented, equally committed people, not least the younger cast.

"It's exciting for me because I was a child actor," Foster says. "I love working with kids.

Always have. You can't bribe them to do things. You can't make them do things that aren't like them. There's never, or very rarely, alternative motives for their choices, like you get with adults. So for me there's a real purity working with kids."

Sister Assumpta marks the two-time Oscar winning actress' first nun. And since her character is seen through the eyes of the boys, expect some variation on the harsh Mother Superior type.

"Oh sure, there's a little caricature in all of this. It's their story, so it colors how we see things. For me, it's been great working with animation. All the longing and everything that's inside these boys is brought out in this crazy, wild, expressive way, even though they may not understand it all consciously.

"Their characters are in the midst of a turmoil they don't understand. The reflection of the reality is very different from reality. So the nun you see on screen will be very different from the animation."

Foster did her customary research before tackling the role, spending time with nuns and realizing how diminished their numbers have become, but encountering "happy, genuinely joyful people."

Yet Foster's portrait, convincing as usual, may have been a bit too on the mark for Culkin.

"I went to Catholic school for the first, second and third grades, and my memory of the nuns is that they were scary. When Jodie appeared for the first time in the nun's habit, chills went up my spine."

....

Charlton Heston: Looking back on '50 Years in American Film'
October 18, 1998

After all the costume epics, the westerns, the Shakespearean plays, after 50 years of work on television, stage and screen, Charlton Heston – ever the heroic figure – pursues a single remaining grail.

"My goal in life is to get it perfect, just one time."

At 74, Heston still is a man of undeniable presence. Stumping for his latest book, "Charlton Heston's Hollywood: 50 Years in American Film" (GT Publishing), the actor who defined the stalwart protagonist of post-1950 historical dramas is looking back on each stage of a remarkable career.

And still hoping for that one flawless performance.

Heston collaborated with Jean-Pierre Isbouts in writing the book, which explores this enduring star's films in the context of Hollywood's evolution, beginning with his early days as a struggling Broadway actor and his breakthrough in live TV of the late '40s, through to the signature movies – "The Ten Commandments," "Ben-Hur," "El Cid" and beyond.

Also chronicled, in modest fashion, is Heston's public service, including his marches with Martin Luther King, his tour of Vietnam, his leadership within the Screen Actors Guild and the American Film Institute, as well as his efforts on behalf of film preservation.

But the work's the thing for any actor. So what stands out?

"You remember, and regard highly, different films for different reasons, "he says. "For instance, I'm very proud of the fact that I've made more Shakespearean films than any other American actor, performances on the stage aside. And the fact that I have done more films about significant historical figures – about a dozen, I think – than any American actor I know of.

"The great men are more interesting than the rest of us, really, and I have had the great good fortune to play presidents and generals, geniuses and tyrants, kings and cardinals. And then I've had my shot to work with any number of great directors and very fine actors and actresses."

The Shakespearean roles mean the most, he says, because they are the best parts. Most recently, Heston starred as the Player King in Kenneth Branagh's four-hour, full-length film rendition of "Hamlet."

"These plays are the measuring stick of an actor's work and what I remember and value most of my own work. It's surprising to me that there are so many fine American film actors who never have done a stage play at all, ever. Of the ones that have, almost all have never done Shakespeare, which stuns me."

Biblical epics and the occasional war story aside, the historical rigor and authenticity Heston brought to many period characterizations was decidedly at odds with Hollywood's general preference for hokum. And continues to be. Not that Heston hasn't played romanticized heroes. But his Gen. Charles Gordon in "Khartoum," the Medieval knight of "The War Lord," the emotionally complex cowboy of "Will Penny" and his superbly observed Cardinal Richelieu in "The Three Musketeers" bespeak an actor who cares about fully fleshed characters.

"I value very much the chance I've had to play so many significant historical figures. If you're playing someone of this stature, you've got to be honest. You've got to find out as much about him as you can. Usually, it's hard to find much that he wrote himself. But you can read the biographies and the history of the period and end up knowing him as well as possible."

Heston also believes he has played more different nationalities than any other American actor, including Anthony Quinn. The most unlikely may have been his Mexican police inspector in "Touch of Evil," the recently restored and rereleased classic by Orson Welles.

"We're all very happy about that (the release)," says Heston, born Oct. 4, 1924, in St. Helen, Mich., where he retains 1,200 acres of timberland. "I think the (revised) version is very close to what I imagine Orson had in mind.

"After he finished his first cut, he left the picture for a few weeks, which of course is a terrible idea. It disqualified him from finishing the film as he wanted to. But he went to Mexico to try to raise money for a film of `Don Quixote' with me. A fine idea but too bad that it resulted in this conflict with the studio.

"All the sound has been redubbed for the entire film and enhanced. `Touch of Evil' is not a great film; it is unquestionably, however, the finest `B' movie ever made."

The original legend surrounding the picture was that Heston, fresh from "The Ten Commandments," took scale pay just for the privilege of working with Welles. Heston, however, says that when he was approached to do the film it had no director. Welles was signed on to play the heavy, and that was all. It was Heston who suggested to the studio that Welles also direct.

"One of my main contributions to American film is that I `bullied' Universal Studios into hiring Orson Welles to direct `Touch of Evil.' "

Though revered by two generations of filmgoers, Heston has weathered criticism that his principal talent was handsomeness, that his acting style, like that of contemporary Gregory Peck, is "stiff" and "inexpressive," that his skills were used to far better effect in such pictures as "55 Days in Peking" than in playing Moses, Mark Antony or Andrew Jackson.

Heston's book gives these critiques a verbal shrug. You do your best and move on, he seems to say. The writing is modest and self-effacing. And the book is enlivened with more than 150 color and black-and-white photos and 50 sketches from the sets of his films, drawn by the actor himself. The text consists largely of Heston's revised journal entries and interviews by Isbouts, who also wrote and produced Heston's "Voyage Through the Bible" on CD-ROM in 1995.

"I took materials I had rethought and had opinions on and wrote a lot of it down, and we taped some of it. Some of my taped interviews are in quotes. And Jean-Pierre himself is knowledgeable about films and was able to give a third-person perspective, which was important I think."

Heston started keeping journals in the mid-'50s, mainly for technical purposes.

"When you talk about the people who work regularly, the film community is actually quite small. Maybe 200-300 people: actors, directors, writers and so on. After you've made 15 films or so, you find yourself working with people you worked with before, and I thought it would be useful to keep track of how it was to work with, say, this cameraman on one picture - in case we would be working with him on another. I would write down day-to-day entries about the work. And it has been very useful for me."

Heston, who next stars with Warren Beatty in the film "Town and Country," credits his longevity to an instinct for survival, to the good luck of having worked with great directors and having learned something from each.

"Of course, I've also gotten some marvelous parts."

Unlike many an actor, Heston insists making movies is not fun. It's hard work. Like Dorothy Parker, who once opined, "I hate writing; I love having written," Heston says the fun part of a movie is having made it.

"Anyway, it isn't supposed to be fun for us. It's supposed to be fun for you guys looking at it. It's my life; I'd do it free if they'd feed me. But this notion of fun on the set is a misconception people have."

Heston has directed films infrequently but enjoys the occasional exercise of different muscles.

"As an actor you may make a significant contribution to a movie. But the director is the real author of the film. I like directing. My problem is, I like acting a little bit more. I do feel as comfortable behind the camera, but to direct a picture takes at least a full year to do all the work. The shooting of it takes three or four months at most. I don't want to give that much time up where I don't get to act.

"Also, I want to find a good part in every film I direct, and that's hard to do. But I like directing, and I admire the people who do it."

Not least his son, Fraser, with whom he has worked on several projects, beginning with the adventure movie "Mother Lode" in 1982.

"He's making a movie now, but I don't think there's anything for me in it. He doesn't offer me work all the time, by any means."

On the other hand, the filmmaker son offers the actor father useful criticism from time to time.

"Both my son and my wife are well-equipped to tell me where I went wrong in a performance. You can always find any number of people to tell you how wonderful you are. What you need are people to tell you how you goofed."

....

Barbra Streisand: Film's Grand Dame reconciles her past.
December 22, 1991

She has been lionized and reviled, called Barbra Strident, worshipped by the gay subculture and dismissed as the most pretentious woman the screen has known. She is that one overpowering talent critics feel obliged to genuflect before, or pelt with invective.

Whatever you may think about her, Barbra Streisand remains an icon, a Diva, the Grand Dame of American entertainment who laid the Platinum Brick Road for Bette Midler and Madonna.

Her image is larger than life. So, it would seem, is her vulnerability.

You expect to be confronted with this imposing, perhaps even abrasive creature. After all, she is the Difficult One, or so it is said. But close up, the ego does not seem so colossal.

Startlingly, your first impression is one of fragility. You want to protect her. It is a moment of incongruity.

Streisand cares intensely about "The Prince of Tides," as director, actress and as a woman born into a dysfunctional family. It is this and this alone that has propelled her to the interview table.

"I've been in the business for 30 years and I've never done a press conference like this. But I wanted to help my movie and give it the best possible shot."

Dressed entirely in smart but funereal black, Streisand looks 10, not 15, years younger than her age, a few hundred days shy of 50.

She is talking about coming to terms with the past, about not dispensing blame. There is a line from "The Prince of Tides": "There is no crime above forgiveness in families." Streisand believes it utterly.

"The quality that drew me to the book was its treatment of the traumas of childhood and how they affect us as adults, how we lead lives that could be much, much fuller if we only have the courage to go back there end face that pain.

"We must realize we are adults now and can deal with the pain. As a child you can't deal with it. You're impotent; you're not articulate. You're dealing with powerful parents and you accept the myths and opinions they have about you. They establish roles for you and you grow up playing out your role unless you really get conscious of the fact that, 'Hey, I'm not the ugly duckling or the bad kid or the weird one. I came into the world pure. I'm OK and I deserve to be happy."

A wounded childhood can be h healed, she says, adding: "To journey into the past is the only way forward." The ultimate goal is to live in the present, but the only way to do that is by conquering, by healing, the past.

"A child is destined to live out the unresolved problems of his parents, which is why you're like your mother or father even if you don't want to be. You have to break those patterns and the way to do that is by having the distance of consciousness that comes with being a genuine adult, knowing you can handle the pain.

"It's so hard to change. But doing this self-exploration, I know, has helped me forgive and has made me a better person. I'm at a pointing my life where I can live with the truth."

It certainly has made her more resilient.

When Pat Conroy's book initially was pushed as prospective film material, almost every major studio but TriStar (Columbia) Pictures gave it the deep six. Robert Redford reportedly had been involved in the early stages as producer, before backing out. Streisand picked up the torch and finished the race. But it required three years.

"I remember my first encounter with the book. A friend of mine kept reading passages to me from the book and I found them so striking I finally bought it. It knocked me out. I just knew I had to make that movie."

Her brow furrows as she attempts to answer a question about a specific technique.

"Two months ago when I was dubbing the film I could tell you every line. But it's a little hard for me to talk about the film, because after I do something I sort of forget it and we finished it last year. I'd have to go back and see it again to remember what I did.

"It's, like, I'm on to something new. That's one of the reasons why I don't sing live anymore, because people always want to hear me sing my same old songs and I can't stand to sing them. I bore myself. I always need new things to inspire me."

Until the soundtrack album for "The Prince of Tides," composed by then-flame James Newton Howard (exit James, enter actor Liam Neeson), Streisand had not sung for more than two years. Other than some last-minute remastering, her involvement in this fall's four-CD career compendium, "Just for the Record," was simply to select the cuts.

"I never sing." Not even in the shower?

"Never. If a year from now I feel like singing, I'll do it in the recording studio. Live performance is a major challenge. I don't know if I have the courage to get up in front of all those people and sing."

Acting and direction have her undivided professional attention.

Streisand's character of psychiatrist Dr. Susan Lowenstein in "Tides," her first film role since 1987's "Nuts" has been changed from a pivotal but secondary character in the book to a centerpiece of the film. She has been accused of padding her character for vanity's sake.

That's the image. But Streisand says that when she produces and directs, as well as acts, the "star" dissolves.

"Actually, I don't consider the star. She doesn't exist for me. The star would have her scenes shot early in the day's shooting schedule so she looks her best. I didn't do that.

"As a child, I longed to be the best, to be famous. But stardom didn't sit well with me. It drove me into analysis. It gave me psychosomatic illnesses. It was tough living up to other people's expectations. Today I'm a worker. I find it interesting to absolutely throw away the star."

Several of Streisand's cast members claim to have been a bit ill at ease about doing screen tests for her as director. Again, the Reputation.

"The idea of reading for Barbra was terrifying initially," says Blyth Dinner, who plays Sallie Wingo. "But she was so accessible and human from the moment you walked into the door that you forgot about that. It was great being directed by her. She understands the fragility of all actors, being an actor herself."

Warren Beatty had been interested in playing the role of Tom Wingo, but couldn't commit, which left the door open for Nick Nolte.

"I knew he was right for the part. Nick, probably above all the other actors who read, was the one who allowed himself to be the most vulnerable and be macho at the same time. And Nick is very male. Viewing his other films, I had never seen this ability of his to be a romantic leading man. He's much more comfortable playing character roles."

What comes naturally to Nolte, Streisand must insinuate into. She may be willing to lose herself in a character part, but will her public accept it? Try as she might to dispel her, the Diva remains, even basic black.

"I love a paradox; things that are true and yet seem opposite."

Including herself.

....

Mighty Mel
May 21, 1995

ATLANTA - Child's play it wasn't, but for Mel Gibson, producing, directing, and starring in the medieval epic "Braveheart" was very much a case of adolescent wish fulfillment.

"It's the film I always wanted to see when I was a kid. And never saw," says Gibson, fairly collapsing into a chair in a meeting room of the Ritz-Carlton. "When I read Randy Wallace's script I thought maybe this was it. So then I went about making it exactly what I'd wanted to see."

Having shed his camera-ready threads in favor of an old blue jacket, stripped shirt and jeans, Gibson ignites that 10-candle-power smile, turns on the azure eyes and invites his questioner in, however briefly.

Though drained by his promotional tour for the picture, which chronicles the 13th-century revolt against England by legendary Scots hero William Wallace, Gibson quickly warms to the subject of his character and the demands of making an old-fashioned historical romance.

He says the idea of choreographing vast battle sequences with thousands of howling warriors was a thrilling prospect to an emerging director as well as to his "inner child."

"Oh, it was exciting! Definitely exciting. Because in preparation I'd watched a lot of battle films, films I really admired. You name it, I saw it. I watched them again to really examine how their battles were constructed. And I found that most of them, even the good ones, weren't very clear as to what was happening. It also wasn't an `experience.' They didn't really investigate a battle from within. They sort of looked at it from a distance. And they didn't have the impact we wanted."

One that did, and which Gibson found highly influential, was Orson Welles' 1967 Falstaffian tale, "Chimes at Midnight."

"It had a terrific battle sequence in black and white. The movie was ahead of its time, and he used devices like speed changes and odd-frame cuts, which gave it a kind of reality and shock value. And if you examine our film closely, you'll say `Hey, look at all the jump cuts! There's hundreds of them.' "

Gibson says one of the reasons most epic films made in the '50s and early '60 failed to have impact was that the violence is sanitized. "Braveheart" may not reflect the full horror of battlefield carnage, but no one will accuse the picture of sterility.

"I don't think what you see in the movie is gratuitous violence. It may be excessive, but also appropriate to the subject matter. The scene where Wallace is being tortured is probably the most horrible scene in the film, so it also had to be the most beautiful scene in the film. I wasn't about to show you entrails or heads being struck off. It was all slowed down and lyrical. The depiction had to be lyrical to take away from the horror.

"And we didn't linger on stuff (in the battle sequences). I think the real thing was much worse than that. I knew where it could go to. In fact, I filmed where it could go to, but I didn't necessarily use it all."

Gibson jokes that if a director's cut of the picture ever is released, it will be only "for really twisted people."

"My assistant made a gag reel – literally – of all the most heinous moments, but set it to all three verses of `These Are a Few of My Favorite Things.' You can't do anything else but laugh because it is so over the top. What I wanted to do was push the envelope but not open it."

"Braveheart" is in many respects not simply an epic spectacle, but an attempt at genuine medieval drama on the order of Franklin Schaffner's "The War Lord" (1965). Gibson says that, insofar as possible, he wanted the movie to reflect genuine medieval sensibilities as well as an authentic medieval look.

Real sentiments

"Even though the dialogue, the language, wouldn't have been quite what you hear on screen, the sentiments behind it suggest what I feel (the people) of that time were like - in a very broad way. You have a main character who is able to regard life in a manner quite different from the way people do now.

"A lot of it is historically accurate, but not right down to the letter. You can even have historical accuracies like the battle of Stirling, which actually occurred and the outcome was the same. Wallace was outnumbered 10,000 men to 2,000, and he won. But the (screen) battle itself didn't resemble the real one. It was devised for cinematic purposes. It was actually called the Battle of Stirling Bridge, though you'll note there's no bridge in our movie, because it just wasn't as exciting."

Gibson candidly admits he was unfamiliar with Wallace before making the film. He knew him "only in a drinking sense," as a frequenter of a suburban Sydney pub in the William Wallace Hotel.

But the historical man, whose exploits have been embellished in almost mythic tales, came to exert a powerful hold on the actor.

"I kind of felt like I got invaded by William. Here was a man who died by the time he was 35. But he achieved so much. And he started all this at 17 or 18 - one of those guys. Like (King) Edward I of England, who he fought to win Scotland's freedom, Wallace could be a monster in the battlefield. He did some terrible things.

"By the same token, he was very educated. He spoke five languages. he didn't do anything corrupt. He was offered money, land, even a crown. And refused it all. He was completely uncompromising in his quest. I tried to find out what his motives were. I read a ton of books, and what it all amounted to is that he wanted to be free. He was on fire, and he was very persuasive, very magnetic. Wallace was successful for a time, for 17 years in fact. We've condensed it."

After reading the initial script, Gibson put it away for a year, focusing on other projects for his Icon Productions Co., including his directorial debut in "The Man Without a Face." Wallace haunted him throughout.

"It (the story) crawled in some place and started whirring around in my empty brain. Before you go to sleep at night you start planning shots. I began to shoot the film in my mind. I've never read anything that affected me quite that much, where I felt I had to start constructing scenes - like the guy building a mountain of mashed potatoes (Richard Dreyfus in "Close Encounters") in the middle of his table. I felt I had to tell the story quite desperately. It was a possession of sorts."

It was also an experience he'd like to repeat, absorption and all.

"Oh, yeah. It was wonderful. I really loved it. I make it sound like hardship, but it was really a ball for me."

Apart from Gibson and Patrick McGoohan (Edward I), famed for the spies he created in a pair of successful TV series, "Braveheart" is noticeably lacking in "name" co-stars. For good reason.

"I figured one prima donna was enough," says Gibson, who may star in a theatrical version of McGoohan's "The Prisoner." "For me it was just a question of getting really great people, which I think I got. As the producer, there was no pressure to sign Julia Roberts, for example, for a lead role. Not that she wouldn't have been good in the part. And she's bankable.

"But you succumb to some of these things: I put myself in it. I was really the only one who brought any baggage to the movie. But it gives you credibility with the studios, and makes them take their claws off the cash and let you have it, because they'll anticipate they have a better chance of getting it back."

As serious as Gibson is about making entertaining pictures, he has an equally well-earned reputation for lightheartedness and on-set mischief. Just ask anyone subjected to his practical jokes. "Braveheart" offered pranksters unusually ripe opportunities.

"We had a lot of fun on the set. But you can't really schedule extracurricular stuff that. It's just evolves, and you do it as they become available. A practical joke is based on making people believe the worst, or finding out their greatest fear is and then playing on it. Which sounds kind of cruel. But there are degrees. You have to do it to the point where they don't get an ulcer. If it is too bad, put them out of their misery quick. The same applies to a joke played on me. I may go eight feet in the air, but I'll at least enjoy it."

Frequently, Gibson isn't the only kid on the set. His own children, ages 5 to 14, are regular visitors.

"Oh, yeah, all the time. They like to come on the set; it's a big treat. I like to horse around with them, and they get a big kick out of it. Like I was when I was a kid, they'll try anything. Maybe more than I would. Between scenes on `Braveheart' they had fun trying out some of the prop weapons, bonking each other over the head. That's when they're not bonking me."

And should his kids get bitten by the acting bug?

"It would be all right. If they really wanted to do it. At the proper age. Certain things have to be gotten out of the way first. Like a high school education. I keep them away from it right now. I mean, they'd like to do it. Most kids would because it seems like a wild idea. They might go through the whole thing with no problem. But there's more of a chance that they'll get damaged."

Gibson was equally concerned about damage to his cast and crew, given the perils of shooting battle scenes. Safety was a paramount concern, and for the actor-director, the technical demands made for an altogether different learning experience.

....

Leslie Caron: Film star recalls her struggles, successes
December 20, 2009

Leslie Caron knew that fame, like happiness, can be fleeting. She did not foresee that the renown she had enjoyed might not last a lifetime.

She was mistaken, of course.

Though producers and casting directors did not come courting as often once the actress reached her 50s, audiences well-remembered the elfin French gamine who enchanted filmgoers as the star of "An American in Paris" (1951), "Lili" (1953) and "Gigi" (1958), then won respect as a dramatic actress for her Oscar-nominated performance in "The L-Shaped Room."

Caron, also nominated for an Academy Award for "Lili," was aware of the fact that not all film stars are destined for immortality. But at the time, the sense of being yesterday's star was one more blow to her feelings of self-worth.

"It was not about fame having consumed me," says Caron. "I was never that way. I had never counted on enduring fame. Wait, that's not quite true. I did not think fame would disappear during my lifetime. I thought it was achieved for good. When I became 50 (in

1981), those years were naturally ones where parts were not being offered. Yet I was quite surprised. The idea of being forgotten during one's lifetime was difficult to imagine."

When she saw that a print of "Gigi" had deteriorated badly, it only compounded her distress.

"I thought, 'This film, too, is ruined, and gone, within my lifetime.' What a shock that was. Fortunately, it was rescued and new prints were made. These experiences were part of the reason I suffered a breakdown."

Yet Caron recovered, professionally as well as emotionally, a passage chronicled in her otherwise optimistic, gracefully written memoir, "Thank Heaven" (Viking).

Step lively!

Beginning as a dancer with the Ballets des Champs Elysees in Paris, where she was "discovered" by Gene Kelly, then wowing 'em in classic MGM musicals such as Kelly's "An American in Paris," Caron rivaled Audrey Hepburn as the darling of Hollywood's European imports of the '50s. In her insightful memoir, which draws its title from the song Maurice Chevalier performed in "Gigi," "Thank Heaven" (For Little Girls)," Caron offers an unsentimental and candid recollection of her life in and out of entertainment. She dissects her three marriages, one of them to British theater director Peter Hall, with whom she had two children, and recalls with some amusement her then-"scandalous" affair with America's most eligible bachelor, Warren Beatty.

While she is generous to such co-stars as Kelly, Cary Grant and Fred Astaire, and diplomatic about other colleagues, she is invariably frank about herself.

Today, with a new generation of audiences having seen her in such pictures as "Le Divorce" and "Chocolat," Caron, who won an Emmy Award in 2007 for her work on "Law & Order: Special Victims Unit," finds her early movies on TV with great frequency. Most of her time now is devoted to operating her hotel in Paris, but she maintains dual citizenship. Few realize that Caron's mother was American, a gifted dancer who hailed from Topeka, Kan.

Curiously, she is more likely to be recognized in the U.S. than in France.

"The place where I am really incognito is in my own country," she says. "In Paris, every now and then someone will recognize me. But that is not common. My films are not discussed, and I am not asked to do any films. It's total anonymity."

Illumination

Revisiting the signposts of her life was, in some instances, as illuminating for her as for the reader.

"It was very surprising, believe it or not, because when I started to put it all together, I thought, 'Well, after all, I am a professional actress,' which I kept doubting throughout my life. I kept telling myself I was not really an actress, but a would-be dancer who never quite made it.

"Years ago, I kept thinking, 'Oh, well, I'll do better next time.' Then finally, when I had a look at a few of those films in order to write about them, I was surprised at how well I thought I had done."

Caron was physically fearless, a tireless worker, but emotionally uncertain. Confidence was a commodity she did not possess in great supply – a legacy of her relationship with her mother. The best foundation a person can have for later in life is the knowledge in childhood that one is well-loved, to have parents who are firm but encouraging. Margaret Petit Caron was not of this bent. And her daughter, growing up in war-torn Paris, felt alienated from the French and Americans alike. Even after winning success in Hollywood, she struggled with insecurity.

"I think I did suffer from her lack of encouragement. With her, whatever I did, it was all right, but not quite good enough. I never seemed to reach a point where she thought it was good enough. I'm not the only artist to have faced that, of course. It was the opposite of a motivating influence. I needed encouragement and did not get it."

These deficits certainly influenced Caron's own parenting approach with her children. "I used the opposite technique from my mother. I said to them, 'You can do it, you're good at this.' "

Fretting's fruits

To this day, she remains something of a perfectionist, a trait reinforced by working so closely with such legendary worriers and perfectionists as Kelly, Astaire and Grant.

"All three were worriers, and all three worked very, very hard. You cannot attain that level of accomplishment otherwise."

Yet one of Caron's most relaxed and appealing performances was opposite producer-star Grant in 1964's "Father Goose," essentially an update of "The African Queen" and quite a segue from the demands of "The L-Shaped Room."

"Cary told me he wanted me in the picture because he liked me in 'The L-Shaped Room,' which was rather surprising. But I have terrific memories of making that film and the wonderful villa we were given during shooting (in Jamaica). I wish it had been a bigger hit for Cary, though. His fans did not like seeing him as a character who was unkempt and scruffy."

Apart from playing cowboys and Indians with her older brother in their youth and doting on American movies, Caron did not feel part of two worlds growing up despite having an American mom.

"Not growing up, no. But after having my Hollywood life and career, I really did feel that way," says Caron, who has never made a pilgrimage to Topeka. "Eventually, I decided to take American citizenship. I am really very pleased to have done so because America gave me so much. I am immensely affectionate toward America."

Assessments

What features of her life and career afford her the most satisfaction?

"In life, the fact that I have two children and two grandchildren. As for movies – the honest truth – the fact that my film career has brought me many good friends."

Yet there is also a sense of wistfulness.

"I think I could have done better. Your eyes open more and more as you get older. You acquire more knowledge, which is a very good thing. I'm not at all jaded, but I think I should have been more daring. And I should have learned that more quickly. I refused a lot of opportunities because I believed I could not have done the role or I would have been miscast.

"I was quite wrong about casting and my capability. It was a lack of faith in myself and a lack of courage. When I see Meryl Streep singing and dancing in 'Mamma Mia!' I realized there is so much I refused because I thought, 'This is out of my range.' I doubt Meryl ever thinks that. I refused a film with Clark Gable, if you can believe it. I refused to make 'Les Girls' with the great director George Cukor, and I even refused a film with Gregory Peck. How silly."

....

Hal Holbrook: A Passion for playing Twain
October 9, 2011

Critics were beside themselves with admiration. The audience was rapt.

Hal Holbrook was stunned, and more than a little unsettled.

In the moments following his off-Broadway debut as Mark Twain in 1959, actress Margaret Sullavan came backstage to congratulate the 34-year-old "unknown." Then came the dreaded words, "Where will you find another character so rich, Mr. Holbrook? How will you ever top this?"

The answer, which soon emerged, was never to relinquish the role. For Holbrook, now 86, playing this icon of American letters would be a life's passion, spanning six decades and more than 2,200 performances.

"The 1959 experience was a shock to me," recalls the veteran stage and screen actor, who spoke to The Post and Courier from his home in McLemoresville, Tenn. "I didn't believe it. I couldn't. How could I have traveled all over this country for five and a half years playing this part, rarely having anyone write a grown-up review, and now have all these big-time New York critics fall all over themselves about it?

"It also scared the hell out of me. I thought, 'If I'm a star, whatever that is, what do I do now?'"

For years, Holbrook and his first wife, Ruby, had been theatrical nomads, a troupe of two who wandered the country in a station wagon, alighting now and again to do summer stock, and accrue a repertoire.

Suddenly, he was a hit, on the Great White Way no less, yet no one had a clue who he was.

"Mark Twain was the star," Holbrook recalls. "Mark Twain was the success. Nobody had any idea who I was or what I looked like unless they saw me on (the daytime soap) 'The Brighter Day.' I had to start all over again, being careful not to get typed into playing old man roles."

This vignette, arriving near the close of "Harold" (Farrar, Straus & Giroux), a candid, first installment in Holbrook's new memoir, belongs more properly to Volume Two, now well under way.

"It is how I open the second book, which has the working title of 'Second Chance,' " he says. "I'm more than 500 pages into the writing, and I'm still trying to discover who I am."

This inaugural entry, which chronicles his life from childhood to age 34, was ushered into print with the aid of Dr. Vernon Burton, a Lincoln scholar and professor of history at Clemson University.

"He got this book going," says Holbrook, a two-time Emmy Award winner and 2008 Oscar nominee. "We were having dinner one evening in Illinois, and the subject of my book came up. When he got home, he called his editor, Thomas Levine at Farrar, Straus, and he soon got in touch with me. I have Thomas to thank for locating the themes of the book."

Also, thank Holbrook's recordkeeping. The actor's longtime penchant for keeping a vest-pocket diary is serving him in good stead. Without these notebooks, the detail embodied by "Harold: The Boy Who Became Mark Twain" would not have been possible.

White suit and a wig

Born in Cleveland and raised in South Weymouth, Mass., Holbrook and his sisters were abandoned at an early age by their mother, a dancer who fled to California to follow her muse, and their father, who spent years in and out of mental institutions before venturing to Hollywood.

Holbrook graduated from Culver Military Academy, where he had his first brush with the theater, and, after service in World War II, from Ohio's Denison University, where that interest intensified.

At Denison, he was introduced to Twain by his drama teacher, Ed Wright, a lifelong influence who Holbrook says is responsible for his career.

"I didn't even know who Twain was. When I first started doing the show, I was just playing an old man, I didn't really know him. When I had to put the solo show together, I started reading other books .... I had no idea! This was great stuff, and I could use it."

Holbrook's first solo performance as Twain was at Lock Haven State Teachers College in Pennsylvania in 1954. Two years later, Ed Sullivan gave Holbrook his first national exposure. The U.S. State Department also sent Holbrook on a European tour, which included pioneering appearances behind the Iron Curtain.

Holbrook's 1959 triumph in "Mark Twain Tonight!" would be followed by still greater ones: a 1966 Broadway smash, and the now-famous CBS special, in front of 30 million viewers, the following year.

"On Broadway in 1966, that was really the big time. I didn't know what to expect when the reviews came out, and was amazed. But I was just very grateful. By the time of the CBS show, I thought we might do pretty well. CBS had a really smart idea. They contacted literature teachers all across the country and got them to make my show a student assignment. So whether they liked it or not, a family had to sit down in front of the TV and watch it. It turned out that they loved it."

Now in his 57th consecutive year touring as Twain, Holbrook still marvels at the writer's intelligence and prescience.

"The Mark Twain show has become a marker for the way I live my life, really. The engine that drove me as a child is still operating very strongly: to go forward, to achieve, to do my best. I don't give up. And I don't give up on Twain, on going out and doing material of his that is not easy for some people to take, even today, like the cleavage between rich and poor.

"Twain faced that social issue and many more in the latter part of the 19th century and the first 10 years of the 1900s. Most people don't realize that Twain also addressed slavery, racism, religion, politics and women's rights. There is almost nothing on which he didn't touch. I toured the South with the show during a volatile period in the 1950s and early '60s, and if I hadn't been wearing the white suit and a wig as Twain, I might not have made it."

His Twain is a characterization, of course, yet Holbrook confides that it scarcely feels that way anymore.

"Not when I'm out there on stage, no. I'm saying things I believe in, and things I believe need to be said. I realize I'm not going to change anybody's mind, but I am interested in talking to everybody, not preaching to the choir."

Survival and discovery

Holbrook, whose most recent film is "Water for Elephants" (2011), has been married three times. He has two children from his first marriage with Ruby Johnston Holbrook, Victoria and David, and a daughter, Eve, with his second wife, Carol Eve Rossen.

Holbrook was married to Dixie Carter (of "Designing Women" fame) from 1984 until her death in April 2010.

The first marriage, and what Holbrook perceives as his failures as a husband and father, are well-chronicled in "Harold."

"What I learned from writing about the first 34 years of my life is that very early on I became a solo person. I liked being alone. I realized I was going to have to make it on my own somehow, though I probably never said it to myself quite that way."

The first book, he adds, is about survival and self-discovery.

"Discovering myself was very difficult because I was always hiding behind these disguises."

But one thing was clear: Holbrook was driven, chiefly by the goals of earning a living and supporting a family.

"We didn't have anything when Ruby and I got married. No money, no one to give us advice. It was a grim business. We had to survive, and work became the No. 1 necessity for me, no matter what. That's not a recipe for a good marriage, unless you happen to find somebody who can deal with it."

Otherwise, says Holbrook, there's an abrasive force within couples in show business that can get worse as time goes on. Children compound the problem.

"I don't know how you match it all together. I was never successful with children until my third child was born. I was so guilty about not having given my two older children the kind of attention they needed and wanted from me every week. That's another thing I learned from writing this book and from my work on the second one. My kids wanted me. And I'm the one who left when Ruby and I divorced. I didn't have time for them. I tried, but it wasn't enough. The damage had been done.

"When I evaluate the first 34 years, it comes down to a single-mindedness about making a living and succeeding, creating some kind of a career you could depend upon. That's a very difficult thing to achieve in my business. Even today I don't know what's going to happen in the next six months, except for the Mark Twain dates."

In a touching epilogue, Holbrook writes that while one tries desperately not to make terrible mistakes in one's personal life, ultimately you have to go with your gut.

"If you don't, you die off somehow. You retreat. And I still don't know how to retreat. I'm having a problem with that now, as an 86-year-old man learning to slow down. I don't know what that means."

....

The Redgrave 'family business' still going strong on screen, stage
November 1, 2007

SAVANNAH - Mainstays of the international stage, TV and cinema, the Redgraves give the term "family business" new meaning.

Compared to their five-generation-long history in entertainment, the Barrymores are pikers.

That Vanessa, Lynn and Corin Redgrave would become actors was, one suspects, a foregone conclusion. Were they not the children of Sir Michael Redgrave, the distinguished stage and screen performer and his actress wife, Rachel Kempson? Were they not the grandchildren of stage and silent film star Roy Redgrave? Have not Vanessa's own daughters, Jolie and Natasha Richardson, continued the tradition, if not the name, having established themselves as worthy inheritors of the dynasty?

Rarefied words for so down-to-earth a family.

Vanessa: 70, lean, strong-willed, daring, with piercing blue eyes and a husky, melodious voice.

Lynn: 64, outgoing, chatty, open, yet with more going on than meets the eye.

Corin: 68, witty, urbane, with a hint of barely suppressed mischief.

The celebrated siblings appeared Saturday evening at the 10th Savannah Film Festival to receive Lifetime Achievement Awards, but they took a few moments earlier in the day to reflect on their careers as working actors, rather than stars. The recognition is not without some irony. That these widely respected actors should have played the lead roles in their films so rarely, yet still have so high a profile, is unusual in motion pictures.

Integral to their success has been the act of staying busy.

"None of us, if I may presume to say it, have ever been in the position to just stick around looking for the perfect role," says Vanessa, who, typically, captured an Oscar for a film (1977's "Julia") in which she had the title role but played a supporting part. "We've done everything we could get our hands on and we've been frightfully lucky."

Adds Lynn: "Our dad used to say work breeds work. By putting out the energy doing something, not being so exclusive that you're waiting for the 'right' thing to plan the perfect move, you need not wait. I've never waited for the right thing, because I've never really been able to afford to. And that's a good thing. Sometimes I have the good fortune that a job that will earn me a living also is with extraordinary people and has a brilliant script, but you do not always possess those ingredients. Sometimes, young actors who become very famous very quickly are persuaded to then wait for the right thing, and it's a terrible mistake."

After baptism on stage in the late '50s, each enjoyed their film debut in 1966. Vanessa erupted into prominence with an Oscar-nominated performance in "Morgan!" and an iconic part in Michelangelo Antonioni's seminal "Blow Up," while Lynn wowed critics with an Oscar-nominated turn as the ugly-duckling title character of "Georgy Girl."

For his part, Corin had a small but forceful role in the Academy Award-winning historical drama "A Man for All Seasons," holding his own with the great Paul Scofield in a picture that also harbored sister Vanessa (as Anne Boleyn).

They have seldom lacked for work since, despite the occasional political dust-up on Vanessa's part. Like most actors trained in the British manner, their approach has been pragmatic, differing in style and mentality from the standard Hollywood arc.

The Redgraves still are having wonderful careers (and have yet to enter their anecdotage). Aren't lifetime achievement awards a bit premature?

"Oh, no," says Vanessa, receiving her first such honor. "It's the perfect time, while we can enjoy it. In our Fall - while we are green and yellow and red."

"Somehow, when one hears the expression 'lifetime achievement' you tend to think, well, these were for people certainly well-advanced toward the end," offers Corin, affecting a doddering tone. "Actually, I don't think the givers of this award mean it in that way. And I have to say, being a first-time recipient, it does make me very proud."

It's the second tribute for Lynn. "I got one at the Palm Springs Film Festival when I had just been diagnosed with cancer but nobody knew. And I began to wonder, does the Festival know something I don't know about my upcoming surgery? But I'm still here."

Of the three, only Corin has had no brush with Charleston. Vanessa shot the supernatural drama "They" on James Island in 1993, while Lynn was flown in by Gian Carlo Menotti to open the 1989 Spoleto Festival. "My luggage had been lost and I arrived with just the clothes on my back," Lynn recalls, laughing. "But I was able to go to one of those delightful boutiques at 7 in the morning - they were so kind to open it up - and replenish my wardrobe."

Of late, the Regraves have betrayed no sign of slowing down. Vanessa riveted audiences on Broadway this year in a one-woman adaptation of Joan Dideon's "The Year of Magical Thinking," earning a Tony Award nomination. It won Vanessa her most glowing reviews since playing the lead in the 1998 movie "Mrs. Dalloway." In 2005, she had the pleasure of working with daughter Natasha and sister Lynn in "The White Countess."

"It was the first time I'd worked with my daughter in a film she was actually in," she says. "We had great fun together, Tasha, Lynn and I." Since then, Vanessa has starred in "Venus" opposite Peter O'Toole and in "Evening" with Meryl Streep. Next up, she stars in the adaptation of Ian Mc-Ewan's "Atonement" and unites with Corin for the Romanian production of "Eve."

Corin's next feature is "The Calling," while Lynn has "The Jane Austen Book Club" currently in theaters and is preparing to make the animated feature "My Dog Tulip."

Retirement? Don't be absurd.

"I don't plan to retire," Vanessa states flatly.

"Nor I," says Corin. "I can't remember who said this, or of what actor, but the expression was 'He made people laugh, and he made them cry.' Why stop?"

Lynn gets the final word: "The only way to go is after a wonderful, wonderful performance. Waiting, mind you, until after the curtain call."

....

Tommy Lee Jones: No shortage of work on the horizon
November 23, 2006

SAVANNAH – The actor stands in the back of a packed Trustees Theater, shifting his weight from foot to foot, engrossed in the movie of his own making.

Occasionally he scans the audience, as if he might absorb its mood, its communal reaction. But the eyes quickly return to the screen, arms fidgeting on a rail, the nervous body language as clipped as the dialogue he silently mouths.

The anxiousness is understandable. "The Three Burials of Melquiades Estrada" is not a conventional Western, and not the easiest film to approach. Released almost a year ago, it has impressed critics but not received the distribution many feel it deserves. The actor in particular.

Tommy Lee Jones, the star, is also Tommy Lee Jones, the director, and he is still out stumping for a movie he believes in. Even with a busy slate of films in post- or pre-production, and a brace of new scripts in development, Jones is more than happy to discuss the virtues of "Three Burials," his first feature at the helm.

Accompanied by his wife, Dawn, a gracious lady and gifted photographer, Jones' appearance at the recent Savannah Film Festival was one of its showcase events.

Jones and screenwriter Guillermo Arriaga clearly are disappointed that the film has not gotten as broad an audience as they had hoped, but the conviction is that this has little to do with the product.

"I think it has good, long legs," Jones said in an interview earlier in the day. "It will always appeal to people, if it's marketed well. It hasn't been so far."

Jones took his own sweet time in observing character and circumstance in "Three Burials." The leisurely pacing, a slow canter on a rocky, twisty trail, paid off artistically if not commercially. Lean and mean, "Three Burials" knows its place, its poetry and its people.

Jones appreciates any acknowledgment of the fact. Unless you want to provoke his prickly side, just don't refer to him as a "first-timer" behind the camera.

"It's not my first time directing. It was the first feature film I've made. People who don't know anything about film drop the term 'first-time director' in full confidence that it makes them sound like they're thinking."

But recognize what went into the making of the picture, how a small movie embraced allegorical content, structural elements of "Lone Star" and "Touch of Evil," the tenor of "The Last Picture Show," the gruff sensibilities of a John Huston or Sam Peckinpah, a smattering of macabre humor, and an examination of ethnicity and justice, and Jones' tone changes.

"Thank you for seeing that, because we worked at it very hard. We were well organized, and we worked on the script for about a year. Guillermo (screenwriter Arriaga) and I were hunting on my ranch some time ago and just decided we wanted to make a movie. He wrote a first draft and I changed it and sent it back. He changed the changes and sent it back to me. Ultimately, he made four or five trips to San Antonio, sat across the table from me in my library, and we worked it out so it was both under control and controllable. This was long before we went into pre-production."

Jones won Best Actor laurels at the Cannes Film Festival for the movie, but he deflects praise to the work of his co-star, Barry Pepper, and to the wizardry of John Blake in fashioning the corpse that the Jones and Pepper characters transport across the border.

"Barry was wonderful in the movie. And John's been working with me on makeup for many years. He did a terrific job on building that cadaver in various stages of decomposition."

There's little chance of disintegration in Jones' career. The actor's been working steadily since graduating cum laude from Harvard University (where he roomed with future Vice President Al Gore) and cutting his teeth on the New York stage. He played an escaped convict being hunted by police in his first starring role in a U.S. film, "Jackson County Jail" (1976). But people really sat up and took notice after the eighth-generation Texan won raves as country singer Loretta Lynn's husband in "Coal Miner's Daughter" (1981) and took home an Emmy Award for playing convicted murderer Gary Gilmore in the TV drama "The Executioner's Song" (1982).

It's been gravy ever since. After touching viewers as Woodrow Call, the repressed Texas Ranger in the acclaimed miniseries "Lonesome Dove" (1988) and winning an Oscar for "The Fugitive" (1993), the craggy, somewhat eccentric star and his distinctive screen presence have been in constant demand.

Up next is a Coen brothers movie for which he has a special affinity. It's an adaptation of the book "No Country for Old Men" by Jones' favorite writer (aside from Flannery O'Connor), Cormac McCarthy.

How did the Coen brothers manage to make all their cockeyed movies without a Coen natural like Tommy Lee Jones is a puzzler.

"I really don't know," says the 60-year-old Jones, considering the thought. "But they're good fellows. I enjoyed their company and we had a wonderful time. We had a house to live in up in the hills above Santa Fe and were very comfortable there. We spent a lot of time in north New Mexico. It was special for me, because Cormac is a good friend and a great writer, and I feel really happy to be a part of bringing his work to the screen."

"No Country for Old Men" is due out next year. Also in the cast are Javier Bardem, Josh Brolin, Tess Harper, Woody Harrelson and Richard Jackson.

In the pipeline for Jones is Paul Haggis' fact-based "In the Valley of Elah" (in pre-production) co-starring Charlize Theron, and another project close to Jones' heart, a new and likely superior screen version of Ernest Hemingway's "Islands in the Stream," which he is writing and directing.

"'Islands' is a very interesting project. I believe we've been working on that screenplay for about a year, and just finished it a few days before coming here. We're going to see where we can take it now."

Any chance of reuniting with director Andrew Davis, who helped summon two of

Jones' best performances ("Under Siege," "The Fugitive")?

"I haven't talked to Andy in a while. I don't know what he's got on his mind at the moment. We've been friends for a long time and I enjoy working with him. So who knows?"

....

Amy Adams: Actress drawn to tragicomic role in 'Junebug'
September 11, 2005

Until Amy Adams came South, the best rendition of a North Carolina accent on film belonged to British actress Janet McTeer in 1999's "Tumbleweeds." No longer.

A native of Colorado – perhaps it's southern Colorado – the star of the Sundance and Cannes film festival hit "Junebug" makes it work so well because, like McTeer, she doesn't try too hard. Much the same could be said of first-time director Phil Morrison, a Tar Heel, and his film.

Front and center in the low-budget independent picture are two striking women. Polished, urban art dealer Madeleine (Embeth Davidtz) has come to North Carolina from Chicago to scout an undiscovered regional artist. Riding shotgun is her husband, George (Alessandro Nivola), whose family will be their hosts. There she meets George's sulky sibling, Johnny (Benjamin McKenzie), and his utterly unrestrained wife, Ashley (Adams), a pregnant chatterbox who's the only family member delighted by the incursion.

Effusive almost to a fault and wholly transparent, she is the centerpiece of the film.

Adams, last seen in Steven Spielberg's "Catch Me If You Can," makes her more than vivid. She says tackling the tragicomic role was simultaneously enticing, daunting and immensely satisfying.

"It was all of that, and I really looked forward to doing it," says the 30-year-old actress, who is preparing to join another N.C. shoot for the untitled Will Ferrell NASCAR movie. "Before 'Junebug,' I had a couple of other roles that challenged me, but I had not gotten the opportunity to explore this wide a range of emotions. I was really, really ready for it."

Adams moved with her family to Minnesota at an early age. She studied dance and toiled in regional dinner theater, often musicals, before securing her inaugural feature film role in the 1999 satire "Drop Dead Gorgeous." An independent comedy with a catchpenny title, "Psycho Beach Party," was next, followed by guest spots on several TV series, among them "That '70s Show," "Buffy the Vampire Slayer" and "The West Wing."

She also was cast as a regular on "Manchester Prep," a TV spinoff of the film "Cruel Intentions." The sexually suggestive series was never televised, surprisingly, though several episodes resurfaced in edited form for the direct-to-video "Cruel Intentions 2."

Rebounding, Adams made four films in 2002, most notably as the starry-eyed wife of Leonardo DiCaprio in "Catch Me," after which everyone expected her career to shift into high gear. It didn't happen. Not right away, at least. Though she won raves for her performance, Adams didn't work in films for a year.

"I have no shame about that now, though I did at the time. To work in a Spielberg movie and think this should make everything start rolling was the wrong attitude to take. I did 'Junebug' because I loved it and had no expectations of what would happen."

In penning his script, which dwells evenhandedly with its underlying culture-clash scenario, screenwriter Angus MacLachlan clearly was taken with his female characters, which are written with considerable more depth and interest than the men. Stereotypes are few, and the quirky quotient is not overdone, even with Ashley.

Adams captured a special Jury Prize for her "Junebug" performance at the 2005 Sundance Film Festival. What makes her character distinctive, apart from how she is written, is the way audiences react to her.

"It begins with the writing, of course. And also Phil's direction. But I wasn't trying to portray a Southerner. I just made her, her. She's such an inviting person that I think she draws the audience in. She is so open, so willing to love. I think the audience sees that.

"When I'm working, I have to throw the intellectual out the window and really relate to the character from an emotional pool. With Ashley, I tried to be as emotionally honest to each moment as I could be. In the manner of a child, but not like a child."

While flattered to be singled out for her work, Adams says she's proud of the entire film and everyone involved in it. Any expectations beyond this centers on continuing to develop a body of work, not renown.

"Being serious about my craft is something I learned since coming to L.A," says Adams, who has two more pictures in the pipeline, "Fast Track" with Zach Braff and "Stephen Tobolowsky's Birthday Party."

"At first, I just wanted to see if I could make it as an actress there in L.A. But the climate and environment of the city made me anxious. When I first arrived, I felt everything had to happen for me quickly. In recent years, and after 'Catch Me,' it's about more than that. It's about the work you do, about a life I've chosen. So I changed my focus."

And found Ashley.

....

For Kevin Costner, it's about possibility
March 22, 2008

MCCLELLANVILLE – It is not the curtain call that Kevin Costner misses – of those, he gets plenty – but the curtain itself, a century-old tradition lost to the multiplex.

"I miss having an actual curtain drawn in a movie theater. There's something really magical about a curtain opening. Every movie has a chance to be great at that moment. And it's all about what decisions were made, be it the script, did people 'settle,' did they cave in to convention? I'm a sucker for the curtain opening. Anything is possible at that moment."

Costner, who is in the Lowcountry shooting "The New Daughter," has moved headlong through a career that has always been about possibility, about seizing a cinematic opportunity even when conventional wisdom says otherwise.

"I've been flying against the conventional wisdom for a long time," he said, "and simply for one reason: What if everybody's wrong? We're still talking about an emotional experience, not something empirical."

Which is one reason why the actor, director and producer disdains test audience screenings, which often compromise a filmmaker's vision and intent - as if Hemingway had asked his readers to rewrite a manuscript.

"It's been our undoing. We're so convinced now what an audience will sit through and what they won't. But there are a lot of reasons why a movie doesn't come together. Either you started with a bad document, or you weren't careful in the post (production), or the conventions of modern filmmaking tore you down: timing, ratings, over-testing. A lot of times what you actually have are pretty good movies, but they're not great. I have some of those. They're pretty good. Why? Because those movies suffered from conventional wisdom."

Directed by Luis Berdejo, "The New Daughter" marks Costner's first return to the Lowcountry since making "The Big Chill" (1983), a film in which Costner's scenes famously found the cutting room floor - thanks to test screenings.

It is also the first horror film of his career, following a picture in which he played his inaugural "villain," the serial killer of "Mr. Brooks." Though his enthusiasm for the new movie is palpable, Costner believes any number of actors could play his role.

"In some of my movies I think I'm probably the guy. There are some movies that I feel like I 'own.' I don't like scary movies personally, but I did want to be in one. I thought this one read really well, and I like the idea of making a movie like this and trying to see if we can raise the bar on it - at least its IQ - a little bit. I know the screenplay is very good. We have monsters, and right at the end we have to fight them. So, is that where we lose it, or do we make it work? I depend on people hanging with it and being able to make that theatrical jump."

If there is one constant in his films, as actor and director, it is that Costner has made movies for men.

"I do. I always make sure there are great women's parts in them, but when I start off my No. 1 goal is, 'Can a man relate to this movie?' It doesn't mean the character has to be butch. It means if I'm a character in a movie where something breaks down, will a man recognize why Billy Chapel (in "For Love of the Game") weeps in his hotel after he pitches a perfect game and there's no one there for him? Will a guy watching go, 'I get it, man'"?

From "A Perfect World" to "Field of Dreams," Costner has given us an array of men with whom audiences might identify, at least on some level.

"And you can relate to them, whether it's a sociopath or whether there's a thread of humanity in any of them. I believe I have this relationship with the audience and people have a feeling that they think they know me. But it's really not quite the case.

Which is one reason why Costner has spent the past two years performing live gigs with his band, Modern West, often in the communities where he's filming. Costner and Modern West will kick out the jams live at the Music Farm on March 29.

"I've found that if I can perform music for two hours on stage, talking to people, it beats a two-second autograph. And anybody who is really watching goes, 'I feel really different about him.' Now, the hope is that they feel something positive."

Costner's sports-themed films, "Bull Durham" and "Field of Dreams" among them, have been a principal propellent in his career. But no less so have been his Westerns, most recently "Open Range." Costner says he harbors a special affinity for them.

"I think they're our Shakespeare, to be honest. And I say that in the sense that Shakespeare can be difficult to understand on the page, but when you see it performed really well, you can understand it. His work lives hundreds of years later and is still vital. I think the reason why you don't see a lot of great Westerns is because they are hard to make. And when people are sloppy with them they do a disservice, because when they're cliched or too bloody they're boring."

Authenticity in a Western, Costner says, swings on the most basic elements.

"'Yep' and 'nope' are not just words. The language of the era had a simplicity to it: 'A man's trust is worth more than a handful of cards.' That's as eloquent as anything written by Shakespeare. And if you believe that, you also believe that it's important for westerns to have those lines. There's an elegance and a poetry in the language, and if you look for it, you'll find it.

"I believe people do appreciate that, although it doesn't always add up to great box office. What it adds up to is maybe a classic. If you can be content with classic and not being No. 1 at the box office, it will probably serve your filmmaking instincts a lot better. In the end what you may have something that we are all looking for, something that endures, that travels through time. You have to have a fundamental belief in your story."

Next: Costner riffs on his return to music and his band, Modern West, as well as the virtues of connecting live with an audience.

Sidebar: Kickin' out the jams with Kevin

Kevin Costner was on the fence. Should he reassemble his old bandmates, recruit some new members and take the stage, or maintain music as a hobby?

His wife, Christine, galvanized him with three simple questions: "'Will you have a good time doing it? Do you think the people in front of you will have a good time?'

"I said yes to both, and she added, 'What could be wrong with that?' That was very liberating. And she's been able to do that for me at moments of my career."

Two years on, Kevin Costner and Modern West still are kickin' out the jams. They'll sashay into the Music Farm on Saturday armed with a posse of their own tunes and musical influences that range from The Pretenders and Talking Heads to Bruce Springsteen and Hank Williams.

Costner, currently shooting "The New Daughter" in McClellanville, says the band's performances begin as a kind of "thank you" for allowing his company to come into an area and film. Whatever the venue, Modern West tries to corral a certain intimacy.

"As much as I can, I like to turn every place I am into a living room, whether it's an audience of 10,000 people or 900 or 200 or 50. I think it's an intimate opportunity to connect with people. It's very personal. You can ride the songs and you can also feel the room. It's a chance to have a party. Because what else is there in life if there's not more good times."

Authentic experience

For Costner, caring about his audience is not confined to filmmaking. But the decision to form Modern West, write new songs and play live gigs also is about having an authentic experience for himself. Being able to communicate with an audience through his music, directly, is at least as gratifying as smiling and signing autographs. Getting past the novelty of Costner fronting a band usually requires just a couple of cuts.

"As I've experienced national and international fame, the handshake and the autograph - mostly the autograph - have become so important. Even very cool people suddenly go. 'I've got to get your autograph; I've got to let them know I talked to you,' as opposed to trusting in shooting the (breeze) for 10 minutes and finding that was so much better. It seemed it was all about the autograph. I love to entertain people, but I found that I had been rendered into a kind of cardboard stand-up. I started thinking that was not a good exchange for me.

"I began to crave the chance to genuinely give something back. I really felt I wanted to do music again. And I found that if I was making a movie in a town like Charleston, that I wanted to entertain on another level. I've had this relationship with the audience from my movies for 20-plus years now. People have a feeling that they think they know me, and it's really not quite the case. So I've found that if I can perform music for two hours on stage, talking to people, it beats a two-second autograph. And anybody who is really watching goes, 'I feel really different about him.' Now, the hope is that they feel something positive."

Should anyone be surprised an actor would have a range of interests? Some filmmakers are accomplished painters and photographers, woodworkers and poets as well as musicians. Costner's mother sat him at the piano at an early age. He's played in pickup groups with old friends many times over the years, but it was always just a pastime, a diversion between films, until his wife encouraged him to do something with the songs he'd written.

"I came to music first. I was trained in classical piano and performed in music halls and stage plays. I was in the church choir. Music was a very dominant thing, so much earlier than acting. When you perform, you have to try to be a rounded person. If you are going to try to make a living as an actor, you certainly have to come to it with as many tools as possible."

Gust of fresh air

Costner says the driving force of his life has been an effort not to be defined or limited.

"I think we're all in search of fresh air. But there's all these small traps that people run into in their lives that keep us from going forward and experiencing something new. I think a lot of people do sidestep these traps. But I've had a tendency to run right up against the things. Interestingly, music was one of the first things I actually backed away from in my career.

"It was right about the time 'Dances With Wolves' was coming out and I was enjoying some success in the movie business. I thought, do I want to endure the criticisms that necessarily come with, 'Oh, you're doing music?' Because I was always doing music. I thought, no, I don't want to have that. It was very unusual for me to back away, but I did. I found later on that I missed it. What was I worried about? I had not been worried about anything as I charged through life."

Accommodating dual schedules as a musician and filmmaker keeps Costner on his toes. The two dovetail to a degree, though to go at one exclusively would eliminate the other, he says. And he's always appreciated the hours of music more than the hours of the movies.

"Movies typically start at 6 a.m. And no one does that in music."

Unwritten rule

Costner and Modern West – Costner on guitar and vocals, guitarist and producer Teddy Morgan, keeper-of-the-beat Larry Cobb, Park Chisholm on vocals and guitar and Bobby Yang on fiddle – provided some original tunes and perform (as the "Half-Nelsons") in his upcoming movie "Swing Vote," shot last August in New Mexico. Yet just because he's the star of the film doesn't mean he's not exacting about what tunes make the final cut.

"That's probably the hallmark, the unwritten rule on our band, that I break all the ties. Some of my songs aren't good enough. I mean, they're good songs but not good enough. That's always been a really easy thing for me because I know the scrutiny that comes with anything, and it's better to be honest. If you really believe in what you're doing, you can live through the scrutiny. Really, that's a great place to be. It doesn't mean you can't suffer a sling or an arrow, but it does mean you're on pretty solid ground, that you didn't just float something out there and hope people like it.

"We've enjoyed such an interesting two-year ride since I put the band together. Two of the guys in the band are from my first band I was ever in. When I contacted them, they wanted to do it but were surprised that I did. Before I started making 'Mr. Brooks,' I began thinking I really wanted to do this. I set my bars pretty high because I have to, because I know who is going to come after me if I don't."

Performing with the band has met Costner's three prerequisites: It had to be fun. It had to be good enough to put in front of people. And he had to enjoy playing live, given the pressure that would be on him insofar as people's expectations were concerned.

"That's a proper edge for me to be at if I want to continue to be an entertainer. I have to deliver. And I don't want to be a wreck for four days afterward. I wasn't sure until I cracked through those things. But whether you make a dime on it or not, it's all about that exchange. It's what happens in that room. That's what will be the most important thing when we play. I don't want to sabotage whatever good will has come before."

....

Milos Forman: Director still focused on character, wit
November 8, 2007

SAVANNAH - All great showmen know that the length of a piece of entertainment should not exceed (as Alfred Hitchcock so delicately put it) the carrying capacity of the human bladder.

Which is one reason why celebrated filmmaker Milos Forman excised 35 minutes from his original print of "Amadeus," which went on to capture seven Oscars (including Best Picture) in 1984. This, despite the fact that even admiring critics felt the 158-minute run time already was too long.

Undeterred, Forman has restored the footage for a Director's Cut of his costume classic, which played at the recent Savannah Film Festival.

"This version was not meant to be played in the theaters because it is well over three hours long," says Forman, on hand to accept an award for lifetime achievement. "It was my decision to cut them; I panicked when we saw the final film. MTV had just burst on the scene in the early 1980s with this quick, fast pacing. Ours was this very long period movie with classical music. So I took out those scenes that were not directly pushing the story forward. Now, I've put them back. They were easy to re-integrate. And it is the film I had imagined."

As well as the one playwright Peter Shaffer had written.

However, Forman is candid enough to admit he is no judge of whether or not the restored scenes enhance the narrative.

"I cannot say. The curse of every director is that we never see our films the same way an audience does. You have to ask the audience, and those who will watch this extended cut on DVD. They can always pause it to go to the (restroom)."

A two-time Oscar winner as Best Director, Forman earlier played a major role in shaping the Czech New Wave of the 1960s, films distinguished by an ironic humor and meticulous observation of character. These traits are echoed in his finest English-language pictures: "One Flew Over the Cuckoo's Nest" (1975), "Ragtime," (1981) and "The People vs. Larry Flynt" (1996), as well as in "Amadeus."

"Character is what all storytellers must develop," he says. "The humor is out of the culture I grew up in. Even the most tragic story can have comic sides to it. Czechoslovakia is a small country. When you have been occupied for hundreds of years by some major power, if you cannot fight back with swords or guns, you do it with humor. This was part of my cultural education."

Though he has made few waves in recent years, Forman remains one of the few foreign filmmakers to have enjoyed major Hollywood success, commercially as well as critically. More importantly, his work set in America has been a case study in how an "outsider" looking in can perceive the truth of a place and a culture in ways those born there may not. For proof, one need only see "Ragtime," an often brilliant adaptation of the novel by E.L. Doctorow.

"There is a certain truth to it," Forman agrees. "I just realize now how beautiful Prague is, because I was not there for 20 years. When I lived there, it was just another city. Suddenly, when I went back and spent four months working there, I discovered things there I had never seen. I never noticed them. You live in a certain environment long enough, you stop seeing the details which make it different."

His second and most famous U.S. film was made with then-TV star-turned-producer Michael Douglas. The multiple Oscar-winning "Cuckoo's Nest" (1975), also may have been most characteristic of his penchant for anti-establishment protagonists. Likewise, Forman, with a deep humanist impulse, often has mined the theme of generational conflict, particularly within families.

While Forman insists he explores the familial theme only when it serves the story, his childhood - he lost both parents in Nazi concentration camps - has had a profound effect.

"I suppose I always envied harmonious families in which the parents lived with their children," he says.

Forman's latest, the recently released biopic "Goya's Ghost" with Javier Bardem and Natalie Portman, possesses a similar edge.

"The nucleus of that film started developing 50 years ago when I was a student at the film school in Prague. I was reading a book about the Spanish Inquisition and could not believe that the same things were happening around me in the middle of the 20th century: people being arrested – nobody knew why. People being accused of crimes they never committed. People confessing under torture. I wondered, 'How is this possible?'

"Twenty years later in Madrid, seeing for the first time his work in the Prado museum, Goya's paintings seemed like illustrations for the book I read in the '50s. Somehow the movie grew out of this experience."

In the early '90s, Forman devoted his principal energies to academe, serving as co-director of the film program at Columbia University, where he had taught since the late 1970s. Since returning behind the camera with "The People vs. Larry Flint," his projects have been surprisingly rare, his work as a screenwriter fitful.

"Goya's Ghost" is his first (and only) film of the new century. Hollywood, hungry for a moneymaker, may have lost interest - for now. But don't expect Forman's fire to stay banked.

....

Lily Tomlin: A talent for staying busy
June 8, 2006

There was enough crossover dialogue to augment a Neil LaBute play. And Lily Tomlin loved every minute.

Robert Altman's cinematic homage to the long-running radio show "A Prairie Home Companion" has, among other features, three principal sets of byplay: between Tomlin and Meryl Streep, Woody Harrelson and John C. Reilly, and Kevin Kline and Virginia Madsen.

Tomlin and Streep play the Johnson Sisters, a country-tinged singing act who are among the headliners for what in the movie (not in real life) is Keillor's farewell show. The Johnsons have more than the usual complement of sisterly issues, but it doesn't affect their harmonies, nor does it make them any less simpatico off stage, where they keep finishing each other's sentences.

"That was sort of like a heightened essence of an Altman soundtrack, and we came to it kind of spontaneously," says Tomlin, who spoke to The Post and Courier by phone from Los Angeles. "It's such a convoluted story. We did one major scene in 20-minute takes on the first day of shooting. If either Meryl or I would forget a part of the dialogue, the other would pick it up."

The cast hewed, for the most part, to Keillor's screenplay. Not to say there was not some elaboration of what was on the page, which is emblematic of an Altman film. Few directors afford their casts such latitude, or room to maneuver.

"We stuck to the spine of the script," says Tomlin. "But Altman just lets you do it. He'd redirect you rather than stop you. It's serendipitous and easy and wonderful and he trusts you. It is a gesture of respect, and the actors love that in him. Altman would never call 'cut.' We'd just keep going."

An Altman feature is marked by more than the presence of gifted ensemble casts. What distinguishes them is that the performers seem utterly absorbed in the story, very much cogs in a collective framework, yet still retaining their individual distinctiveness.

"It's so intuitive, and he lets us be intuitive," Tomlin says. "He trusts his own instincts and somehow he trusts ours. It (embellishments) could be something as simple changing a character's hair color from the way it's written, which I took as license to make my hair red. Often it's playful things. That little unbuttoning of the blouse that Meryl does was inspired, I had that to play off of and to ad lib, 'Button up.' "

For Tomlin, who maintains a demanding schedule of live concert dates each years, singing with Streep was as much fun as acting with her.

"Listen, I took lessons for two months. I didn't know I'd sing that well, either. I had sung with a kind of gospel group in 'Nashville,' But this was different. I was really turned on to it. This time I got to sing in what is a real voice for me. I'm proud of what I did."

Winner of the Mark Twain Prize for career achievement, among Tomlin's inspirations have been such renowned comedians as Lucille Ball and Imogene Coca. But she has always been pure Lily. The Detroit native continues to star in television and theater, animation and video, as well as features. She is the recipient of six Emmys, two Tony Awards, a Drama Desk Award, a Cable Ace Award, a Grammy and a pair of Peabody Awards. Quite a haul.

But Altman holds a special niche in her film work. Tomlin's earlier outings with the director include the former "Laugh-In" star's aforementioned motion picture debut, "Nashville" (1975).

"It was probably most enjoyable working with him this time, because I'm a better actor now than I was when I made 'Nashville,' " says Tomlin. "I'm always excited to be in his films. I was excited to be in 'Short Cuts,' too. Even the small part I had in 'The Player' was fun."

Having the most fun on set, apparently, was Kevin Kline, who stars as the radio show's head of security Guy Noir, an ex-private eye given to suggestive remarks, pratfalls - and stealing scenes. Who else would have taken Keillor's familiar character and made him a cross between Sam Spade and Inspector Clouseau?

"Often, we knew that Kevin was doing something behind us. Apart from being actors and knowing you're being upstaged, you also just wanted to see it because he was constantly inventing something physical to do. Kevin really gave life to the character Garrison wrote."

With TV's "The West Wing" having closed up shop after a successful run, Tomlin turns her attention to new projects.

"I still do concerts all the time. I'm also in the movie "Ant Bully" in August, and in an upcoming Paul Schrader movie. I stay busy."

....

Sayles pitch: Writer-director has political bone to pick
September 23, 2004

His unhurried voice belies the publicist tugging at his shoulder. With the remnants of Hurricane Ivan bearing down on north Georgia, John Sayles is being hustled from his hotel to Atlanta's Hartsfield Airport, one step ahead of the deluge.

But the stumping must go on.

The director may dodge a storm, but he's never ducked an issue. Certainly not in any of his films, of which "Silver City" is the latest. It's a noir-ish political mystery with an accomplished ensemble cast and many a bone to pick with those in the corridors of power.

Chiefly, the Bush administration.

There is no ambiguity about point of view in Sayles' pointed pictures, though he achieves a heightened state of message with infinitely more grace and care than a Michael Moore. Where the latter uses a bludgeon, Sayles employs a scalpel. And the result tends to be far more persuasive. If it's sermonizing, it is sermonizing of a high order, with characters that are more than mouthpieces.

Fitting for a fellow whose production company is called Anarchists Convention, which was named for his first collection of short stories. Sayles takes no prisoners. And he reads no reviews. Not anymore.

"I just don't," he says. "They interfere with my process. You start focusing on the wrong things."

For Sayles, 54, that process has been in development for more than a quarter century. Among his 15 movies are several of a political nature, including "City of Hope" (1990). In the broad sense, all of them are, not least his last two, "Sunshine State" and "Casa de los Babys."

But each is defined by two things: solid writing, and superior performances. Sayles draws full-blooded, three-dimensional people who come alive on the page as well as the screen. Combined with his versatility, it makes all the difference. Here is a filmmaker who may be said to have created, at once, one of the best family films ever made ("The Secret of Roan Inish"), among the finest police procedurals ("Lone Star"), an altogether unique science-fiction allegory ("Brother from Another Planet"), one of the most trenchant exercises in American film history ("Matewan"), and an anthem for the Sixties generation ("The Return of the Secaucus Seven") that reduced the otherwise sterling "The Big Chill" to the status of imitator.

Sayles does not fret that "Silver City" is coming out at a time when theaters are awash in such politically driven films as "Fahrenheit 9/11," or that many may have grown weary of calcified ideology. Newmarket Films, the company that happily took a risk on such pictures as "Whale Rider" and "The Passion of the Christ," relishes the edge he brings to bear.

"Well, of course, none of these films were out when I wrote and directed this picture, and the film finding its audience doesn't really concern me now. I believe that it will. One of the things our movie deals with is the way people see the world differently. One of the things that creates drama is not just that characters want different things or think different things, but that they see the world in a totally different way. So you can't expect movies to be received in a uniform perspective."

What Sayles does expect, or at least hopes for, is that viewers will see the movie with an open mind.

"There are some big issues here. I want to make sure people can draw a line from 'Silver City' to the Bush administration. But a bigger issue is, what do we expect from our politicians? Do they work for us, the voting public, or for the corporations that help put them into power? Also, the movie asks what we expect from our news media. More and more they are so embedded or compromised that they're only thinking about the corporation that signs their paycheck, and not the basic idea that they are supposed to go out and dig up the truth and present it."

Shot by the peerless Haskell Wexler, a frequent Sayles collaborator, "Silver City" takes us to a mythic "New West," wherein doltish born-again gubernatorial candidate Dicky Pilager (Chris Cooper), son of Colorado's Sen. Jud Pilager (Michael Murphy), is shooting an environmentally friendly TV spot. The filming is interrupted when Pilager, snagging something on his fishing line, reels a cyanide-laced corpse to the surface of a lake.

This renders his campaign manager, Chuck Raven (Richard Dreyfuss), positively apoplectic. Accident, or diabolical prank meant to deep-six his hand-groomed candidate? Raven isn't sure, but he retains a once-idealistic journalist-turned-private eye named Danny O'Brien (Danny Huston) to investigate. The Pilager family's political foes are many, some of whom are Cliff Castleton (Miguel Ferrer), a slavering right-wing radio host; Casey Lyle (Ralph Waite), a former EPA crusader; and even the family's own Maddy Pilager (Darryl Hannah), the candidate's black sheep sister.

O'Brien's digging unearths a complex and unsavory well of influence peddling and corruption involving powerful lobbyists, media barons, resource plunderers ("Pilager," get it?), and migrant workers.

"It has a lot of that kind of scope of classical Raymond Chandler, 'Chinatown' kind of mystery, including that the investigation starts to turn back toward the detectives' employers. Which is pretty classic. And I do like the way in which, although I hadn't thought about this very much when I was writing and directing it, that Danny's character, the detective, is kind of like the American voter.

"He starts out very apathetic and cynical – 'I don't do politics anymore' – and by the end of it he's at least gotten his sense of moral outrage back. And he's done it by digging a little.

"I'm afraid that we, the American public, can't just sit back and watch one news broadcast or read one newspaper. We have to dig a little if we are going to be informed citizens."

Also starring in one of Sayles' larger ensemble casts are Tim Roth, Maria Bello, Billy Zane, Thora Birch, Kris Kristofferson and Mary Kay Place.

The best actors in the business clamor to work with Sayles, usually for scale. The director commands great loyalty from some of our most distinctive performers, including some he has worked with again and again: Cooper, Waite (who was so memorable in "Sunshine State"), Mary McDonnell, Joe Morton, David Strathairn, Angela Bassett, Miriam Colon and Tom Wright, among others.

Arguably, it all stems from the writing, and people's respect for it.

"That loyalty and friendship is very special to me. Working with such people so often is the most gratifying thing about my job," says Sayles.

A graduate of Williams College, the Schenectady, N.Y., native began his career as a novelist and short-story writer with the 1975 release "Pride of the Bimbos," followed in 1977 by "Union Dues," a National Book Award nominee. A short-story collection, "The Anarchists' Convention," surfaced in 1979, the same year he began working as a screenwriter for Roger Corman's pinch-penny New World Pictures.

In Corman's company, Sayles learned his lessons well, such as how to make movies for a pittance. Sayles plowed that money from his "creature features" into generating his first film as writer-director and editor, "Secaucus Seven" (1980), made for $40,000 and winner of the L.A. Film Critics Award for Best Screenplay. Many regard the movie as instrumental in setting American independent film movement in motion.

He has used the same modus operandi since, writing screenplays for big-ticket, mainstream features (the forthcoming "Jurassic Park IV" is next) and doctoring scripts of all kinds for other filmmakers to underwrite his own, considerably more intelligent pictures.

"I'm lucky as opposed to most directors that I know, in that I get to work with a lot of other directors," says Sayles, a sometimes actor known to make the occasional cameo appearance. "Actors get to work with each other, and writers get to work with directors. But directors don't generally have that experience. I've worked for Steven Spielberg, for Ron Howard, Rob Reiner and a long list of interesting directors."

Sayles' new collection of short stories, "Dillinger in Hollywood," will be out in October. What's in the works cinematically?

"Plan B is always to write something cheap."

Sayles revisited (2007)

One may disagree with his politics, or find the occasional fit of sermonizing to be unseemly, but there is one undeniable fact of the career of John Sayles: He has never sold out. It's hard to imagine that he ever will.

Although the staunchly independent filmmaker's uncompromising approach has seen him struggle to get his films financed, finding top-drawer actors to star in his films (for scale) seldom has been a problem. Serious actors clamor to work with him, even if it means passing on a lavish payday.

"The biggest compliment that we get," says Sayles, "is when we ask these well-known and well-paid actors to be in our movies knowing they're not going to be well-paid because we don't have the budget, and they say, 'Yes.'"

An indy icon, Sayles has proved an inspiration to scores of writers and directors whose vision exceeds their purses or their powers, but one can also discern the influence of his storytelling techniques in much bigger mainstream movies.

His new film "Honeydripper," a music-infused drama set in Harmony, Ala., in 1950, follows the owner (Danny Glover) of a faltering juke joint who reluctantly hires a young electric guitarist in a last-gasp attempt to attract patrons. To a large extent, the film captures the transitional moment from the blues to rock 'n' roll.

"It's that moment in one place and one time that we heard the first couple of notes that anyone had ever heard of a solid-body electric guitar, the spread of which was so rapid and so quick to change the sound of music that you forget that it didn't exist in the public way until 1949," says Sayles, honored for lifetime achievement at the recent Savannah Film Festival. "It was developed on the East and West Coast at about the same time and spread like wildfire. In the movie, the kid builds his own guitar, and it's like Frankenstein's monster in the beginning."

Sayles and his companion/producer Maggie Renzi had a whole five weeks to shoot the picture. Nothing new; as Renzi says, they've experienced 30 years of making good movies inexpensively, "carving sculptures out of gravel."

"Because time and film are money, you don't want to do too many takes if you don't have too," says Savles. "It's important to edit in your head. It's not theater; it doesn't have to be a great or even a complete performance of a scene on the set. It can be made into a great performance in the editing room."

Sayles began as a fiction writer, producing two novels, "Pride of the Bimbos" (1975) and "Union Dues" (1977), and the aforementioned short story anthology, "The Anarchist's Convention" (1979). Switching to screenwriting and script doctoring (in part to fund his own movies), Sayles took the plunge in the late '70s. Taking $60,000 in screenwriting income, Sayles directed his first feature, "Return of the Secaucus Seven" (1980), a poignant look at a reunion of 1960s activists on the cusp of adulthood. It put him on the map. He followed with "Lianna" (1982), a daring examination of lesbian awakening.

The highly original "Brother From Another Planet" (1984) was followed by a pair of pet projects, "Matewan" (1987) and "Eight Men Out" (1988). Sayles continued to forge an uncompromising path in the '90s with films such as "City of Hope" (1991) and the Oscar-nominated (Best Original Screenplay) "Passion Fish" (1992). Shifting gears, Sayles delivered one of the most evocative children's/family films ever made, "The Secret of Roan Inish" (1994).

Sayles enjoyed a rare commercial breakthrough with "Lone Star" (1996), a somewhat atypical film that earned him a second Oscar nomination for his original screenplay. It remains his most thoroughly realized picture, and a tough act to follow.

Films of more recent vintage – "Men With Guns" (1998), "Limbo" (1999), "Sunshine State" (2002), "Casa de los Babys" (2003), "Silver City" (2004) – all were well made, with solid performances.

It's the least one expects.

....

Natasha Richardson: 'Countess' rewarding for actress
November 20, 2005

SAVANNAH – In the muted light of a backstage green room, Natasha Richardson glows.

It is not so much the warmth of her smile – a genuine, inviting thing – or some practiced actorly radiance. It is an incandescence of personality and of bearing. An approachable dignity, call it. One that glimmers as she speaks or regards a question. Born of a regal family of British thespians, this accomplished actress of stage and screen shares much with her character in "The White Countess," the last of the Merchant-Ivory pictures, and one of the best.

The making of the film, set in Shanghai, was a bittersweet experience for all concerned, given the sudden passing of producer Ismail Merchant on location earlier this year.

"It was very sad for me personally because I've known Ismail a lot of years, though we had never worked together," says Richardson, feted at the Savannah Film Festival recently. "I remember him coming into my dressing room one evening after a play I was doing and handing me a manila envelope. He said, 'Here's this wonderful movie that we're going to do together.' And I thought, 'Yeah, yeah, I believe that.' But then I read this beautiful story and this wonderful part.

"Getting this film made, and making this film in China, was so tough that you could see it take a toll on his health on a daily basis. It really knocked the stuffing out of him. Now, it's just hard to believe that he is not here anymore because he was such a life force."

Richardson enjoys one of her finest roles as Countess Sofia Belinsky, the only working member of a family of White Russian nobility exiled to Shanghai in the 1930s. Despite having been reduced to a sordid life in the city's bars and dance clubs, with all that implies, the young widow never loses her stately comportment with clients. At home, amid the pregnant silences of a less-than-approving family (which she supports), it is only her daughter who holds Belinsky in unquestioning esteem.

Enter American man-about-town Todd Jackson (Ralph Fiennes), a former diplomat blinded by the explosion that killed his child. His idyll of opening a swanky watering hole, enlivened by a certain political tension in the air, needs only one critical component, a living emblem whose style the club embodies. Jackson meets Belinsky at one of the halls she frequents and promptly makes a proposition. It is not sexual favors he wants. Rather, it is her resigned, world-weary, but polished presence. An echo of old Europe. Skeptical at first, she accepts out of need. Yet instinctively, she trusts this unusual, soft-spoken man.

"Sofia is a woman of great sadness and grace. She has lost everything in her life. She has lost her home. She's lost her country, her husband, her status and is having to live in a foreign land keeping her family alive by not being the aristocrat she was, but by working as a dance hall girl-cum-prostitute and bearing that humiliation with dignity."

....

Robert Wagner: The career of a thankful 'lucky man'
October 5, 2008

It was director Fred Zinneman who taught Robert Wagner that the mark of a gentleman is how he treats people he does not have to be nice to.

In a career spanning 60 years, Wagner has been not only a generous actor on screen, but a consistently gracious and appreciative fellow off camera. In one of the most telling observations in his memoir, "Pieces of My Heart: A Life" (Harper), he wonders if his ability to sustain a long career has been at least partially the result of his capacity for sustaining long-term relationships.

"That's why I wrote the book, because I wanted to acknowledge all the people who have been kind to me, acknowledged me, and made me aware of what I could do, where I could go," says Wagner, who spoke to The Post and Courier from Los Angeles. "I've really been so fortunate, and I constantly say to myself what a lucky man I am, because my dream came true."

At 78, Wagner has journeyed nimbly, though not without setback, through modern American film, television and popular culture, and continues working today in such productions as the "Austin Powers" pictures. Celebrated in his mid-20s as a hot, young Hollywood property, and half of one of the most glamorous young couples Tinseltown has ever known, the Michigan native made a mark in features before finding his most enduring success with three popular television series: "It Takes a Thief," "Switch" and the long-running "Hart to Hart." The latter was inspired by the "Thin Man" films of the 1930s and their blithe, debonair sleuths, Nick and Nora Charles.

Wagner does not pull his punches when the occasion warrants, but in the main, "Pieces of My Heart" is warm and magnanimous. Wagner chronicles his personal life in considerable detail and with an eye toward self-discovery. He does not shrink from recounting the darker times, especially the death of his wife, Natalie Wood, in 1981, which left him a shattered man. But his resilient optimism and the responsibility of caring for his three daughters helped Wagner reassemble the pieces. And thrive.

Sage counsel

In his early 20s, Wagner was counseled by his chief mentors – Spencer Tracy, Clark Gable and 20th Century Fox mogul Darryl F. Zanuck – to learn to get out of his own way and not be so self-conscious. Writing a memoir required a different strategy.

"There are so many ways in which you can go with it," says Wagner, married since 1990 to actress Jill St. John. "You have to be selective. I tried to use as a model David Niven's books 'The Moon is a Balloon' and 'Bring on the Empty Horses.' I liked his approach, and the way he could make a reader roar with laughter. If I could get that kind of quality and seamlessness in telling my story, I was going to be happy. It's not a big story, but it is a story of hope and believing in people who guided me in the right directions."

Having completed the book was a signal moment for the actor.

"It was a strange feeling to let it go, I can tell you that. But the response has been gratifying. I have a collaborator, (film critic) Scott Eyman, with whom I worked on the book for three years. He was so helpful to me in going back in time. He knows Hollywood and the industry so well, and he put me right back in there when I was 18 years old, trying to get started and get my foot in the door."

With one foot in the Old Hollywood of the studio system and another in the modern era, Wagner knew and befriended a pantheon of the greatest names in show business: Gable, Tracy, Niven, Bette Davis, Cary Grant, Frank Sinatra, Laurence Olivier, James Cagney, Audrey Hepburn, Fred Astaire, Gary Cooper, Robert Mitchum, Noel Coward and Deborah Kerr - to name a handful.

Before (and between) his marriages to the great love of his life, Wood, Wagner dated women as diverse as Debbie Reynolds and Joan Collins, married again, and enjoyed a relationship with Elizabeth Taylor. But one of his more influential experiences was a clandestine four-year love affair - in his early 20s - with Barbara Stanwyck, then in her mid-40s.

One lucky man

Wagner is keenly aware of what a privilege it was to have known and worked with so many extraordinary people, many of whom he first met as a star-struck boy who was a classmate of their children, or as a caddie at the Beverly Hills Country Club. Add to their number all the top-flight character actors, directors, producers, writers and crew with whom he has been associated.

"Isn't that amazing? To have had the opportunity to have been with all these people and for them to have taken time with me is extraordinary. And also to have worked with some of them. They were responsible for getting me going. They represented father figures in some cases. In some cases they had great caring for me, and I appreciate it so much. I'm so thankful that I was able to recognize the importance of friendship and to carry it with me."

With the recent death of good friend Paul Newman, Wagner may not be the last man standing of his generation of stars – contemporaries such as Christopher Plummer and Robert Vaughn also have memoirs out this fall – but it doesn't take as long to call roll.

"I was friends with Paul for 50 years. He was a very special human being, and I had great affection for him. He was obviously a tremendous talent, but also a marvelous husband, father and citizen.

"I'm far from the last man standing of our generation of actors, but it was a tremendous, sensational era, the last of the studio system. It had its negative side, too, but all I needed was for someone to tell me, 'You can do it, and we can help you.' And they did. It was all a family in those days. They tried to make you better."

Tracy exhorted him to learn the trade, not the tricks of the trade. After 50 movies, the brisk pace of TV freed Wagner to be himself. More, he discovered that for an actor, good TV is better than bad movies. Wagner found his real metier in comedy, winning his most loyal fans on the small screen with a trio of successful series, two of them playing lovable rogues.

"They were all characters that were written for me. I was told they would bring me into people's homes and they would embrace me. And the public did, certainly Stefanie (Powers) and me on 'Hart to Hart.' We stole liberally from William Powell and Myrna Loy (of "The Thin Man") on that one. But doing a series like that is not so easy today. It's harder for people to get involved with you. It was a lot of work, but also a lot of exposure. The chemistry was there, and I loved it."

Retire? Bah!

The Los Angeles he grew up in is long gone, and Wagner finally bid it adieu as a residence. But the echoes remain. Though Wagner has yet to enter his "anecdotage," his powers of recall are impressive.

"I had a lot of film and still pictures to look at for the book. And that brings back a lot of memories. You start to think about when it was taken and where you were."

Wagner, who had a somewhat difficult relationship with his father, views his life as a search for the closeness and intimacy of family. He often found it on the set, making movies and TV series. He found it most profoundly with Natalie Wood and his daughters. Today, a first-time grandfather, with Jill St. John he has recovered much of what was lost.

Years ago, like the jazz musicians he reveres, Wagner found a note and a tone all his own. Professionally, he has no interest in retiring.

"As long as I can touch and move an audience, or make them laugh - which is the greatest reward an actor can have - I'll keep going. I always have some projects in the fire."

....

British actor Tom Wilkinson is a pro's pro

December 26, 1999

Tom Wilkinson groans, failing to suppress the glimmer of a smile.

Is it true, he is asked, if his performance as Gerald in "The Full Monty" heralds the rebirth of James Cagney, song and dance man?

"You can be cruel, you people."

Among the most familiar of British actors to grace the screen - on both sides of the Big Pond - Wilkinson, currently in Charleston shooting "The Patriot," is widely respected for his way with a script, but his artistry as a hoofer was heretofore unknown.

Playing Fennyman, the theater owner and aspiring actor of "Shakespeare in Love," by contrast, did not require him to do the Hustle. What his character's seamless transition from villainy to innocence did reveal, once again, is the 51-year-old actor's considerable versatility.

Enjoying a somewhat more leisurely work schedule than is customary, Wilkinson stars as British Gen. Cornwallis in director Roland Emmerich's Revolutionary War-era drama, which features Mel Gibson in the lead. Will "The Patriot" afford him the opportunity to portray a man who was also governor-general of India and viceroy of Ireland, or will we get the Hollywood version?

"What you have to deal with is not the historical character, but the character presented in the script," says Wilkinson, a veteran of the National Theater and Royal Shakespeare Company. "I'm not a great researcher, but I do know a little bit about the character. I didn't want to play him as a villain, and he's written slightly villainously. I wanted to take the edge off that.

"I think people will be quite astounded by this picture in many ways. But of course, (a truly historical film) never happens. It's not meant to be a documentary. It's meant for people to go and see it."

Although such brief but comparatively juicy parts as the bristling autocrat he played in "The Ghost and the Darkness" have established Wilkinson's facility for sinister roles, he says doing a sympathetic figure can be more fun, provided he is furnished with complexity.

"Playing baddies in Jackie Chan movies is so easy and a little bit dull. Goodness is much more challenging to play. But whatever the part is, it is about professionalism. What you get from English actors of my generation is this: They've done a lot and they know what they're doing. They turn up on time, they know their lines, they have an idea of who they're playing and they're cheap. Which makes them very attractive.

"But that's the least thing you can offer to a director. You should be able to take something that is lackluster on the page and give it something more. That's what you are meant to be as an actor; an actor should an expert."

In the United States, until fairly recently, there was always a stigma attached to acting in television, at least for those who aspired to features. Only a few, like James Garner and Steve McQueen, were able to elude it. Now, things are wide open. But such artificial distinctions between stage, screen and TV performers never truly existed in England, where actors have moved freely from one medium to the other.

Oddly, Wilkinson says this may be changing.

"It is less the case now than it used to be. That sort of snobbery (regarding TV) is developing slightly. When I first started, you did theater. Your career went in two stages. You did theater and then you did television, and then you went back to theater and played leading parts. It's only in the past 10 years or so that English actors, as a group, have gone on to make movies. It's a serious proposition."

And if you are serious about it, Wilkinson insists, you don't rush over to America just to put your hands on as many dollars as you can.

"I do films now exclusively. I wouldn't dream of doing television, because the television scripts that I see are hopeless. Never say never, of course, but that's not really an option at this time. The jumping between theater and movies that people like Alan Rickman do, is nice to do. But I haven't done stage for eight years. I'm enjoying doing what I do at the moment, so I don't miss it much. It was a conscious choice to make films, not something I just drifted into. It's worked quite well. You get to a point when people know who you are and better things are offered you."

And there is always that lingering sense, he says, that America is the major leagues.

"I'm not free of it, either. If you do OK in films here, you've made it. You can say `I'm at the top of the hill.' Somehow, having a lead role in the National Theater, or having your own TV show - both of which I've done -- does not have the same cachet."

Today, Wilkinson is as busy as he wants to be, though he wishes he could make more films in England to be close to his family.

"The problem, of course, is that though there are more films being made there, they are being made under the most crippling of circumstances. Basically, they never have enough money. It's rather dispiriting, and I don't see it changing. I mean, the only time you have any money is when an American company like Miramax or Fox Searchlight is involved."

Wilkinson has made one other feature in North America this year, the comedy "Shiny New Enemies" in Canada, where he grew up. And where he almost became a farmer.

That idyll ended early on. His parents had emigrated to Canada with their own dream of forging a successful farm. The roots did not take.

"They went to find the promised land, but it didn't work out. They returned to England and ran a beautiful, picturesque country pub in the early '60s. But in those days you made nothing, but nothing, in such a business. It was then that I realized I would do something else."

Wilkinson happened upon acting at age 19 when he was asked to direct a play at school.

"I immediately knew how to do it. Exactly how. It was the Swinging Sixties in England, Everything had been sort of freed up. Youth suddenly had a voice. Suddenly the most important people in the country were under 25 - designers, poets, painters, actors, writers, musicians, entrepreneurs. If you were young, everything was thrown up for grabs.

"I thought `I love this so much. I'm good at it.' And that's what I've done ever since. No regrets."

Wilkinson's performance in "The Governess" won him the 1998 BAFTA award (England's hybrid of the Oscar and Emmy) for Best Supporting Actor. Still, it was "The Full Monty" and "Shakespeare in Love," both of which were nominated for a Best Picture Oscar ("SIL" winning), that may have won him a broader following in the States.

"I am very good at choosing scripts, I think. I generally pick the right ones to do. You get offered a lot of things, and you have to be careful. A big part is not necessarily a good one to do. But I certainly had a feeling that `Monty' was a good film that accomplished what it set out to do. It was not an ambitious film, but it had a good script and was made in an economical way.

"As for `Shakespeare in Love,' there are lots of actors' jokes in it and I thought initially that it might appeal mainly to a small coterie. Romantic comedy is very hard to do well. But it had broad appeal."

While, as Wilkinson reminds us, it's harder being a failure than a success, remaining a success is difficult. It depends, he says, on what is presented to an actor and at what age it is presented.

"If you are young and a big star is put on your dressing room door, it's difficult to accept several years down the road that the big star is no longer up there. I don't have that problem. The big star is yet to be put on my door, and perhaps it never will be. But that doesn't matter. I do what I do, and I'm comfortable financially. It's given me the most wonderful life I could have possibly dreamt of."

....

Ossie Davis: Actor has commanding presence
February 14, 1993

Dominant. Imposing. Resolute.

These are the qualities which come to mind when recalling the gallery of characters essayed by Ossie Davis over the span of a 45 year career. He is among a select group within a generation of actors who have exhibited an unusually commanding screen presence.

One thinks of George C. Scott, James Earl Jones, Sean Connery, Anthony Quinn, Burt

Lancaster — men who project forcefulness and integrity with equal aplomb, men whose power is as much spiritual as physical.

"I do have a sense of that," says Davis, currently starring in "Queen," a six-hour CBS miniseries based on the book by Alex Haley. "And I have a sense that I am fortunate enough to be one of those to have a specific gravity that stands me in good stead, a kind of in-built authority that comes from God knows where, that uses an actor's body and voice to express itself."

If only he understood the mechanism.

"It's one of the great puzzles of my life, the nature of this thing, how it works and why. I wonder why a man like Dr. Martin Luther King Jr., with the cadences in his voice, eventually has such a sway over such a large mass of people, while someone of equally brilliant accomplishments will remain unknown. To the degree that I have been fortunate enough to play a part in that, I am thankful and grateful."

A product of the New York stage, Davis, born Dec. 19, 1917 in Cogdell, Ga., made his debut with "Jeb" in 1946, the same year he met his bride-to-be, actress Ruby Dee. His first significant roles in film came with "No Way Out' (1950) and "The Joe Louis Story" (1953).

Four decades later, he is garnering a whole new audience in TV's "Evening Shade," and trenchant screen roles in pictures such as Spike Lee's "Jungle Fever," the latest in a line of films pairing Davis and his wife of 44 years.

As with contemporary Sidney Poitier, Davis' work has almost always had a provocative and unsettling component. No less so does "Queen," the Civil War-era chronicle of a mulatto woman's struggle for identity and independent life.

Davis, a long-time friend of the late Alex Haley, hopes audiences will gain something of lasting value from the miniseries, which features a starry cast led by Halle Berry, Jasmine Guy, Paul Winfield, Danny Glover, Ann-Margaret, Martin Sheen and Tim Daly.

"I think, and I hope, that viewers will begin to accept the fact that bloodlines of both our peoples have been intermingled for a long time and that there is nothing shameful about it. Alex Haley not only had a proud black bloodline but a proud, strong white bloodline. We in America have to recognize this duality, accept it, and get on with the business of establishing peaceful, equitable society. This truth doubles the importance of 'Queen.'"

Davis was interested in the project from the start, on both the professional and personal levels.

"I was intrigued in the beginning not only by the story, but by being a personal friend of Haley and (producer) David Wolper. I was predisposed toward doing this piece. It was my wife who first put David and Alex together. So I was definitely chomping at the bit when the offer came.

"The second thing that intrigued me was that I knew there were other elements of the story of our (African-American) sojourn here that needed to be addressed. Queen, Haley's paternal grandmother, is one. She is the child not only of a slave mother but of the white plantation owner. And she is compelled to press the case of her humanity."

Combined with "Roots," Haley's profoundly influential recollection of his maternal bloodline, the writer's impact will continue to be felt for many years, Davis believes.

"It's easier often times to look at the heroes and heroines that are more in the physical line of battle, people like Dr. King, Malcolm X and Thurgood Marshall, but often we forget that there are other heroes that worked in other vineyards, but produced work every bit as necessary as agitators and movers and shakers.

"Alex was one of those leaders and deserves to stand shoulder to shoulder with the best we have. He showed all of us a whole new side of ourselves that has too long been hidden. I had no idea of my particular African heritage until Hailey. These are things I needed to know."

At 76, Davis seems to have lost none of his zest for acting, or his abiding appreciation of his colleagues. This is especially true of the excellent ensemble cast of which he is a part in "Evening Shade." Even the regular commutes between his Los Angeles and New Rochelle, N.Y., residences are taken in stride.

"The series is great fun, to think of it is to laugh. To me, it's the closest TV is going to get to heaven because I get to work with such stellar performers as Elizabeth Ashley and Charles Durning, just to mention two. Topping it off, I get to work with a very old friend I admire in Burt Reynolds."

Davis also is appearing in the theatrical film, "The Ernest Green Story," released in January, a story harboring great meaning to the veteran actor.

"Both as an artistic experience and re-living of the civil rights struggle in which I was caught up, this film helped in one sense to put into perspective some emotionally very wrenching and disturbing facts with which I and a whole generation lived. Even now doing it, I get a bit of the shakes. But it's a chance to share with my kids something of what it was like, what this whole struggle has been about. We celebrate so much, but we take some things for granted. Some people gave their lives to achieve what progress we have today."

Davis says he has no plans to resume directing, which he did with considerable frequency in the 1970s ("Cotton Comes to Harlem," "Kongi's Harvest," "Gordon's War," etc.).

"The thing about directing is that it requires a tremendous amount of energy and withstanding an assault on one senses. You must become more of a monster than a man. This was more acceptable when I was younger, but I'd burn myself out in a couple of weeks today."

The vanguard of talented young black filmmakers led by Spike Lee, Carl Franklin, the Hudlin brothers and John Singleton doubles is impressive. But Davis, while encouraging, is reserving judgment.

"I'm particularly impressed with their potential. But I don't think any of them, Spike included, have come within sight of the true fulfillment of their possibilities. This is not the time to rest on your laurels — especially when you haven't got them yet. They just got the toe in the door. It's a chance to learn their craft.

"One of the critiques of American culture is that we have no 'second act.' We are sort of flashes in the pan, making a brilliant first statement and then not following it up. The odds favor long and steady application. I would hope for these young people to be so respectful of the art that they push aside even the impediment of their own fame and strive for excellence. To be celebrated so soon can be corrupting. And it is very unfortunate that we do this to our youthful talents. The corrective is to be mindful of one's goals and be humbled by what you have not yet done."

Davis and Ms. Dee apply this dictum to the personal lives, echoing the famous Paul Newman comment, "Just because you have a Screen Actors Guild card does it mean you stop being a citizen."

"I have an assignment that I've given myself. In our prisons reside 25 percent of our young black men, men who should be out working and marrying my daughters. I have to find a way to reach over those walls and put something in their minds and hearts that will change them. How can I as a writer and actor feed motivation over those prison walls? It's an ongoing thing. Poverty begins and ends in the mind, and soul. My task is to try to do what Malcolm and Martin tried to do: provide a sufficiently rich motivation."

....

Ruby Dee: Busy actress reflects on memories of King
January 26, 1992

Ruby Dee makes few concessions to age. If anything, the distinguished veteran of stage and screen is busier today, at a robust sixtysomething, than she was a decade ago.

"Life doesn't get gray hair or graybeards, you know. It just is. It's eternal and forever. One of the things about getting older is the recognition of this being a glorious time. There's a freedom you enjoy. You have to pinpoint the tasks, of course, but there are chances we can take that our kids can't take. There are things we can do that they can't do."

Such as exerting the kind of influence that only maturity affords.

Dee was in town last Sunday to serve as keynote speaker for the YWCA of Greater Charleston's 21st Annual Martin Luther King Celebration Ecumenical Service at Morris Street Baptist Church.

The figure of King remains of vital and illuminating one for Dee and her husband of 43 years, actor Ossie Davis, who collaborated on the 1987 television special

'Martin Luther King: The Dream and the Drum."

"We knew him mostly through (Harry) Belafonte, and also through a drug store and hospital workers union with which we were associated. Belafonte did a lot of fund-raising in his house and we were always there as a part of that scene. We came to know Dr. King well.

"Dr. King — and Malcolm (X) as well — had a presence that went beyond reality. If they seem present and real to us even now it is because we are dealing with their words, their thoughts, which are indelible. And I love coming to places like the YWCA here, for these reasons. It's also sort of the environment in which I grew up."

The daughter of a railroad porter and a schoolteacher, Ruby Ann Wallace was born in Cleveland and raised in Harlem. Although she made a mid-course correction from speech and drama to major in languages at Hunter College, acting seems almost preordained.

Dee, who studied with the likes of Paul Mann, broke in with the storied American Negro theater in New York. Her widely held Broadway debut came in "Anna LaCosta," in 1946, the same year she met another young thespian hopeful, Ossie Davis. They were married two years later.

Her first film was 1950's "No Way Out," one of several pictures co-starring Davis. Dee repeated her stage role in the film version of Lorraine Hansberry's "A Raisin in the Sun," (1961), the picture for which she is best known. More recently, she has impressed in "Cat People" (1982) and this past year in Spike Lee's "Jungle Fever, " again teaming with her husband.

The couple's permanent residence is in New Rochelle, N.Y., but Davis, a regular on the Burt Reynolds situation comedy "Evening Shade," also maintains an apartment in Los Angeles. She also is obliged to travel widely in her capacities as actor (the Great Lakes Theatre Festival is next), producer and speaker.

"Ossie comes home every two or three weeks. And we make the most of our time together, personally and professionally. I've always enjoyed working with him immensely. We collaborate as writers, and naturally have struggled in this area. We write well together, but we had to learn to do that. We offer different things to the package. He's a little bit more independent and much better read than me, with a great historical since about things, so I'm the one who most often compromises."

Which is not to say that Dee won't fight for her vision. Several projects under the aegis of their production company, Emmalyn Enterprises, have begun to catch fire.

"I'm busier now than ever. And I'm so grateful because at my age it could be the opposite. I could be retired. In addition to acting, I'm working with several novelists now on film treatments. I have a workshop as well. I love these projects, but I'm involved because I want to improve the situation. It's frustrating to see so many good works optioned by the film industry but never done. I hope to do a book a year in this area."

Dee says the stage generally presents greater opportunities to attempt themes challenging material, but that film has untapped potential.

"Movies cost so much now that few people are willing to take chances, but I'm hoping that will change because film has the potential to be as powerful as stage. I will be in a play at the Great Lakes Theatre Festival this year, an unconventional story called "The Ohio

State Murders, " which I think could make a great film."

What King, Malcolm X and other black leaders of the 1960's might have made of the new wave of motion pictures by such directors as Lee and John Singleton (Boyz in the 'Hood") is uncertain.

"I don't know. It is interesting to ponder what perspective Dr. King and Malcolm might bring to this time. I think they would put it in context. Things do not exist in a vacuum. Too many movies glorify guns, making a way of life out of violence. Others establish as values only what you can get, what you can acquire.

"That's how movies tend to define us as human beings now. It's not about the spiritual elements in various peoples; it's about making money. But Dr. King would not have attached the negatives alone. He was not an absolutist, which was one of the things I most respected about him. He would say that a system in disrepair had the duty to correct itself."

Dee says she is delighted to see this young filmmakers getting a chance to do significant pictures, but would like to see more movies like "Wall Street," which argue that more violence is being perpetrated in the corporate boardroom than on the mean streets of the ghetto.

"When I think about corruption and greed and murder I wish we could examine the daytime world and the well-dressed set, the white male questions. These crimes affect everybody. If there is something missing from the spectrum in exploring what's wrong in America, that's it. Too many people want to blame things on the victims. And you see little attacking the roots of our problems, unless it's exotic in some way."

....

Fonda mines gold as Ulee in new film
July 6, 1997

They've flung Freud in his face, jostled him with Jungian archetypes and pretty much dissected his every gesture for hidden meaning - or echoes of his famous father.

After a string of probing yet oddly superficial interviews, Peter Fonda is getting used to it.

The psychic mining of "Ulee's Gold" – and Fonda's performance – so irresistible in implication, moves on apace. Catharsis, pure and simple, we're told: Peter coming to terms with his demons. Peter's remote, taciturn character, Ulee Jackson, as the embodiment of his dad, Henry. Peter, matured at last, no longer the icon of rebellion.

It's been almost three decades since Fonda, then 28, zapped the public consciousness with 1969's counterculture anthem "Easy Rider." He was never to hit the stratosphere again. But at 57, with the success of Victor Nunez's "Ulee's Gold" assured and Oscar being whispered about, his career has taken a sudden surge skyward.

There's been much ado about his physical resemblance to his father in middle age, and even more about his exorcising the ghosts of the past.

"When it gets to be the psychobabble, it does get a bit old," says Fonda, speaking by phone from his hotel in Manhattan. "But you know, the movie's so good I don't care so much about that. After all, they're comparing me with Henry Fonda, who was a fantastic actor. And that's not too shabby.

"What was therapeutic about playing Ulee had nothing at all to do with my dad. It had everything to do with my ability as an actor. This time, I stood in front of the audience and pulled the rabbit out of the hat. That was great therapy for me. People are seeing that and seeing a whole different me. I've never been offered this opportunity before. I got to do this - that was the catharsis."

The publicity swing has been exhausting. There's a distinct sense of deja vu in being the subject of such widespread - and double-edged - media scrutiny. But Fonda, sounding quaintly (and appealingly) the old hippie, is taking these exertions in stride.

"I can use that old line from Bob Dylan's `Shelter in the Storm': `Burned out by exhaustion, buried in the hail, ravaged in the bushes, hunted on the trail.' It's the business of show business and I don't mind doing it at all, because I can do it well."

In writer-director Victor Nunez's "Ulee's Gold," Fonda has what many consider the role of his life, playing an emotionally withdrawn North Florida widower forced to take care of two young granddaughters while his son is in jail. Ulee is proud, stern, inflexibly independent - and the sole survivor of an Army unit obliterated in Vietnam.

That this solemn man makes his living at beekeeping, precisely the activity Henry Fonda enjoyed as a hobby, is only one of the reasons that amateur shrinks have licked at the performance like bears on honey.

The similarity in mannerism, gait and body language between father and son is startling at times. But if the notoriously taciturn Henry was the inspiration for his son's characterization, it's more roundabout than most would have you believe. Fonda told one interviewer, offhandedly, that Ulee was a composite of the characters Henry played in "On Golden Pond" and "The Grapes of Wrath."

"That was misunderstood. I said I went to the well of Norman Thayer and I went to the well of Tom Joad, then I finally went to my own well. I was waxing poetic and shouldn't have been. As my darling sister said after reading it, `Now remember, this is a great chance for you. But you're not there to entertain them (media).'

"She hasn't seen the film yet, by the way, but she calls whenever she reads another review and she gets real weepy eyed."

In preparing for the part, Fonda says he put himself into the character of Ulee's younger granddaughter, Penny, and imagined sister Jane in the part of rebellious elder child, Casey.

"And the two of us looked back at Ulee, not so much as our father - though both of us had gone through an experience of having very reticent and rejecting parents - but remembering how we felt. Then I put myself into Ulee. He's closed off, but he still has a way with his grandchildren. They respect him. He's taught them much of what they know of value.

"I didn't go into my father's characters, but I did go into the man we knew as our father that nobody else knows. People saw my father as a certain kind of decent man who stood for everything that democracy was supposed to be - and he was in his own right. But at home we had no idea. It was silence at the table."

Life with father

Fonda, who today lives on a Montana ranch with wife Becky and their sons Justin and Thomas, recounts one vivid domestic scene from his childhood that, though poignant, makes the listener feel somewhat the voyeur.

"Mom would be crying, Dad remote. Jane and I would whisper to each other, `Why is mother crying? Did we do something?' He'd give us a real stern look, and we thought he really hated us."

A few days ago, while taping an interview for television, Fonda was shown a clip from "On Golden Pond," a scene that leaps off the celluloid and helps balm the memory of the past.

"It was a wonderful moment. Jane's character in the picture is trying to talk to my father's, and he doesn't want to. Frustrated, she exclaims, `Why were you always mad?' And he replies, `I was never mad at you. It was something else.' I don't think our dad was ever really angry with us. Disappointed from time to time, with me for example. He thought I was going to be a fullback when I was born. So I was a failure from the get-go.

"But that scene was him for sure. It was the closest he ever got to playing himself. Before that happened I had already got him to come around to the point where I could hear the words, `I love you very much, son.' But seeing the movie still had a great impact on me. Today if I went to see it I'd have to take a box of Kleenex."

Nunez's script for "Ulee's Gold" contained parallel elements, though in far less sentimentalized terms than those of the sometimes syrupy "On Golden Pond."

If it ain't on the page it ain't on the stage, goes the theater maxim. Nunez's Ulee was there, in every detail.

"It was all on the page, from the first. Marvelous. I looked at that part carefully and I said, `I can play that. But they're not going to let me have it.' They'd typecast me so well. My own fault, of course; `Easy Rider' was such a hit that it made me an international icon of sorts."

It was a great stroke of luck that Nick Nolte turned down the part, and no small irony that Fonda's "Easy Rider" co-star, Dennis Hopper, also was considered for the role.

Fonda twice had seen Nunez's previous movie, "Ruby in Paradise," first as a director looking at Ashley Judd. It never occurred to him that he'd eventually cast his lot with the filmmaker.

"Then I got the script through my agent. Was I interested? Well, of course. Blood on my knees, give me the part! This could change my whole career around. People just don't know that I can do this kind of stuff. And I know how to do it very well.

"At one point, the script has Ulee walking into the room `with a gentle sorrow.' There's so much that can be done with that as an actor, so many places to go and find that emotion and find that moment and tell it. I thought, `This is unbelievably cool.' And I needed just one read-through to know how well it could be shot. It's a joy to read something so well-written, especially in an emotion that was slow."

The admiration is mutual between Fonda and Nunez, who refers to his star as a "synthesis of sage and fool," a phrase Fonda loves.

"Victor is a very gifted filmmaker, extraordinarily independent. He writes, he directs, he edits, he operates the camera. We used to call that an auteur, but if you use that word these days people say, uh oh, here comes Mr. Ego. Of course, you have to have an ego. In Victor's case, the way he works is that he spreads his ego around his wonderful company that have been working with him for years.

"I'm thrilled to be in it, but it's Victor's film, his magic, his words and his heart that stand out: All the things that allow him to see the extraordinary in ordinary people and bring it to the screen in a way that I've never seen before."

Comeback kid

After 30 years of sporadic work in films, directing the occasional picture such as 1971's well-received "The Hired Hand" and performing in a spate of mostly forgettable pictures, Fonda's long-standing "attitude" regarding Hollywood - and the indifference with which the industry replied - seem fated to keep him forever at a remove from studio productions.

"It wasn't disdain for Hollywood so much as disappointment," he says. "I love to make movies. Not all the work I did all these years was fine, but some of it was. I just got more and more disappointed as I realized the deals were becoming more important than the films. But as soon as I read the script for `Ulee's Gold' I realized it was my ticket to be invited back inside the walls and be able to play the parts that Clint or Paul Newman would play when they were my age, and still have access to independent films.

"It's remarkable. When I run into some of the movers and shakers at the Hollywood studios today they're so happy. They want me to be the comeback kid."

Some critics point to "Nadja," the campy 1995 vampire flick in which Fonda's Van Helsing won raves, as a career turning point. But the actor insists he began re-inventing himself as a performer in 1993.

"It was as if I had been riding this bicycle and looked over to the right where you see these 18 gears, and for the first time I looked on the left side and saw there were another 18 gears there. Let me try some of these. I've been having a blast doing my work. Waiting for it, of course, my phone doesn't ring off the hook, except for really terrible films."

That may change, especially if Oscar comes knocking. And if there is heightened respect for Fonda's range as an actor, it's matched by his seriousness of purpose. "I respect the skill of acting and the amount work it takes: finding the moment, as many moments as possible, and filling them. That's the trick of a film actor," says Fonda, who lectures in theater arts and media at Montana State University in Bozeman. "On stage, you can't take your time that way.

"One of the first things I learned on stage is when you're playing a scene, and you have to make the audience cry, whatever you do, don't cry before they do. If you do, they'll let you, the actor, do their crying for them. If you wait, they'll go Niagara."

Ulee's plight and passage are custom-designed to loose the flood. But for Fonda, putting the finishing touches on his memoir, "Don't Tell Dad," his own Ulyssean journey appears to have found home port.

....

Oliver Stone: Shining a light on survivors
August 6, 2006

ATLANTA – Oliver Stone, provocateur.

Over the years, it's seemed like a job description. Not "director," not "filmmaker," but a purveyor of inflammatory theories, of conspiracies in places high and low. From "Salvador" to "Platoon" to "JFK" to "Nixon" – corrosive, controversial.

No longer, says the man who was hardly the first choice to make "World Trade Center."

Opening nationwide Wednesday, the film has been made at a respectful distance from the events of Sept. 11, 2001, but for many it remains an open wound. No one would dare exploit it. Least of all a culturally aware director coming off an embarrassing flop in "Alexander."

"I know you think of me as political, but you have to realize I think of myself as a dramatist," says Stone, stumping for a picture that has his harshest critics throwing rose petals in his path. "I'm not running for office. I react to people. People take me to the issue. I don't look for the issue then try to find the people.

"I've always said controversy isn't such a great thing. It's nice to have people talking about a movie, but when it alienates a certain degree of the population without them even having seen it, that's no good. I'm not for controversy. I'm for making good movies that bring people in and get people talking for the right reasons. My problems have been between movies. I have spoken out on political issues between films but not within the films themselves. If you look at them, they are about people. And I really think that in this film, the light should shine on the survivors, the rescuers and their families. I don't want to get between them and the audience."

Large canvas, small story

Stone says he subordinated any other consideration to the task of telling the true story of the survival and rescue of two New York Port Authority policemen - John McLoughlin (Nicolas Cage) and Will Jimeno (Michael Peña) - who were trapped in the rubble of the World Trade Center after going in to help evacuate the towers. "World Trade Center" also follows their families as news reports terrify, anxiety mounts and information about the fate of their loved ones is slow in coming. The stories of those who risked all to worm through the debris and rescue the survivors – 20, out of almost 3,000 dead – are given no less respect in a film that is far less an entertainment than a testament to courage.

"There is a potentially big audience for this movie," agrees Stone, "but it has to be handled very delicately. It's an issue that inflames people very easily. I think the hope of the film is that it is fresh; it doesn't have political baggage. Everyone thinks of 9/11 politically now because of the five years that have passed. But 'World Trade Center' is clean. It is what it is. It's about those 24 hours."

McLoughlin and Jimeno, as well as their wives, Donna (Maria Bello) and Allison (Maggie Gyllenhaal), all say the film takes few liberties with their experiences. Producers Michael Shamberg, Stacey Sher and the late Debra Hill sought their approval from the start. "World Trade Center" began to evolve when Hill read about McLoughlin and Jimeno in a newspaper article, met with the men and listened to their stories.

An emotional shoot

Stone came aboard rather late in the game, well after screenwriter Andrea Berloff had made a pitch to Shamberg and Sher.

"It was late in 2004 when Andrea's script was sent to me," says the three-time Academy Award winner. "It's a very rare instance in my business when you get something that immediately inspires you to say, 'I want to make this.' Usually, it's a more drawn-out process. But it hit this horrific event in a way I had not seen before, in a way that deeply personalized it for me.

"I put myself up for the job, but they weren't ready to go with me at that time. They wanted somebody else. But you can't take that too personally in Hollywood. Six months later, they came back to me and I said yes again. I thought it was a great story from the beginning. It was true, and you don't get stories like this every day."

After filming the bloated "Alexander," living in his own Iran and Iraq of 2,500 years ago, telling a smaller story appealed to Stone.

"I've done small movies. Remember, 'Talk Radio' and 'Natural Born Killers' were small films. I follow the people. I follow my heart. This was a moving story. These two guys were among only 20 who survived. And they are lucid enough to share their feelings. It's an amazing stroke of luck."

Berloff and Hill had won the families' trust, encouraging others involved during that harrowing 24 hours to sign off on the project and, in some cases, participate. Berloff, especially, allayed their fears, spending long sessions in the Jimenos' home in Clifton, N.J., and with the McLoughlins in Goshen, N.Y.

Stone would not betray that trust.

"Their involvement was crucial," he says. "And it took time. I estimate it took John and Will two years to recover from their injuries and be able to talk about and process their experience, and another year for the script to develop. Then it languished a bit, because the timing wasn't right. Then when I came on in May of last year, it went into another phase because I brought Nicolas Cage in. John and Will were already aboard. There was a lot of politicking going on: all of the families, the mayor's office. It turned out the Port Authority was our best ally.

They wanted the story to be told because it honors the PA, which everybody forgets about. They had a lot of people killed."

The right time?

The movie opens in a stark, wrenching manner, shorn of any hint of melodrama. For some, it may be a bit too realistic, and unsettling.

Was the timing right? Stone thinks so.

"I think it's too late in some ways. Let's get real here. The consequences of that day are far worse than that day. Worse things have happened. You have more death from terror, more fear, more war, more constitutional breakdown."

But with raves from the Right, even from such conservative political columnists as Cal Thomas, Stone's certifiably apolitical film may quiet some of the criticism that has dogged such pictures as "JFK" and "Nixon."

" 'JFK' was not original to me. It was based on research by many citizens who had gone out as individuals to investigate without government money. I thought the right wing would like that film. I was shocked at the vitriol attending it. 'JFK' was not a hatchet job. 'Nixon' was not a hatchet job. I've been made out to be a left-wing looney. I'm not. I consider myself an independent. I don't vote Democrat because I'm anti-Republican or anything like that. My father raised me Republican. I understand conservatism. I understand liberalism. But I think there's a blend to be had. I do believe in evolution; I will say that. And it is the only thing I will say politically."

Stone says minor changes have been made to actual conversations for drama's sake in "World Trade Center," but nothing is created from whole cloth, no event fundamentally altered.

"I would say it is a dramatization of a gripping and exciting event that transports you, hopefully, to pity and tears and maybe a cleansing catharsis. It reminds you of the feelings of that day. We did overcome fear. We did respond well. We helped each other. The Jimenos and the McLoughlins, as well as the ex-Marine Dave Karnes (Michael Shannon)

- the first to find the men, and the character who represents the American public on that day - helped each other in extraordinary ways.

"I tried to make as realistic a film as possible," adds Stone, who shot a film in New York for the first time since "The Doors" (1987). "Making it in New York assured its authenticity. Two men, buried in the rubble in the middle of those towers for 24 hours. What made them survive? These lived because they were able to communicate with each other, to help each other, and to draw strength from their love for their families." Stone pauses.

Then, "We included the world's reactions to the events in the film because I think America was empathized with that day. A very special day. The world was with us in the war in Afghanistan, too. Let's not forget that. People today who walk around in denial and watch 'American Idol' - that's not the way to respond to the situation the world is in right now. You can't bury your head in the sand because you live in a geographically blessed country."

Any more than you can stop having a point of view.

....

Jeff Daniels: A career actor, just not a career star
October 27, 2005

Jeff Daniels prefers to live in the world. The real one, minus the cadres of fawning assistants, shorn of superficiality and tabloid prattle. They invented the term "regular guy" for fellows like the 50-year-old actor, though there is nothing commonplace about his versatility or skill.

Like "Good Night, and Good Luck" co-star David Strathairn, Daniels is an actor noted not only for the instant believability of the characters he plays, but for the way he has kept himself grounded in a sometimes surreal business.

Daniels plays (CBS executive) Sig Mickelson to Strathairn's Edward R. Murrow in director George Clooney's chronicle of the McCarthy "witch hunt" of the 1950s, one of two major movies Daniels currently has in theaters. He enjoys a much larger role, one of the best of his career, Daniels says, in Noah Baumbach's celebrated "The Squid and the Whale."

Daniels will discuss both pictures Monday during an appearance at the eighth-annual Savannah Film Festival, in between rounds of golf with his parents on Hilton Head Island.

The notion that the actors' approaches to their personal lives (Daniels and his family live in Michigan, Strathairn's in upstate New York) inform their performances is an intriguing one.

"That's an interesting point," says Daniels, who spoke to The Post and Courier from New York. "I think whatever that grounding is, whatever David's doing, whatever I've chosen to do, it helps you to keep it about the work. It allows you to play unsympathetic without thinking twice about whether you should be likeable or not.

"With a character like the husband and father in 'Squid,' it never crossed my mind to try to be sympathetic, though Noah was kind of waiting for me to ask the question that, in screenwriting, they call 'When can I pet the dog?' Or, as in a hospital scene in the movie, 'When can I hug my kid and cry and tell him how much I've screwed up and basically be likeable to the audience?'"

Being likeable is what they teach actors in Star School, says Daniels, who has played his share of clueless jerks. He and Strathairn went to acting school.

"So that doesn't enter our vocabulary. By being grounded, it becomes about the character, about the work you're doing, and not about whether someone's going to like us or not, critics or audiences or producers. Nor is it about 'I have this image to uphold as a star/celebrity/actor.' Our job as actors is to play the character as honestly as possible, not worry about image. I certainly have, and the career certainly reflects that. When you dive into something like 'Dumb and Dumber,' I mean, can you worry about image?"

Stumping for films of quality is much more palatable to an actor than being compelled to do publicity for lesser pictures. With "The Squid and the Whale" particularly, Daniels is all enthusiasm.

"It's a lot easier to talk about, that's for sure, compared to something that's mediocre and you're just in it. But, yes, it's a great time for me. It really is. I'm real proud of 'Squid' and 'Good Night, and Good Luck.' Bernard in 'Squid' is certainly the most complex role I've ever had to play. There are many traps in the part. It's very tricky. How do you play a guy who comes off fairly harsh to everyone he's around, and yet you don't play to that? You have to find ways to make him a human being. It's the kind of basic acting that they teach you: If you're playing the hero, find the flaws; if a villain, find the strengths. That's what you do. With Bernard, underlying everything he does is a guy who thinks he's right and truly believes he's right, that he did everything to save his (failing) marriage, that it's not his fault and that he's the victim."

Daniels' leading lady in the picture, Laura Linney, increasingly is regarded as one of our most accomplished stage and screen performers, a marvel of the naturalistic style.

"She really is, and she's one of these people who make you better, if you let her," says Daniels, born in Athens, Ga. "If you just play off her, it's almost like ping-pong. As actors, she and I both work on instinct, and it's really moment to moment. If she goes one way, you go with her. It really is act/react. I just loved working with her."

The movie, which also stars young actors Jesse Eisenberg and Owen Kline, reunites Daniels with the now 20-something Anna Paquin, with whom he had made two earlier films, memorably, as her father in the family classic "Fly Away Home," when Paquin was 12. That makes seeing the actress stroke his cheek seductively in a still from the new film a trifle jarring.

"She has grown up. Thank God. It's always good to see Anna. I did another movie with her called 'All the Rage.' She was no longer the 12-year-old girl then. And she's in her 20s now. As long as there weren't any geese outside the window (a reference to "Fly Away Home"), I was all right."

Daniels says what makes "The Squid and the Whale" so distinctive, for performer and audience alike, is its realistic focus on family dynamics.

"What makes the story so tragic is the deterioration of a family and the way all four of them struggle to cope with a lot of pain. Noah did a great job with the script. He launches it so well with an early scene where the parents say we're going to separate, that we're going to have joint custody and we're all going to live happily ever after and here's how it's going to work. It just deteriorates from there. You watch as these people with flaws, but with good intentions, fail miserably."

Family values

Daniels' marriage and family life, by contrast, appear to be blessed. They live near Chelsea, Mich., where the actor and sometimes writer-director founded The Purple Rose Theater (named after the film he made with Woody Allen).

"My wife Kathleen and I chose to move to Michigan and put family first, career second. That's what we did with our three kids (now 21, 18 and 15). We just wanted to raise them outside the industry in a place we were comfortable in. It was home to both of us before and it became home again. Now there are ways to live in California and still raise your kids outside the industry so that they are fine, but the joke is that your kids wind up going to Easter egg hunts at Sly Stallone's house, and that's just not real.

"The kids know there's a whole world out there; they've seen movie sets and met some really interesting, creative people. And yet they live in a part of the country that is, you know, a very feet-on-the-ground kind of thing."

Next up for Daniels is "RV," an adventure comedy with Robin Williams about "an average, dysfunctional American family" that sets off on a harrowing journey: two weeks together in an recreational vehicle. Daniels identifies, if only with the driving.

"My family has kind of a poor man's tour bus, which I love. I'm a big fan of RVs, and when (director) Barry Sonnenfeld was doing this movie, for personal reasons I wanted to get on it. Kathleen and I drove the bus out from Michigan to Vancouver, and the rest of the family flew out later. I arrived at the location after driving five straight days through the Rocky Mountains, and as I pulled up the (Teamsters) transportation captain turned to the assistant director and said, 'You can cancel his RV driving lessons.' I loved that."

Daniels devotes what time he can to the Purple Rose Theater, where, among other productions, he has debuted plays of his own. At the moment, he's helping fund the theater company by selling a CD of his live musical performances. It may also serve to underwrite a new play Daniels has written, "Guest Artist," which debuts in January.

"I only got into the live performances because it was a way to raise money. The CD came after that. We taped all the shows. So why not? We've sold 10,000 or so and now it's on iTunes and XM radio has picked it up. I just played Joe's Pub last night in New York. It's fun. We've got 30 more songs recorded live we can put on another CD, and eventually we will."

Daniels made his screen debut playing P.C. O'Donnell in Milos Forman's "Ragtime" (1981), his breakthrough role coming two years later as Debra Winger's inconstant husband in "Terms of Endearment" (1983). The last 25 years have seen him navigate a wide variety of roles. With rare exceptions, he's played characters sunk to the knees in authenticity.

"I was talking to an actor once who said 'I just hope I get one movie that outlives me.' I think I have half a dozen or so.

"I've been real lucky and I've worked with some of the best people in the business. And the phone keeps ringing. Longevity for a film actor is a big deal.

"I met (actor-director) Forest Whitaker for the first time this year at the Toronto Film Festival and I said to him 'We're part of that group of people who have careers in this very fickle business that allows us to work over decades. That's a special room to be in.'

"And I'm proud to be in it."

....

Anthony Minghella: 'Cold Mountain' director on hardships and rewards
December 14, 2003

An actor in an air-conditioned sound stage in Burbank or London might be sufficiently skilled to convey the hardships his character endures, without suffering those slings and arrows himself. Place the same actor with cast and crew on a long, cold, rain-drenched location shoot, and the shared miseries are all the more convincing on screen.

Anthony Minghella can laugh about it now. But the writer-director who undertook the task of adapting Charles Frazier's celebrated Civil War novel, "Cold Mountain," says five months of logistical nightmares and relative privation in Romania made the film company's two-week shoot in Charleston feel like lolling on the Cote d'Azur.

"I must tell you, the crew in Charleston felt that though we were working very, very hard, it was as if we had come on vacation," says Minghella, whose film opens Christmas Day. "We were so happy in Charleston because suddenly we had all this film infrastructure, we had a lovely hotel, we had great craft services, and because it was all so comfortable, we really felt like we were visiting somebody else's movie. We were lulled into this wonderful ease where we could swim and go out to wonderful restaurants. Then we had to go back to Romania, and it was appalling."

Minghella, best known for his previous adaptations of "The English Patient" and "The Talented Mr. Ripley," spent 10 months total in Romania, whose landscape doubled for Petersburg, Va., and the North Carolina uplands in which "Cold Mountain" is set.

"In Romania we couldn't get hot food on the set and it was so cold and rainy. There simply wasn't the support system that could keep a film of that size going. So we had a couple of weeks of bliss in South Carolina and 25 weeks of purgatory.

"But there is an upside to that, because it breeds an enormous esprit de corps. You're all in it together. I think it 'stains' the film in the best way; you really see that it's real. We grew the farms, we built the farmhouses. There is something about the shabbiness and the lack of beauty, which seemed to me to be able to summon some of the realities of that war. It was a terrible war for the South and for those living in the mountains in North Carolina. I felt we were duty bound to reflect some of that."

Dream cast

Minghella and his team composed an uncommonly gifted, and deep, cast. Apart from the leading roles played by Jude Law, Nicole Kidman and Renee Zellweger, a who's who of character actors made significant contributions, chiefly Philip Seymour Hoffman, Donald Sutherland, Brendan Gleeson, Ray Winstone and Eileen Atkins. Younger performers, such as Natalie Portman, were given meaty, albeit brief, parts to play.

This was not by accident. As another director famously remarked, "I cast actors correctly in order to liberate me from having to direct." Minghella clearly took great care.

"That was a very clever man or woman, that director," Minghella says. "People are always saying how a good director can make actors better. But actors make directors better. And these actors certainly made me better. I know I will never have a cast like this again in my life.

"One of the reasons it worked out like that was the trick of the film in a way. The movie is both a big story and a very small one, and the small one is really a series of duets. The character of Inman (Law) meets various people (on his odyssey home from the front), and while they are in the film, these actors are all central characters. Then they disappear, which means that in terms of casting I could aim very high with who I approached to be in the film, because I was coming to them to play a big role for a few days, as opposed to a small role for a lot of days. Because of that, and because I'm lucky enough to have some repeat visits by actors and get some of them early on, it meant that other actors were happy to work with people they admired. The casting was joyful."

Period Dress

"Cold Mountain" might seem to be of a piece with Minghella's earlier adaptations, yet, as screenwriter, chronicling the intertwined lives of the Confederate soldier Inman, his sweetheart Ada (Kidman) and Ada's salvation, Ruby (Zellweger), presented him with an enviable opportunity. As producer Sydney Pollack puts it, "Anthony was able to make his adaptation completely his own without ever violating the author's intent. In a way, he re-imagined and re-dreamt the whole world of the novel in his screenplay," earning Frazier's blessing in the process.

Minghella views Frazier's National Book Award-winning novel as a lost book of the 19th century, noting that 19th-century novels were in thrall to the job of telling a story.

"A lot of those books were serialized. They required a sufficiently muscular narrative to get a reader going back to buy the next installment. They were much more concerned with the quality of story and the quality of character. And so when I came to adapt 'Cold Mountain,' it wasn't about fixing anything; it was about how to do justice to the power of the storytelling in the limited amount of time a filmmaker has to lasso the preoccupations and journeys of these characters in a way that makes sense.

"Essentially you're trying to distill an American 'Odyssey' into 150 minutes, which is no small task. The real job was getting enough of everything in that it was satisfying without being overwhelming to an audience."

Total Immersion

It was Minghella who often felt overwhelmed during the four years he invested in the picture, a period only now coming to a close. It was not merely a matter of absorption in the work at hand. He says it also had to do with what he brought to bear from his own life, willfully or otherwise.

"What happens when you make a film is that it becomes your life. And it also becomes the sum of your feelings about where you are in your life. I'm sure it's the same with a novelist. Everything enters the book. And so everything enters the film. I was striving to do justice to the book, striving to do justice to the South, and also striving to do justice to where my own feelings and thoughts were at this point. I've been doing a great deal of personal writing about pilgrimage and about walking as atonement, and I think that's very much reflected in the way the story tells itself.

"It is asking questions about spiritual destinations, about where we're all heading and why we're heading that way, what is the reason why human beings are so tribal, electing to solve so many of our problems with violence - the perfunctory solution of a gun as opposed to the fuzzier solutions of dialogue and compassion."

Playing Southern

When Minghella shoots a movie, location scouts must think creatively. And actors check their passports at the door. Nationality is irrelevant. The British Isles and Australia are well represented in this cast, as they were in the war itself.

"There was a sort of imperative at some level to be literal and say, 'Well, who are the Southern actors, where are the Southern locations?' But I'm looking for fellow travelers, I'm looking for actors I admire, and I'm not looking at their passports. It's my job to give myself a safety net of apparent authenticity. But the reality is that truth in films is not about passports or about geography, because it's a fact for me that I've never shot a film in the place it's been set. My very first film ("Truly, Madly, Deeply") was set in London, but I shot it 100 miles away. With 'The English Patient,' the scenes in Cairo were actually shot in Venice.

"The truth that you're trying to get has got nothing to do with the museum of period work. It's to do with creating something that is a kind of time travel, taking the audience into an imagined past. Notwithstanding that we shot the siege of Petersburg some 6,000 miles away from its real location, what we were able to create just outside of Bucharest might have been more recognizable to a Confederate soldier than the real place is today. Where we were in Romania also seemed to me enormously redolent of the Appalachians. It's authenticity by the sleight-of-hand of filmmaking."

In this, Minghella had the complicity of an Academy Award-winning production team with whom he has worked for years: director of photography John Seale, editor Walter Murch and costume designer Ann Roth, among them. They are joined this time by production designer Dante Ferretti. All of which affords the director and his stars a wellspring of confidence.

"Exactly right," Minghella says. "I'm lucky in so many ways, but the luckiest thing is that I have this crew, who are so good to me and stay with me and support me. They set the tone for the actors, because they are so resilient and determined and dedicated that it's easy for that to spread to the people in front of the camera. They see the willingness of all of the crew who have been with me now for 10 years and are very loyal.

"Sometimes I think it is perfectly appropriate when the director gets the blame when a movie doesn't work, but sometimes the director gets too much credit when it does work, because it's the sum of the work of a lot of people, and I've got the best people around me."

....

Malcolm McDowell: Still going strong
January 29, 1998

Malcolm McDowell is perfectly willing to sacrifice for his art, within reason. But he draws the line at dyeing his now fully gray hair. The gifted British-born actor figures he's earned every frosty lock.

At a youthful 54, those few lines which do crease McDowell's once boyishly handsome face form an interesting topography.

And there remains that mischievous glint in the eye, the same that flashed provocatively at audiences a quarter-century ago in "A Clockwork Orange."

The picture earned McDowell widespread acclaim. Yet, like Anthony Perkins' characterization in "Psycho," the actor's portrait of the violent leader of a gang of futuristic toughs was so vivid and indelible that many had a hard time separating McDowell from the character. Not the least casting directors.

"That's absolutely true," says McDowell, who makes his home north of Santa Barbara, Calif. "Perhaps if I had stayed in England a bit longer after that it would have been different. But much the same sort of thing was going on there, even then.

"If you make a characterization too powerful and too good, it can have that effect. But it was a great film, with a great director. And it came at the right time for me. But it was strange, as well. After I did `if...', I was offered almost every script in Europe. After `Clockwork,' I got almost nothing. There was also a period of about three years when I didn't do a film. I'm not quite so fussy these days."

McDowell was in Charleston on Wednesday in the company of producer Barbra Ligeti and actress Cathy Moriarty, his co-star in writer-director Robert Downey Sr.'s picaresque comedy "Hugo Pool."

Described as "a flighty comic allegory about love and death in contemporary Los Angeles," "Hugo Pool" marks the return of one of the more celebrated independent filmmakers of the '60s and '70s, noted chiefly for the movies "Putney Swope" (1969) and "Greaser's Palace" (1972).

Downey, father of Robert Downey Jr., who also stars in the film, tells the tale of a romance between Floyd (Patrick Dempsey), an unusual young fellow who suffers from Lou Gehrig's disease, and Hugo (Alyssa Milano), a swimming pool cleaner.

McDowell weighs in as Henry, Hugo's out-of-control dad, but he shares most of his scenes with co-star Sean Penn: the "bad boy" of one generation bantering with another.

"Maybe there are parallels," McDowell says. "Sean's a wonderful young actor, of course. Wonderful to work with, as was everybody. Most of the cast is involved in a series of vignettes, and the whole thing is a little out of the mainstream. All power to it for that. One can see mainstream films any day of the week.

"This is a very personal film to Bob, funny, yet also dealing with a serious subject. It's a wonderful, whimsical kind of film that you rarely see anymore."

The character of Floyd is based on Downey's late wife, Laura Ernst Downey, who co-wrote the script and was, with Ligeti, a driving force behind the picture until her death from Lou Gehrig's disease.

McDowell's Henry is a man whose life is in ruin. Fighting drug addiction and a fractured past, he is charged with the task of driving a water truck to the Colorado River, filling it and making it back to the home of one of Hugo's customers (Richard Lewis) in time to avert catastrophe. Penn plays a rather outsized leprechaun who rides with Henry and helps him undergo catharsis.

"Henry is trying desperately to gain control. He's gruff, but he has tremendous vulnerability and heart. His new therapy is to inject a puppet with heroin rather than himself. Just because he's an addict doesn't make him a bad person. We rush to judgment so quickly about these things."

In 1994, when he was doing press for "Star Trek Generations," McDowell said he believed his career was at a stage in which he could bring the most to the kinds of richly nuanced parts Anthony Hopkins was doing. Roles not easily come by.

"I still feel that way. But I have yet to convince others. In this business, you just have to get the one part and then – boom – everything follows. Most of us are used to that. The whole procedure of casting means you have to have a pretty thick skin and not take things personally. You can't be bitter. You use it (disappointment) in the next role.

"Still, I must say I have been very lucky. I had a wonderful experience doing the 22 episodes of the (CBS) TV show `Pearl' with Rhea Perlman."

While the sorts of feature film roles he might prefer have been few of late, McDowell has not lacked for work. And like most stage-trained British performers, he scoffs at the notion of a role being "beneath him."

"It's ridiculous to say that. You're a working actor and can't afford to get too precious about your career. I often think I get these somewhat underwritten parts because they think I can make something of it.

"But the more complex the role, the more fun it is. I have a very interesting script now called `The Big Brass Ring' by (writer-director and WorldFest-Charleston alumnus) George Hickenlooper, with layered characters. I'd love to do it."

Upcoming are "My Life So far," with Colin Firth and Mary Elizabeth Mastrantonio. McDowell calls it "a lyrical, gentle comedy" of family life in Scotland as seen through the eyes of a 12-year-old boy, and "2103: The Deadly Wake."

There's also the nine installments of "Our Friends in the North," a British TV series that explores four generations of the political scene in the United Kingdom. Shot two years ago and already the recipient of most major English awards, the series was written by Peter Flannery and may yet make it to American TV. McDowell plays Cockney porn baron Benny Barrett.

....

McDowell, revisited (2008)
October 23, 2008

Malcolm McDowell, O lucky man.

A self-described working actor who started in films as big as could be, and of late has been at his busiest in years, the 64-year-old star was keen to give a little something back. Especially to a man few recall with the resonance of the past.

"Never Apologize," a filmed one-man show, is McDowell's tribute to the late British filmmaker Lindsay Anderson, celebrating a friend and colleague whose career deserves renewed attention. McDowell discusses Anderson's work, illustrated by clips from some of the latter's movies, such as "If..." and "O Lucky Man!" They were McDowell's first two features, Anderson's second and third. Both had enormous impact in 1960s England.

"I've always felt very indebted to Lindsay, who was such a good friend," says McDowell, who will receive a Lifetime Achievement Award during Saturday's opening night festivities at the Savannah Film Festival. "I was very lucky. He was my first director, and I really admired him. I started with one of the greats."

As so often happens with the passage of time, many were cloudy on who Anderson was. McDowell was determined to refresh their memory, keep the director's name alive. Those involved did it entirely out of pocket.

"People didn't remember the films, and I felt it was a great shame. Lindsay was unique. He was a great director who was also a poet. His vision was extraordinary, and his mirroring of what was happening in Britain at the time was really spot on even though the British hated it. 'If...' assimilated a rebellious feeling and was one of the watershed English films of all time.

"I wanted to bring attention to him and his films, which, of course, are my films, too. He gave me so much and changed my life forever. So I was very happy to put this show together. I can't believe the life it's had."

Born in Horsforth, Leeds, McDowell's career has spanned five decades in film and, more recently, on the small screen in series such as "Heroes" and the hit HBO comedy "Entourage."

But his signature movie, "A Clockwork Orange," contained a performance so potent and unsettling that it both ignited international stardom and risked limiting the sort of roles he would be offered. For years, and even now, despite such exceedingly sympathetic roles in movies such as "Time After Time" and "My Life So Far," casting agents persist in seeing him chiefly as a "heavy."

"Stanley's film was so vivid that people had a hard time knowing what to do with me after that. Had I not made 'A Clockwork Orange,' I would have had a very different career."

His films may have been of variable quality over the years, as with all actors, but the attitude McDowell brings to the tale has not wavered.

"I still get offered the 'heavies,' but I'm not complaining," says McDowell, who says he feels completely "Americanized."

"One is a working actor. You are not going to make masterpieces every time out. The peaks and valleys of a career happen to us all. Even the great John Gielgud went through a few rough patches. And he was a man I always admired for his extraordinary career. But if you want to wait for just the good stuff, you're going to have a very slim career.

"And also, you're not learning anything if you wait. You learn by doing crap, too. You have to do it; you can't teach it in a drama school. To keep practicing your craft is critical. An experienced actor can take a somewhat underwritten part and make more of it than is there on the page. But you have to be prepared with a point of view and a readiness to flesh things out."

With the likes of Robert Wagner, Tony Curtis, Robert Vaughn, George Hamilton and other contemporaries having recently published memoirs, might a book be in the offing from McDowell, though he is a decade their junior?

"Yes. I've been asked. But this film about Lindsay is my book, in a way. It's free form. I'm up there with no script, really not knowing what I'll be saying next. The stories I chose to tell varied from night to night during the five live performances of it I gave."

With several features and a host of TV appearances in the can or in production, bestowing upon him a Lifetime Achievement Award might seem a trifle premature. But McDowell appreciates the honor.

"It means I've been around a long time. But I'm still working. There's a lot of work right now for me. I don't know why. I guess most of my competitors have retired or dropped off the perch, as they say."

English Language Film Reviews

English Language Film Reviews

I grew up with movies in the English language, among the world's richest and most expressive.

I also grew up with a certain mindset about the filmgoing experience. How things have changed.

Today, we go to see a movie. Quite a different thing from going *to the movies* – the full, rich experience of the thing, in a darkened theater, with an audience. To be rapt, not merely diverted. To participate in a communal event. To be delighted by the grandeur of the theater and overwhelmed by the vastly larger-than-life presence of images on the screen.

A *really* big screen, mind you, not some 21st-century postage stamp.

Of course, we still frequent the bijou – at least many of us do – and it's still a pleasure, especially in an age of Netflix, Amazon and all those other streaming services that would have us stay at home or be tethered to our laptops, tablets or phones.

For the simple truth is that no matter how large the TV screen, to see a great movie on TV isn't really to have seen that film. It is not the way the director intended it be experienced, unless it was designed to go straight to video. The movie may still be entertaining, perhaps even edifying (and you can pause the flick to go to the bathroom or make a snack). But you will not be transported. You will not be truly immersed. Not the way we once were.

Not every innovation is an advance. On the other hand, here's something to be said for having choices.

The age of the true cinephile may have come and gone, apart from a handful of publications that try to sustain the intellectual depth and cachet of such bibles as *Film Comment* and *Cahiers du Cinéma*. But the simple love of movies and of visual storytelling endures, even in spartan surroundings.

And for that we should be grateful.

....

A poet's love: Film about John Keats is a triumph in every department
"Bright Star"
September 24, 2009

After the deserved critical pasting she absorbed for the austere and airless "Portrait of a Lady" (1996), New Zealand born writer-director Jane Campion all but disappeared from view, no longer riding the crest of her Oscar for "The Piano."

None of her subsequent films -- the failed literary adaptation 'In the Cut' and a brace of little-seen ventures -- helped restore the lost luster. Until now.

'Bright Star,' based on the three-year affair between 19th-century English poet John Keats and Fanny Brawne, is a thing of beauty that may be a joy forever. Painterly, sensual, and intensely romantic (as befits her subject), Campion's latest is a return to form: an engrossing, exceptionally literate character study that beguiles and touches in equal measure, dominated by beautifully rendered performances and a visual eloquence we've not seen from the director in years.

Set in an era when poetry was revered -- even if Keats, at the time, was not -- when people gathered in parlors to read and quote verse as often as we'd discuss the weather, the film is successful at re-creating a vivid sense of place (and sensibility). The movie does not dither, but gets to the business of character exposition from the start. There is little in the way of plot to deflect the viewer from this; nevermind that the leading figures are in their 20s, not possessed of the deepening of character that time confers.

No matter. Ben Whishaw (as Keats) and especially Abbie Cornish (as Brawne) deliver layered performances, ably supported by a fine ensemble cast.

With Lord Byron and Percy Bysshe Shelley, Keats (1795-1821) was one of the greatest poets of the Romantic movement, though it was not until his final days that he was rewarded with anything approximating critical acceptance. Renowned today for the brilliance of his Odes, his influence on the likes of Alfred Tennyson would prove profound.

That Campion takes some artistic license is understandable, and she is judicious in doing so. Although the film suggests that this secret romance between the penniless genius that was Keats and a well-born, headstrong young woman was restorative to the poet at a melancholy moment in his life, history tells a rather different story, that the affair was not an entirely happy one for Keats, his love for her bringing him more consternation than comfort as his feelings intensified and his tuberculosis progressed. He would die in Rome, a continent away from Brawne, at 25.

The correspondence between Brawne and Keats was published posthumously, scandalizing Victorian society. Although her letters to him were, as he had requested, destroyed upon his death, a collection of 31 missives written by Brawne to Keats' sister, Frances, was unearthed in 1937 and published by Oxford University Press. Campion's hymn to young love is an admirable companion piece.

While Whishaw is excellent as Keats, Cornish has the more challenging role. And she gives one of the year's most accomplished performances as the bright, obsessive, highly fashionable Brawne. It does not diminish the skill and nuance of her portrait to note that the actress also has a costume change in every scene, without exception, not simply a nod to Brawne's creative flair, but a clear indicator of the principal target of the picture.

Kudos to costume designer Janet Patterson, whose sumptuous work complements that of art directors David Hindle and Christian Huband and the lensing of cinematographer Greig Fraser.

....

Bigelow grows up, and then some
"The Hurt Locker"
June 28, 2009

A searing document on the chaos of war — and of soldiers trying to keep their sanity inside the maelstrom — Kathryn Bigelow's "The Hurt Locker" is tense and believable, first scene to last.

This gritty, ground-level approach, made frighteningly real with the help of hand-held cameras and stunning special effects, is of a kind seen in such remarkable films as "Black Hawk Down" and "Children of Men." Until now, it has eluded Bigelow, who finally has stopped trying to out-boy the boys and has made what is by far her best film.

Set in Baghdad in the summer of 2004, a three-man U.S. Army unit specializing in handling homemade bombs is counting down the last 38 days of its duty rotation. Sgt. J.T. Sanborn (Anthony Mackie), Specialist Owen Eldridge (Brian Geraghty) and team leader Sgt. Matt Thompson (Guy Pearce) are at the highly volatile center of the urban war, their task to locate and disarm (with a minimum of military and civilian casualties) the Improvised Explosive Devices (IEDs) that account for more than half of American "hostile deaths" and have claimed thousands of Iraqi lives.

Bomb disposal is an excruciatingly pressurized, extraordinarily risky proposition under the most controlled of circumstances. But when a sniper, an innocent with a cellphone or any number of potentially disastrous variables come into play, the job of the elite Explosive Ordnance Disposal (EOD) squad takes on a whole new dimension of hazard.

Thompson won't make it through the day. And his replacement, Staff Sgt. William James (Jeremy Renner) doesn't exactly go by the book. Sanborn and Eldridge consider him able but reckless. They are appalled by his disregard for protocol and basic safety measures.

Yet there is more to James than a high-wire act. Although at times it seems like he has a death wish, he is skilled, nervy, uncommonly precise. His unconventional style is not mere bravado. Only an encounter with an amiable Iraqi boy dents his unflappable exterior.

Meanwhile, with each day's new mission in the fog of war, the odds stack against them.

Renner is surprising, often brilliant, as James —a stark portrait of how war can make men crazy, or impel them to find reserves of courage and resolve. Geraghty and especially Mackie are no less convincing, and together the three drive the action throughout, reducing star cameos by Guy Pearce, David Morse and Ralph Fiennes to the status of footnotes.

"The Hurt Locker," with Amman, Jordan and Kuwait standing in for Baghdad, is nearly flawless on the technical end, with riveting photography by Barry Ackroyd and his team, propulsive editing by Bob Murawski and Chris Innis, and exceptional, grimly horrifying effects devised by Richard Stutsman.

That said, this is Bigelow's show, with a considerable assist by screenwriter Mark Boal, a journalist who had been embedded with a bomb unit in Iraq. Although Bigelow still telegraphs a few scenes with unnecessary visual cues, the film is otherwise confident, surehanded and efficient, a major step up from the tiresome macho posturing of "K-19: The Widowmaker" (2002) and the leaden tripe of "The Weight of Water."

The promise she demonstrated in the taut (if gaudy) "Strange Days" way back in 1995 finally may be coming to fruition.

....

'Bashir' a landmark combination of animation, story
"Waltz with Bashir"
February 26, 2009

Seldom has animation been employed to such sobering ends.

A rare and riveting motion picture experience, "Waltz With Bashir" is arguably the most haunting, most troubling movie of the past year, documentary or feature. Favored to win the Oscar for Best Foreign Language Film, that it lost in a stunning upset to the Japanese-made "Departures" in no way diminishes its honesty, its clear-eyed observation or its impact.

The story opens one evening in a bar in Israel, where an old friend confides to writer-director Ari Folman about a recurring nightmare in which he is pursued by 26 ravenous dogs. Always, it is the same number. He does not know what to make of it. But two men surmise that the dream is linked to their Israeli Army mission in the Lebanon War of 1982.

Folman realizes, to his considerable surprise, that there are unexpected gaps in his own memory of that time, more than 20 years ago when both men were 19 and stupefied by the chaos of war. Intrigued at first, then finding himself increasingly disturbed, he determines to visit and interview other comrades now living in places around the world.

Folman also speaks to friends who are psychologists, hoping to interpret strange images of his own. As he delves deeper, old events and old horrors resolve into shape and take hold. It is a meld of the real and surreal, of literal occurrences and fragments in which memory fills the fissures.

From melancholy beginning to unforgettable climax, "Waltz" works brilliantly on so many levels: as a moving personal account, as a study of the dynamics of memory, as an expose of the myths that glorify war, as a scathing attack on tribalism, as an examination of how men deal with the experience of urban combat (or don't), how they make sense of it (or don't), as a chronicle of unspeakable mass murder.

More, the film is a landmark in the use of animation to enhance the potency of a true story. The narrative techniques, framing devices, emotional content, character study and sheer visual invention of Folman and director of animation Yoni Goodman recall Vincent

Paronnaud and Marjane Satrapi's "Persepolis" (2007), yet surpass it.

The title refers to Bashir Gemayel, the Lebanese president who was assassinated during the 1982 war. His death led to a monstrous retaliation on the part of the Christian Phalangist militia: a wholesale massacre of Palestinian civilians at the Sabra and Shatila refugee camps. What terrible irony that the film was released on Christmas Day.

Folman, who had witnessed the aftermath and suppressed the memories of it, chose to tell his story via a graphic novel approach, moving back and forth in time, reasoning that "animation functions on the border between reality and the subconscious," one of the film's principal themes.

He succeeds to an astonishing degree.

"Memory takes us where we need to go," a psychologist tells him. If we are to understand the psychic costs of war, it is where all of us need go.

....

Withering study of an American dreamer
"There Will Be Blood"
Jan. 6, 2008

An intense and progressively dark character, Daniel Plainview seems at first blush a classic early 20th-century mogul in the making: personable and plain speaking on the outside, ruthless within. He is a driven man, possessed of vision and a blueprint to make it happen.

Plainview is first and foremost a pragmatist, able to ingratiate himself with almost any crowd. But pity those who get in his way.

As played, masterfully, by Daniel Day-Lewis, the pioneering oil man also is something else: a misanthrope, the embodiment of a slow-acting poison that gradually erodes the man. One of the year's most accomplished performances, it is the centerpiece of Paul Thomas Anderson's withering study of an American dreamer, "There Will Be Blood." Watching Anderson and Lewis develop this fascinating figure is not unlike observing a cook peel away each "leaf" of an onion to reveal the new layer beneath. They may seem uniform, apart from diminishing size, but they are not. Each is distinctive, a part of the whole. Just don't expect Plainview to shed a tear.

Loosely based on the muckraking novel "Oil" by Upton Sinclair, the movie is sprawling in the best sense. Set on the frontier of California's turn-of-the-century petroleum boom, it assays the life and times of an ambitious man who transforms himself from a dirt-poor silver miner into a self-made oil tycoon, inheriting an orphaned baby boy en route.

Working as a wildcatter, Plainview is visited one afternoon by a young man who claims his family is sitting atop an ocean of petroleum on a small goat farm out West. It's just oozing out of the ground, he's told. All the stranger wants is a $500 finder's fee. Whether there's a real sea of oil below the seepage remains to be seen.

But the signs are promising enough for Plainview and his now 7-year-old son H.W. (Dillon Frasier) to investigate. The farm rests on scrub land a stone's throw from the minor burg of Little Boston. Locals have little to entertain them, save for the caterwauling to be heard at the church of charismatic preacher Eli Sunday (Paul Dano), whose family owns the farm and whose twin brother was the mysterious lad who gave Plainview the tip.

Plainview is nothing if not efficient, and after reaching an agreement with the family, buying up every neighboring parcel of land and promising to lift everyone's fortunes, he has a derrick up and drilling in short order. He acidly rejects a proposal by corporate giant Standard Oil to buy his holdings and make him a millionaire — "Just what would I do with myself?" he asks, derisively — instead beginning work on a 100-mile pipeline to the coast and a more favorable contract with Union Oil.

But with the flow of oil comes rivulets of corruption, deception and murder.

The fifth film from writer-director Anderson, whose "Magnolia" and "Boogie Nights" were among the most intelligent, atmospheric and unpredictable pictures in recent memory, "There Will Be Blood" has faint echoes of "Citizen Kane," not only in its plot development but in such technical areas as camera placement. Some key scenes are presented in long shots, with the characters in the near distance. At other times, cinematographer Robert ("Good Night and Good Luck") Elswit's generally organic, unobtrusive photography employs fleeting metaphorical images, such as shadow creeping over the landscape to suggest the encroaching darkness. It's a rather obvious gambit, yet isolated and effective.

A fine, classically infused score by Radiohead guitarist Jonny Greenwood marries well with the action, which Anderson renders with intimacy, as well as epic sweep and scale. Kudos, too, for the gritty production design of Jack Fisk.

But towering over it all is Day-Lewis, who makes the other actors — even the first-rate Ciaran Hinds, as his chief lieutenant — seem like extras observing a one-man show. He's that good. Day-Lewis does comparatively few movies these days, but he pours himself into those he does make. This Oscar-worthy performance is one of his most riveting.

....

A beautiful marriage: Ensemble-driven movie classy in depiction of race relations
"Rachel Getting Married"
November 6, 2008

Colorful, unconventional nuptial preparations serve as the backdrop for Jonathan

Demme's "Rachel Getting Married," scenes somewhat reminiscent of "Monsoon Wedding" in their casual though sumptuous elaboration.

But while "Monsoon" was a comedy girded by serious undertones, "Rachel" is a raw and corrosive drama that dissects a young woman's war with addiction and her difficulties in dealing with the swirl of her sister's impending marriage.

It is one of the year's best independent films, lent immediacy and intimacy by hand-held camera work - there is, throughout, a sense of being a member of the party - and an ensemble-driven structure suggestive of a Robert Altman picture.

Finally emerged from the chrysalis of her adolescent roles, Anne Hathaway gives a searing performance as Kym Buchman, edgy child of a prosperous family, and an addict in shaky recovery. Her issues with soon-to-be-wed sibling Rachel (Rosemarie DeWitt), estranged mother Abby (Debra Winger) and father Paul (brilliantly played by Bill Irwin) obscure the root cause of her agony, a tragedy that director Demme and debut screenwriter Jenny Lumet (daughter of Sidney) take their time revealing.

The film unfolds over the course of a weekend in Connecticut, with two very different kinds of gatherings going on: people joined in the fun and folderol of the wedding party, and others caught in a quagmire of past events, struggling to draw strength from the parallel community.

A probing director, Demme wants to show (and generate) respect for the honesty of their emotions as well as their displays of self-delusion and courage. He succeeds. Lumet's script is admirably devoid of formula or manipulation. She cares less about making her people likeable than she does about helping us understand them, so that in the end we are concerned with their fates. With rare exceptions, scenes that might have slipped into theatricality are instead shorn of histrionics. Kym may be a drama queen, but you believe every moment of it. There is humor in the story, to be sure, but it is just as often painful for the characters as it is a source of relief.

Hathaway, fragile, jittery and combative, does the most accomplished work of her young career (in what is admittedly a showy role). DeWitt's subtle portrait is one of the film's strongest and more nuanced. But the most impressive actor on view, arguably, is Irwin, who quietly, generously turns in a delicate balancing act of a performance, rich in emotion yet restrained.

The supporting cast, led by Winger, Tunde Adebimpe (as the groom) and Anna Deavere Smith as the sisters' stepmom, also delivers the goods. Among the principal pleasures of the movie is the wedding party's large and boisterous cast of friends and relations, assembled for an idyllic interlude of feasting, affection and music. And what music, a festive, multi-cultural score by Zafer Tawil and Donald Harrison Jr.

Production designer Ford Wheeler's lively sets couldn't be more engaging, and the photography of Declan Quinn, especially in close-up, does much to draw us in and enthrall the eye.

If there are quibbles with the film, they reside in overlength, and in the warm-and-cozy way in which it depicts this interracial marriage, with its breezy integration of black and white. Very appealing, and certainly possible, but perhaps a bit gauzy. It is the way race relations should be, and, sadly, so seldom are.

....

Bieber burnishes Garland legend in 'Crazy'
"Crazy"
May 15, 2008

Biographical films of the Hollywood variety tend to be problematical, especially when the subject is a musician.

Too often they are freighted with the same story arc of tough childhoods, hard living, fractured relationships, drug or alcohol abuse and painful recovery. Even when true, it feels trite.

Then there's the tendency to play fast and loose with the facts, to amplify this, downplay that, and inject fictionalized characters and situations to augment the dramatic potency of the picture.

Sometimes, in the right hands, this works, as was the case with Taylor Hackford's "Ray" (2004) and James Mangold's "Walk the Line" (2005), to cite two recent examples. Other times, it's hackery or worse, an abomination.

"Crazy," written and directed by Rick Bieber, resides comfortably in the former category. The name Hank Garland may not be nearly as familiar to audiences as Ray Charles or Johnny Cash, but within the recording industry his musicianship and creative drive were legend. A virtuoso studio sideman turned star act, the Cowpens, S.C., native, excelled in country and western, rockabilly, R&B and jazz in the late '50s and early '60s before an automobile accident derailed his career.

Working chiefly out of Nashville, Garland's playing was revered by Elvis Presley, with whom he made recordings from 1958 to 1961, but he was no less respected and sought after by the luminaries of country music (Patsy Cline, Hank Williams Sr.), rock (the Everly Brothers, Roy Orbison) and, after a gig in Chicago exposed him to the great jazz artistry of the day, some of the finest musicians who have ever taken a stage and hatched a note.

Bieber makes it plain from the start that dramatic license has been taken, yet he is so conscientious about the key details of Garland's life, informed by hours of conversations with his subject and Garland's family, that "Crazy" has a bedrock feel of authenticity. More, it is the work of a filmmaker who genuinely cares about the story he is relating and the man at its core. It is all the more impressive for being Bieber's first stint as a director. A long-time producer and writer with extensive film and TV credits, he has rendered a lively, emotionally resonant movie, with wonderful music, that is an uncommonly seamless meld of character study and period recreation. But the real surprise is not so much Bieber's deft execution - you expect a certain polish from someone of his experience - as it is the casting.

Starring as Garland is relative newcomer Waylon Payne (godson of Waylon Jennings), among whose previous film roles was Jerry Lee Lewis in "Walk the Line." Payne, possessed of considerable screen presence, also brings the kind of gravity to the performance that one usually associates with a far more seasoned actor. He gives us a flawed but principled man for whom professionalism and loyalty meant something. We also discover a musician who risked his livelihood (and perhaps more) to fight for musicians' rights in an era when they had few.

But at least as integral to "Crazy" is the story of Garland's stormy relationship with his wife, Evelyn, played to the hilt by Ali Larter (TV's "Heroes"). Formidable, fragile, voluptuous and complex, Larter's Evelyn may open some eyes. It is a zesty, largely sympathetic portrait that is deserving of attention. There is also strong support from the likes of John Fleck, Raymond O'Connor, Lane Garrison and, in the most touching turn in the film, Scott Michael Campbell as Garland's ill-fated cousin.

A fine script, co-written by Brent Boyd, is girded by the atmospheric photography of Craig Haagensen, the meticulous production design and sets of Philip Toolin and Linda Spheeris, and original compositions by Larry Klein, which add much to the recreation of classic musical hits of the era.

Garland, age 74, died in Jacksonville, Fla., in 2004, two weeks before Bieber began principal photography. At least he had the pleasure of knowing that a new generation might be introduced to his innovative music, that a thoughtful film was at hand. And in good hands.

....

'Atonement' just can't pick up the pace
"Atonement"
January 3, 2008

Some will rave, others curse, but there's is little in "Atonement" to get worked up about, one way or another.

A prestige picture with a fine literary pedigree, the film is one part story to five parts sumptuous (but showy) photography. Although affecting at times, with fine production values, director Joe Wright's adaptation of the novel by Ian McEwan is too self-consciously "arty," diluted by surprisingly thin characterization and mired in "women's picture" inertia.

The film is so lethargic and over-studied that it drains even the herculean evacuation of Dunkirk of its drama.

Exploring the minutiae of life is one thing, lending commonplace occurrences absurdly large import is quite another. It does not help when your leading lady, Keira Knightley in this case, is almost as irritating as her character is sympathetic. Or when one of the better young actors to emerge in some time, James McAvoy, is stuck in the purgatory of what feels like a lesser "Masterpiece Theater" rerun.

"Atonement" opens in 1935, with 13-year-old Briony Tallis (Saoirse Ronan) having completed her first play. Her family, occupants of an immense English mansion, exhibit the classic signs of the privileged enjoying their privileges. Her headstrong (what else?) older sister Cecilia (Knightley) may feel cosseted by this opulent hothouse existence, but she is too busy thinking about Robbie Turner (McAvoy), the son of the family's housekeeper (Brenda Blethyn, wasted). Turner, who was put through Cambridge by Cecilia's father, carries a torch for her as well.

Briony, meanwhile, has a potent adolescent crush on Turner. So much so that, interrupting Turner and her sister in high ardor, she accuses Turner of a crime he did not commit. Cecilia and Turner are torn apart when he is convicted and imprisoned just before the onset of World War II. Heartbroken, Cecilia defends Turner steadfastly, eventually leaving her family to take up residence in a tiny flat in London. There, she works with incoming wounded at a local hospital, soon learning that Turner was given the option of getting out of prison if he'd join the army.

Briony, who comes to realize what she has done, the consequences her bearing false witness has brought, seeks forgiveness for her misdeed as the years pass and she, too, volunteers for work in a London hospital. One day, she will realize her dream to become a writer, a novelist, as it happens, and it is through the conduit of fiction that she finds penitence.

If all this sounds rather melodramatic, it is.

Someone kindly tell Wright and his cinematographer Seamus McGarvey that evocatively lit, painterly close-ups are not acting. And longing looks do not compensate for limp dialogue. There are beautiful images piled on beautiful images, but too many call attention to themselves in an unseemly way.

Just as disappointing is the script. Screenwriter Christopher Hampton ("The Quiet American") may be a lion of the British theater, but his work here falls short, burdened with a plot that turns on a single moral dilemma.

Where is the freshness, the snap, Wright and Knightley brought to their first collaboration, "Pride and Prejudice"? Where is the richness of characterization of McEwan's book? The film shares much with another gorgeously filmed but shallow period adaptation, the superior "Wings of the Dove."

Knightley plays her part like someone just out of acting school, investing Cecilia with unnecessary flourishes that reveal almost nothing of character. McAvoy ("The Last King of

Scotland") already had a Austenesque costumer under his belt this year with "Becoming Jane," and might have been better advised to stick with more modern drama, the kind that suits his edgy talents.

Ronan is adequate as the younger Briony, but Romola Garai, so good in "Amazing Grace," renders a frustratingly one-dimensional Briony at 18. Only Vanessa Redgrave, appearing in a brief coda as the elderly Briony, registers as more than a glorified drawing-room type.

Kudos to production designer Ian Bailie for his recreation of Dunkirk, which is very effective at conveying the grimness, exhaustion and initial disarray of that episode. But Wright simply doesn't take it anywhere. It's just a set piece, a backdrop.

In the end, the film is another case of much ado. A movie paced this sluggishly needs to have a sharp script and a sense of purpose to sustain interest.

"Atonement" offers not enough of either.

....

Writer-director Penn paints expansive yet intimate canvas
"Into the Wild"
October 18, 2007

"I will exchange a city for a sunset, the tramp of legions for a wind's wild cry, and all the braggard thrusts of steel triumphant, for one far summit blue against the sky." – Ben Saunders in "The Middle of Nowhere."

It is no mean feat to render a film that is both intimate and expansive, one quality enhancing the other. That writer-director Sean Penn has achieved it - and more - demonstrates a rebellious spirit seasoned by maturity, a painterly way with the medium and an insistence on layered characterization.

"Into the Wild," Penn's finely balanced adaptation of the 1996 book by Jon Krakauer, echoes of everything from "Jeremiah Johnson" to "Never Cry Wolf," but it is very much its own film, a hymn to the exuberance of youth, to daring and possibility, to wanderlust.

But it is also a cautionary tale, based on the true story of Chris McCandless, a freshly minted Emory University grad who chucked it all to discover a genuine sense of self on the roads of the American West and in the Alaskan wilderness.

Idealism is a laudable, perhaps necessary, facet of the conscience of youth. The problem is that the innocent and inexperienced are even less likely than their elders to distinguish between authenticity and romantic illusion. McCandless, played with thoughtfulness and verve by Emile Hirsch, was a case study in black-and-white thinking, a 23-year-old romantic imbued with Thoreau's notions of self-reliance and Jack London's sense of adventure, but repelled by the "false security of material success." He was determined to emancipate himself - from the prison of a suffocating future, from parents (William Hurt, Marcia Gay Harden) living a lie, from a way of existing he found poisonous, even from a sister (Jena Malone) who came as close as anyone to understanding him.

For all the satisfactions of living life on one's own terms, the reality of a vagabond's life is not a walk in the park. But driven by his own brand of glorious arrogance, McCandless embraced uncertainly, rolled with the punches (literal and figurative) and stayed focused on his ultimate goal: Alaska. After 18 months of hoofing around the West and Mexico, encountering a menagerie of folks vibrant (Vince Vaughn), quaint (Brian Dierker, Catherine Keener), sweetly 16 (Kristen Stewart) and grandfatherly (Hal Holbrook), he's still convinced he has all the answers.

Finally in Alaska, he thrives for a time, his resourcefulness helping him endure a harsh winter, creeping loneliness and the specter of privation. Soon that specter takes on definable features, and despite McCandless' grit, the wilderness claims him. McCandless died on Aug. 18, 1992, found by hunters in the abandoned bus that was his camp. He had never contacted his family. Their only link to his experience was his journal.

Passionate and visually spellbinding, this beautifully shot, carefully edited paean to the wild also understands its perils - and those of hubris. Moving back and forth in time, it pivots on an exceptional portrait of a man whose fierce moral code, while admirable in many ways, was also a form of blind self-absorption.

Hirsch, reunited (albeit briefly) with his "Dangerous Lives of Altar Boys" co-star Malone, plays this passage into manhood unusually well, if not quite as brilliantly as some rapturous notices might suggest.

No, the most impressive feature of this film is the filmmaker, Penn.

It's his finest hour as a director, from storytelling to composition to casting. In another director's hands, the supporting characters could have been types scissored from cardboard.

Not here. The performances of Dierker, Keener and Holbrook in particular are rounded and touching. They are integral to the narrative.

Penn's movie, like his people, inhabit the moment.

....

O'Toole still a lion in winter
"Venus"
March 1, 2007

This lion in winter still has a certain majesty.

His face ravaged by years of hard living, but his talent as expansive as ever, Peter O'Toole will not go gently into that good cinematic night. Not when there's a ripping good role to play, a chance to exchange rejoinders with some gifted contemporaries and, oh yes, flirt with a female character one-fourth his age.

Some things never change. The great reprobate is every bit the rascal he always was, and just as disarming.

While some have found "Venus," the story of an elderly actor drawn to a 20-something Pygmalion, to be a wee bit creepy, that's a too-literal reading of the tale, which is really about the pleasure and comfort an aging man takes in a young woman's company, especially when he can help her find a path to the larger world. There's more poignancy than prurience.

Much of the credit for the film's success must go to screenwriter Hanif Kureishi ("My Beautiful Laundrette") and director Roger Michell ("Notting Hill," "Persuasion"), who together crafted a witty script peppered with tart, telling dialogue. It's also mercifully free of sentimentality.

"Venus" explores the unlikely relationship between a once-well-known stage actor of suave bearing, now in his 70s, and a less than polished young woman five decades his junior. But it's no conventional May-December romance. In fact, the relationship they develop all but defies categorization.

On the one hand, it seems Kureishi is getting at those things in life that are achingly transitory, fleeting, as elusive as wisps of smoke. But look (and listen) closely. You find that the story is more about connection, friendship and the many manifestations of love, about the passing of the baton of wisdom and knowledge. Particularly the knowledge of what it means to live fully and well, of how to deal with how we age.

This is skillful storytelling, expertly handled by Michell and his marvelous cast, whose crisp line readings are rendered with perfect inflection.

Subtle is not a word commonly appended to the work of seven-time Oscar nominee O'Toole, who's always seemed larger than life, more leading man than leading actor. The average movie could not confine him. Not so here. His character, Maurice Russell, is a case study in craft.

Age 74 but looking far older, O'Toole has stolen most of the attention from cast mates Leslie Phillips (as Maurice's prickly pal Ian) and Vanessa Redgrave (as his ex-wife). Fine as O'Toole's (perhaps valedictory) performance is - and it ranks among his best - the most enjoyable work in the film may have been turned in by Phillips, whose long-suffering asides give the movie so much of its humor.

As Jessie, the grand-niece who arrives to upend Ian's orderly life and fascinate Maurice, Jodie Whittaker, a recent grad of London's Guildhall School of Music & Drama, gets a plumb role from the get-go and makes the most of it. Without her character's growth, the film goes nowhere. Whittaker's work is surprisingly unforced and relaxed in such august company. Like character, like actor: Whittaker's co-stars are imparting a lifetime of experience to their young collaborator.

Still, it is O'Toole who towers. Maurice thinks of himself as a "scientist of the female heart," but at this stage of his life, it is not lechery that drives him. It is a yearning for his lost youth, and a vicarious (if envious) delight in Jessie's.

....

Outstanding film a restrained, measured 'Letters' translation
"Letters from Iwo Jima"
February 1, 2007

Like most battlegrounds, it is a haunted place. Echoes and ghosts. Voices in the wind. On the Pacific island of Iwo Jima in 2005, a team of Japanese archaeologists are paying their respects at a World War II memorial site, marveling at how untrained soldiers could have dug such expansive tunnels to escape enemy artillery fire. Strewn about are remnants of abandoned gun emplacements, but it is the tunnels that fascinate the men. Suddenly, one of their number finds an officer's leather folio buried shallowly in a cave. Undisturbed for 60 years, it contains maps, letters and other artifacts.

Segue to 1944. A young Japanese soldier (Kazunari Ninomiya), a simple baker in civilian life, is taking a break from digging trenches to write to his wife back home. He wonders if he may be digging his own grave.

So begins Clint Eastwood's Oscar-nominated "Letters From Iwo Jima," one of the past year's truly outstanding films.

Enter Gen. Tadamichi Kuribayashi (Ken Watanabe), who has just arrived to assume command of the island's defenses. Humane, intelligent and unconventional, he ignores the sweltering heat and the barren landscape while trying to motivate weary, ill-fed troops.

Having lived in the United States for a time, and well aware of American industrial ingenuity, Kuribayashi immediately suspends the excavation of trenches and erecting of bulwarks on the beach, knowing they will prove ineffective. Instead, he orders tunneling in the island's network of caves. The decision is not popular with his officers, especially the older ones, who regard him as a desk jockey.

About the only army officer on his side is the recently arrived Baron Nishi (Tsuyoshi Ihara), a gallant Japanese noble and former Olympic equestrian champion whose sudden appearance temporary boosts the soldiers' morale. But he also brings with him dire news: a Japanese naval task force has suffered crushing defeat, which all but eliminates the prospect of close air support or re-enforcements. Iwo Jima, it is clear, is a lost cause.

The first rumblings of that futility arrive with aerial bombardment and battleship fusillades, pounding the island for days on end before the actual amphibious assault.

Meanwhile, the general dutifully writes letters to his wife, as much for his peace of mind as hers. They deal less with the hopelessness of his position or new tactical problems than with mundane household affairs, apologizing to her that he was unable to finish laying the new kitchen floor before shipping out.

What he doesn't write, at least not at first, are his orders to fight to the last man

The companion piece to Eastwood's "Flags of Our Fathers," "Letters" completes the director's magisterial two-part saga of World War II. Has any film ever been made by an American that has so much empathy for a people that once were a mortal enemy?

Produced by Eastwood with Steven Spielberg, it achieves a number of singular goals, not the least of which is humanizing Japanese soldiers long stereotyped as "yellow demons" fanatically devoted to the Emperor.

The screenplay by Iris Yamashita, from a story by Yamashita and Paul Haggis (based on the book "Picture Letters from Commander in Chief") cocks a knowing ear to the age-old grousing and complaining of enlisted personnel. It is a very different picture of the Japanese foot soldier - common men, not professional warriors - than we are accustomed to seeing in films of World War II. With a few pointed exceptions (the code of Bushido still ruled), the movie is shorn of the sinister, rabid countenance typical of films of the '50s.

Some may question the inclusion of (seemingly) gratuitous examples of Japanese and American barbarity in the field, but it is well to remember that both sides were guilty of such expedients.

The film generally skirts politics in favor of character, and the story provides some indelible ones. Watanabe, imposing in "The Last Samurai" and "Batman Begins," could not be better. His is a rounded, fully fleshed portrait of an honorable man in an impossible situation, dedicated to his duty and his country but mindful of the extraordinary human cost. No less outstanding are Ninomiya and Ryo Kase in pivotal supporting roles.

As in "Flags," Eastwood and cinematographer Tom Stern opt for a curiously sanitized, washed-out color palette: mere hints of brown on a soldier's belt; the pale blue of sky; snatches of sepia and occasional flows of blood in muted red. It is a device at once distancing and starkly intimate.

Stern captures the claustrophobia of the caves and their connecting tunnels, cul-de-sacs and corridors riddled with dysentery, ferocity and fear. The carnage outside is even more graphic and horrifying: a slaughterhouse on both sides. Death descends arbitrarily on individuals, not just massed troops on a distant beachhead.

The interplay of combat sequences and lulls in the action are exemplars of choreography and, especially, film editing (Joel Cox and Gary Roach), as effective as any since Spielberg's "Saving Private Ryan."

One may quibble over some of Eastwood's narrative choices, but few can question his mastery of the medium.

In "Letters," more so than in "Flags," Eastwood's vision is restrained, measured and painstakingly precise. He knows exactly what he is after on screen, and secures it.

"Letters" casts an unflinching gaze at war. It may at times be unavoidable, but it is never less than horrific.

....

Winslet delivers a fine performance in 'Little Children'
"Little Children"
January 4, 2007

It is a conceit of the urban dweller that all of suburban existence is a bland monotone coma divorced from the real life of the cities.

When vibrance and culture infuse the metropolis, who in his right mind would dream of wasting away in the 'burbs, those Stepford-like enclaves of little (or massive) boxes all in a row, with their hissing sprinklers, manicured hedges and desperate housewives?

Not to mention an increasingly insular mind-set.

This condescending image - not totally removed from reality, of course - has been fodder for numerous novels, nonfiction tomes, TV series and films generally produced by people who've seldom set foot anywhere near a suburb. It's like those well-meaning folk who (rightly) decry the violence visited by humans on animals yet have some Bambi-esque notion of how nature functions in the wild.

To date, the best of the films to plumb this theme of slow suburban rot have been Ang Lee's dour "The Ice Storm" (1997) and "American Beauty" (1999), Sam Mendes' fascinating satire of an American dream curdled at the edges. Mendes' movie could be scathingly funny as well as sharp and melancholy. By contrast, Todd Field's winning ensemble piece, "Little Children," is more of a rumination on how the real lost boys and girls of the title aren't the overweight suburban munchkins who have to be driven to every outing, but the adults who do the carting.

It's a worthy follow-up to Field's first directing effort, "In the Bedroom," propelled by a script the director co-wrote with Tom Perrotta, drawing on the latter's popular novel. Stylistically, the new picture has trace elements of the work of Douglas Sirk: idyllic on the surface, unfulfilled yearning underneath, with some parallel archetypes. But the analogy breaks down quickly. Field has no interest in Sirk's burnished visuals and dreamlike torpor. And he gets more from his actors than the melodramatic posturings typical of Sirk's (overwrought) characters.

Although Field breaks no new ground, one thing that does set his movie apart is that it has the temerity to question that hallowed constant of American culture: that motherhood is the ultimate experience.

You'd get a major argument on that score from Sarah Pierce (Kate Winslet), a wife and stay-at-home mom who has allowed herself to settle, not just settle down. She is palpably unhappy: bored with her life in a cookie-cutter Massachusetts subdivision, tired of her self-involved husband and not particularly insane about the task of tending her young daughter.

She is also a duck out of water among the gaggle of judgmental hens who safeguard the suburban realm. The biggest moment of their days is sitting in a communal park with their strollers, speculating on the buff physique of Brad Adamson (Patrick Wilson), aka The Prom King, a Mr. Mom who can't muster much enthusiasm for yet another crack at the bar exam.

Adamson is married to Kathy (Jennifer Connelly), a gorgeous public TV producer who is not insensitive to his issues with the role reversal (He's actually pretty comfortable with it.) but wishes he would show more initiative. He loves her, but the wife's firm control of their lives and her nit-picky budgeting lectures make him feel emasculated.

Back in the park, none of the assembled moms dare speak to him. Leave that to Pierce, who, though doubting such a hunk would ever find a "frump" like her attractive, nonetheless makes a bold move. Introducing herself, she impishly suggests Adamson kiss her just to shock their onlookers. The two lonely hearts are unexpectedly stirred, and it's one short step to an unlikely but seemingly inevitable affair that embodies their emotional frailty - and essential immaturity.

Field whisks in several subplots: chiefly that of a former cop (Noah Emmerich) and his campaign to fan outrage over a convicted sex offender who has moved to the neighborhood after a stint in prison. A genuinely creepy fellow, the ex-con (Jackie Earle Haley) triggers a spasm of fear and loathing, attended by the specter of violence. His only bulwark is a staunchly protective mother (Phyllis Somerville), who fights for him to have a fresh start.

The entire cast delivers the goods, with especially fine work from Somerville, Haley, Emmerich, Jane Adams and Mary B. McCann. But in the end, Field's film belongs to Winslet in as polished a performance as the past year produced.

....

Fine performances fit for 'Queen'
"The Queen"
November 9, 2006

When the fairy tale becomes accepted as reality, print the fairy tale.

That seems to have been the approach adopted by the British tabloids, and some hyperventilating fellow travelers, in the aftermath of the death of Princess Diana.

Darling of the Empire - the new Guinevere of a new Camelot - and the young, lovely breath of fresh air beloved of fashion houses and rock stars, Diana was adored even more by the British people. Her divorce from Prince Charles mattered not a whit. As far as they were concerned, she was still Princess.

Nevermind that she often courted the kind of microscopic scrutiny she railed against. Diana has been portrayed as the victim of royal indifference and of a predatory press for so long that the "truth" of it is engraved in stone.

There is another side to the story. Several in fact. And in "The Queen," Stephen Frears tells them with the inestimable aid of Helen Mirren and Michael Sheen, affording us a more rounded and subtle version of events. Though not necessarily more accurate.

A nation in mourning needed comfort from its Queen, she was admonished. Where was the Royal Family in this time of grief? Why were they silent? Day after day, as the flowers piled high by the gates of an empty Buckingham Palace, and the outpouring of tears reached flood stage, the voices of dismay over the Queen's silence turned to outrage, fanned by media overkill. An orgy of attention out of all proportion, many would argue, to Diana's actual significance.

Frears' tale turns on Queen Elizabeth II's (Mirren) inability to comprehend the depth of the public's response to the death of the former Princess, who had been divorced from Prince Charles (Alex Jennings) barely a year before, and on new Prime Minister Tony Blair's respectful, if relentless, insistence that the Royal Family make some gesture. If for no other reason than to save the monarchy from itself, to recognize that the world and its expectations had changed.

"The Queen" opens with Blair (Sheen) just having taken office as the 10th Prime Minister (Winston Churchill was the first) to serve this Queen and country. Labor is triumphant, the Tories in eclipse, and Blair has thrilled his constituency with his vow to "modernize" Britain. The Queen is not enamored of him or his attitudes, and their initial meeting is strained.

Diana's sudden death soon exacerbates matters.

Though the family thought her more than suitable at the start, Diana was not long in being an "embarrassment" in the Windsors' view, a bit too modern to be countenanced and prone to errors of judgment. She is actively disliked by Prince Philip (ably, coldly, played by James Cromwell) and, apparently, oft given the cold shoulder by the Queen and Queen Mother, not to mention suffering betrayal at the hands of her husband.

Blair is convinced that however distasteful it may be to the Queen, or difficult for Diana's young sons, nothing will appease the public short of a public expression of grief, and a public ceremony - anathema to the Royal Family. They deem it an intensely private matter, for them as well as for Diana's kin. In this respect, Elizabeth is behaving in precisely the way she was taught to behave since taking the throne as a young woman. It is what is expected of her, she believes. She could not possibly be so terribly "out of touch" with her people, could she, a people in whose sound judgment she has great faith?

Initially, Blair believes Diana deserves better. But as the clamor increases in volume,

Blair, no romantic, begins to sense an ugliness about the way the Queen is being bullied. Still, the pressure mounts, and when the people's long-standing love of the Queen at last seems at risk, even from ardent supporters, she capitulates. Whisked from the refuge of her country retreat, the Queen must endure the humiliation of a public statement of grief and admiration she does not feel, live and broadcast globally. The experience leaves her shaken. But only for the moment. Her family may spend pounds like they're going out of style, yet in matters political, Elizabeth II is practical to the core.

She is wonderfully played by Mirren, an actress who grows better, deeper, more gutsy by the decade.

Not for 35 years, since Glenda Jackson drew on the vestments of Queen Elizabeth I in the matchless TV miniseries "Elizabeth R," has a British actress worn the purple with such assuredness and skill. Mirren gives us both an impenetrably regal bearing and a complex portrait of a woman one may admire anew, for all one's misgivings about the anachronism of royalty and its conceits.

It is a measure of the strength of Sheen's performance that he in no way falls in the Queen's (or Mirren's) shadow. He never falters, nor does the remainder of a fine cast, in an absorbing film with no wasted scenes.

In his best work in some time, Frears ("Dangerous Liaisons," "The Grifters") takes a balanced approach. He has the decency to give most characters the benefit of the doubt, even the ineffectual Charles. Of course, since Peter Morgan's script is said to be largely fictionalized, with much supposition augmented by "palace insiders," the film's take on what was actually said and done could be just as open to question as the tabloids'.

It's feel of authenticity could be the greatest fiction of all.

....

This 'Bettie' fetish film done with taste, innocence
"The Notorious Bettie Page"
May 25, 2006

Human sexuality will out. You can repress it, suppress it, try to legislate against it. You can pound away from the pulpit. You can smother it with psychology. But like a blade of grass that works its way through concrete, the most basic of all natural drives will surface -- in all its manifestations.

That's one not-so-coded message of Mary Harron's atmospheric biopic "The Notorious Bettie Page," a partial history of the fabled "Pin-Up Queen of the Universe" that shares its subject's particular brand of innocence, despite all the nudity and fetishistic trappings of the story of her rise.

Yesterday's scandal is today's absurdity.

It took decades to recover Page from the kinky cubbyholes of pop culture to the prominence she enjoys today, but the sweetly seductive lass from rural Tennessee has attained full iconic status, thanks largely to collectors of her '50s photos, a vibrant Internet underground, hordes of admiring artists and the long-time championing of such publishers as Playboy's Hugh Hefner.

After several desultory documentaries, and several published biographies in recent years, most of which dwelled on the "seamy" side, now comes writer-director Harron's surprisingly upbeat feature, which takes a paddle to hypocrisy and empty moralizing. It even suggests the importance of restraint in matters sexual. All while showcasing a bravura lead performance by Gretchen Mol, who plays Page as both benefactor and victim of her beauty.

Trained as a teacher, but hoping to become an actress, Page fled an abusive marriage and the legacy of child sexual abuse to arrive in New York in 1949, hoping to make a fresh start. She supported herself with generic modeling gigs and secretarial work while taking acting classes. As depicted by Harron, she did have talent. But that was not what most people saw. Page had an uninhibited personality, notwithstanding her Christian beliefs, and its wasn't long before she graduated from playful pixie to cheesecake.

The black carpet to fame (and notoriety) was unrolled by pin-up mavens Irving Klaw (Chris Bauer) and his photographer sister Paula (Lili Taylor), an inoffensive pair of business partners who transformed Page into a sensation - at least to the many thousands of American men who frequented a certain kind of newsstand. A goddess was born.

But this was the 1950s. The great monotone coma of conformity held a nation in its grip. Rectitude and wholesomeness above all - in theory, at least - and peril befalling anyone not "right thinking" about God, country and the evils of sex.

That could not stop Page from becoming "The Pin-Up Sensation That Shocked The Nation!" Or at least shocked the blue noses (most of them well-meaning) in the federal government of the day. One was the sanctimonious would-be porn eradicator Estes Kefauver (David Strathairn), a U.S. Senator and fellow Tennessean who, not without irony, continually irked his own constituents with his progressive stance on such issues as consumer protection laws, antitrust legislation and civil rights for African-Americans.

Apparently, the senator drew the line at pictorial expressions of unconventional sexuality - almost comically tame by today's standards - and its "disastrous" effects.

Meanwhile, Page had met renowned glamour photographer and former model Bunny Yeager (Sarah Paulson) while vacationing in Miami Beach. Yeager forever cemented Page's image with a breezier, light-hearted approach. She also saw Page's allure more clearly: "Even when she's nude, she doesn't seem naked."

While the Klaws were obliged to destroy most (but not all) of their vast library of stills and film, Page continued to flourish for a time.

Kefauver's 1955 committee hearings essentially ruined Klaw. Soon enough, its canards also compelled Page to turn her back on "show" business and find herself anew in the church. The story ends there, with Page in her mid-30s, bobby socks having replaced garters and hose. She is happy and not a bit ashamed of her past. "Adam and Eve were naked in the Garden of Eden," Page insisted. "It was when they sinned that they put on clothes."

Harron, who wrote the screenplay with Guinevere Turner, does not deal with Page's troubled later years or her eventual recovery.

She didn't need to. Fifty years later, Page remains the exuberantly voluptuous muse of photographer and artist alike. And Mol ("The Shape of Things," "The Cradle Will Rock") effectively captures her in a performance that is both gutsy and skilled. Mol projects that blend of freshness and fragility, optimism and sadness, exceptionally well. They are qualities the real Bettie Page -- a nice, somewhat naive Southern girl -- knew all too well in a life that had its share of tragedy.

For their part, Bauer plays Klaw with a splendid nervousness, Taylor is her customary edgy self, and Paulson makes a quick impression, but Strathairn barely gets to stretch his acting legs. Jared Harris also contributes a minor, eccentric role as the soon-to-be-famous fetish artist John Willie.

Harron ("I Shot Andy Warhol," "American Psycho") succumbs here and there to a regrettable penchant for stereotyping, especially of men, but on balance her film - shot mainly in period-perfect black and white, with bursts of color - is fair, measured, and tasteful.

But definitely not for every taste.

....

This 'Austen' is no plain 'Jane'
"Pride and Prejudice"
November 24, 2005

Love's anguish, love's ecstasy -- the eternal themes of the "women's picture" -- underscored by class consciousness, gender politics and the folly of snap judgements. Can there be a more perfect embodiment than Jane Austen?

No, and despite the narrow, pinched world of its characters, "Pride & Prejudice" reminds us why.

Deft direction, gorgeous visuals and an exceptionally fine central performance by Keira Knightley make this latest rendition of the Austen classic one of the most satisfying. It's a lady pleaser extraordinaire, though one may have a few quibbles with the authenticity of its period sensibilities. Not to mention its length; such delicate minuets can seem to go on forever. After an exuberant opening, the movie settles into an agreeable canter through the passages of the heart and some of the most beautiful (computer-augmented) countryside ever captured on film.

"P&P" modernizes some of its 18th-century dialogue, which won't be to everyone's taste. Nor is the heroine in the film exactly the same person as on the page, which might be of concern only to purists. What is true to form, apart from the sumptuous sets and costumes, can at times be tedious: the depictions of men as clueless shadow figures and of women as either giggling meemies or calculating ciphers. The last, of course, with the customary proto-feminist justification: A woman had no choice, and little recourse.

But Elizabeth Bennet (Knightley) does. The second of five daughters born to Mr. and Mrs. Bennet (Donald Sutherland, Brenda Blethyn), country gentry whose circumstances are comfortable if less than grand, Elizabeth is a self-possessed woman of ready wit and understanding heart. Her honesty is as unassailable as her courage, though it seems she takes first impressions too seriously.

Elizabeth desires love as ardently as her sisters, yet intends neither to make husband-hunting her chief occupation or settle on just any monied clod who finds her enchanting. Yet, in the end, she too will fall prey to sister Jane's dictum, "We are all fools in love."

Screenwriter Deborah Moggach does a generally good job with the adaptation of Austen's novel, but it lacks some of the elegance of Emma Thompson's Oscar-winning script for "Sense and Sensibility." The male characters are drawn much too thinly, with Matthew MacFadyen obliged to play the stolid Mr. Darcy as if he is perpetually constipated.

Knightley's Elizabeth, by contrast, is dead-on: emotionally rich, unfailingly intelligent and sparkling with personality. It is among the year's best performances from an actress demonstrating heretofore unseen range.

The supporting cast was hand-picked. Notwithstanding what you may have heard from the rapturous blurbs, however, Blethyn's acting is not "genius, " not does the glorified cameo by Judi Dench amount to much. Blethyn (an excellent actress when she wants to be) is in her hysterical, over-the-top mode, and Dench is simply standard-issue crusty. Far better are Rosamund Pike as eldest daughter Jane Bennet and Sutherland, a fellow content to wade in a sea of estrogen. For all the potency of the climactic scene between Elizabeth and Darcy, the most poignant moment is the one shared near the close by Elizabeth and her dad.

Joe Wright's first motion picture outing comes after extensive directing experience in British TV, which is almost indistinguishable from film. His work here is nuanced, unobtrusive, often superb. The same superlatives may be applied to Sarah Greenwood's production design and the photography of veteran cinematographer Roman Osin, which immediately go to the forefront of likely Oscar nominations.

In sum, "Pride & Prejudice" may have a few blemishes, but is no plain Jane.

....

Hoffman, 'Capote' likely Oscar contenders
"Capote"
November 10, 2005

November 1959. Rural Kansas. Bare trees and a vacant horizon are backdrops to a shadowed farmhouse. They are also a portent. Within, a spasm of violence will shatter the tranquil isolation of this place and horrify a neighboring community.

The savage murder of a family of four shocks millions. It simply intrigues Truman Capote, who one morning happens upon an item on the killings in The New York Times. Over the course of the next four years, he will mine this story for all it is worth. And he will change the ways in which the line between journalism and fiction is perceived.

His seminal "In Cold Blood," melding nonfiction with the techniques of the novel, proves to be a title that cuts both ways.

A riveting dissection of complex personalities and motivations, debut director Bennett Miller's "Capote," brilliantly adapted by Dan Futterman from the 1988 book by Gerald Clarke, trains a dispassionate eye on the period in which the Southern-born darling of New York literary circles researched and wrote "In Cold Blood" (1965), and in the process reinvented himself. Though universally hailed, it would be the last book he ever finished.

Philip Seymour Hoffman gives the finest performance of an already distinguished career as Capote, though it is acting of such consummate skill and emotional detail that it risks overwhelming the film itself. No mean feat, considering how well made a movie this is. It's lone flaw, a minor one, is overlength. At times, Miller seems not entirely sure how to bring matters to a head.

In exploring the nature of the rapport Capote established with one of the two killers, Perry Smith, whose intelligence and sensitivity were unexpected, the film delves into a key question raised a few years ago by journalist Janet Malcolm. Malcolm, with characteristic overstatement, contended that reporters who are honest with themselves must eventually recognize that, in the end, they always betray their sources and their subjects.

It was certainly true of Capote in this case, who misled Smith at many points along the line of their relationship, about his book, his approach in writing it, and his reasons for helping the two convicted killers gain new counsel and stays of execution.

Was it chiefly, as the film asserts, that Capote mainly wanted to keep Smith alive long enough to get the truth of that night, and complete a book he knew might be his best work? Yes and no, it turns out, and it's this ambiguity, and this ambivalence, that the filmmakers exploit for potent effect.

One moment we see Capote visiting Smith on Death Row, solicitous and encouraging. The next he is blithely regaling his coterie at a Manhattan cocktail party with the course of events, including the connection he and his "research assistant and bodyguard" Harper

Lee (Catherine Keener) made with the family of the chief investigator (Chris Cooper), back among the bumpkins in Kansas.

But Capote himself is not completely confident of his rationale, or his desires. Lee, whose pleasure at the news that her "To Kill A Mockingbird" is being published falls prey to Capote's moroseness, wonders if perhaps he's fallen in love with Smith. Capote, identifying with Smith's harsh childhood, replies, "It's as if Perry and I grew up in the same house, and one day he went out the back door and I went out the front."

In the end, Capote's compulsiveness and his art trump his compassion, as if there was ever any real question of the outcome. Then again, the homicidal Smith also was duplicitous, perhaps willfully.

But Capote -- charming, cunning and ruthless -- was never the same.

As superb as Hoffman is in the lead, he is expertly augmented by a supporting cast whose seriousness of purpose is unquestioned. Keener and Cooper are pitch-perfect; they usually are. But the surprise here is Clifton Collins Jr., whose portrait of Perry Smith commands, however grudgingly, some particle of sympathy. There are also solid contributions from Mark Pellegrino as Smith's accomplice, Richard Hickock, and from Bruce Greenwood, Bob Balaban, Amy Ryan and Marshall Bell.

Technically, the movie has unusual polish for a first effort, no doubt helped by its atmospheric photography, and most of its studied effects are well-judged. Yet it's the people who are vivid and indelible, something that will be remembered come Oscar time.

....

This 'Flow' right on the mark
"Hustle and Flow"
July 21, 2005

A small-time pimp and drug dealer in the slums of Memphis, DJay is treading water, buoyed only by the faint hope, likely futile, that his main chance may come.

"I'm trying to squeeze a dollar out of a dime, and I ain't even got a cent," he moans, struggling to lay down a track in a makeshift recording studio

For DJay, a thoughtful if unschooled man, has talent. What he hasn't had - not for years, anyway - is a way out of (or at least above) the mean streets.

Those possibilities passed him by with every quick buck, with every bad choice and every ruthless act.

As played by Terrence Dashon Howard, he is perhaps the most compelling character to appear in a film this year. What makes "Hustle and Flow" such a riveting experience is that it is a movie brimming with such convincingly realized characters.

It is not merely the meditative quality of the story or a fully engaged ensemble cast that sets "Hustle and Flow" apart from the many half-furnished films that capitalize on hip-hop culture. Rather, it is in delineation of character, the way in which such standard figures as a pimp and his "girls" are humanized. They may not be entirely sympathetic, but they are genuine, recognizable.

In only his second film following 2003's "Water's Edge," writer, director and co-producer Craig Brewer has rendered a confident, authentic picture. Though not above indulging in a smattering of character "types" and letting his optimistic outlook lead him toward a questionable plot resolution, Brewer's missteps are few.

"Hustle and Flow" is exceedingly well-acted, so much so that one forgets within minutes that these are performers, not the people they play. The deceptively skilled Howard sets the stage with an opening monologue that, if its promises more than the film ultimately delivers, is nonetheless a star making moment.

DJay uses his "working girls," mainly the willowy Nola (Taryn Manning), to help fund the recording project. As he waits in his car, he writes down freestyle raps, the "flow" of the title, while plotting how he is going to hustle platinum-selling rapper Skinny Black (Ludacris), a hometown hero, into helping him secure air play - or a contract. DJay persuades old chum Key (Anthony Anderson), a church musician and recording engineer, to run the technical end. Key, whose middle-class wife (Elise Neal) is at first appalled, recruits the assistance of Shelby (D.J. Qualls), a gawky white vending machine loader and part-time musician, to lay down the bass.

As matters proceed, DJay's progress is reflected in those around him, not only in Nola, who yearns to do something important, but in the pregnant Shug (Taraji P. Henson), a woman who seems to embody the thwarted hopes of all those we meet. All find ways to add to the creative process, save for a smart-mouthed stripper named Lexus (Paula Jai Parker, in the picture's chief comic relief), whom DJay gives the, ahem, heave-ho.

In the end, it's up to DJay to pull off the final ploy, even when the result seems a foregone conclusion. Comparable to "8 Mile," which had the advantage of a substantial budget, a marquee rap artist and a director (Curtis Hanson) as experienced as he is gifted, Brewer's Sundance Film Festival hit film comes off remarkably well on minimal resources. But then maybe it didn't need them.

"Hustle" echoes the in-your-face timbre of the early work of Brewer's production partner and financier, John Singleton.

Still, the movie won't be for every taste. For all its invention, rap culture can seem straightjacketed by what is often a sullen, belligerent tone, a singular lack of humor and its frequent objectification of women. Not to mention a preoccupation with the power of cold hard cash.

Youthful rebellion? A mirror held to realities of the street? Certainly. But it is not the only reality. And Brewer's film sets most of the antagonism aside for larger aims. Not to say the music isn't a principal, and arresting, component.

"Every man has to contribute a verse," says Key in a trite but true aside to DJay.

In "Hustle and Flow," Brewer offers us stanzas to burn.

....

This shade of 'Lavender' full of color
"Ladies in Lavender"
May 26, 2005

A gift from the sea proves a mixed blessing, enriching yet complicating the settled lives of two aging spinsters in Charles Dance's gracefully played "Ladies in Lavender."

Sisters Ursula (Judi Dench) and Janet Widdington (Maggie Smith) enjoy a serene if uneventful existence on a beautiful stretch of the Cornish coast, their principal concern being what offshore storms may do to their carefully tended garden.

The year is 1936, with rumblings of war on the continent invading the radio but otherwise seeming at a great remove from the Widdingtons and their fellow villagers.

When a half-drowned young man washes up on the beach after a violent storm, they take him into their cottage and, soon, into their hearts, nursing him back to health with the aid of a local doctor (David Warner) and their irascible housekeeper, Dorcas (Miriam Margolyes).

This mysterious fellow, a boyish lad by the name of Andrea Marowski (Daniel Bruhl of "Goodbye Lenin!") speaks nary a word of English, but as he begins to recover, they learn he is a Polish Jew and a supremely gifted violinist. This gift does not go unnoticed by another foreigner in the village, visiting Russian painter Olga Danilof (Natascha McElhone), sister of the globally renowned violinist Boris Danilof.

Whether from misplaced maternal protectiveness or simple mistrust, the sisters give Danilof short shrift when she passes by their cliff-top dwelling one day, praising the music emanating from Andrea's bedroom window. Fearing they may lose Marowski to the attractive, 30-ish woman, who can communicate more easily with him, they also hide a letter Danilof writes expressing her wish that she might introduce him to her esteemed brother.

Andrea hopes to find his way to America, a land the sisters refer to as "the sweepings of Europe." But this is neither as intolerant or malicious as it sounds. The Widdingtons are the soul of generosity, but there is a certain loneliness, too, and subterranean longing.

The aforementioned Dr. Mead is a different matter. He is drawn to the lovely Danilof and comes to see the young man as a potential rival, or worse, a spy.

The town, which greeted Marowski's arrival with muted wariness, eventually embraces him and his music. But the sisters' possessiveness turns counterproductive, especially for Ursula, whose feelings for Andrea turn out, however irrationally, to be more than motherly.

Those who haven't followed the acting career of writer-director Dance may know him only as the cold-eyed villain of films such as "China Moon" (1994) and "The Last Action Hero" (1993), but here is an actor who could bring sympathy to a fallen character in the otherwise execrable "Alien 3" (1992) or astonishing sensitivity to the real-life character of pioneer filmmaker Robert Flaherty in "Kabloonak" (1994).

In "Ladies in Lavender," he captures the timelessness of Cornwall and the immutable toil of its farmers and fishermen. He also coaxes wonderful performances from two doyennes of the British pantheon, his script furnishing their characters with rough-cut simplicity and complexity that actresses of this caliber can polish into jewels. Dench is especially fine in one of the most tender and vulnerable roles of her career, while Smith, the practical sister to Ursula's romantic, proves the perfect foil - and counterpart. For his part, Bruhl is an excellent stranger in a strange land, bringing just the right mix of puzzlement, patience and gratitude to the table.

There is also much pleasure to be had from a hand-picked supporting cast. Apart from the versatile Margolyes ("The Age of Innocence," et al), an appealing McElhone ("Solaris") and Warner (poor chap, still typecast as a bounder), the supporting players include veteran character actor Freddie Jones.

Violin solos are by Joshua Bell.

Dance based his film on the short story of the same title by William J. Locke. He may or may not have been faithful to the original. One suspects he was. If the pace of the picture feels a trifle slow, it's by design, the better to relate a relaxed pace of life where a beam of sunlight after a storm is the height of sensual pleasure. If the happy ending seems just a bit pat, it can be excused. We would not settle for anything else.

……………………

'Merchant' stays true to the original
"William Shakespeare's The Merchant of Venice"
March 17, 2005

What, did we think it was Hemingway's? The motion picture industry's silly insistence on appending William Shakespeare's name to the titles of his classic plays, or, for that matter, any other universally known writer's name before one of his or her most famous works, continues its preposterous march.

"The Merchant of Venice" … excuse us, "William Shakespeare's The Merchant of Venice" is the latest example.

Perhaps the distributor wants to deflect any intimation of anti-Semitism toward filmmaker Michael Radford ("Il Postino") in his adaptation of the Bard's most troublesome play. Troublesome not only because of the sometimes discordant clash of tones exhibited in the telling - a putative "comedy" shot through with all that nasty business about "a pound of flesh" - but also because of the disturbing aftertaste left by its resolution.

The new film version, first since Trevor Nunn's in 2001, is faithful down to the last iambic syllable and tonal shock. Beautifully mounted, and expertly performed, it may be the definitive movie incarnation. That doesn't mean it sits well with 21st-century sensibilities

Set in the 16th century in the economic powerhouse that was Venice, the story focuses on the plight of Antonio (Jeremy Irons), who offers to go perilously into debt for a loan so that his friend Bassanio ("Shakespeare in Love's" Joseph Fiennes) can wield the fortune necessary to impress the object of his affections, well-to-do Portia (Lynn Collins).

Despite Bassanio's misgivings, Antonio agrees to the unconventional terms of the bond proposed by Shylock (Al Pacino), the forfeit of which will result not only in the loss of worldly goods, but in a pound of the flesh of Antonio, who has scorned and vilified Shylock for being a Jew in a community that confines them to a "ghetto" after dark. Already stricken by the fact that his daughter has fallen in love with the young Christian nobleman Lorenzo, a friend of Bassanio's, and eloped with Lorenzo and a huge portion of her father's gold, Shylock seizes on the news that Antonio's ships have all been lost at sea.

Now that Antonio cannot pay back the loan, Shylock insists on the literal interpretation of Venetian law.

The pound of flesh from Antonio will be taken "nearest to his heart," and it is not likely he will survive the penalty.

As newlywed Bassanio rushes back to Venice from Portia's estate in Belmont to defend his friend, the clever Portia determines that she and Nerissa (Heather Goldenhersh) will go to court disguised as a young male judge and his clerk, thereby to save her new husband's friend with some wily re-reading of the bond.

For all the light-hearted folderol between the lovers, the film, like the play, has as its central figure that of Shylock, a wronged man undone by his hunger for vengeance and "justice." These bleak, cautionary scenes do not co-inhabit well with all the mirthful romantic banter and usual bits of Shakespearean misdirection and irony.

Pacino skates the periphery of overacting in his highly theatrical performance, yet is penetrating all the same, evincing the torment of the man as well as his vindictiveness. But there will be those who think Shylock's fate is decidedly unjust.

Still, it is a worthy film, nicely shot by cinematographer Benoit Delhomme and buttressed by a flock of fine supporting players, among them Allan Corduner ("Topsy Turvy").

Shakespeare, one suspects, might even be pleased to have his name associated with it.

....

One 'Sunset' you'll want to catch
"Before Sunset"
July 22, 2004

Richard Linklater's engrossing "Before Sunset" is a great rarity, not only for its modest 80-minute length but for a screenplay and acting so naturalistic and genuine that it gives you the sensation of eavesdropping on a private conversation, one that hits achingly close to home. Usually, in the vicinity of the heart.

The picture offers more than a nice touch of verisimilitude. "Before Sunset" encapsulates so many of our most ardently held beliefs (and fears) about love, about people and possibilities. Through two highly appealing, very human characters, we meet ourselves in many guises, from hopeless romantic to hopeful cynic.

Driven by virtually uninterrupted dialogue, and beautifully so, this sequel trumps the 1994 original for the very reason that its stars and director, who wrote "Sunset" together, are nine years older: wiser about the deceptions and vicissitudes of life; about the nagging anxieties, unspoken thoughts and sustaining moments of the day-to-day; and shrewder about the bittersweet tang of love and longing.

For all the tensile strength conferred by the years, they are no less vulnerable, and perhaps more conflicted. Now in their early 30s, life is decidedly more complex. They are experiencing that first glimmer of mortality, the knowledge that time - and opportunity - are fleeting.

In the first film, "Before Sunrise," a young American (Ethan Hawke) traveling through Europe via train chances to meet a lovely French student (Julie Delpy) in Vienna and persuades her to spend a dreamlike day with him. It's instant chemistry, instant connection, and before they know it, they are falling in love. But it is like wraiths who pass in the night, in a city to which neither of them belongs. Their plan to meet again in Vienna runs afoul of fate.

The two do not see each other again for nine years - the set-up for "Sunset" - with Jesse Wallace (Hawke) in Paris for the last stop of his book tour, and environmental activist Celine (Delpy) back home after several years in New York. She appears as if out of the ether in the bookshop where Wallace is meeting the media and, after their tentative first few minutes of reunion - accompanied by flashbacks to the first film - they launch into a wide-ranging and ultimately heart-baring conversation, strolling the city as Wallace waits to take a plane.

Was his book inspired by their brief encounter, and the disappointment over how it turned out? Is the female protagonist created by Wallace really Celine thinly veiled? What of all the songs she has written? Are some of them about him? Very likely, though the movie is a bit coy on the subject (as it should be). What is certain is that Wallace, trapped in a lukewarm marriage, and Celine, with a globe-trotting boyfriend and a checkered romantic history, suddenly desire some kind of resolution (as did the actors).

Which won't be a simple matter, since the attraction between them is little changed

The script composed by Linklater, Delpy and Hawke (with two novels to his credit) owns a number of arresting features, not the least of which are its perceptiveness, its sense of irony, and its clear-eyed generosity. The writers also are well aware of their characters' occasional spasms of glibness, which they pillory on the spot.

The performances are pitch-perfect, something seldom said of the often one-dimensional Hawke. But here, revealing aspects of himself we haven't seen before, he's close to flawless. As is the enchanting Delpy ("Three Colors: White"), an actress of such incandescence and depth of personality that you can't take your eyes off her. Not that she permits beauty to upstage talent, which she has in abundance (she also sings several of the songs on the soundtrack).

Their exchanges have the texture of truth. You believe them, and their story, first scene to last.

After his ambitious but only moderately successful experiments with "Waking Life" and "Tape" in 2001, followed last year by the hit comedy "School of Rock," we weren't quite sure what to expect from Linklater, who erupted on the scene a decade ago with "Slacker" (1991) and "Dazed and Confused" (1993).

No worries. He's in fine form, giving us a tale told in real time with winning characters, a resonant setting in an off-the-beaten-path Paris, and writing that cuts ever-so-carefully to the quick.

It's intimacy and universality in one package.

....

Gibson's 'Passion' nearly drowns in gruesome violence
"The Passion of the Christ"
February 25, 2004

Mel Gibson's "The Passion of the Christ" vividly portrays the suffering and sacrifice of Jesus during the last 12 hours of his life.

Perhaps too vividly.

The message is almost drowned in a bath of blood.

Make no mistake, the realistic depiction of violence in motion pictures serves a vital purpose. When we see the real, hideous face of human brutality, we are far less likely to be inured to violence when we witness it firsthand. But by the time we reach the moving final scene of "Passion," many filmgoers may feel as if they've been subjected to nauseating excess.

While it is certainly true that gruesome details of Christ's scourging are in the Bible, Gibson's movie, with its needless slow-motion effects, horror film tricks, and maniacally cackling Roman tormentors, falls into the grotesque, even the repulsive.

And it is so unnecessary. The power of the cinema comes from restraint, but Gibson has spent so many years and so many films wallowing in gratuitous displays of violence that he seems unable to do anything else.

It may seem hypocritical to criticize "The Passion of the Christ" for its over-the-top violent content when hosannas of praise have fallen on, say, "The Lord of the Rings: The Return of the King," itself a three-hour orgy of sometimes repellent combat.

But it is a question of context, degree and purpose.

The film is said to be based on a variety of sources, including the diaries of St. Anne Catherine Emmerich (1774-1824) as collected in the book "The Dolorous Passion of Our Lord Jesus Christ," "The Mystical City of God" by St. Mary of Agreda, and the New Testament books of John, Luke, Mark and Matthew.

Jim Caviezel is well cast in the role of Jesus, and the actor reportedly endured no end of injuries and other miseries during shooting. His performance is stoical and humanized, limned with grace notes. But Christ is seldom presented as more than a two-dimensional character, and almost everyone else is either a stick figure or a caricature, save for Maia Morgenstern as Mary. For believers, this may not be an issue.

Others may find the more rounded and, yes, complex figure of Pontius Pilate to be the most compelling. The Roman governor is played with depth and fine understatement by Ivano Marescotti, ably supplemented by Claudia Gerini as his wife. Rosalinda Celentano also makes for an exceptionally creepy Satan.

There is no doubting Gibson's lofty intent, and this technically proficient film -- Caleb Deschanel's photography is expert, as always -- does have fleeting moments of beauty and uplift.

Yet it also seems deficient in the one thing one would have thought it must contain: spirituality.

Is there anti-Semitic content in "Passion," as had been feared? We see little of it, yet that, naturally, depends on one's interpretation.

The Pharisees, a Jewish sect devoted to strict observance of holy law, are shown as Jesus' principal -- and rather bloodthirsty -- antagonists, the same people who had welcomed the prophet into their midst mere days before his crucifixion. But "Passion" portrays this as more about entrenched power feeling threatened – a universal human failing -- than having any real religious motivation.

That said, Gibson's subtitled, self-financed, self-distributed (with Newmarket Films) picture is undeniably an indictment of our capacity for barbarism. It is also a fervent lesson in the possibility of redemption.

....

Moviegoers will bask in this 'Splendor'
"American Splendor"
September 11, 2003

While mainstream movies often supply characters you love to hate, it is left to the independent cinema to provide characters you hate to love.

But you do, in spite of yourself. Even someone like Harvey Pekar.

To call Pekar prickly or eccentric is as much an understatement as saying Liberace was gaudy. He is also a slob, an irritant and utterly self-absorbed.

Funny-sad, obnoxious and endearing, Pekar inhabits "American Splendor" like a great gloomy ogre, albeit a principled and highly intelligent one with a wide, deep fissure of vulnerability.

Filmmakers Shari Springer Berman and Robert Pulcini have produced a movie tailor-made for the festival circuit, one that breaks all (or at least most) of the rules of construction, and in very ingenious ways. If it doesn't quite live up to all the attendant hype, it's not the fault of those involved. Few films could. But it comes awfully close

Based on the real-life story of a comic-book legend - a "hilariously grumpy observer of life's strange and unpredictable pageant" - and drawn from Pekar's ongoing series of the same name, the film is a clever intersection of re-enactment, interview, file footage and animation. It follows Pekar (Paul Giamatti) as he toils (testily) in obscurity as a file clerk in a VA hospital in Cleveland, meanwhile writing comics about the mundane moments, small victories and cruel twists of fate that mark his everyday existence.

But "American Splendor" is more than an imaginative chronicle of Pekar's rise to fame (if not riches). It's also a smoothly integrated interplay of techniques and styles, showcasing the filmmakers' nimble wit, as well as of the artwork of some of Pekar's notable friends, like Robert Crumb, whose life inspired Terry Zwigoff's extraordinary 1994 documentary "Crumb." (Pekar was/is no draftsman; he needed others to flesh out the stick figures that accompanied his text balloons.)

Pekar serves as narrator and is both subject and periodic co-star of a picture that also depicts Pekar/Giamatti in animated guise. In one brief but arresting scene, the actors step out of character to view (on the set) the people they're playing, as the latter riffle through a tray of jelly beans. For a moment, Giamatti, the performer, is a bystander, and it's the kind of audacity that defines the film.

Character actress Hope Davis stars opposite Giamatti as Eve, Pekar's neurotic (and equally functional/dysfunctional) compatriot, who gladly gives up her home in Delaware and her comic-book shop to be his (third) wife and collaborator. She's the sort of self-diagnosed feeb who can size up a personality disorder in a heartbeat (she thinks), and is profoundly bored with her husband's new celebrity, which has gone from underground renown to a series of high-profile, if cantankerous, appearances on "The David Letterman Show." If she can ever lift herself off their futon, she might actually get something accomplished. When she does find motivation, however, Pekar (characteristically) believes it's at his expense. In what turns out to be a blessing in disguise, Pekar is diagnosed with cancer, and it is the graphic novel generated from the ensuing battle – "Our Cancer Year" – that rounds out the story and makes for something of a Pekaresque happy ending.

Unconventional to the last, "American Splendor" certainly is one of the most engaging pictures of the year.

The performances of Giamatti, who paints a three-dimensional portrait of a two-note character, and Davis almost certainly will be short-listed for an Oscar. And there is excellent supporting work from Judah Friedlander, James Urbaniak, Earl Billings and Madylin Sweeten. Each has an important part to play in a film that's a dyspeptic swipe against synthetic Hollywood sentimentality.

....

'Seabisquit' cast, director, script, go distance
"Seabisquit"
July 27, 2003

Great actors, saddled with a poor script, sometimes can carry the day through sheer force of personality. But bet against it.

Give them a great story, though, and it's off to the races.

With its familiar, even predictable rags-to-riches elements, Gary Ross' "Seabiscuit" might have been ordinary, a jaunty but unremarkable trot to the paddock. It isn't. Suggestive of both John Ford and Frank Capra, this stirring adaptation of the book "Seabiscuit: An American Legend" by Laura Hillenbrand is a quintessentially American shaggy colt tale about possibility, second chances, endurance and grit.

Amid all the spavined swaybacks of summer, this film explodes down the stretch with confidence.

It's the true story of a one-time bicycle repairman, Charles Howard (Jeff Bridges), who made a fortune imposing the automobile on the American West.

"I wouldn't spend more than $5 for the best horse in America," Howard tells one prospective car buyer in the heady days of the 1920s. But after the accidental death of his son, the disintegration of his marriage and a chance meeting with a kindred spirit (Elizabeth Banks), Howard just happens to buy a horse. This small, lazy, ungainly looking animal is destined to change his life -- and become one of horse racing's most celebrated steeds, the toast of a nation emerging from the throes of the Depression.

Howard's unwavering belief in the future, his faith in half-blind, angry, oversized jockey Red Pollard (Tobey Maguire), and his rescue of former mustang breaker Tom Smith (Chris Cooper) to be Seabiscuit's trainer would make history.

Winner of the Horse of the Year laurels in 1938, Seabiscuit was one of the most electrifying and popular "athletes" ever, but not before cantering through the lowest levels of racing as Smith and Pollard coaxed his dormant abilities to the fore.

Seabiscuit was a populist hero, producing more newspaper ink than Roosevelt, Hitler, Mussolini or any other public figure in 1938. Every detail of his rise and championship run was recorded with a fervor the mass media later reserved for Michael Jordan or, more recently, those hordes of Japanese journalists shadowing baseball's Hideki Matsui. Seabiscuit also filled tracks to bursting with nontraditional race fans. When Seabiscuit dueled the mighty War Admiral -- the Man O' War of his day -- 40,000 showed up at Pimlico to cheer him on.

In fealty to Hillenbrand's book, the film maintains a deliberate pace, focusing not on Seabiscuit so much as on the people behind him. Howard, haunted by the death of his child, embraces Pollard as much more than a rider. Pollard, a literate but troubled young man, has never recovered from a wrenching parting with his parents as a boy, and a hardscrabble life on the dole and in the boxing ring has left him unprepared for the generosity extended by both Howard and his new wife. Smith, meanwhile, belongs to another era, tough, gentle and savvy, a horse whisperer nursing his own private disappointments.

Three isolated men, and one strong, good-hearted woman, who instinctively reach out to each other as family. It makes all the difference.

This is solid thematic turf for director Ross, who co-wrote the script with Hillenbrand and Charlie Mitchell. Ross directed "Pleasantville" (1998) and wrote "Dave" and "Big," each film assaying a strain of American myth -- and American virtue. Here he proves you can make a "patriotic" movie without smug sloganeering or flag-waving. "Seabiscuit" is about what a country and a people might *aspire* to be.

Ross opens and intercuts the picture with documentary elements somewhat in the Ken Burns vein, and the narrative ploy works, girded by newsreels, archival images and the splendid live-action photography of cinematographer John Schwartzman, whose pastoral framing is as engrossing as his race footage. Jeannine Oppewall's production design is likewise impeccable, as are the costumes by Judianna Makovsky.

While the dramatic arc of the film does betray a degree of patness, this does little to impede our enjoyment. Ross' orchestration is deft, and the performances are uniformly outstanding. Bridges remains the most unsung great actor of his generation, and he's never been better. His boyish innocence now sporting an edge, Maguire continues to impress with each outing, and here he demonstrates a steadily increasing range. Cooper delivers his customary slow-speaking, deep-thinking Everyman, very much in the mold of another Cooper, Gary. He lends a layer of somber gravity to which William H. Macy's manic radio personality is a lively and amusing counterpoint.

Banks may be a trifle young for her role opposite an aging war horse like Bridges, but she handles it with brio, never breaking stride. There is also a touching supporting performance by first-time actor Gary Stevens, a Hall of Fame jockey with more than 4,700 races to his credit.

The can-do spirit that made, and salvaged, a nation also invigorates this film. Overhyped, but deserving on merit, it's the best big studio movie of the year to date, leaving all its competitors in the dust.

....

'Adaptation' a winning insider comedy
"Adaptation"
January 12, 2003

So much for placing one's self in the best light.

Operating on the theory that as long as there are skeletons in the family closet, you may as well make 'em dance, screenwriter Charlie Kaufman reveals himself as a herd of galloping neuroses amusingly and sometimes touchingly, in Spike Jonze's winning insider farce, "Adaptation."

Those who feared that Kaufman and Jonze might turn conventional after the success of "Being John Malkovich" may rest easy. It's an even more off-the-wall movie, a meld of self-awareness and delusion, vanity and vigor, insecurity and kick-out-the-jams performance.

If "Adaptation" shares the one-joke scaffolding of "Malkovich," it remains one heck of a sturdy framework.

In the movie, Kaufman (played by Nicolas Cage) agonizes over adapting New Yorker writer Susan Orlean's (Meryl Streep) best seller, "The Orchid Thief," for the screen, and we do mean agonizes. It's precisely the quandary that the real-life Kaufman confronted after he and Jonze took on the task after making "Malkovich."

Desperate, Kaufman turns to writing quasi-fictional characters. He even inserts himself ("I have no understanding of anything but myself.") into the story, as well as Orlean. He already has transformed her into a predatory journalist and incipient orchid junkie who's having an affair with her book's wild- man protagonist, John Laroche (Chris Cooper), a jabbering orchid hunter who risks life, limb and karmic health to obtain federally protected species.

Kaufman also gifts (or curses) himself with an imaginary identical twin brother named Don (Cage again), and renders him as almost his polar opposite: aggressive, confident, utterly unself-conscious.

The result is among the most playful films to come along in some time. Indulgent? Sure. But who cares? The real-life Kaufman co-wrote the screenplay with real-life Orlean, and both have had great acid fun at their own expense. Apart from the filmmakers' Möbius strip of a set-up and their manic time-shifting. "Adaptation" is chock-full of ideas and daffy asides, which Jonze keeps spinning like juggler's plates. Audacity is fast becoming the partners' stock-in-trade.

In his dual role, Cage trips effortlessly from frazzled to frenzied to depressed to exultant. It's easily his best work since "Leaving Las Vegas." And Streep gives us a delightful antidote to her dramatic heroines of recent vintage, satirizing the more voyeuristic and vicarious aspects of journalism, as well as Orlean's own insecurities. In vivid supporting roles, Brian Cox (as a maven of screenwriting seminars) is supercharged, and Cara Seymour (as Kaufman's could-have-been girlfriend) is sweetly vulnerable.

But the chap who steals the show — as advertised — is Cooper. His Laroche is a jumble of contradictions: profane and learned, gentle and ruthless, pompous and unaffected. It's a bravura comic performance, well-drawn and richly played.

"Adaptation" won't be for everyone. A taste for the certifiably insane is a prerequisite. The kick is that Kaufman and Co. are playing with our heads as much as theirs. We can only wish them continued consternation.

....

Crowe convincingly portrays genius and madness
"A Beautiful Mind"
January 6, 2002

"A Beautiful Mind" would have been a terrible thing to waste.

Director Ron Howard, whose forte is straightforward narrative without so much as a hint of complexity, almost undermines this sober but terrifying study of schizophrenia by succumbing to a feel-good resolution - the sort of formula tailored to win Oscar attention at the expense of story.

But another impressive performance by Russell Crowe, which eschews flamboyant theatricality for a more grounded portrait, lifts the movie above the Hollywood conventions of Akiva Goldsman's uneven script.

Neither Howard nor Goldsman, whose track record has been dominated by such feeble efforts as "Batman Forever" and "Lost in Space," would be the first choice to adapt - however loosely - Sylvia Nasar's biography of Nobel Prize-winning mathematician John Forbes Nash Jr.

It's a subject demanding unconventional treatment. Surprisingly, for much of the movie Howard manages to think "outside of the box," like the troubled genius whose life he details. But he fails to achieve what Nash's career was all about, the pursuit of one truly original idea.

In the end, a good film is rendered just a little too pat, complete with manipulative tear-duct finale.

"Despite my privileged upbringing, I am quite well balanced. I have a chip on both shoulders," Nash tells a fellow student upon his arrival at Princeton University in 1947. A West Virginia man of modest background, he is uneasy amid his more socially prepared counterparts. At first, his colleagues in the mathematics department view him as a backwoods misfit without a clear academic focus. But Nash is impatient with wasting his time on classes and books that are the province "of lesser mortals."

Soon it all comes into focus, and Nash leaves his fellows in the dust with a breakthrough in game theory that one day will influence economic analysis, global trade and even evolutionary biology.

It's as much a triumph of the will as the imagination, but with a bitter legacy to come.

These early scenes of "A Beautiful Mind" are the most convincing. Nash's progress from eccentric outcast to esteemed (if reluctant) lecturer at MIT is rendered vividly. You can almost smell the musty walls and chalkboards of the Ivy League surround, and feel the competitive tension and overweening drive for success.

It is at MIT in 1953 that Nash attracts the attention of Alicia (Jennifer Connelly), a brilliant young student with the patience to shepherd the awkward Nash into the first real relationship of his life.

Only belatedly is it learned that Nash suffers from schizophrenia, and as the illness overpowers that fabulous mind and distorts its grasp on reality, Nash, once the star of the new mathematics, disappears from the scene, stabilized though dulled by medication and becoming useless to his wife and new baby.

Everything adds up except his life.

In time, Nash will learn to keep his curse at arm's length, his determination augmented by modern drugs and the love of his wife. By the mid-'90s, he will regain control of his life and again be a productive scholar, a role the real-life Nash fills to this day.

Crowe plays him to the hilt. His Nash is a distillate of clumsiness and slashing wit, surpassing ambition and nagging fear, genius and madness - all embodied without a trace of histrionics. He is ably supported by co-star Connelly, who has waited years for the kind of meaty leading role she navigates so well here, and by reliable old hands Ed Harris and Christopher Plummer.

While Howard shrinks from touching upon Nash's intermittent experiments with homosexuality, and romanticizes elements of the mathematician's story, he avoids many of the pitfalls that could have ruined the picture. One may begin to roll the eyes over all the clever little aphorisms couched in dialogue, but the power of the film is in its larger details: how Nash's extraordinary mind saw definable patterns where others saw chaos, and glimpsed order in the enigma of the universe.

....

Film shows insecurity
"The Anniversary Party"
July 12, 2001

A knowing and sometimes nasty reflection of Hollywood angst, "The Anniversary Party" gives one the feeling of having wandered into a bash to which one was not invited — and cannot escape.

Too long to sustain interest, too whiny to be sympathetic and too strident in its concerns to be effective satire, this slice of life from Jennifer Jason Leigh and Alan Cumming is well-acted but ultimately tedious.

What, they needed two hours to communicate the revelation that writers, actors and directors tend toward insecurity (with a capital "I")?

Accompanied by a dozen or so of their famous real-life chums, Leigh and Cumming wrote, directed and star in the picture, which isn't quite the vanity production it might appear to be on the surface.

They play Joe and Sally Therrian, a recently reconciled couple who are celebrating their sixth anniversary, "celebrating" being a relative term.

They throw a party in their fashionably chic canyon home with (mostly) fashionable friends, but Sally, an A-list actress whose star is dimming, isn't overjoyed with some of the invitees. Especially Skye Davidson (Gwyneth Paltrow), an effusive young movie goddess who has usurped a role Sally believes is rightfully hers.

Joe doesn't agree. And novelist trying his hand at directing a movie — albeit on a shoestring — he has adapted his own book, whose protagonist seems patterned on his own wife.

The last thing an already resentful Sally needs to hear is the 25-ish Davidson gushing "You're my icon! I worship you. I've seen all your movies since I was a little girl!"

Ouch. Sally is ancient all right, creaking along in her mid-to-late 30s. But hubby has pinned the part for a woman in her 20s. Can you spell friction?

"That character isn't really you," insists her best friend, Sophia Gold (Phoebe Cates), an actress who gave up her career to be a mom. "She's possessive, fragile and remote."

"But I AM possessive, fragile and remote!" replies Sally.

So the party starts with at least as much awkwardness as high spirits, exacerbated by the less-than-neighborly folks next door (Mina Badie, Denis O'Hare); the arrival of Joe's ex-love and confidant Gina Taylor (Jennifer Beals), whose photographs dominate the Therrians' walls (and are a constant reminder to Sally of the past); a neurotically stressed-out new mother (Jane Adams) and her husband (John C. Reilly), who is directing Sally's faltering new film; and the undercurrent of Sally's outward excitement but inner ambivalence about having kids.

Gold's not so cheery herself. Early on, she expresses relief that she's left all the glamour and pressure to her star actor husband Cal (Kevin Kline). Later, she tearfully tells Sally that motherhood is equal parts joy and hellish prison.

The final catalyst is an unexpected anniversary gift, which plunges the party into complete turmoil and results in a torrent of anguished confessions.

The climax of "The Anniversary Party" is meant to be an examination of tenuous marriage on the brink. And the confrontation between the Therrians near the close is exceptionally well-played. But the fireworks come too late. We've long since lost our sense of involvement, and feel uncomfortably like voyeurs.

....

Merchant-Ivory succeeds again
"The Golden Bowl"
June 7, 2001

"The Golden Bowl" is a gilded film set in a gilded age. But its echoes of Edwardian deceit and honor are not without relevance to the present day.

Another triumph for the team of director James Ivory, producer Ismail Merchant and screenwriter Ruth Prawer Jhabvala, this gorgeous picture does justice to the Henry James' novel that some consider his crowning achievement.

While James' story plays out as an elaborate literary soap opera, someone forgot to tell the cast, which, with the single exception of Uma Thurman, rejects bathos to invest these characters with profoundly human features.

The story pivots on a single act of introduction, albeit one with unforeseen consequences. Fanny Assingham (Anjelica Huston) is the wife of an aristocratic British colonel (James Fox) and an expatriate American pillar of London high society. She is so taken with the handsome, but penniless young Italian prince Amerigo (Jeremy Northam) that she is determined to play matchmaker. What better combination, she thinks, than the good-natured, cultivated Amerigo and sweet Maggie Verver (Kate Beckinsale), beloved daughter of widowed American tycoon and art collector Adam Verver (Nick Nolte), who made a vast fortune in coal.

The match is a successful one, and the two are soon wed. Amerigo is a principled man, not an unscrupulous gold digger, though the restoration of his decaying Italian palazzo will certainly benefit from his father-in-law's millions. Maggie is deliriously happy, yet there is a shadow over the marriage. She has married the prince without knowing that her oldest and best friend, fellow American Charlotte Stant (Thurman), previously had an affair with Amerigo and remains madly in love with him. Like the prince, she was well-connected but without money.

Stant meets and eventually marries Maggie's father, a man so utterly devoted to his daughter (and she to him) that even their respective spouses can feel excluded. Stant, who was willing to marry Amerigo for love, marries Verver mainly to be close to Amerigo - with unsettling results.

There are lies upon lies, but also, in the end, a hunger for truth.

James' people do not always exhibit sound judgment, but they do value strength of character and regard for the feelings of others. So do the filmmakers, and it is a worthy reminder in our own age of self-obsession.

As a willful, if reckless, woman somewhat ahead of her time, Thurman's Stant dominates the screen, but the usually reliable actress somehow seems transparent and out of sync. There is something rather forced about the performance, which too often spills over into histrionics when subtlety is called for. A demure Beckinsale and a shrewd Huston, however, deliver more balanced work, convincing from first to last.

Though titularly a "women's picture," Nolte and Northam not only match their female co-stars stride for stride, but in some ways they surpass them. Northam delineates the prince's inner conflicts with practiced skill. Nolte, in one of his best performances, embodies all those early 20th-century titans of industry who were ruthless in business but upstanding in their private lives.

Apart from his daughter, Verver's only competing passion is his dream of building a great museum back home in the states to house the art treasures he has purchased throughout Europe. This, ostensibly, for all the migrant workers who slaved to make him a potentate but who have "never in their lives beheld beauty."

We behold it in every scene.

With the sun-splashed lushness of its lawns and gardens, its opulent costumes and grand interiors - all captured in exquisite detail by cinematographer Tony Pierce-Roberts - "The Golden Bowl" is unquestionably one of the most ravishing films to be made in many years. One reason Andrew Sanders' production design is so impressive, and impeccably tasteful, is that the filmmakers employed real homes and real interiors in England and Italy as principal locations.

Ivory ushers us inside massive London mansions like Belvoir Castle and to estates such as Syon House, a large country home outside of London whose drawing room is lighted like a Sargent painting come to life.

Framing, lighting and camera movement are no less impressive for being unobtrusive. Ivory's meticulous composition renders rich, deep colors that are lent striking contrast in several brief black-and-white, newsreel-like inserts. These add social contrast as well, comparing the established elements of European high culture with young America's energy, ingenuity and burgeoning industrial might.

Pierce-Roberts' photography and John Bright's costumes are all but guaranteed Oscar nominations, while Richard Robbins' fluid, excellent score does much to temper rather than inflate the melodrama.

This is moviemaking of a high order.

....

A Deceptively clever 'Memento'
"Memento"
April 26, 2001

As always, art flourishes where there is a sense of adventure.

In "Memento," British-born director Christopher Nolan pushes the envelope of narrative invention with a tale not simply told backward, but with the kind of edgy kaleidoscopic detail that seems to absorb you into the frame itself.

And keeps you quite literally in suspense.

The film succeeds chiefly on the strengths of audacity and performance, despite a relatively slender, noir-ish, B-movie storyline. You may suspect how it's all going to play out in the end, but you're never quite sure.

Nolan, who adapted the film from the short story by his brother Jonathan, is another representative of a generation of young filmmakers with an exhilarating command of cinematic language and the imagination to add to its vocabulary.

Nolan should be counted among contemporaries Steven Soderbergh ("Traffic"), Paul Thomas Anderson ("Magnolia"), David Fincher ("Fight Club"), Darren Aronofsky ("Pi") and David O. Russell ("Three Kings"). If, as a group, their triumph is in many respects a visual one - not all of these directors or writer-directors have an equal gift for storytelling - they each approach the medium with great vigor and a willingness to take risks.

"Memento" stars Guy Pearce as Leonard Shelby, an insurance investigator who is out to avenge his wife's rape and murder. The problem is, he is a man who lives in a continual present tense. Ever since suffering a head injury in a failed rescue attempt, he can't make new memories. While he owns total knowledge of his past and who he is, he can't retain fresh memories for more than a few moments. He either must write everything down on paper and Polaroids or use his body as a bizarre data-retrieval system covered with tattoos - clues to his pursuit of the mysterious "John G."

As Shelby tracks his quarry he is either aided, exploited or duped - depending on one's suspicions - by Teddy (Joe Pantoliano), a guy who may or may not be a cop; bartender Natalie (Carrie-Anne Moss), who may or may not be a drug dealer's moll; and the scraggly motel manager Burt (Mark Boone Jr.), who may or may not be sympathetic to Shelby's plight.

As the story keeps looping back on itself like a Moebius strip, slipping in fragments of back story and making us rethink our guesses, Nolan toys with the notions of shifting truth and perceptual illusion.

Nolan's second film, like his first ("Following"), has been referred to as "leaner, meaner" Hitchcock. Indeed, "Memento" does bear a similarity to the stories and novels of father-of-noir author Cornell Woolrich, whose famed exercise in paranoia, "Rear Window," was one of Hitch's most masterful adaptations.

The cast adds conviction.

Pearce's outstanding performance in 1997's "L.A. Confidential" was somewhat overshadowed by the hubbub over Russell Crowe and Kevin Spacey in the same film. Here he inhabits the role in every sense, in every scene, making us live in his world - where even revenge achieved may not be remembered.

Pearce's bravura work is augmented by a small but no less skilled ensemble of supporting players. Especially good is Pantoliano, a top-drawer character actor who is as distinctive, crafty and dynamic as ever.

There are also significant contributions from Stephen Tobolowsky and Harriet Harris as a married couple whose tragic experience both haunts and shapes Shelby's thoughts. Cinematographer Wally Pfister ("Stuart Little") executes Nolan's visual embellishments with assurance and verve, while David Julian's score lends an effective aural parallel to Shelby's alternately jittery and confident state of mind.

Who knows if this film, with dazzling style but not as much substance, will be retained in our own memories for long. It may or may not leave a lasting impression, but it's so deceptively clever that you're content to live in the moment.

....

'Requiem for a Dream' is a grim portrayal of drug addiction

"Requiem for a Dream"
December 14, 2000

Darren Aronofsky is nothing if not bold. His nightmarish "Requiem for a Dream" is one of the more vehement anti-drug films ever made, a grim human carnival flecked with mordant humor but driven (chiefly) by the writer-director's visual invention.

Adapted from "Last Exit to Brooklyn," the 1978 novel by Hubert Selby Jr., it is a movie few would attempt. But Aronofsky, 31, composing his second film after 1998's impressive "Pi," approaches matters in a fractured and dizzyingly reassembled narrative style that suggests a kinship with Tom Tykwer's "Run Lola Run" and David O. Russell's "Three Kings."

The subject matter, however, is more akin to Paul Schrader's superb "Light Sleeper," though considerably more bleak.

Ellen Burstyn gives one of the better performances of her career as Sarah Goldfarb, an aging widow whose life is confined to a dingy apartment and a set of friends no less at loose ends than she. Goldfarb is hooked on memories, chocolate, a motivational TV infomercial and, soon enough, diet pills.

Her son Harry (Jared Leto) is a once-promising 20-something-turned-drug-slacker, not yet hooked but well down the thruway. He comes to see her only when he needs to "steal" her TV set to pawn it for cash.

Comic actor Marlon Wayans turns serious as Harry's best friend and cohort, Tyrone, a fellow who consumes grass and smack recreationally, but is addicted to the game of dealing.

Then there's Marion (Jennifer Connelly), Harry's girlfriend, whose cocaine habit fuels — and undermines — her dreams of being a dress designer. Harry and Tyrone delude themselves into believing they can sell enough dope to live the highlife while helping Marion open a dress shop.

Early on, they're not in so deep that they can't exhume themselves. But as dependency grows, so do the various degradations to which the characters will submit themselves.

Aronofsky and cinematographer Matthew Libatique employee whiteouts as fades, and, by extension, as symbols for the oblivion of heroin (and cocaine) addiction. Aronofsky's use of split screen and accelerated film speeds, sometimes with foreground action in normal mode, effectively convey the distance between these supposedly intimate characters, as well as the desperation or frantic opportunism they embody. Quick cutting and time shifts are done not simply to divert the eye, as in action movies, but to communicate his people's mounting frenzy.

An original score by Clint Mansell, played by the Kronos Quartet, lends the perfect complement of edginess and energy.

Occasionally, Aronofsky's message feels labored and a bit gratuitous, with an excess of shock value. What humor does intrude on these dark proceedings derives from Sarah's food fantasies: Trying to resist, she is assailed by a dementia of cakes and pies, not to mention a demonic refrigerator.

When she is chosen to be an audience member for her favorite infomercial, she begins popping pills to drop pounds, only to fall into a trap of her own.

Unrated despite explicit sexual content and some rather gruesome elements, the film offers a brilliantly rendered montage as its final "scene," bombarding viewers who likely have cried "uncle" much earlier. But for those who can handle the film's shock value, there are rewards to be had, not least the fine acting Aronofsky extracts — there's no better way to put it — from a hand-picked cast.

Somehow, their characters win your sympathy.

....

Cool jazz, sweet movie
"Sweet and Lowdown"
February 17, 2000

Emmet Ray is the sort of self-made man who worships his creator.

Such is the nature of conceit, and of the artist convinced of his own genius. In Woody Allen's sweetly engaging "Sweet and Lowdown," Ray (Oscar nominee Sean Penn) is presented as a real-life figure from the '30s jazz age whose legend as a guitarist is second only to his idol's, the immortal gypsy Django Reinhardt.

Did we say idol? Make that "fixation." Ray is so consumed with Reinhardt and his wizardry with the frets that the only two times he's been in his presence he's fainted dead away. Ray's loathe to actually meet him, some suspect, because he's afraid to learn that Reinhardt's merely mortal. Somehow it would tarnish Ray's standing as No. 2.

Ray is not a sympathetic character, at least not in the conventional sense. Drop the "sym" and you've got the photo. He is a drunk. He is a compulsive womanizer. He is a vain, irresponsible, thoughtlessly cruel and self-absorbed egotist who defends his bad behavior by declarations of his own brilliance. As if being an artist absolves him from all responsibility.

At the same time, he is possessed of a touching innocence. And for all his cluelessness about human feelings, his guitar sings with the full spectrum of emotions. As does the love of his life, the mute and almost angelic laundress Hattie, wordlessly (and poignantly) played by Oscar nominee Samantha Morton, whose alternately ardent and mousy child-woman was inspired by Fellini's muse Giulietta Masina.

But Ray can't square his affections for Hattie with his ambitions - or his insistence on sexual freedom.

Less appealing is Uma Thurman as the socialite and would-be writer who marries Ray shortly after he runs out on Hattie. Her hammy take on the young Lauren Bacall is one of the film's few discordant notes, even if it does provide Allen with a vehicle to satirize writers and their pet delusions.

Penn, by contrast, invests a despicable lout with subtle shadings. And he reminds us that while many great artists may have been cads and bounders in their personal lives, in the end what matters to history is their art.

Allen, well known for his love of jazz, cobbles Ray from a composite of genuine jazz musicians and places him with a wholly convincing world of seaside resorts, dingy roadhouses, railyards and opulent nightclubs. Vintage cars as well as flawless period sets and clothes combine with a delicious soundtrack of the era's music to give "Sweet and Lowdown" the feel of effortless authenticity.

Allen also recruited Chinese cinematographer Zhao Fei ("Raise the Red Lantern") for the film and the warm, intimate radiance of the picture is among its most appealing features. Appearing in cameos as supposed jazz historians and music experts are Allen, Ben Duncan and Nat Hentoff, among others, who serve up their own retrospective tales about Ray.

Penn fakes it with aplomb, but the real playing is done by the masterful Howard Alden. Anyone who ever savored the work of Reinhardt and his long-time partner Stephane Grappelli and their Quintet du Hot Club de France will swoon along with Ray.

And that's the lowdown.

....

Cruise exceptional in a film littered with damaged souls
"Magnolia"
January 9, 2000

A third of the way through Paul Thomas Anderson's startling "Magnolia," you may be wondering "OK, so what's the point?"

Be patient. It becomes apparent soon enough. And the point of it all is going to nail you to your seat.

A bleak, if sometimes darkly funny, meditation on human frailty, Anderson's third and most accomplished film offers, first and foremost, a smorgasbord of fine performances from a hand-picked ensemble cast.

Structurally, and to a certain extent in tone, it's reminiscent of Robert Altman's "Short Cuts." But the similarity ends there. Instead of an array of contemporary themes, "Magnolia" is concerned with a single, universal one: We may be through with the past, but the past isn't through with us.

Guilt, regret, grief and rage assail Anderson's characters from every quarter, almost all of it rooted in past transgressions and weaknesses. In "Boogie Nights," Anderson explored a community of people united in their disarray, in being wounded by life and in desperate need of some semblance of family. The damaged souls of "Magnolia" have all the family they can handle, and then some.

Set within a 24-hour period in California's San Fernando Valley, "Magnolia" presents nine main characters in the throes of personal crisis. Their stories sometimes connect and twine, but each is a definable individual with sharply drawn features. What they share is isolation.

Anderson's script brims with vivid set-pieces and audacious touches. Unsparing and candid, it does not look away when characters aching for absolution despise their own need. But also like "Boogie Nights," even the most painful moments are leavened with compassion and, at least in some cases, the hope of forgiveness.

There is so much good acting on display here that you hardly know where to begin.

Start with Tom Cruise, who over the past several years has shown surprising indications of developing, at last, into an actor.

He does the best work of his career as a strutting male dominance guru, who has tried to bury the memories of youth and now must confront the past – and present – head-on. Furious and vulnerable, loathsome and sympathetic, it's exceptional work.

The same is true of Julianne Moore, riveting as the young wife of a dying elderly husband (Jason Robards) whose guilt (and drug abuse) has her waltzing on the brink. You expect Robards to be excellent; he always is.

But there also are consistently compelling portraits by Philip Seymour Hoffman, John C. Reilly, Philip Baker Hall, the young Stanley Spector, Melinda Dillon, William H. Macy, and Melora Walters, with engaging tidbits from Henry Gibson and Alfred Molina.

The movie is not without flaws. It's too jumbled, for one thing. It gets frantic at times with its excess of quick-cutting. You also can fault Anderson's screenplay for a gross over-reliance on a certain curse word: It's the dominant element in everyone's vocabulary, and grows tiresome.

That said, Anderson is unquestionably a gifted filmmaker. If "Magnolia" is a trifle over-furnished - three hours is an awful lot of misery to support - it is so involving that its length seems to whiz by in a (fractured) flash.

....

House 'Rules' made to be broken
"The Cider House Rules"
January 06, 2000

Lasse Hallstrom's sentimental though quietly effective "The Cider House Rules" may be the most satisfying film translation of the work of novelist John Irving.

For the first time, Irving adapted his own story for the screen. His careful attention to detail, to nuance, marries beautifully with Hallstrom's unhurried and deeply humane approach. The filmmakers telescope some events from the book and successfully compress relationships while dealing soberly with a complex of moral issues.

Any movie which concerns itself with abortion, incest, the racial divide, suicide, betrayal and the tension that can exist between medical ethics and patient needs might be weighted with ponderous "messages" and gobs of melodrama.

But while melodramatic elements do exert themselves in what is essentially a coming-of-age tale — not least in the bitter sweet love affair between the principal characters — the larger matters are handled with organic calm, and no overt inflection. The film chooses to document, not preach, with the result that its central metaphors are all the more persuasive.

The narrator, Homer Wells (Tobey Maguire), grows up within an atmosphere of love, as opposed to the more familiar Dickensian cruelty, in the St. Cloud Orphanage in rural Maine. But the affectionate care so deftly dispensed by the pragmatic Dr. Wilbur Larch (Michael Caine, in a memorable performance) and his nurses (Jane Alexander, Kathy Baker) is somewhat offset by the orphans' purgatory.

Day after day, year after year, they wait, as perspective parents file in and out, interested chiefly in the infants Larch delivers. It is not his only service. In part to foil the butchers that pray on desperate women, Larch also performs abortions — a considerable (yet plausible) irony. Wells, a surrogate son, has been trained by Larch as his medical assistant. By 1943, he has gained much experience, if not formal credentials, but he declines to assist his mentor with abortions.

Wells, who has never ventured far from St. Cloud's, finds his role there a rewarding one, and the children adore him. Still, as manhood looms, he yearns to experience the larger world. These feelings are intensified when young Air Force pilot Lt. Wally Worthington (Paul Rudd) and his girlfriend, Candy (Charlize Theron), come to Larch to terminate her pregnancy.

Wells abruptly joins them on their trip home. Larch, having groomed the boy as his replacement, is crushed.

Worthington and his mother (Kate Nelligan) offer Wells a job in the family apple orchard and cider brewery, learning the business under the tutelage of one Mr. Rose (Delroy Lindo) and living with a group of migrant workers in a crude, functional dorm.

It is here that Wells discovers more of the harsh realities of life outside St. Cloud's. It is also on the dorm's walls that the "cider house rules "are posted.

Trivial, petty and completely ignored, by movie's end they represent the necessity of sometimes breaking the rules and the inevitability of compromise.

The latter is brought home painfully when Worthington returns from the war. In his absence, the friendship shared by Wells and Candy has evolved into love. Guilt, and feelings of responsibility, return her to Worthington's side.

Where does Wells, who has maintained a correspondence with Larch, go from here? The decision is not long in coming.

Hallstrom, best known for "My Life as a Dog" and "What's Eating Gilbert Grape?," elicits a bevy of understated, pitch-perfect performances, chief among them the first American character ever played by Caine. Maguire's aura of naïveté and gentleness of spirit is put to surprisingly convincing use in the central role, while Theron and Lindo continue to impress. One might wish Alexander, Nelligan and Baker had more to do, but Paz de la Huerta as a young girl with a crush on Wells, musician Erykah Badu (in her film debut as Rose's daughter) and a host of children deliver touching portraits.

Irving's distilled but vivid dialogue is key, as is the writer's penchant for melding pivotal personal events with a keen sense of place, then setting them against sweeping backdrops. Together with Hallstrom, he has rendered a faithful film that resonates well after the final act.

....

Superb leads make 'Anna' a magnetic movie
"Anna and the King"
December 19, 1999

As Andy Tennant's sumptuous "Anna and the King" opens, imperial arrogance, in the person of English schoolteacher Anna Leonowens, meets Oriental reality, in the imposing presence of Siamese King Mongkut.

Leonowens, a recent widow, has been ushered from her home in colonial India to teach the forward-looking monarch's eldest son, only to learn all 58 of his children will be in her charge.

It is not the only source of her indignation.

Yet soon, the king's own imperiousness softens to respect, then affection, while the spirited but proper Victorian lady's notions of "civilized" behavior are forever changed. Could love not ensue?

A timeless development, from an enduring story.

Two actors of great versatility, Jodie Foster and Chow Yun-Fat, deliver charismatic performances in the most handsomely appointed movie of the year. A triumph of production design and photography, it is also an impressive achievement in direction.

The film is based on the memoirs of the real-life Leonowens, which inspired the making of the 1946 film "Anna and the King of Siam." It includes trace elements of the 1956 Rodgers and Hammerstein's musical "The King and I," largely in its score.

If Tennant's telling, co-written by Steve Meerson and Peter Krikes, occasionally slips from drama into melodrama, it can be forgiven. Told with intelligence and verve as well as delicacy, this intensely romantic movie manages to meld epic sweep with intimacy against a backdrop of political intrigues and wrenching social change.

Denied permission to shoot in Thailand, the former Siam, the makers of "Anna and the King" scouted locations throughout Asia before settling on Malaysia, chiefly the pristine beaches and lush interior of Langkawi Island. A magnificent choice, as it turns out, offering breathtakingly exotic scenery.

Cinematographer Caleb Deschanel, currently shooting "The Patriot" in Charleston, captures these landscapes in an alternately simple and ethereal splendor, while the genius of Oscar-winning production designer Luciana Arrighi and Oscar-winning costume designer Jenny Beavan, who worked together on such films as "Howard's End,"

"The Remains of the Day" and "Sense and Sensibility," is apparent in every frame.

Foster pulls off her British accent without a hitch, but it's the quality and clarity of the emotions that startle. Chow, meanwhile, makes it a superb pairing of leads with a magnetic turn. The byplay between the characters, moving from the first clink of foils to the full clash of steely resolve, could not be better.

When devoted King and reawakened lady must make the inevitable sacrifice, we are reminded of what another of the picture's indelible characters (beautifully played by Bai Ling) has said: "If love was a choice, who would ever choose such exquisite pain?" We all would. If you are not now in love with someone, "Anna and the King" will make you wish you were.

....

Being John Malkovich' wacky, fun
"Being John Malkovich"
November 11, 1999

All puppeteer Craig Schwartz ever wanted to do with his art was to see through the eyes of another, to feel what he feels.

Wish granted.

As played by John Cusack, the gifted-but-nerdish street puppetmaster, gets more than he bargained for in Spike Jonze's utterly beguiling "Being John Malkovich," as original a picture as you'll see this year.

Jonze, directing his inaugural feature from a script by fellow first-timer Charlie Kaufman, delivers a delightful spoof on Andy Warhol's prediction that everyone is destined for 15 minutes of fame. The film also plays into the notion of an actor being absorbed into a character and, of course, characters taking on a life of their own.

"BJM" is a totally off-the-wall experience, which, despite a few draggy interludes, sustains a rare degree of comic invention from start to finish. From the first scene, you know you've placed yourself in the hands of certifiable madmen, and you couldn't be happier at the prospect.

Chronically unemployed, Schwartz lives with his eccentric pet shop employee wife Lotte (a de-glamorized Cameron Diaz) and their growing menagerie in a cramped New York apartment.

But his domicile is cavernous compared to the claustrophobic confines of Lestercorp, a goofy filing business wedged between the seventh and eighth floors of an office building. Like all but his most diminutive co-workers, new employee Schwartz must stoop when not sitting down. The president of the company, Dr. Lester (Orson Bean), is weird enough. A man who believes he's 105 years old, he's also convinced he has a speech impediment, not quite realizing that his receptionist (Mary Kay Place), a speech therapist with a kind of hearing dyslexia, is the one with the problem.

One day, while moving a bank of filing cabinets, Schwartz discovers a secret door low in the wall. It opens onto a strange tunnel, which in turn becomes a portal which whisks him headlong into the mind and body of actor John Malkovich.

Malkovich is unaware of the intrusion at first, but Schwartz retains his own consciousness while in Malkovich's body. This bit of transcendental voyeurism lasts only a quarter of an hour, after which Schwartz is hurled out - onto a greensward by the New Jersey Turnpike.

When Schwartz relates the phenomenon to Maxine the Ice Queen (Catherine Keener), his chilly and self-absorbed colleague for whom he has developed an infatuation, she finds a way to capitalize: charge $200 a pop to give people the chance to be a star, however fleetingly.

But things get complicated, especially when Lotte takes the ride and winds up lusting for Maxine - as John Malkovich. The feeling is mutual.

Then things really get wacko.

"BJM" is an obvious riff on "Alice Through the Looking Glass," but this is a film that throws you a curve ball about every, well, 15 minutes. It's a carnival ride through a series of unexpected trap doors and fits of narcissistic delirium.

The real Malkovich, merely a vessel at first, eventually rules the film through a dandy exercise in self-parody. Or rather, a parody of the self-parody he's already undertaken in some of his recent roles. It's daring work. Frizzy-haired and as plain as they can make her (which isn't very), Diaz shows yet again that she has strong comic instincts. Cusack (unkempt and obsessed) and Keener (blithely shallow) likewise play it to the hilt.

There's also a handful of cameos (an inside joke involving Charlie Sheen is particularly amusing) and some uncommonly clever set design.

Jonze, a sometimes actor who made a name for himself in music videos, has given us a movie loaded with ideas, complete with fresh takes on the cult of celebrity, the malleability of gender, and the dangers of vicarious experience.

Great writing and execution, plus accomplished acting from a cast unafraid to take risks. What more could one ask? Well, nothing against Mr. Malkovich, but next time: how about a ride into the consciousness of Ms. Diaz? Equal time for us guys.

....

Acting raises level of gritty film about urban paramedic
"Bringing Out the Dead"
October 24, 1999

Lights flashing and siren wailing, an ambulance races through the netherworld of New

York at night.

Behind the wheel is EMS paramedic Frank Pierce (Nicolas Cage), a man who can't sleep, can't eat, and who survives on cigarettes and booze. Throw in a shot of adrenalin. He hasn't saved anyone in months, and now the ghosts of the dead - one young woman in particular - keep coming back to haunt him.

Pierce is a man on the edge, in one of the most stressful occupations there is. And he can't even get himself fired.

"In the last few years, I've come to believe in spirits leaving the body and refusing to come back," says Pierce, who narrates.

Martin Scorsese's "Bringing Out the Dead" is Paddy Chayefsky by way of Dante's "Inferno," an alternately stark and delirious take on the urban paramedic's reality.

It's "The Hospital" meets "Taxi Driver." Scorsese and screenwriter Paul Schrader have returned to their mean streets, and they don't look any kinder than they did 25 years ago.

The film is an adaptation of the cathartic novel by Joe Connelly, based on his 10 years as an EMS worker in Manhattan. As the movie makes abundantly clear, it can be the greatest job in the world - the doctors of the streets - or one of the worst.

Nothing matches the high of saving a life. "Saving someone is like falling in love," says Pierce. "It's the best drug in the world. God has passed through you - why deny it?"

But it's a high that fades as the body count multiplies.

Cage ventured into this grueling world with paramedics in both New York and L.A. to bring authenticity to the role, and it has helped produce one of the best performances of his career.

We get three days in the life of a man at risk of becoming one of his own clients. Pierce grows more haggard and hollow-eyed with each passing hour as the array of cardiac arrests, drug overdoses, gunshot and knife wounds, attempted suicides, broken bones and imagined emergencies mounts beyond the human capacity to deal with them.

Only one thing is different as we meet our protagonist. Responding to a heart attack call, he has met the daughter of the victim, Mary Burke (Patricia Arquette), a recovering drug user who, like Pierce, chose to stay in the neighborhood where she grew up.

As a madhouse of a hospital keeps her comatose dad alive artificially, the two develop an edgy rapport, taking solace at arm's length. He tells her he has begun to feel like a "grief mop." She says she has just spent the last couple of weeks before her father's attack wishing he were dead.

Also in the mix are a trio of Pierce's rotating partners: a Jesus-channeling lothario (Ving Rhames), a violence-prone wild man (Tom Sizemore) and a Chinese food-gorging giant (John Goodman), none of whom makes the process of burnout any easier.

Eventually, Pierce achieves an element of grace, but first he has to drive through to the other side of the night, realizing the guilt that plagues him is self-applied.

"Bringing Out the Dead" is bravura filmmaking, bleakly fascinating yet overlong and somewhat repetitious, like most of Scorsese's work. We get the point pretty early on, then spend the next two hours-plus hearing it reiterated. As dark comedy, there aren't that many laughs, even rueful ones. Though there is ample gallows humor - the lone insulation paramedics have against the often grisly reality of their work - it isn't always up to Schrader's standard.

It's the acting, not all the camera tricks and flashes of angelic light, that really carries the film. Cage and real-life spouse Arquette perform together for the first time, and it's an auspicious match. One of the more underrated young actresses around, she invests Mary with lots of inner conflict and suppressed emotions.

Of the supporting players, Rhames and Sizemore stand out, while there is fine work in small roles by singer-actor Marc Anthony and Cliff Curtis, who play a frenzied addict and a becalmed and philosophical drug dealer, respectively.

....

'Fight' both knockout and dive
"Fight Club"
October 17, 1999

A bored Yuppie locked in a deadening job, Jack (Edward Norton) is having a premature midlife crisis at age 30. His posh high-rise condo and fits of conspicuous consumption no longer cut it.

Beset with insomnia as well as ennui, Jack will do anything to feel alive and connected, like faking illnesses to gain entry in a variety of support groups.

"When people think you're dying, they really, really listen to you," says Jack, who narrates the film.

It is in one of these assemblies he meets Marla (Helena Bonham Carter), a fellow poseur. But the encounter that changes his life - and propels us into the bizarre world of David Fincher's "Fight Club" - occurs on a plane. Jack is seated next to one Tyler Durden (Brad Pitt), a garishly attired soap maker with a compelling philosophy of life: total freedom.

If this dazzling but disturbing film proves anarchy can be funny - and wildly witty at times - it also is guaranteed to ignite the most ferocious controversy since "Natural Born Killers."

"Fight Club" weds manic invention with such extreme violence it makes "NBK" look like "Bambi."

The director's morbid fascination with the grotesque, which first oozed to the surface with "Alien 3" and "Seven," was tempered in his last outing, "The Game." Not so here. Fincher and screenwriter Jim Uhls have kicked out the jams in adapting the kaleidoscopic debut novel by Chuck Palahniuk.

There is nowhere Fincher's camera fears to tread. Graphic, macabre and extraordinarily intense, its depiction of how a single urban underground fight club morphs into a mayhem-minded cult is Guy Movie to the nth degree - a manifesto of male rage in the modern age which serves up a brutal kind of emancipation.

When Jack's apartment is mysteriously blown up, he flops in Durden's dilapidated house in "a toxic waste part of town." There, liberated from all the possessions that possessed him, he adds Hyde to Jekyll, helping Durden found the first of what will become a national network of bare-knuckle clubs - hidden rooms where members pound each other senseless for the camaraderie of it.

"Fight Club is not about winning and losing," Durden intones, "It's a communion."

But Durden, a Svengali who wants to take his show on the road, has more in mind. An army of skin-headed anarchists, for starters. A cacophony of chaos as his ultimate goal - urban terrorism as art form.

Despite scene after scene of blood-spurting, sometimes nauseating violence, "Fight Club" is disarmingly funny for much of its length. But when this blacker-than-black comedy turns really dark, it sails past excessive to border on irresponsible. Even those who dismiss the idea that violence on screen begets violence in life may be compelled to reconsider the possibility. "Fight Club" could give genuine crazies ideas. It's that alluring, in a perverse sort of way.

From a narrative standpoint, the picture also gets a little too clever, a little too contrived, in some of its details, which blunts the satire in favor of visceral sensation. Of course, that's largely intentional.

As cinematic derring-do, the movie is a remarkable achievement, from opening credits to inside jokes (check out the "Seven Years in Tibet" marquee) to twist ending. And it is underscored by excellent performances, especially those of Norton, brilliant again in a complex characterization, and Bonham Carter, who is about as far removed from her refined Merchant-Ivory roles as can be imagined.

Pitt, dead-eyed and bland in "Meet Joe Black," is formidable here, declaring war on white-collar slavery and exuding an exhilarating, hair-trigger menace.

"Fight Club" is both knockout and dive, amusing and corrosive. One wonders how much further Fincher, a gifted filmmaker, can go in indulging himself. Or how successfully he will weather what is already shaping up to be a firestorm of controversy.

Where do you go from here?

....

'Moon': Love for grown ups
"A Walk on the Moon"
April 29, 1999

In the golden summer of 1969, a few miles from Woodstock, N.Y., and the festival of hedonism that is to come, is a vastly different world of bungalows, bar mitzvahs and immutable tradition.

As Apollo 11 approaches lunar orbit, and the Hippie Nation's defining moment is at hand, life is unchanged in the Catskills resorts, where Jewish families form the city vacation as they have for decades.

What happens when conventionality collides with the unfettered spirit is the subject of Tony Goldwyn's beautifully observed "A Walk on the Moon," a feast of exceptional acting wed to a mature script.

Pamela Gray's balanced, finely crafted screenplay is her first for the big screen. Infused with equal measures of yearning, humor and heartbreak, it centers on the dilemma of one Pearl Kantrowitz (Diane Lane), an attractive young housewife who married too soon and now feels the times are passing her by.

"This whole decade's gone by and the biggest decision I've made is where to shop at the A&P or some other grocery," she confides to a friend.

Try as she might to communicate her longings to her husband Marty (Live Schreiber), an overworked TV repairman, Pearl can only articulate them in vague terms. As the Kantrowitz family arrives at Dr. Fogler's Bungalows for their yearly sojourn, matters are coming to a head, even if Pearl is only beginning to recognize the signs.

In tow are the couple's urgently adolescent daughter Alison (Anna Paquin), her precocious kid brother Daniel (Bobby Boriello), and Marty's mother Lilian (Tovah Feldshuh), a meddlesome if warm-hearted woman who believes she's prescient.

Marty's job forces him to go back and forth from resort to city, which provides the opening filled by strappingly handsome Walker Jerome (Viggo Mortensen), a quasi-hippie who peddles his wares from his mobile store, a vintage bus that makes the rounds of the resorts.

The Blouse Man, he is called, and it's not long before he and Pearl prove a perfect fit. She is smitten — not so much with Jerome, perhaps, as with what he represents. At first.

Compared to Pearl's squarish spouse, Jerome is a figure straight from a romance novel, all sensuality and animal magnetism. He's just as intrigued by her. As the very moment astronauts set foot on the moon, Pearl takes her first fateful steps onto the new ground. The affair is conveyed in scenes that will transport anyone who lived it back to a magical time — but the feeling is more wistful than nostalgic.

Meanwhile, as Janis Joplin wails provocatively in the background, Pearl's awakening is rivaled by that of her daughter, awash in boy craziness. Alison gets her first period and first date the same day, and soon after slips off to Woodstock.

What she doesn't know is that her mother will be there, too, with Jerome.

Things quickly unravel for Pearl, whose husband learns of her dalliance and, stricken, leaves.

Then comes a heated exchange between mother and daughter, who accuses her of irresponsibility.

"I'm the teenager, not you!" cries Alison. "You *had* your chance."

"No," her mom replies, "I didn't."

And that's the crux of Pearl's problem, as well as her fling: She is living out her adolescence as an adult, compelled to discover the self that was never allowed to flower, even if it destroys her family.

Lane, who is wonderful, never has shown this kind of range as an actress. From flawless line readings to achingly eloquent body language, she gives the performance of her career.

Mortensen plays it tender rather than tough this time, though exuding the same charisma, and stage actress Feldshuh makes a rare film appearance a memorable one. Schreiber, however, impresses almost as much as Lane.

One woman's personal sexual revolution may be oft-trod terrain, but seldom has it been done in such a compassionate and grown-up way. Bravo.

....

The mighty Quinns make impressive film
"This Is My Father"
July 22, 1999

A small, beautifully drawn story of love and tragedy in an Irish village, "This Is My Father" marks a remarkable screen debut for stage director Paul Quinn, and an equally impressive turn by his brothers Aidan, who stars, and Declan, whose camera captures the Emerald Isle as few have done before.

Though there is nothing especially original in the director's script – many an unavoidable cliche rears its head – this film set in 1939 and the present day is pointed, poignant, and brimming with fine performances.

Among the best is by James Caan, who has his meatiest role in years. Caan plays widower Kieran Johnson, a disillusioned high school history teacher in Chicago with more than his share of disappointments in and out of the classroom. When Johnson stumbles upon an old photograph of a strange man arm in arm with his mother, a stroke victim now living with his sister (Susan Almgren), he suspects it may be the father he never knew.

His mother (Francoise Graton) is bedridden and uncommunicative. So Johnson decides to go to Ireland and uncover the man's identity. His harried, divorced sister urges him to take his troubled nephew Jack (Jacob Tierney) as well.

Once there, Kieran and Jack take a room at a small inn run by Seamus Kearney (Colm Meaney) and his fortune-teller mother (Moira Deady), who recount the fateful tale of his parent's love affair.

As her narrative unfolds, the film slips back to a time just before the onset of World War

II. Fiona Flynn (Moya Farrelly), the daughter of an embittered but proud middle-class widow (Gina Moxley), has just been sent home from boarding school, having had a row with the nuns. One evening she invites childhood friend Kieran O'Day (Aidan Quinn) to a dance. Adopted at age eight and carrying the stigma of being a "poorhouse bastard," he and his foster parents (Maria McDermottroe, Donal Donnelly) are tenants on the widow's land.

The two soon fall in love, and as the relationship intensifies, so do the forces aligned against it, chiefly the widow - superbly played by Moxley - and a pair of fire-and-brimstone priests (Stephen Rea, Eamonn Morrissey). The life O'Day and Flynn so looked forward to sharing, is shattered instead.

Although "This Is My Father" invests much of its length in a rueful attack on the tyranny and hypocrisy done in the name of organized religion - in this case Irish Catholicism - as well as its incapacity to see its own contradictions, the picture really has less to say about the church itself than the extremist tendencies betrayed by the all-too-human people who interpret it.

In this respect, the Quinns' film is more a lament. The brothers grew up hearing the story from their own parents, and they have rendered it as a touching lesson on taking the secrets of the past that bind the future and releasing them in the present.

Paul Quinn gracefully handles these familiar yet potent elements, and he is aided by what is perhaps the most deceptively rich, nuanced acting of Aidan's career. But the entire cast, which also includes small turns by John Cusack and Brendan Gleeson, is simply flawless. Apart from Moxley and gifted young Irish actress Farrelly, standouts include Donnelly, Deady and Joel Gordon.

Declan Quinn, whose credits as cinematographer include "Leaving Las Vegas" and "Vanya on 42nd Street, makes this first collaboration of the Quinn brothers a memorable one, strengthened both by literary values and heart-felt emotions.

....

'Husband' is ideal Wilde
"An Ideal Husband"
July 08, 1999

"I love talking about nothing. It's the only thing I know anything about."

This characteristic *bon mot* comes courtesy of Lord Arthur Göring, an archly amusing upper-crust dandy who's life's mission is never to be serious about anything.

As played by Rupert Everett, he is the perfect stand-in for the playwright whose line he utters. But Oscar Wilde's "An Ideal Husband," like many of his most delightful works, is not without its serious points.

Writer-director Oliver Parker has taken things a step further, maintaining the elegant but airless Wildean world while enriching the story's emotional base and — let this heresy stand — devising a resolution that is an improvement on the original play.

The privileged still get to enjoy their privileges, but they have a finer grasp of the contradictions of human character.

Some may see the story as diluted, yet with political and sexual blackmail, a variation on insider trading, and the specter of death by tabloid, this 1895 melodramatic comedy looks a great deal like 1999.

Sir Robert Chiltern (Jeremy Northam) has a dark secret, a malfeasance on which his fortune is based. A certain Mrs. Cheverly (Julianne Moore), a calculating expatriate now living in Vienna, returns to England with a not-so-veiled threat. Unless Chiltern reverses his position and sponsors of corrupt Argentine canal project, in which Cheverly has invested heavily, she will expose his past and ruin not only his career in parliament but his happy marriage to the worshipful Gertrude (Cate Blanchett).

Goring, his best friend, urges him to confess to her, not mentioning the fact that he once was engaged to the conniving Mrs. Cheveley. While the advice is genuine, Chiltern is a man forced to relearn the values by which he has lived his life even as his wife comes to realize the folly of placing her husband upon too lofty a pedestal, rather than appreciating him as a good man subject to human frailties.

An incomparable wit, Wilde often seemed to write for the stage simply to provide a vehicle for his eminently quotable asides and dialogue. Parker has distilled the wordiness, strengthened the people and added a degree of naturalism to the mix.

The acting is impeccable as a silk cravat, with performances from Everett and Moore that alone are worth twice the price of admission. Yet everyone involved — with the possible exception of Minnie Driver — is ideally cast in a film that is a decided improvement on Alexander Korda's 1948 screen version. Blanchett, maybe the finest young actress now working, again is strikingly good, while able support comes from veteran character actors John Wood, Peter Vaughan, Marsha Fitzalan and, in a brief appearance, Jeroen Krabbe.

Costume designer Caroline Harris manages to lend a modern feel to the rigidly formal look usually associated with the late Victorian Age.

And the contributions of production designer Michael Howells — those enormous Belgravia houses never looked so grand — and cinematographer David Johnson can't be minimized.

Some may prefer their sociopolitical satire weighted more towards the political, as Wilde did in this particular case. But kudos to Parker for emphasizing the romance.

....

Nolte is a man afflicted
"Affliction"
March 11, 1999

Wade Whitehouse is a man incapacitated by life, by a dark and violent family history. He lives and works, as a part-time cop and full-time flunky, in the economically depressed town of Lawford, N.H.

His parents are broken people, especially his abusive, alcoholic father, and there seems little doubt that Whitehouse (Nick Note) is powerless to sidestep a similar path to destruction.

It's hard to say which is the greater desolation in writer-director Paul Schrader's "Affliction," the wintry landscape or that embodied by the central characters. Like the town they inhabit, these are people with a nondescript past and no future.

Based on a novel by Russell Banks, a harrowing story which was equal parts thriller, psychological study and indictment of the ways in which violence is passed down from father to son, the film is as cunningly crafted as it is bleak.

Few, if any, directors meld the allegorical with grim realism as deftly as Schrader. "Affliction" starts out as a minimalist character study, every gesture pregnant with meaning (or seeming to be). It then segues into a sort of murder mystery before delving into deeper waters with the realization that no murder, in fact, has been committed. More dreadful crimes are involved.

Schrader's film may be set in 1990s northern New England but its pedigree extends back to those centuries when life was organized and utterly controlled through the threat of male violence.

This is the affliction of the title, a heritage of emotional bankruptcy and familial terrorism fueled by booze and kept under wraps. And no one familiar with Schrader's work ("American Gigolo," "Hardcore," "Light Sleeper") expects an epiphany.

There will be no redemption, no salvaging of damaged human goods. Not even Margie Fogg (Sissy Spacek), the waitress and childhood friend who loves (and pities) Whitehouse, can rescue him from himself and the legacy of his dissolute father (James Coburn).

Only Wade's kid brother Rolfe (Willem Dafoe), a history instructor at Boston University — and the film's narrator — will survive the past's lock on the present, though he remains indelibly marked by it.

Whitehouse is far more complex and self-aware an individual than he first appears. There is a family heroic (if hapless) quality to the man as he struggles, chalked with rage, to resurrect his life and avoid becoming his father — only to compound his miseries. Nolte, who over the years has specialized in playing characters wavering on the edge, gives a masterful performance, his best since "Q&A." The actor's grizzles, deeply lived-in-face, the haunted eyes and weary body language, combine with impeccable delivery to limn a fatally crippled character.

Perhaps even more impressive is Coburn, who has the role of his life. Glen Whitehouse is a sodden but animated snarl, incapable of remorse. He is a man so poisoned by the antiquated notions of masculinity hammered into him by his own father that he long ago became impervious to change. Not even his wife's death moves him. Wade? He has always, been, and remains, Glen's whipping boy. This is acting of amazing economy and power.

Apart from Spacek, who can capture the screen even with as sketchily a drawn part as this, strong support also comes from Mary Beth Hurt as the ex-wife with whom Whitehouse is at odds, Brigid Tierney as the daughter with whom he can forge no link, Dafoe in the understated role of Rolfe, and Holmes Osbourne as Whitehouse's boss.

The classic "prop" of Whitehouse's throbbing toothache is another of the small fillips of artistry we've come to expect from Schrader, who, like Atom Egoyan ("The Sweet Hereafter") before him, has adapted Banks' difficult work with professionalism and finesse."Affliction," at base, is a story of someone who simply wants to be a good man but can't divine how. The gulf between his imagination and his capacities simply is too great to bridge, and time has run out. His personal tragedy, brilliantly told, makes for an unforgettable film experience.

....

The Bard triumphant
"Shakespeare in Love"
January 10, 1999

Love looks not with the eyes but with the mind; And therefore is wing'd Cupid painted blind. – "A Midsummer Night's Dream."

William Shakespeare was more than the greatest poet and playwright in the English language. He was also its most insightful psychologist, possessed of an extraordinary ability to describe the subtlest emotional state.

Surely, no one before or since has written more brilliantly, more expressively, on the nature of love.

And few have mused on the man and his times with more stylishness than the makers of "Shakespeare in Love," a romantic comedy bursting at the seams with wit, with ideas, with sheer exuberance.

Abetted by a wonderful cast, director John Madden and screenwriters Tom Stoppard and Marc Norman have fashioned a flawless film that is at once intensely romantic, howlingly funny and a feast for the eyes. Intelligence glimmers from every quarter thanks to the year's best script, one festooned with sly references and unexpected pleasures.

The movie turns on a single, speculative notion: What, in fact, do we really know of the Bard's life? Very little, as it happens. We assume that he was as respected in his day as we revere him now. Not necessarily.

London, 1593. Young Will Shakespeare (Joseph Fiennes) is an actor and struggling playwright suffering from a wretched bout of writer's block. Try as he might, he can't seem to get untracked on his latest comedy, "Romeo and Ethel, the Pirate's Daughter." Even the title seems wrong, somehow.

While Shakespeare longs to leave the life of "a hireling actor," noblewoman Viola De Lesseps (Gwyneth Paltrow) longs to be nothing but an actor in an age where women on stage are deemed indecent.

Smitten with the Bard's poetry, and soon to fall for the man himself, Viola believes female characters should be played by women, not by "petticoated boys." In a move that anticipates all the cross-dressing masquerades of the Bard's plays to come - and heralds a gender revolution - Viola poses as a boy and auditions for a role in the new play - and promptly is given the part of Romeo.

Viola dreams of a love "that overthrows life ... such as there has never been in a play." Will finds his dream of love embodied in her. Block broken, he is inspired (with a little help from his friends) to transform his play into the tragedy "Romeo and Juliet," turning real life into some of its most memorable scenes.

Shakespeare the writer may be wise in the ways of love, but what of Shakespeare the man, his heart no longer his own? And what will be their fate, since Viola has been promised in marriage to the dour Lord Wessex (Colin Firth) by none other than Queen Elizabeth (Judi Dench) herself?

Madden keeps it all moving at a brisk pace, helped immeasurably by the photography of Richard Greatrex and David Gamble's exceptionally creative editing. Not to mention Oscar-caliber costumes from Sandy Powell ("Wings of The Dove") and accomplished production design by Martin Childs.

The performances are impeccable. Never more luminous, Paltrow seems lit from within, but it is her deftness as an actress that impresses most. It is her finest work in a career that's only scratched the surface. As featureless and bland as Fiennes was in "Elizabeth," he's dynamic here, handling the title role with admirable aplomb.

Of the supporting players, Dench and Geoffrey Rush are first among equals, but the richness of the screenplay allows for contributions by all, among them Firth, Ben Affleck, Imelda Staunton, Tom Wilkinson, Jim Carter, Martin Clunes and Rupert Everett (as Christopher Marlowe).

This is one occasion when modern sensibilities are woven seamlessly into period trappings, rather than intruding. Mixing subtlety with slapstick, the beautiful with the bawdy, acuity with action, "Shakespeare in Love" is a triumph, superb in every respect.

....

'Elizabeth' is royally dull
"Elizabeth"
November 26, 1998

By themselves, meticulous production design and great costumes do not a movie make.

Someone kindly inform Shekar Kapur, director of the dreary "Elizabeth," a self-consciously arty period soap whose brand of "revisionist" history betrays small regard for the genuine article.

Where the movie does succeed is in affording us an alternate and more realistic view of the early years of Elizabeth's reign. We get not the supremely confident monarch of previous films, but a courageous young woman initially beset with uncertainty, reluctance, and a weakened realm. Not to mention various plots against her life by the movie's slavering villain — the Catholic Church.

Yet what strengths "Elizabeth" does possess are deposed by Kapur's operatic direction, more reminiscent of a horror film than an historical drama, by a wildly uneven script by Michael Hirst, whose spasms of wit are buried under the same tired old intrigues-within-intrigues cliches, and by simple tedium. Little of consequence happens in this unrelievedly gloomy enterprise.

A first-rate cast, including the gifted Cate Blanchett in the title role, can't save it.

Among the chief irritants is Remi Adefarasin's agile but hyperactive camera. Continually calling attention to itself with showy flourishes — white-outs, gauzy distortion, lightning flashes, shadows upon shadows — the photography also is dominated by interminable up-angle/down-angle vantage points which ultimately detract from the story and reduce it to that of an opulent music video.

One with an annoyingly overwrought score courtesy of David Hirschfelder.

In style, tone and execution, what "Elizabeth" most resembles is Francis Ford Coppola's "Dracula," another monument to excess.

The whole business is so overdone you almost forget how fast and loose "Elizabeth" plays with history. Revisionism is one thing. Disregard of fact another.

The most glaring foolishness is the depiction of William Cecil, played by Richard Attenborough as a doddering old man forever beseeching the young queen to marry and secure her throne. Cecil was a vigorous and ambitious 38 when the 25-year-old came to the throne in 1558, not a creaky advisor near the end of his days. For 40 years, they maintained one of the most enduring and productive partnerships between minister and queen in European history. In this movie, he's mere footnote, hardly the most accomplished statesman of the Elizabethan era.

Blanchett, brilliant in "Oscar and Lucinda," manages a credibly vulnerable-tough performance amid all the "modernist" liberties. And it should offer considerable contrast to Dame Judi Dench's rather matronly portrait of the queen in the upcoming "Shakespeare in Love." But the screenplay lacks the depth of characterization that marked her role in "Oscar and Lucinda."

Otherwise, only Blanchett's Australian countryman Geoffrey Rush delivers genuinely effective work as the composed and coolly sinister spy master Sir Francis Walsingham. Fanny Ardant, last seen in "Ridicule," and John Gielgud as the Pope, at least get to chew some scenery.

Christopher Eccleston is too dour and brooding as the Duke of Norfolk, while Joseph Fiennes plays Robert Dudley, Early of Leicester and apple of the young Elizabeth's eye, with smoldering sincerity and a fatally bland sameness of affect.

At its best, "Elizabeth" gives us its heroine's passage into confidence after a difficult beginning, from the reviled "bastard queen" to the adored Virgin Queen, who supplanted the Virgin Mary as the object of her Protestant nation's worship.

....

Getting under the skin (heads)
"American History X"
November 19, 1998

Tony Kaye's riveting "American History X" offers a simple message – tolerance – powerfully told.

Intelligent, provocative and stunningly shot, the film trains it's light on the roots of neo-Nazism and the rest of the white supremacy movement. Both its illumination of the darkness and it's appeal to "the better angels of our nature" are underscored by an electrifying performance by Edward Norton as a skinhead who gets wise.

Norton turns in the most intense acting of his career in the role of Derek Vinyard, an unusually bright and promising youth in Venice Beach, Calif., who is seduced by hatred. The murder of his firefighter father, gunned down while putting out a fire in a drug den years earlier, and his own seething frustrations are manipulated by an neo-Nazi demagogue (Stacy Keach) who exploits Derek's natural leadership to lure others to the fold.

The film courses down two tracks, both lain by the narration of Edward Furlong as Derek's kid brother Danny, now caught in the same morass of explosive racial bigotry. Flashbacks charting Derek's missteps toward prison - and the horrors of life in stir - are presented in black and white. Present day sequences are in highly saturated color. And Kaye, serving as his own cinematographer, handles the transitions brilliantly.

Derek is being released from prison after having served three years for killing three blacks who tried to steal his car. They called it manslaughter. It was execution.

The years behind bars have convinced him of the cost of hate-mongering and the violence it spawns. Now he wants no part of the twisted thugs who regard him as a hero, and he'll do anything he has to do to extricate his brother from the grip of the sinister Cameron Alexander (Keach).

"American History X" is especially effective in reminding us of the pool of fear, ignorance and thwarted hopes from which hate groups recruit. But it also helps us understand how such resentments can evolve into perverse interpretations of people and events.

The picture falters from time to time. Some of its characters tend to be crudely drawn. Aside from Derek, people undergo fundamental attitude reversals in a manner that's a bit too facile and pat. Also, while most questions are treated soberly, some complex issues are oversimplified. On the other hand, the filmmakers didn't have five hours to dissect the history and causes of racial and class bitterness.

So compelling is Norton's delivery, and so charismatic is his presence, that some of the less toxic doggerel he espouses early on actually has you listening with an disarmed mind. That is, until these reasonable-sounding words translate into action. Kaye and screenwriter David McKenna set this trap intentionally, to force is to examine the depth of our own "enlightenment."

All in all, "AMX" is a blisteringly truthful film that pulls few punches. Why, then, did Kaye want to have his name expunged from the credits?

The first-time feature director, whose only previous experience was in making flashy tire commercials for European television, reportedly feuded with Norton throughout filming. He claims that the film was butchered in the editing room and that Norton's own retooling of the script rendered something quite different from the movie he envisioned. Naturally, Norton and the producers disagree.

He should be proud of the final cut, not disparaging.

Fresh from his fine turn in "Rounders," Norton impresses yet again. Only more so. In "AMX," it's hard for anyone to adequately complement, much less compete with, the performance of the buffed-up star. But there is solid work from Furlong (his best since "American Heart), from standup comic Guy Torry as the affable black inmate who gets under Derek's skin (and ultimately saves his life), from Ethan Suplee as the most obese and pathetic of the skinheads, from Beverly D'Angelo as Vinyard boys' mother and from Elliott Gould as her would-be lover.

The greatest contrast is between the parts played by Keach, who is superbly oily, and Avery Brooks, as a sober, committed high school principal trying to salvage both Vinyards' future. Brooks helps supply the film with its moments of calm, the better to apprehend its frenzies.

The climax is shocking, but not because you don't see it coming; you're waiting for the other shoe to drop throughout the final third of the film. As in "AMX's" spiritual cousin, "Menace II Society," its inevitability in no way undermines its impact.

Nor is the scariness of the movie compromised. More than its prison rape scene, more than the often grisly hate crimes, it's the awareness of how readily a political cause can "legitimize" gangsterism that chills one to the bone.

....

'Happiness' is a myth in this satirical film
"Happiness"
November 12, 1998

Call him the Wizard of Ooze.

Like many young writer-directors of his generation, Todd Solondz appears to have made it his life's mission to expose the comforting myths and suffocating fictions of modern suburbia.

Understandably, given his perception that behind the surface contentment lurks emotional detachment, obsession, and cruelty.

But as he proved in "Welcome to the Dollhouse," Solondz is a deft satirist. And he applies the skewer with a trace more compassion than his contemporaries.

In his second film, the ironically titled "Happiness," Solondz may have gotten in touch with his inner sadist, but he has melded humiliation with darker-than-dark humor to produce a picture that, at its best, is as poignant as it is funny. The juvenile gross-out gambits, somewhat resembling those of "There's Something About Mary," generally are in aid of something more than a cheap chuckle.

It's been widely reported how the filmmakers formed the company Good Machine to distribute "Happiness" after Universal Pictures compelled its "independent" subsidiary, October Films, to drop the film like a live grenade due to its sympathetic portrait of a pedophile. Even though it captured the International Directors Prize at Cannes earlier this year, it was considered film non grata.

Yet the character of psychiatrist Bill Maplewood, played with exceptional sensitivity and understatement by Dylan Baker, is sympathetic only in the sense that the man is not demonized. In no way does Solondz offer an apology for Maplewood's monstrous actions; quite the contrary. But neither does he engage in overheated moral outrage. Maplewood's admirable qualities are not ignored, among them a touching relationship with his own 11-year-old son, Billy (Rufus Read). He is an otherwise decent man being consumed by perversion.

As it happens, the film pivots to a far greater degree on the experiences of three sisters living in close, if uneasy, proximity in suburban New Jersey.

Helen Jordan (Lara Flynn Boyle) is a successful author who believes she is "living in a state of irony." Her exterior cool masks compulsive promiscuity and acute self-loathing. She's also the target of a spooky computer-nerd neighbor's (Philip Seymour Hoffman) obscene phone calls, which she counters with husky appeals for phone sex.

Diffident, hapless, ever-optimistic Joy (wonderfully played by Jane Adams), is a heart-rendingly lonely teacher of English who continually takes it on the chin from dippy or exploitive men (Jon Lovitz, Jared Harris) and her unappreciative, often hostile students. She also must suffer her sister Trish's (Cynthia Stevenson) sugar-coated put-downs.

Trish, Maplewood's wife, is a study in self-deception. The perfect housewife, she believes she has it all. But she has a lot more than she suspects. Namely, a husband who is drugging and molesting their son's playmates.

Much in the manner of Robert Altman's "Short Cuts," Solondz employs the farcical and tragic to twine their stories together with that of other, no less frustrated characters, searching in vain for love.

The Jordan sisters' parents, Lenny (Ben Gazzara) and Mona (Louise Lasser) are enjoying what appears to be a pleasant Florida retirement. Yet Mona is miserable. Her husband's indifference is not about infidelity, as she suspects. It's about boredom. Lenny's so glumly lifeless that even the prospect of a tumble with a neighboring widow (Elizabeth Ashley) leaves him cold.

Meanwhile, the aforementioned computer geek is being "wooed" by a portly murderess (Camryn Manheim) of such transparent vulnerability that you ache for her - even as she gives you chills.

If the tale were set in Orlando, they'd dub it Dysfunction World.

For all of this, most of the people in Solondz's complex, finely observed film stubbornly cling to a certain hopefulness. Joy, who both belies and justifies her name, borders on the heroic. Things may seem bleak, but tomorrow, after all, is indeed another day. It just takes the guts to face it.

It likewise took courage to embody several of the roles in "Happiness," which has its share of indelible moments. Above all, there is the measured scene in which the pedophile father, finally exposed, quietly and honestly answers his son's (graphic) questions. Baker, and no less so the young actor Read, handle it without a hint of sensationalism, yet still produce one of the most wrenching scenes in any film this year.

Solondz's sophomore effort not only shows marked improvement, but an unblinking vision: one unafraid to take that skeleton out the closest and make it dance.

....

Modern teens in '50's town make for fine feel-good film
"Pleasantville"
October 25, 1998

Gary Ross is a master purveyor of honest feel-goodism, as demonstrated in his screenplays for the gently disarming films "Big" and "Dave."

Yet in each of Ross' pictures, things happen to his characters that expand reality and broaden their hearts as well as their perceptions. The first-time director reiterates the theme in "Pleasantville," a breezy fable whose "Ozzie and Harriet" trappings lend contrast to serious concerns.

Tobey Maguire stars as David, a slightly geeky teen-ager from a contemporary broken family who finds a reassuring sense of normalcy and contentment in reruns of a '50s TV sitcom — a hybrid of "Father Knows Best" and "The Donna Reed Show" — where amity is the norm and no problem endures past the half-hour.

After a steady '90s diet of diminishing expectations, AIDS, global warming, homelessness and manifest doom and gloom, who wouldn't want to seek refuge in a simpler time? Even a fabricated one.

As seen on a "Nick at Nite"-styled cable channel, the town of Pleasantville is a wholesome, lily-white, numbingly dull place of fixed smiles and gee-whiz innocence. It is a place where sex is unknown, library books are blank, and no one is aware of a world outside of the burg's environs.

David is an authority on "Pleasantville" trivia, much to the dismay of his way-cool sister Jennifer (Reese Witherspoon), who thinks he's from the shallow end of the gene pool. Imagine her chagrin when the two of them are whisked into their TV set and onto the stage of Pleasantville's black-and-white universe. This, thanks to the manipulations of a mysterious TV repairman (a perfectly cast Don Knotts).

There they find themselves in the roles of Bud and Mary Sue, teen offspring of George and Betty Parker (William H Macy, Joan Allen), a married couple so upright and proper they make Jim and Margaret Anderson seem like the Manson family.

While Jennifer wants to play subversive, bent on modernizing her friends, David insists on maintaining Pleasantville's genial integrity — at first. But the kids' presence soon upsets the town's clockwork regularity. Ripples of change begin to course through the community. Suddenly, late one night, a red rose blooms — a lone splash of color in the B&W world, and a harbinger. Little by little, more hues emerge, as well as vague feelings of dissatisfaction, until Pleasantville undergoes a technicolor explosion, complete with burning bush.

Resistance to change and fear of "difference" turns dark as those townsfolk still in black and white begin to distrust and ostracize the "coloreds," blocking them from certain stores and banishing them to the balcony of the courtroom during the mayor's (J.T. Walsh) last-ditch effort to restore conformity.

David/Bud bows to the inevitable and, with the aid of his friend and fellow soda jerk Mr. Johnson (Jeff Daniels) — a painter who's just discovered the rainbow — foments an insurrection.

"Pleasantville" is packed with solid performances and clever — if not terribly subtle — touches. But the supposed parallels to "The Truman Show" are superficial. "Pleasantville" is a steady-state town doubling as a TV series.

Ross reminds us that knowledge, like new experience, is a disruptive force, upending dearly held beliefs and coloring one's view of the world. But one might have wished for a bit more bite in the film's "exposé" of a synthetic, Never-Never Land of '50s America that never truly existed. Yet the film doesn't so much pillory the myth as re-enforce it — not that we object to a little praise for civility.

The lines between sweet and cloying, pointed and pointless, touching and schmaltzy, are rather thin at times. Still, "Pleasantville" is a graceful, well-made move with equally graceful performances.

Allen and Maguire play mother and son for the second time, having been paired in Ang Lee's "The Ice Storm" last year. Although McGuire is the focus, Allen, Hollywood's most underrated actress, is its emotional center. Allen's Uber-Mom is all crinolines and blueberry pancakes until flesh tones appear on her cheeks and the wider possibilities of life become evident. She's wonderful.

Macy, already our reigning Everyman, lifts the bar a notch, while Daniels and Witherspoon play their parts to the hilt. Daniels' scenes with Allen are especially fine. And who could ask for a better emblem of simple, insular, small-town life than Barney Fife himself? He'll tie you in Knotts.

Add top-drawer supporting players and witty production design, and you have a film that's pleasant indeed.

....

As D-Day approaches...
Saving Private Ryan
July 26, 1998

Through the meat-grinder.

No more apt description could be devised for the horror of Omaha Beach.

For the first half-hour of "Saving Private Ryan," Steven Spielberg's monumental re-creation of D-Day and its aftermath, we are utterly immersed in the furious, deafening, blood-soaked, nauseating horror of combat.

Men shot in midstride drop like sacks of grain. Body parts are strewn in a sea of gore. Believable, even necessary, gore. The violence of this remarkable film is never gratuitous; it is appallingly realistic. The Omaha landing and its nightmarish slaughter are shot at ground level, very much in human scale, and in an almost documentary style.

This is no Technicolor extravaganza of World War II. There are no swooping crane shots that distance us from the hallucinatory chaos of battle, no cartoon carnage and Hollywood heroics, and a bare minimum of wisecracks.

If anything, the style of the picture suggests newsreel footage from the '40s. Its dominant color: a dusty brown, cut with red. It's "The Longest Day" with a tighter focus and an intensely personal story.

The brilliance of "Saving Private Ryan" is not simply the movie's brutal honesty or its attention to detail and refusal to glamorize. It is how it puts us inside the hearts and minds of the foot soldiers: average men who are wet, cold, tired, miserable and just want to go home.

"Every man I kill, the farther away from home I feel," intones the enigmatic Capt. John Miller (Tom Hanks), commander of a company of Army Rangers whose life back home is a source of consistent speculation by his men.

After the hell of Omaha Beach, on D-Day plus 3, Miller is ordered to lead a squad of men behind enemy lines to rescue Pvt. James Ryan (Matt Damon), a paratrooper whose three brothers have been killed in battle. Army Chief of Staff Gen. George Marshall (effectively played by Harve Presnell) has decided he will not inflict a fourth casualty on the Ryan family and orders him found and sent home.

The problem is, Ryan, among those holding a critical bridge, doesn't want to leave. And Miller's squad, already having lost two of their number in an attempt to locate Ryan, are deeply resentful of the mission. Why is one man's life worth more than all of theirs?

"Saving Private Ryan" is not an anti-war film in the strict sense of being a pacifist statement. It seeks only to present war as it really is, even World War II, the Good War. The noble qualities war extracts are given as much currency as the madness. And it is through this crucible of insanity that we grasp the nature of genuine heroism. As such, the film is much more in the vein of a "Das Boot" than an "Apocalypse Now" and serves as a useful corrective to the legion of movies glorifying war.

Spielberg again teams with cinematographer Janusz Kaminski ("Schindler's List," "Amistad") to compose a visual narrative that, for all its gruesomeness, is startlingly lyrical. The genius of it is how the camera sees as though through the eyes of a G.I. under fire. The battle sequences, especially the last, in which Miller's men fight alongside Ryan's, are unquestionably the finest ever committed to film and a triumph over daunting logistical challenges. But no less impressive are the quiet moments, especially the interchanges between Miller and his old comrade-in-arms, Sgt. Horvath (Tom Sizemore).

The cast is so uniformly superb it is difficult to single out an individual actor. And there is a reason the performances ring true.

Spielberg put his actors through a grueling six-day boot camp under the not-so-gentle tutelage of retired Marine Capt. Dale Dye, a veteran of Vietnam and Beirut whose three Purple Hearts testify to his knowledge of the pain of combat. All the actors, that is, except Damon, to fuel a little genuine resentment on the part of Hanks and Co.

Notably impatient with war movie fraudulence, Dye, who first worked as a consultant on Oliver Stone's "Platoon," combined with author Stephen E. Ambrose and screenwriter Robert Rodat to ensure battlefield realism and historical rigor.

The one constant in a foot soldier's life, says Dye, is deprivation. "Saving Private Ryan" underscores the fact, frame after frame.

To his eternal credit, Hanks vetoed a showy speech from the original script - one any actor might kill to have - for the purposes of sustaining the integrity of his character. It pays off handsomely. This, more than "Philadelphia" and "Forrest Gump," may prove the defining role of his career.

The film opens with an echo of a real-life event experienced by Spielberg, who, in Normandy in 1972 to promote the release of "Duel," visited the cemetery at Omaha Beach

Spielberg witnessed a veteran accompanied by his family, walking by the graves of those who perished. The man collapsed, sobbing inconsolably. Spielberg never forgot it.

Neither will we.

....

Enter the Land of Zs
"The Mask of Zorro"
July 18, 1998

Zounds!

With its flashing blades, daZZling acrobatics and siZZling romance, "The Mask of Zorro" is nothing less than Zensational.

En garde, and enter the land of Zs.

It's got Zest, it's got Zing, it's got Zoom. Not to mention Zip and Zap, Zig and Zag, and a touch of Zaniness. "Zorro" blows onto the screen like a Zephyr (that's the West Wind, compadres).

It's even got a few explosions for those who can't live without them.

Armed with the most splendidly choreographed swordplay and gymnastics since Richard Lester's "Musketeer" films of the '70s, director Martin Campbell has unsheathed a spirited new adventure of the fabled swashbuckler and righter of wrongs. In pure entertainment terms, it's in the Zone.

Two Antonios, Hopkins and Banderas, give us two Zorros. One lends gravity and class. The other, vigor and dash. It's a terrific combination, in a new telling very much in keeping with the old – which is to say, Old World romanticism joined to Old West themes.

Perhaps the most refreshing thing about the movie is, in terms of violence, its restraint. Like previous Zorros, the valiant swordsman doesn't romp about killing scores of villains. He's too adroit, too clever for that. Mainly, he disarms them, humiliates them, renders them impotent.

"The Mask of Zorro" manages to generate excitement without the gratuitous mayhem and bloodletting of most action films of the '90s. Campbell ("GoldenEye"), who replaced Robert Rodriguez at the helm before production got underway, blends the fencing and fisticuffs with equal measures of humor, passion and, yes, operatic virtues. All the emotions are writ large, and so are the performances.

One difference between the Zorros of past and present, aside from the fact that a Hispanic actor finally gets to play the lead, is that Banderas isn't in the role of Don Diego de la Vega – the original Zorro's alter ego (as embodied by Douglas Fairbanks Sr., Tyrone Power, Alain Delon, Guy Williams and George Hamilton).

Here, de la Vega is inhabited by Hopkins. It was he who was the thorn in the side of Spanish oppression in Alta California 20 years earlier. Caught in 1821 and imprisoned for two decades, the first Zorro has escaped, vowing vengeance on the man who killed his wife and stole his infant daughter, the nefarious governor Don Rafael Montero (Stuart Wilson).

Montero, who has raised de la Vega's child, Elena (Catherine Zeta-Jones), as his own, believes his nemesis long dead. Recapturing power after years in Spain, he has returned with a scheme to forge an independent California under the iron rule of the nobles. And he's quite Zealous about it.

Montero has not counted on Alejandro Murrieta (Banderas), a roguish bandito who de la Vega grooms as the new masked avenger. But Banderas' Zorro is not a caballero's son, as in previous incarnations. He's a ruffian and thief. Alejandro's relationship to Don Diego more resembles young King Arthur's to his mentor, Merlin. Together they try to foil the governor's plan to buy California from Mexican President Ge. Santa Anna – now at war with the United States and in dire need of dinero.

Will they win an ally in Elena? Will they Zero in on Montero and reduce his plot to Zilch? What do you think?

"The Mask of Zorro" is the first major Hollywood theatrical treatment of the hero in 40 years. But it's the same fandango: leaping off parapets, wooing the fair senorita (who also wields a mean rapier), laughing in the face of danger. Even Fairbanks would approve.

The League of Zorros Past has met to judge their Zuccessor.

The verdict: Ole!

....

Carrey takes hard bite of reality
"The Truman Show"
June 7, 1998

LIVE, from the world's largest sound stage ... seven days a week, 24 hours a day, it's "THE TRUMAN SHOW"!

And a really big show it is, a disturbing echo of a prefab America, wherein manufactured "reality" is more real than reality itself. Not unlike our own corporatized, lobotomized, strip-malled culture, you might say.

Peter Weir's provocative fantasy-within-a-fantasy is a "Twilight Zone" episode as imagined by Terry Gilliam - or George Orwell. It's paranoia on steroids, a coolly sinister nightmare vision that fascinates and repels like few movies before it.

Jim Carrey stars as Truman Burbank, an affable 30-year-old insurance salesman who dwells in the postcard-perfect Florida community of Seahaven Island, a hamlet populated by other cheerful, easy-going, "How ya doin'!" folk who are just pleased as punch to be where they are. Here, Burbank shares an idyllic if uneventful life with his Donna Reed-ish wife, Meryl (Laura Linney), a nurse.

But lately, curious and inexplicable things have been happening. Burbank is beginning to experience a vague sense of disquiet. And he can't shake the feeling that he's being watched.

It's no delusion. Our hero is being observed - and by hundreds of millions of rapt television viewers worldwide. For each hour of each day for all of his years in Seahaven - a place whose sun, moon, stars and ocean are merely elaborate constructs - Burbank has been the unsuspecting "star" of history's longest-running and most popular documentary-soap opera.

And he's never even left the confines of the "studio," a vast set ruled with Olympian omnipotence by one Cristof (Ed Harris), creator and puppet master of the show and a man convinced of his rightness. Seahaven is festooned with thousands of hidden cameras, including one on each of the townspeople. Not only his family and closest friends, but everyone Burbank chances to meet, are actors. Straight from the womb, Burbank has been raised to be a character in a show that brings a unique brand of entertainment, as well as comfort, to a devoted audience.

He is, in short, an institution. "It feels like the whole world revolves around me somehow," he confides at one point. Yet why, in all this time, has he never discovered the truth?

"We accept the reality with which we're presented," explains Cristof to a fawning interviewer. How true.

Better than anyone, Cristof also understands the show's enduring success: "We've become bored with actors giving us phony emotions." Although Burbank exists in a fabricated world, all his responses and reactions are compellingly real.

Adds Marlon (Noah Emmerich), Burbank's longtime "best friend," "Nothing you see is faked on the show; it's just controlled."

As are we. The genius of "The Truman Show" is not so much its dark, "Zone"-like satire as the way in which we're drawn into Burbank's reality. Watching the movie, you're almost as much a captive of Weir's orchestrations - and Andrew Niccol's nimble screenplay - as Burbank is a prisoner of Seahaven. When Burbank finally realizes what's going on, we feel the same sense of urgency to escape and follow our dreams.

For the first time, Carrey holds forth as a straight actor, minus the rubber-faced gyrations. Not that the performance is bereft of mugging, but these brief forays into the familiar have an eerie quality that render them more bizarre than comic. Overall, it's surprisingly solid work.

Comparisons with "Forrest Gump" probably are inevitable, for Carrey and the film itself, but "The Truman Show" takes media-age madness one better, with fewer contrivances. And its mood suggests the suffocating, steady-state delirium of Patrick McGoohan's old '60s TV series "The Prisoner" far more than some feel-good hokum.

Weir's direction is simultaneously understated and calculated for effect. It's the hand of an expert. The writing, if not wholly original, comes darned close. Of the performances, Harris, as usual, stands out.

If there's a weakness, it's three-fold: the blandness of Linney as Burbank's spouse, an unrequited love subplot (featuring a rebellious former cast member played by Natascha McElhone), and the uneasy sensation that the film's ending may be a bit of a cop-out.

Also, no film could live up to such overheated hype.

But these are quibbles. For an age shorn of privacy and good taste, "The Truman Show" is a welcome antidote. It tops the ratings.

....

Long Island showcase for engrossing comedy-drama
"Love and Death on Long Island"
April 16, 1998

For Giles De'Ath, a cloistered, erudite British writer sublimely ignorant of the modern world, the radio interviewer's question has taken him aback.

"Does the 20th century play any part in your life, Mr. De'Ath? For instance, do you use a word processor?"

(Quizzical look) "I am a writer. I write. I do not process words."

Nor, in his stodgily ordered existence, does he process much of life. But the hermetically sealed De'Ath (pronounced Dee-AH, despite its none-too-subtle reference) is about to get plugged in.

"Love and Death on Long Island," writer-director Richard Kwietniowski's engrossing adaptation of the Gilbert Adair cult novel, is an eccentric comedy-drama suffused with cleverness and wit. More than anything, it's a showcase for the finely honed talents of actor John Hurt.

Entering a movie theater for the first time in two decades, De'Ath (Hurt), expecting to see an E.M. Forster adaptation, mistakenly buys a ticket to a shlocky American teen picture called "Hotpants College II." Appalled, he is just about to leave when the young actor Ronnie Bostock (Jason Priestley) appears on screen. De'Ath, a middle-aged widower, is halted in his tracks, transfixed.

Intrigue becomes obsession, with this chance incident compelling De'Ath to scour gaudy fanzines, construct an elaborate photo album, and eventually embark on a quest to meet the object of his desire. His preoccupation, no matter how peculiar, has invigorated him, and soon he is jetting off from London to Long Island where Bostock supposedly lives.

De'Ath is sufficiently self-aware to realize that his reverie "has brought me into contact with everything I have never been." But he is hardly prepared for the Long Island "cafe culture" in which he finds himself immersed. Staying in a small motel, he tracks down the Bostock residence, yet is chagrined to discover a resident girlfriend, a model named Audrey (Fiona Loewi).

De'Ath turns cunning, ingratiating himself with the woman as a path to Bostock, who turns out to be a rather dim sort with a distaste for his celebrity and a hunger to do more "serious" work. De'Ath insinuates himself into their lives as the celebrated writer-who-would-be-mentor, flattering a self-involved Bostock for his minor abilities and convincing him of his potential.

It takes a while before Audrey, who likes De'Ath considerably, catches on to his masquerade.

With echoes of "Lolita" and "Death in Venice," the film is both a splendid example of how the absurd, the comic and the tragic can mesh. It is also a perfect vehicle for Hurt, his great lined road map of a face lending itself beautifully to the character's easy charm, genuine yearning, and blend of innocence and guile. No contemporary actor could have done a better job in this tailor-made role - gracefully written, as is the film itself, by Kwietniowski.

There is no overt sexuality involved in "Love and Death on Long Island," which at base is a valentine to the liberating power of pop culture. Indeed, the sexual is only implied until the final moments, which, in any case, are far more expressive of the purity of love than of the libido.

Priestley does a nice job of spoofing his own teen-rave persona, mainly through a series of snippets from Bostock's cheesy repertoire of movies, and Loewi is fine as the supposedly cynical beauty so easily melted by De'Ath.

There are also effective turns from the supporting players, among them Maury Chaykin and Sheila Hancock.

But if the movie belongs to Hurt, one has to be impressed with the polish shown by Kwietniowski, whose inaugural feature after a number of award-winning shorts heralds a thoughtful and provocative talent.

……………………

Film takes wing, falls to Earth
"City of Angels"
April 12, 1998

The celestial wings beat softly, seductively in "City of Angels," so much so that when Brad Silberling's nearly unique American film finally does crash to Earth, we still feel suspended aloft.

Silberling and screenwriter Dana Stevens have attempted one of the most difficult balancing acts in memory, grafting the textures, tone and visual motifs of a European art film to the sensibilities of an old-fashioned Hollywood melodrama. It is an uneasy marriage of poetry and prose held together by the performances of Meg Ryan and Nicolas Cage.

"City of Angels" is a loose adaptation of Wim Wenders' "Wings of Desire" (1988), a lyrical, fascinating meld of meditation and fairy tale involving a pair of angels who wander the streets of West Berlin observing the life around them and pondering what it would be like to be human.

Like "Wings of Desire," Silberling explores the nature of existence, the meaning of love, the relationship between the spiritual and the corporeal, though with considerably less depth than the movie that inspired him.

Cage stars as Seth, a sad-eyed angel of deep compassion and whispering voice who falls in love with a mortal woman, Maggie (Ryan), a cardiothoracic surgeon suffering a crisis of confidence after having lost a patient. Seth wants to help her, but he has no real physical being and cannot touch or be touched. The only way he or any of the other angels hovering about can be seen is by a demanding exercise of free will.

Seth also has become intrigued by the universe of sensation — the taste of a fruit, the feel of water flowing over the body, the sensory vistas of smell. This, and his passion for Maggie, compels him to make an irreversible journey to mortality. Pinocchio reborn.

Cage plays it in the most minimalist fashion possible, every gesture, reaction and a verbal exchange delivered with solemn understatement. The only chink in Seth's benevolence is our vivid recollection of Cage in his other roles as a maniacal killer. From time to time, even as he gazes longingly at Ryan, we half expect him to slice and dice.

Ryan, by contrast, has never been better, or more believable as a secular nonbeliever whose cool professionalism conceals a fragile heart.

The supporting roles handled by two of TV's best cops, Dennis Franz (re-creating Peter Falk's role from the Wenders' film) and Andre Braugher (as Seth's angelic colleague and confidante), are woven seamlessly into the fabric of the tale.

But how much you savor this romantic drama may hinge on your appreciation of, or tolerance for, the metaphysical: the belief in a heavenly corps of angels who look over us and look out for us, who are there to ease us as death draws near; the triumph of faith over the rational, the heart over the head. That, and how much calculated sentiment you can stomach amid the effusions of innocence. Some will consider the film's conceits to be a bit smug.

There's also an excess of banal dialogue. Steven's script doesn't always live up to

Silberling's ambition.

For two-thirds of its length, "City of Angels" is literate, measured, and utterly haunting. Reinforcing the narrative is the work of Oscar-winning cinematographer John Seale ("The English Patient"), who invests even the most mundane settings with an ethereal cast, achieving the small miracle of affording a pit such as L.A. a surreal, even idyllic beauty.

Then comes a disappointing nosedive into conventionality. Namely, the formulaic tear-jerker territory of the movie "Ghost." While Warner Brothers has begged reviewers not to reveal the film's ending, it hardly comes as a surprise. The climax is telegraphed long before the final fade.

Likewise a balancing act is Gabriel Yared's soundtrack, which inexplicably segues from captivating to schmaltzy.

Again, it is a measure of how successful the filmmakers are in the first two-thirds that the movie doesn't disintegrate altogether. We are left with a picture that is not as powerful as it might have been yet achieves a semblance of grace.

....

'The Borrowers' brings out the child hiding in us all
"The Borrowers"
February 12, 1998

Rare is the "family" film that captivates children without boring adults. Rarer still is one which makes grown-ups feel like children again.

Agnieszka Holland's 1993 remake of "The Secret Garden" and John Sayles' "The Secret of Roan Inish," released a year later, are the two most recent examples of charming, meaningful, beautifully told tales whose appeal crosses all age and ethnic lines. It's no coincidence that they were drawn from superior books by gifted authors. The same holds for "The Borrowers," a thoroughly delightful remake of the 1973 made-for-TV movie based on the enduring Mary Norton novels.

Directed by Peter Hewitt ("Tom and Huck") from a screenplay by Gavin Scott and John Kamps, the picture also represents the latest offering from Working Title Films, which in its brief existence has produced such quality fare as "Four Weddings and a Funeral," "Fargo" and "Dead Man Walking."

Borrowers, for the uninitiated, are tiny, inches-tall people who co-exist discreetly (and undetected) with us big folks. In fact, they live right under our noses in the cracks and crannies, crawlways and cubbyholes of your average home.

Have you ever misplaced a thimble? A spool of thread? Postage stamps? A set of screws? Were you ever baffled by the mysterious disappearance of other common everyday objects? Chances are they were "borrowed" by these resourceful and utilitarian little families, daunted only by the danger of being squished underfoot.

Teenager Arietty Clock (Flora Newbigin), her kid brother Peagreen (Tom Felton) and their parents Pod (Jim Broadbent) and Homily (Celia Imrie) are a happy, peaceable clan of Borrowers who dwell under the floorboards of a venerable old house owned by Joe and Victoria Lender (Aden Gillet, Doon MacKichan). That is, until Arietty is discovered "prospecting" in the room of the Lenders' son, Pete (Bradley Pierce), who has long suspected a foreign agency in the vanishing of household goods.

Fortunately, Pete is kindly disposed, and keeps their secret to himself. But their newfound friendship is threatened by the designs of diabolical banker Ocious P. Potter (John Goodman), who is plotting to destroy a will which grants title of the home to the Lenders. Potter intends to evict the residents and demolish the house to clear the way for a garish development.

But this villainous lout, however formidable, doesn't know with whom he is dealing. Madcap missions and heroic deeds soon win the day, through not without setbacks and suspense.

Like most contemporary film fantasies, "The Borrowers" is loaded to the rafters with special effects. But, like the Disney films of old, they are so unobtrusively integrated and done with such endearing cleverness and panache that they further the story rather than distracting from it.

Hewitt does a wonderful job of pulling all the elements together, seldom tipping his hand and almost always emphasizing wit over slapstick. There's inventiveness everywhere you turn, some of it clearly inspired by the "Wallace and Grommit" films, some an echo of the successful "Borrowers" BBC television series (likewise done by Working Title).

The cast, which also includes Mark Williams as the comical Exterminator Jeff, Hugh Laurie ("Jeeves and Wooster") as a mild—mannered policeman and Raymond Packer a the Peter Pan-ish "street" Borrower named Spiller, couldn't be better. Broadbent and Imrie are a joy as the Borrower mom and pop, and Goodman camps it up deliciously.

Stealing the show, however, are Newbigin and Pierce. Especially the former, as a plucky young girl chomping at the bit to explore the larger world.

Go with her.

....

Sea of bathos drowns acting in 'Acres'
"A Thousand Acres"
September 21, 1997

In the Everything-But-the-Kitchen-Sink school of melodrama, nothing bleeds like excess.

Witness Jocelyn Moorhouses's "A Thousand Acres." Is there anything missing? We've got alcoholism, breast cancer, child sexual abuse, brutalization, mental illness, infidelity, betrayal, scandal sibling schisms, courtroom histrionics, ostracism, fearless womanizing, the demise of the nuclear family and the death of small-time agriculture.

Just your average couple of days on an Iowa farm.

At least no one shoots the dog.

Adapted from the Pulitzer Prize-winning novel by Jane Smiley, "A Thousand Acres" may be seen as a contemporary take on "King Lear." The Bard was no stranger to melodrama, either. But Moorhouse, working in her usual plodding, "naturalistic" style, again proves that more is less.

Remember the director's "How to Make an American Quilt," that uneasy mix of female bonding and mystical realism? "A Thousand Acres" offers the same first-rate ensemble acting — and the same emotional overkill.

As in the Shakespearean tragedy, the tale unfolds with a family patriarch (Jason Robards Jr.) announcing that he intends to divide his lands among his children, in this case a large and flourishing farm.

Also as in "Lear," the seemingly wise and even-handed father errs by shutting out his most devoted daughter (Caroline, played by an uncharacteristically subdued Jennifer Jason Leigh).

In Smiley's novel and in Moorhouses's film, the father is not merely arbitrary and tyrannical, but a drunk prone to rages, a monster who routinely had sex with his own daughters in their teens.

Now grown, only Rose (Michelle Pfeiffer) seethes with the memory, while elder sister Ginny (Jessica Lange) has buried the knowledge so deeply that, when confronted by Rose, she adamantly rejects the truth of it. At first. Both farm wives, for years they have waited hand and foot on their dad — a man beloved in his community. But matters soon come to a head after his announcement.

Such frankness about child sexual abuse never would have seen the light of day a decade ago. And it is one of the movie's strengths that the subject — and its implicit feminist statement — is handled with relative sobriety. That, and the outstanding performances of the four principals, especially Lange.

Other themes prove less successful, and the movie ultimately disintegrates into familiar soap opera trappings. Where Smiley's book was a mediation, Moorhouse's film is a sudsy wail.

And as expected, the male characters hardly figure in at all, certainly not with anything like the complexity contained in the novel. Save for Robards' poisonous father, none is afforded any real dimension, and only Keith Carradine, as Ginny's decent but boring husband, is not a worthless bum.

The excellent British actor Colin Firth is simply wasted.

You expect, and want, the women to be the film's centerpiece, but "A Thousand Acres" dilutes the power of its message by pouring on the bathos, one-sidedly at that.

Much of the blame falls on the screenplay by Laura Jones, whose last outing, "The Portrait of a Lady," also drowned the intricacies of a great novel in a sea of soap.

....

'Contact' gives out mixed signals
"Contact"
July 10, 1997

"Contact" is a film of great strengths and jarring weaknesses.

While director Robert Zemeckis' adaptation of the novel by Carl Sagan communicates the late astronomer's hopeful outlook, the thoughtful and deeply humane philosophy that defined his life, it is a film so over furnished with ideas — most of them superficially presented - that dramatic cohesion is all but impossible.

Jodie Foster brings characteristic conviction to the role of Ellie Arroway, a scientist with SETI (the Search for Extraterrestrial Intelligence) who is the first human to receive a message from alien beings across the gulfs of space and time. More, she becomes humanity's first emissary to the stars.

Passionate to the point of obsession, Arroway may be singlemindedly devoted to her work, but her motivations are complex. To some extent, she looks outward as a way of avoiding looking in.

Orphaned at age 9, Arroway always has reached out, seeking voices other than her own, from ever more distant sources. As a child she glued herself to her beloved father's shortwave radio. As an adult, she fights for computer time at the Very Large Array of linked radio telescopes in the New Mexico desert, scanning the heavens for signs of civilization. Like her colleagues, Arroway is dismissed by many scientists as a pie-in-the-sky dreamer intent on squandering a promising career.

Until that day a transmission is received from the star Vega. Deciphered, it contains an apparently benign greeting — and the blueprints for a vehicle to carry a single traveler back to the source. This astounding scientific find promises to be a transforming moment in our history. At astronomical cost, of course.

Vindication is hers. But now David Drumlin (Tom Skerritt), the very project manager who belittled her research, wants to be the first in line to take the trip. Now national science advisor to the President, he already has claimed the lion's share of credit for the discovery, and he's just unscrupulous enough to usurp the voyage, too.

Arroway becomes a lightning rod for controversy. In her corner, however, is an eccentric billionaire (does Hollywood know any other kind?) named S.R. Hadden (John Hurt), an engineer turned industrial magnate with enough clout to win Arroway a ticket to ride.

Complicating matters is the reappearance of Palmer Joss (Matthew McConaughey), a respected religious scholar and Presidential confidante who also happens to inhabit a romantic page from Arroway's past. Their mutual attraction is renewed as the construction of the vehicle moves forward, but Joss objects - not without rationale - to her as Earth's envoy. He believes the agnostic Arroway's scientific detachment, without benefit of spiritual grounding, is inadequate to represent all mankind.

Inadvertently, Joss supplies Drumlin with the God card to play. But privately, his objections to Arroway's sojourn are as much personal as religious: There's no guarantee she'll ever come back.

After a spellbinding opening sequence - a swift transit of the solar system that ends in the mind's eye of a child - "Contact" establishes the basis of Arroway's fervor, then takes us on a tour of the giant radio telescope at Arecibo in the Puerto Rican rain forest.

Shifting to New Mexico, the story takes flight. The scenes at the Very Large Array, as Arroway and her breathless co-workers intercept, verify and try to translate the mathematical transmission, are absolutely riveting - the frenzy of contact after years of empty static.

This, combined with the almost palpable tension of those moments just before launch - and Arroway's kaleidoscopic odyssey to Vega - are the high points of a picture that frankly tries to do too much.

What the movie does well it does exceptionally well. The same goes for what it does badly.

Sets, music and the marriage of models and miniature shots with digital computer work are all superb. So is the Steadycam work.

"Contact" also gets fine performances from Foster, Skerritt, William Fichtner and the inimitable Hurt. It gets disappointingly one-dimensional support from Angela Bassett, James Woods and David Morse (as Arroway's father), who are forced to play sketchwork characters.

But theme, not character, is paramount in "Contact."

What mattered most to Sagan was the pursuit of truth, not merely what makes us feel better. He never tried to reconcile science with faith, as this film does, knowing that the tension between them might forever defy accommodation.

Although his elevation of science to an almost celestial plane made him occasionally seem like, yes, an apostle, this gifted popularizer of intricate concepts never spent too much time examining the mythology surrounding science, or the hubris that can pervert its most valuable advances. Sagan's "faith" in the uniquely self-correcting nature of the discipline was too profound.

One doesn't expect dissertations on the complexities of science in a popular entertainment. And the earnest but rather simplistic musings on science and religion in "Contact" seem largely those of screenwriter James V. Hart. His script further polarizes the argument, unnecessarily making it an either/or proposition.

In any case, it's highly unlikely that Sagan would have peppered his novel with so much illogic or so many tiresome cliches: conspiracies in high places, mad bomber cultists, lame-brained military and government types, et al.

The silliest convention is the climax itself. Though lovely and ethereal, not to mention "heart-warming," it makes no sense whatever. Why, if a superior race has deemed us ready for direct contact, do they transport a human envoy on a vast intergalactic journey yet refuse to reveal themselves? Then erase all evidence that the meeting ever happened? How many "Star Trek" episodes ended precisely the same way, with aliens thinking us too intellectually and emotionally fragile to behold their true form, much less their reality. This gambit is as old as the hills. And it's a cheat.

It is known that Sagan and Zemeckis often disagreed on the direction of the picture, with the latter opting for dramatic effect. And, for all his skills as a storyteller, Zemeckis is just too slick, too Hollywood. He also clutters his film with irrelevancies.

We get utterly superfluous characters such as supposed love interest Joss - while the affection and chemistry between Arroway and longtime colleague Kent Clark (Fichtner) is infinitely more believable. We get amusing but arrant jokes (Rob Lowe as a leader of the Christian Coalition). We get passing mention of the critical tug-of-war between pure and applied science, between discovery and commerce, delivered with all the subtlety of a laser blast.

But the most fundamental mistake made by "Contact" - Sagan would have been appalled - is equating science with a search for meaning in the philosophical or theological sense of the word. Science is not strictly about meaning; it is about discovery, about understanding. These goals are not necessarily synonymous.

Sagan believed that divining the nature of the universe was the greatest of adventures, and that the possibility of communication with other beings might be the ultimate achievement. Just as fascinating - if not more - was what the experience might teach us about ourselves. How would humanity's self-perception be altered? Never did he suggest that true vision was the union of fact and faith.

Zemeckis affords us a flawed version of the vision that was Sagan's.

Warner Brothers' timing is, as they say at Mission Control, optimal. The movie lifts off just as the Pathfinder probe begins its own close encounter with Mars, seeking signs that life once existed - and still might - on the Red Planet.

Life certainly exists in "Contact," but it's terribly confused.

....

Nicholson plays a perfect louse
"Blood and Wine"
April 13, 1997

When he's not laying on heavy helpings of ham, Jack Nicholson is an unmatched interpreter of the corrupt but sympathetic louse.

Nicholson assays a refreshingly complex part within the fairly conventional film noir "Blood and Wine," the eighth collaboration between the actor and longtime friend Bob Rafelson. And it's good performances, not the prefab script from Nick Villiers and Allison Cross, that make this companion piece to "Five Easy Pieces" and "The King of Marvin Gardens" more than an absorbing crime drama.

Like its predecessors in Nicholson's and Rafelson's informal trilogy, the darkly cynical "Blood and Wine" is as much about dysfunctional families and the seamy side of the American Dream as it is about a failed jewel heist.

Nicholson plays Alex Gates, an outwardly prosperous wine dealer who hawks his wares to the South Florida elite. The reality is that Gates has blown his dough on extravagant living and an assortment of mistresses. Not only his own money, but that of his boozy, embittered wife Suzanne (Judy Davis).

Add a hostile stepson, Jason (Stephen Dorff), to this uneasy family unit, and it's not surprising that Gates is looking for an out. His plan: to pilfer a million-dollar necklace from a client's home and escape with his expatriate Cuban girlfriend, Gabriella (Jennifer Lopez), who just happens to be an employee of the estate.

But Gabriella has no inkling of his scheme. Gates' real accomplice is Victor (Michael Caine), a veteran safecracker dying a slow, racking death from emphysema - even as he puffs compulsively away.

The necklace, finally in hand, is their ticket to Easy Street, until, of course, matters go terribly awry.

Following a bloody confrontation with his wife, which leaves Gates unconscious, he awakens to find that his wife, son - and necklace - have fled. Only mother and child don't know they have it, at first.

Gates and Victor track them to Key Largo. Yet while Gates' attention is consumed by the jewels, Jason's is drawn to Gabriella, unaware of her liaison with his stepfather. For her part, Gabriella is torn between the promise of the good life with Gates and an honest relationship with his stepson.

Curiously, the most riveting sequence involves a car chase. Or, more properly, a car crash. Pursuing their quarry down a desolate backcountry road at night, Gates and the increasingly agitated Victor force Suzanne and Jason into a violent tailspin. In a scene both disturbing and gruesomely funny, Gates' larcenous heart overcomes what residue of affection he feels for his wife as he sweetly coaxes the dying woman to give him the necklace, weeping all the while.

Jason survives, eludes his stepdad and returns home, lying in wait to exact vengeance. He also has the jewels, setting up a climax that satisfies despite its overly familiar elements.

Star power carries the old fashioned "Blood and Wine" over the top. Nicholson, in particular, hits all the right notes in a caustic, nuanced portrayal of man whose moral bankruptcy is not wholly complete. And a disheveled Caine is equally adroit in animating what is to all intents and purposes a caricature of the British thug.

Davis, though on screen only briefly, gives the brittle Suzanne an unexpected reserve of resiliency and strength. So compelling an actress is Davis at her best that one wishes she was in every scene. Dorff, in scruffy contrast to his drag queen in "I Shot Andy Warhol," more than holds his own, especially mano-y-mano with the menacing Nicholson and Caine. Lopez' characterization pinballs from sultry cliche to that of an honest immigrant who wants only to fashion a better life and rescue more of her family from Cuba. It's not her fault that the filmmakers seem more attuned to her curvaceous form than her obvious talent.

Rafelson's direction is focused and taut, showing a sure hand with genre materials. Here, his work with Nicholson is a far cry from their last film together, the abysmal "Man Trouble." In "Blood and Wine," they seem like an old married couple who are so familiar with each other that they not only finish the other's sentences, but the other's thoughts as well.

....

'Suburbia' needs urban renewal
"Suburbia"
April 10, 1997

The monotone coma of modern American suburbia, with its soulless, cookie-cutter houses, neatly manicured lawns, strip malls and disaffected youth is prime turf for a probing cinematic examination.

"Suburbia" isn't it.

Although not without its strengths - mainly, character development - the latest film from director Richard Linklater ("Slackers," "Dazed and Confused") is simply too inert to offer much in the way of social comment and too plodding to sustain interest. That is, unless your idea of entertainment is to stand on a street corner by a convenience store for hours on end listening to a bunch of whiny slackers.

The whole movie can be summed up in a single line uttered by the convenience store operator, a Pakistani engineering student (Ajay Naidu) dismayed by his unwelcome loiterers' aimlessness: "You are all so stupid. You stand here and you throw it all (opportunity) away."

To get to this unremarkable epiphany, we have to slug through two tedious hours of self-absorbed twentysomethings bemoaning their lot - and doing nothing about it.

One expects a great deal more bite from a script by Eric Bogosian ("Talk Radio"), who adapted his own play - and his own memories - for the screen.

The flashpoint of "Suburbia," if you can call it that, comes when a successful rock singer named Pony (Jayce Bartok) returns to his suburban hometown of Burnsfield, N.J., with publicist (Parker Posey) in tow, following a major national tour. All he wants is to reconnect and shoot the breeze with his old buddies.

Among them are Jeff (Giovanni Ribisi), Sooze (Amie Carey), Buff (Steve Zahn), Bee-Bee (Dina Spybey) and Tim (Nicky Katt), who, as an Air Force dropout, is the oldest one of the group.

Pony inadvertently lights a slow-burning fuse that ignites in violence.

Trying to find a sympathetic character is not easy although Jeff, with his occasional fits of conscience and decency, comes closest. Listen attentively, and you realize that Jeff (with whom Linklater and Bogosian strongly identify) is more complex a person than his mates. Yet he is just as trapped in his ennui.

"Anything is possible, as long as you don't care about the result," he says with a sigh. Fitting for a film that is one long sigh of alienation.

"Suburbia" is about one generation's dream - the (illusionary) safety and idyllic lifestyle of suburbia - and the reality as experienced by their children - a cultural vacuum that offers no place to go and nothing to do.

It is also about frightened people struggling to cross the bridge from youth to adulthood without getting detoured onto a dead end street. Doubtless, Linklater and Bogosian have the patter, the tone and the angst just right. But somehow it just doesn't come off. "Suburbia" may be the best movie argument yet for not having kids.

....

Campion's `Portrait of a Lady` is disappointing
"Portrait of a Lady"
January 19, 1997

Jane Campion's eccentric rendering of "The Portrait of a Lady" is a sumptuous, visually breathtaking interpretation. Odd that it is so uninvolving.

Are these people or chess pieces pushed about with veiled purpose by a director too wrapped up in being stylistically inventive to really bother with character?

Apart from a rich performance by Barbara Hershey, the principal roles are so numbingly underplayed that Martin Donovan's frail, tubercular Ralph Touchett seems positively volcanic by contrast.

Unlike many more worshipful filmmakers, Campion, a risk-taker, does not adapt Henry James' 1881 novel as if it were a sacred duty. She is as challenging and provocative in her filmic vocabulary as she was in "The Piano." And her frank treatment of female sexuality is about as far removed from James' prose as could be imagined

Yet technique aside, this lushly furnished film leaves much to be desired. Ultimately, it seems little more than a Jamesian version of "Smart Women, Foolish Choices."

As far as the characters are concerned, rigor mortis sets in rather quickly. Isabel Archer (Nicole Kidman) is a young American abroad, a woman of independent mind who intends to live life on her own terms, regardless of what European society deems proper.

Rejecting a marriage proposal from the courtly Lord Warburton (Richard E. Grant), she tells her admiring cousin, Ralph, that she may never marry. Archer also has a confidante in Mme. Serena Merle (Hershey), something of a role model in her apparent autonomy.

But sinister forces are afoot. Merle is in league with the calculating Gilbert Osmond (John Malkovich), a "sterile dilettante" (in Ralph's estimation) who dazzles Archer with his refinement but has decidedly unrefined aims on her newly inherited fortune.

How easily the proto-feminist Archer turns to putty, relinquishing her ambitions to live in Rome as Osmond's hermetically sealed wife, suffocating in her gilded cage. The trap closes, the marriage is loveless and Archer appears doomed - enslaved to her husband's manipulations.

Her lone rebellion is to try to subvert Osmond's plan to marry his young daughter (Valentina Cervi) to a nobleman she does not love.

Kidman weeps well, but her performance here is unconvincing, a far cry from her work in such pictures as "Dead Calm" and "To Die For," which used her contemporary look and style to the full. As Archer, she lacks the spark of life, seeming more a mannequin than a person.

But where Kidman is a mild disappointment, Malkovich almost sinks the movie. Obscuring his talent behind a bored demeanor and an excess of mannerisms, Malkovich insists on playing the same part he's played in most of his recent pictures: the detached, faintly effete aristocrat with a taste for mind games.

Donovan's character, however, is full-blooded and entirely sympathetic, a recognizable human figure who carries his generous nature and sense of humor even to his death bed. Hershey has never been better, giving the film its most complex portrayal in a supporting role that feels more like a lead.

Although Campion's approach is too austere, the photography of Stuart Dryburgh ("The Piano") is exquisitely composed, a painterly feast of light and shadow. Likely, it will duel with "The English Patient" for a cinematography Oscar.

But "The Portrait of a Lady" fails in its primary task: to convey its subject's inner life in a way that sustains our interest.

....

'Kabloonak' a triumph served on ice
"Kabloonak"
November 3, 1996

The most creative filmmakers of the 1920s either devised new strategies for their art or injected their own personal vision into existing ones.

Robert Flaherty did both. Generally acknowledged as father of the documentary form, Flaherty had been taking his camera to the wintry desolation of Hudson Bay since 1913.

Here, he enjoyed the freedom of the solitary artist, keeping his own counsel and molding his material according to his own perceptions.

The result was "Nanook of the North" (1922), a cinematic milestone - and an international sensation - which focused on the daily life of an Eskimo hunter

Armed with primitive photographic equipment, and beset by fearful hardships, Flaherty spent the year 1920 sharing the life of Nanook (Kabloonak, in Inuit) and his family, taking a passionate interest in filming unscripted, everyday scenes.

Nanook, a humorous, uninhibited and big-hearted fellow, was only too happy to oblige, even at the risk of his life.

He neither posed nor acted, but went about his business as Flaherty recorded it and wrote commentary.

Seventy-five years later, director Claude Massot and cinematographers Jacques Loiseleux and Francois Protat set out to recapture these events.

And they have succeeded beyond anything they might have hoped in the spellbinding "Kabloonak," the story of the making of "Nanook."

Massot, who died not long after completing his film, has fictionalized some characters and occurrences. But this in no way detracts from the achievement.

"Kabloonak" is at once an intimate tale of a bond between two men, a sweeping, exquisitely photographed epic, and, like Flaherty's original, a remarkable document of a nearly vanished culture.

A joint Canadian-French-Russian production which, due to internal squabbling, sadly may never reach a broader audience, the picture is utterly absorbing from start to finish.

The bleak, often featureless landscape of the high Arctic is itself a character. Keenly aware of nature's power, Massot conveys a chilled-to-the-bone feeling for these white vastnesses without ever losing touch with the human scale.

He does so, in part, by subjecting cast and crew to conditions almost as brutal as those under which Flaherty worked.

"Kabloonak" benefits hugely from its naturalistic performances, chiefly those of erstwhile film villain Charles Dance ("China Moon," "Alien 3"), an underrated actor whose Flaherty at last affords him a sympathetic role, and the marvelous Adamie Quasiak as Nanook.

Expertly staged, Massot's is many films in one, not least a joyous celebration of motion pictures. Its humor derives from familiar sources – the contrasts between disparate civilizations – yet is so offhandedly presented as to seem of fresh coinage. In style, tone and execution, it is quite nearly perfect.

It would be a grievous loss for "Kabloonak" to be consigned to politically inspired oblivion.

For here is a capstone to a superb director's career, and a picture in which any filmmaker would take pride.

....

'Basquiat' paints N.Y. artist in gray
"Basquiat"
September 19, 1996

More than anything, "Basquiat" is a monument to the utter self-absorption of artists, to their absolute confidence in the truth of the world view they present.

The singleness of purpose that makes many a painter transcend the ordinary often diminishes them as people. It's as if obsession excises an integral piece of their humanity, leading artists to exploit and discard those who love them. It's the Picasso syndrome — creator and destroyer.

Of course, this is irrelevant to art history, not to mention something of a cliché. The work, ultimately, is what matters, not how wretchedly or with what indifference one possessed of genius treated others.

To his credit, artist and first-time filmmaker Julian Schnabel does not gloss over the less admirable characteristics of his subject, the late, lamented Jean Michel Basquiat, who rose to prominence in the 1980s during the heady days of Manhattan's downtown art scene only to die of a heroin overdose in 1988.

Unfortunately, Schnabel leaves a lot to be desired as a writer-director. Too many scenes are hollow or completely lacking in energy, an astonishing shortcoming given the vibrancy of the artist whose brief but incandescent career traced the trajectory of a shooting star. When not flaccid, sequences are propped up with pretense or are downright amateurish.

Worse, the film is needlessly cryptic, undercutting a strong performance by Jeffrey Wright in the title role. Though the young Tony Award-winning actor occasionally plays things a bit too wraith-like, so gaseous you expect him to drift away at any moment, for the most part he imbues Basquiat with an innocence and gentleness of spirit that has much appeal.

But what forces drove Basquiat, who went from a street artist emblazoning his universe with graffiti to a celebrated member of Andy Warhol's coterie and international sensation? How did a middle-class kid wind up sleeping in a cardboard box in a park? What did he think? What did he feel? What, pray tell, was he trying to say? Schnable never bothers to ask these fundamental questions, and it's not like he replaces them with anything substantial.

That is, unless one considers the film's "revelation" of the sham that pervaded the gallery swirl of the '80s to be news.

It's never quite clear if Schnable is satirizing the art business — that rarefied realm wherein back-stabbing is the modus operandi, where unscrupulous dealers see artists merely as product to be bought and sold — or if he simply can't decipher the ironies inherent in his own movie.

And let us not overlook the clumsiness of the director's chief visual metaphor — injected again and again — that of a giant wave on whose crest rides a daredevil surfer.

Could it be that Basquiat, like so many artists, glides triumphantly but precariously on the edge of oblivion, and that life is about to spill him from the heights and crush him to a pulp? Heavens, what subtlety.

There are some fine supporting performances tucked away on this rather slippery canvas, chiefly from Michael Wincott as Rene Richard, Gary Oldman as Albert Milo, Claire Forlani as Basquiat's lover Gina Cardinal and Benicia Del Toro as his old friend Benny Dalmau.

As Warhol, the usually reliable David Bowie is a caricature of a caricature, and Dennis Hopper, who pays the art dealer Bruno Bischofberger, has summoned one of the most absurd teutonic accents in memory to complement a lifeless presence. The various cameos by Willem Dafoe, Christopher Walken, Paul Bartel, Tatum O'Neal and Courtney Love are just pointless.

To the degree "Basquiat" succeeds, it is due to the talents of Wright. He alone is reason to watch the film, which, given a spectrum of colors with which to explore, settles for gray.

....

British hit arrives on these shores
"Trainspotting"
August 22, 1996

"Trainspotting" is tough stuff, but is it tough enough?

Unsparing, to a point, and injected with a rush of stylistic invention, this headlong dive into grunge delirium arrives in the U.S. courtesy of the team of director Danny Boyle, screenwriter John Hodge and producer Andrew Macdonald, whose first film together was "Shallow Grave."

The subject is heroin addiction. But "Trainspotting" also is a window onto the bleakness of life for one segment of the Scottish underclass in post-Thatcher Britain - the youth for whom there is no work, no future and nothing to live for but the next high. Or so they have convinced themselves.

Based on the novel by Irvine Welsh and shot as a series of sketches, the film opens with Renton (Ewan McGregor), an unemployed slacker and the movie's narrator, making a pact with his Edinburgh mates to kick the habit and take a stab at living clean.

Easier said than done, especially for the likes of Spud (Ewen Bremner), who gives fecklessness new meaning; the blissfully amoral Sick Boy (Jonny Lee Miller); and Begbie (Robert Carlyle), whose misogyny is exceeded only by a barely suppressed psychotic rage. Nice chaps.

But the straight life, with no passageway to paradise, is hard time to pull. And it's all too human to despise that to which you believe you cannot aspire: middle class normalcy.

"Trainspotting" (a colloquialism for killing time) follows the quartet as they get on and off the heroin merry-go-round. Whether they're clean or blitzed, an aura of doom hovers above them like a grumbling thunderhead; it's only a matter of time before their flirtation with death becomes a love affair.

Meanwhile, several peripheral characters beat them to death's altar.

The film does not glamorize heroin, as some claim. Nor does it condemn the drug or its use, as others insist it should. To its credit, "Trainspotting" presents its own generation of Dead End Kids spiraling into the abyss and lets the audience make up its own mind on the issues of degradation, morality and failed social engineering.

What does strike a false chord, especially for a movie which prides itself on honesty, is the superimposition of youthful anti-materialism – generally the province of the comfortable middle class – on the rants of working class kids. It's rather ironic that a movie whose characters rail at conspicuous consumption should have spawned a bonanza of ads for athletic shoes and T-shirts.

Also, while "Trainspotting" spends a lot of time wallowing in the muck, the scenes depicting the horror of Renton's withdrawal seem curiously sanitized. Then there are the obligatory drug culture cliches the filmmakers can't resist invoking. They do little to strengthen the story.

Still, there are many things "Trainspotting" does well.

Exuberantly dark, it stretches the definition of black comedy well past the breaking point. Indeed, it's difficult to think of it as comedy at all. What is does do is forcefully communicate the seductive power of drugs, which instantaneously deliver on the promise of nirvana or oblivion, while obscuring the price you pay.

These kids may have acquired the drug habit merely to alleviate the pointlessness of their lives – the sheer boredom of aimless knocking about slaked by smack, booze and anesthetized sex. But they've become as hooked on the purity of the experience – the freedom from striving – as they are on the chemical. For them, having a "sincere and truthful" junk dependency bespeaks a kind of needle-borne integrity.

When you're off heroin, Renton confides, "you have to worry about bills, about food, about some football team that never … wins, about human relationships and all the things that really don't matter when you've got the habit."

A visual complement to the characters' state of mind, Brian Tufano's camera plunges the viewer into a gritty, sometimes grotesque world that frequently tips over into the surreal. Employing lots of quick cutting, at times "Trainspotting" comes across as an extended (if perverse) music video, fueled by a soundtrack of contemporary British bands and pre-Punk godlings like Iggy Pop and Lou Reed). There are also sly little references to the Beatles' "Abbey Road" and the film "A Hard Day's Night."

A phenomenon in Great Britain, where it has engendered furious debate - adored by the hip, reviled by anti-drug crusaders - the film may or may not take off in the States. Much will depend on whether American moviegoers can decipher an almost incomprehensible string of Scottish slang - delivered with a heavy burr - and stomach some of the more nauseating bits of a picture that's determinedly offensive.

Many will "Just Say No." But that would be a mistake. "Trainspotting," though not without flaws, reveals one terrible consequence of people immobilized as much by despair as by poverty.

....

John Sayles' 'Lone Star' is honest, riveting film
"Lone Star"
August 1, 1996

Orson Welles' baroque "Touch of Evil" still reigns as the ultimate sleaze movie, a brilliantly filmed "B" picture that said all there was to say about border towns, corrupt cops and pliant city bosses.

Until now.

In "Lone Star," peerless writer-director John Sayles has produced a more clean-cut – if not streamlined – version for the '90s, and peopled it with some of the most understated but effective characters in any American film this year.

Sayles is the standard by which intelligent independent cinema is measured. His ensemble films generally concern everyday people dealing with outsized problems, but are so remarkably varied in style, tone and setting that they seem to derive from radically different filmmakers.

Their one common denominator: quality.

Combining richness of visual detail, narrative complexity and a strong but even-handed social awareness, "Lone Star" takes what could be desultory material and gives it 10-gallon depth.

The fulcrum of the story is Sam Deeds (Chris Cooper), the divorced, rather reluctant sheriff of the fictional Texas border town of Frontera. A decent but melancholy man, he's the son of the near-legendary Sheriff Buddy Deeds (Matthew McConaughey), who years ago rid the town of his homicidal predecessor, Charley Wade (Kris Kristofferson).

When Sam learns of a skeleton that has been unearthed nearby at an old Army firing range, he suspects the remains are none other than those of Wade, who mysteriously disappeared 40 years earlier. Did Sam's late father run Wade out of town, or did he use a more permanent deterrent?

The issue is complicated by Sam's ambivalence toward his father. He seems all too ready to assume Buddy's guilt, his suspicions fanned by the selective memories of the mayor (Clifton James) and a black saloon keeper (Roy Canada) as well as the town's too-worshipful recollections of his dad.

The monstrous Wade (chillingly played by Kristofferson) is shown in a series of flashbacks - demanding kickbacks, brutalizing minorities, gunning down people with a blithely cavalier malice. No one in modern Frontera mourns him in the least. Nor do they wish to see Buddy's name dragged through the muck.

But Sam is dogged, and layer by layer the truth begins to emerge, though not without a few twists and turns. Scraping away at the Texas topsoil, Sam discovers more about the past than people want revealed, and not all of it has to do with Charley Wade.

Sayles tells his tale slowly and painstakingly. The drowsy pace is calculated in the best sense, for it enables Sayles to introduce and develop a number of arresting characters with the feel of real, three-dimensional people. It's another Sayles trademark, one which distinguishes him from almost every other filmmaker currently at work.

Aside from Cooper, who is both solid and a bit stolid, and McConaughey, whose screen presence suggests the young Paul Newman, the film is loaded with high-caliber performances. Elizabeth Pena is superb as the young teacher and widow Pilar Cruz, the great love of Sam's teenage years who now deals with teenagers of her own. Miriam Colon, majestic in late middle age, portrays Pilar's mother, Mercedes, a restaurant owner whose calcified pride and disdain for her heritage mask a perverse self-loathing. She, too, has buried a few secrets from the past.

A second father-son schism forms a parallel storyline. Delmore Payne (Joe Morton) is a stiff-backed Army colonel assigned to oversee the dismantling of a base on the outskirts of town. His estranged father, Otis, the aforementioned bar owner, left his wife and infant son in the lurch years before. Not surprisingly, Delmore regards him with contempt. He uses rigid military discipline to deflect emotional involvement not only with Otis, but with his own family. This shield begins to crumple, however, when Delmore's son forms an attachment with his grandfather.

As the film evolves, these plot elements coalesce in surprising ways. Some strain credulity a mite, and at least one scene involving Sam's hyper ex-wife (a manic-depressive Frances McDormand) is as superfluous as it is out of place. Otherwise, whether Sayles is exploring the hidden chambers of the human heart or a compost of Anglo fears and Mexican-American frustrations, his shrewd, potent dialogue invariably rings true.

The deceptively straightforward cinematography by Stuart Dryburgh ("The Piano") is a major contributor to Sayles' storytelling, as is the musical propellant of vintage blues, Latin and rock `n' roll standards.

"Lone Star" is an anomaly for summer consumption. It's not about computer tricks and bombast. There is no special effects budget, no gargantuan hype, no Disney-esque deconstruction of literary classics.

What it is, is honest, riveting filmmaking. Like the work of the Coen brothers, "Lone Star" takes an oblique look at genre conventions and invests them with startling originality.

....

Surprises and delights await in 'Fargo'
"Fargo"
March 21, 1996

You expect the unexpected in a movie by the Coen brothers, as eccentric and original a team of filmmakers as exists.

Rarely are you disappointed.

Forget formulas. Forget beat-them-over-the-head cues for the audience. The work of writer-director Joel and producer/co-writer Ethan eludes categorization. No two films are comparable, save for their utter unpredictability and the inspired quality of small, telling details.

The Coens defy fashion even as they access the fashionable, taking genre conventions and re-imagining them in the most off-kilter ways. Their films brim with irony and an infectious sense of humor that ranges from gentle to macabre.

"Fargo" is arguably their most perfectly realized film, a worthy successor to "Barton Fink" and "Miller's Crossing" and light years better than their striking but failed 1994 experiment, "The Hudsucker Proxy."

Based on actual events, "Fargo" tells the tale of a hapless suburban car dealer (William Macy) who, hungry for the main chance, plots to have his wife abducted and split the ransom with her kidnappers. Of course, the scheme goes horribly awry, with corpses piling up like kindling.

The filmmakers utilize a traditional true crime framework to introduce a menagerie of characters in the most unconventional manner, then let their story go sledding off into the surreal.

Calling "Fargo" a black comedy or a farcical film noir is to oversimplify. Rather, it's a dark film sewn together with slyly, sometimes outlandish,- comedic threads. Not to mention some quite realistic violence.

Much of the film's abundant humor comes from turning a keen ear to the world it depicts: the broad Scandinavian accents, matter-of-fact patter, small-town provincialism and, above all, the cheery, chirpy wholesomeness of its protagonist, Brainerd police Chief Marge Gunderson (Frances McDormand). In fact, everyone is so bright-eyed wholesome in this burg (You're darned tootin'!) that even the B-girls seem fresh-scrubbed and rosy.

Only the Bunyanesque statue of a lumberjack, a somewhat demonic-looking sentinel at the gates of the town, suggests the evil that lurks nearby.

McDormand, Joel Coen's real-life spouse, is ideally cast as the chief, seven months pregnant and clucked over by her mother hen of a husband, Norm (John Carroll Lynch). She is a deceptively shrewd investigator whose technique is at least as disarming as Colombo's, and considerably funnier. She is drawn into the case by fate, when a deputy discovers three bodies – including a state trooper's – on the outskirts of town.

Macy, who plays his part to the hilt, is the supreme set-up: a mild-mannered, faintly corrupt everyman (complete with bowling trophies) who is intimidated by his father-in-law (Harve Presnell), bullied by irate customers, and desperate to escape his own fecklessness.

He doesn't stand a chance against Gunderson, who gradually tightens the noose. Nor do his accomplices: the constantly put-upon Carl (Steve Buscemi) and the quietly homicidal Gaear (Peter Stormare). Buscemi, making his fourth picture with the Coens, is as hilarious as ever.

Presnell, it should be noted, is making his first film appearance in 25 years. His gruff, domineering Wade Gustafson is a far cry from the bounding youth he played in early '60s musicals, and totally believable.

The Coens always convey a remarkable sense of place. But here they know the territory intimately. Joel and Ethan grew up in the Minneapolis suburb of St. Louis Park in the '50s and '60s and are well acquainted with the vastnesses of the neighboring Dakotas. The landscape of "Fargo" is so uniformly, featurelessly white it's like living inside a cotton ball, albeit one festooned with telephone poles. And it provides an admirably empty canvas for the filmmakers' trademark visual invention, replete with intriguing camera angles and fresh perspectives. The Hitchcock influence is readily apparent, but here, too, the Coens impart a different spin to it.

One could think of "Fargo" as a hybrid of Carl Franklin's "One False Move" and Martin Scorsese's "After Hours," but to do so misses the point. The best way to appreciate the Coens is on their own, exceedingly playful, terms.

....

'Georgia' takes sisters through the wringer
"Georgia"
February 25, 1996

There's something eternally seductive about a free spirit, even, or perhaps mainly, a self-destructive one.

It's easy to admire their unfettered, full-out dynamism - the badge of mavericks and loose cannons everywhere, a ravenous caprice that turns life on edge and cares not a whit for the consequences.

Including, too often, the consequences borne by others.

There's a vicarious charge in living through such a person; most of us are far too timid or sensible to really throw caution to the wind. Yet sometimes there's a core of desperation behind that blithe exterior.

In Ulu Grosbard's "Georgia" we meet a troubled elf well down the road to oblivion. Sadie Flood is well-named, for emotions pour out of her in a torrent, inundating everyone in their path. Not least her sister, Georgia, a beloved folk-rock singer and songwriter who plays to packed houses but prefers to retreat into her own

The contrast between Sadie (Jennifer Jason Leigh) and her sister, Georgia, (Mare Winningham) could not be more vivid. Sadie is reckless, passionate, wildly ambitious to become a star, but lacks talent. She's a boozed-up, raccoon-faced punker stumbling through a marginalized career on the fringe of the Seattle grunge scene, doing gigs in low-rent bars, bowling alleys and the like. When she can stay on her feet, that is.

Though remarkably gifted, Georgia is an earth-mother, serene, responsible, and unimpressed by the trappings of fame. She lives with her husband and children in the same old farmhouse where she and Sadie grew up.

Each to her own. Which would be fine, if only Georgia wasn't constantly bailing her kid sister out of jams.

The scenes between them are riveting. Yet the depth at which screenwriter Barbara Turner, Leigh's mother, explores the relationship of these siblings only occasionally probes far beneath the skin. We're shown a range of jealousy, generosity, resentment, affection, pettiness and loyalty. But as soon as we pause to examine them more closely, the filmmakers spirit us back to the dives.

Leigh, whose character is loosely based on her real-life sister, Carrie, all but ignites in one of the most flamboyant, and effective, performances of the past year. She walks away with the picture and certainly seemed deserving of the Academy Award nomination that everyone assumed was a lock (but wasn't).

While Sadie dominates, the film actually is about the yin-yang of Sadie's sister-worship. About Georgia, in other words (the movie's title is no accident).

If Winningham had been nominated for best original song, we wouldn't have a quibble. She performs her own compositions and has a lovely voice, a mix of Mary Chapin Carpenter and Shawn Colvin by way of Emmy Lou Harris. But while Winningham conveys Georgia's prim, bottled-up nature with admirable subtlety, the performance is unnecessarily bland. In some ways Winningham's is a more complex character to play. And something's missing.

Leigh's voice, by contrast, is an excruciating screech with which we're endlessly subjected. We get the message of the futility and self-delusion of her dream from the very first number. Why does Grosbard feel it necessary to torture us throughout?

You respect Leigh's talent and fearlessness but wonder if she is in danger of being typed in such "edgy" roles, just as her father (the equally edgy Vic Morrow) was typed as a tough-guy. Excess impresses over the short term, but ultimately limits one's career.

The movie succeeds best in capturing the down-on-their-heels milieu of aging small-time rockers, which it does with great authenticity. There are excellent supporting performances from John C. Reilly as a drummer wasted on heroin, Max Perlich as Sadie's sweet but childlike husband and from real-life rocker John Doe, founder of the punk band X.

"Georgia" puts you through the wringer. And you may love every minute of it. On the other hand, you may also feel a lot like Georgia herself, drained by Sadie's insatiable needs.

....

Film perfectly balanced study of good and evil
"Dead Man Walking"
February 4, 1996

Ambivalence. You don't find much of it in a Hollywood movie. Especially one styled as a "message" picture.

Which is one reason Tim Robbins' "Dead Man Walking" is so remarkable. About the last people in filmdom from which one would expect balance or circumspection are Robbins and his wife/star Susan Sarandon, whose fervent espousal of liberal causes is well known.

Yet here is a movie of great distinction, at once a quietly impassioned plea for the abolition of capital punishment, and a moving consideration of the anguish visited on the families of victims and perpetrators alike.

Adapted by Robbins from the memoir by Sister Helen Prejean, "Dead Man Walking" is the true story of the relationship forged between an unrepentant death row inmate (Sean Penn, in an outstanding performance) and a nun (Sarandon) who overcomes her own fear and revulsion to become his spiritual adviser.

Sister Helen works with children in the projects of a small Louisiana town. She has never so much as set foot in a prison when she agrees to correspond with Matthew Poncelet (Penn), a man convicted of a particularly heinous rape-murder. When she first visits him in the penitentiary, the meeting of innocence and evil is almost palpable.

She must contend not only with her own confusion regarding this monster of a man and his dwindling chances for redemption, but with the rigidity of a conservative prison priest, the doubts expressed by her own family ("A full heart should not follow an empty head," her mother counsels), and the acrimony that pours forth from the parents whose children Poncelet killed.

Prejean is stricken by the unimaginable grief of the families, who chastise her for comforting the killer and ignoring their plight. The more deeply she is drawn into the various families' suffering, the more conflicted she becomes. In the end, however, she is resolute in her faith.

"Dead Man Walking" reveals the primal hate that underlies so many of society's simplistic arguments, exposes the hollowness of get-tough rhetoric, and offers a convincing indictment of the reality of "justice for those who can afford it." More, it also eliminates the comforting distance between us and the horror of execution. The viewer cannot stay at an antiseptic remove from the act, however justified; that which is acceptable in the abstract becomes less palatable in the flesh.

These are difficult themes that defy easy answers on either side of the issue, and Robbins' grim but superb screenplay assures that the film is no mere political tract. "Dead Man Walking" so easily could have slipped into stridency and become a polemic. It does not. And it is a measure of Robbins' maturity as writer-director that he has moved from the facile preachiness of "Bob Roberts" to such sober and thoughtful work.

Its balance is achieved not simply by virtue of seeing both sides, but by letting them exert their own weight, without manipulation. Carefully modulated performances by Sarandon, Robert Prosky and Raymond Barry complement Penn's beautifully.

And the questions remain unresolved: Does society have a right to vengeance? Is it the only thing left to us when the "cancer" is inoperable? The movie allows you to make up your own mind, while showing the human face of the malign. Poncelet is a vile but pathetic creature. Yet "Dead Man Walking" demonstrates that even one such as he, at death's door, may achieve a state of grace.

....

'Sense and Sensibility' is a triumph all around
"Sense and Sensibility"
January 18, 1996

Ever since David Lean, Ismail Merchant and James Ivory renewed Hollywood's faith in the marketability of literary classics, we've enjoyed a decade-long boom of the sort of films the BBC regularly delivers to British TV — even if the locals do tend to dismiss them as "Laura Ashley" pictures.

Such derision is misplaced, of course, in time and otherwise, for what strength of emotion, depth of intelligence, and delicacy of gesture we have gleaned from the cinema the past 10 years has derived largely from these movies.

Even in the most august of company, "Sense and Sensibility" is an outstanding contribution, lifted above the requisite Masterpiece Theatre trappings of gilded parlors and verbal indirectness by means of deft characterization, good humor, and a remarkable range of feeling.

Actress Emma Thompson wrote the screenplay – very much a labor of love – and stars in this lively adaptation of Jane Austen's first published (1811) novel. It is directed, impeccably, by Taiwanese director Ang Lee ("Eat, Drink, Man, Woman"), who had never heard of Austen before reading Thompson's script.

"Sense and Sensibility" tells the tale of the Dashwood sisters, the restrained, rational Elinor (Thompson), and the ardent, impetuous Marianne (Kate Winslet), and the suddenly diminished circumstances of their family – banished from their estate in Sussex to the modest confines of a cottage in Devonshire.

Hugh Grant and Greg Wise play their suitors, Edward Ferrars and John Willoughby, respectively. Alan Rickman, always a wonderful villain, here shifts sides as a romantic wild card, the looming Col. Brandon.

The theme: heart vs. head, passion vs. reason - a familiar Austen concern.

Austen's world is, as one wag put it, "all sly nuance and silk-garbed malice" culminating in the harmony of good marriages for people we care about and lousy ones for those we don't. It's a universe fashioned of melodrama, of course, and all rather absurd. But beguiling nonetheless. And you needn't be female to appreciate it.

Austen's humor can be gentle or merciless, conveyed as much by rhythm as the meaning of the words. Her characters display spirit and real intelligence as well as artifice, and the actors who embody them show a keen instinct for the comic possibilities woven through the writing.

The movie has been in development for four years, beginning when its producers saw several TV skits written by Thompson in period dialogue. Consider it time well spent. Great care is revealed in terms of casting, overall production design (Luciana Arrighi), costuming (Jenny Beavan and John Bright), and, above all, in Thompson's witty, meticulously crafted script.

Michael Coulter's photography is lush and magical, from the painterly composition of its interiors to its depiction of the incomparable English countryside as a realm so verdant as to seem almost surreal.

Thompson's performance is the film's binding agent, and it is an admirable one indeed, layered and complex. Winslet positively gleams, her youthful exuberance controlled and channeled by the director into what promises to be a breakthrough role.

Yet it is Rickman who all but steals the movie and provides it with a certain irony: the distinction of a man being the most poignant figure in an archetypal "women's" story.

Rickman is an old hand at scene-theft, but his very lack of flamboyance in this instance makes all the difference.

Grant is his usual bubbling, diffidently charming self. While suitably ingratiating, his character grows insubstantial alongside Rickman's Brandon and Wise's dashing but flawed Willoughby.

Fine supporting performances are sprinkled throughout, none better than those by Elizabeth Spriggs and Gemma Jones. Also enjoyable are Hugh Laurie (of TV's "Jeeves"), and Imogen Stubbs, star of A&E's "Anna Lee."

"Sense and Sensibility" is a triumph all around, one of the very best films of this or any other year.

....

Matthau's 'Grass Harp' sings exquisite song
"The Grass Harp"
November 5, 1995

Listen to the wind blowing through the grasses. Open your heart to it. One day it will whisper the story of your life.

Charles Matthau must have lent an ear for some time, for he has brought Truman Capote's semi-autobiographical novel "The Grass Harp" to the screen with exquisite sensitivity.

This tender, beautifully rendered adaptation of Capote's Depression-era work tells the story of young Collin Fenwick (Edward Furlong), who, following the death of his mother, is sent to a small Southern town to live with his two aunts.

Verena (Sissy Spacek) is a shrewd, rather pinched businesswoman for whom "nothing matters so much as the owning of things - and people." She is the most powerful (and forbidding) figure in her community. Sister Dolly (Piper Laurie), by contrast, is a whimsical hot-house flower who seldom has been permitted to bloom. They are attended by Catherine (Nell Carter), a cantankerous but loving family cook.

Dolly and Catherine spend most of their time in the kitchen, removed from Verena's withering gaze and dictatorial judgments. Collin soon finds it the most comforting place to be. And the most instructive.

When Verena seeks to absorb the one thing that is Dolly's - the secret to a homemade herbal medicine - the trio determine to escape to a old treehouse. Cozily ensconced, and blithely oblivious to the shock of the townspeople, Dolly, Catherine, and Collin are visited by a variety of eccentric folk: a free-wheeling evangelist (Mary Steenburgen) who thinks she's Mother Hubbard, a chatty barber (Roddy McDowell), Collin's footloose pal Riley (John Patrick Flanery), and, above all, a singularly wise retired judge (Walter Matthau) who wants Dolly to be his wife.

Naturally, the humbugs want to bring them to their senses. Enter a cunning reverend (Charles Durning), a reluctant sheriff (Joe Don Baker), and, of course, the formidable Verena.

"The Grass Harp" is a simple story, but with such resonances. In part, it is about how propriety, meant to regulate and civilize life, too often stifles it. It is a love story whose sentimentality is leavened by humor. It is about maturity and our capacity for change. It is also a parable of how life and love may link us all, if we let it.

The script by Stirling Silliphant and Kirk Ellis hews closely to the original tale, though the focus, despite Collin's narration, is shifted largely to Dolly.

The cast is sublime. And what an inspired move to team Laurie and Spacek, who played mother and daughter almost two decades ago in "Carrie." They are wonderful. Laurie, who has turned in one jewel after another since her "comeback" in "Children of a Lesser God," has all the fodder necessary to steal the picture, and does. Though she and Matthau, as Judge Charlie Cool, at times skirt the precipice of excess, they never fall over the edge. And the scenes between them are as expert as they are touching.

"The Grass Harp" is a model of professional filmmaking and acting, respectful of its source material yet canny enough to have something of its own to say. You simply cannot ask for more.

....

'The Usual Suspects' offers chills of unusual caliber
"The Usual Suspects"
September 3, 1995

Round up "The Usual Suspects" and make them your own. It may not be the beginning of a beautiful friendship - these guys stick out their neck for nobody - but we guarantee you'll be riveted.

Director Bryan Singer has engineered an absolutely Byzantine crime thriller: an intricate coil of wheels within wheels that brilliantly spins characters and multiple plot elements while keeping us guessing throughout.

Told largely in flashback, "Suspects" in at least one respect is an homage to Akira Kurosawa's "Rashomon," in that each of its principals has a piece of the puzzle, none of which quite fits.

Chazz Palminteri stars as David Kujan, a U.S. Customs operative who's interrogating one of only two survivors of a drug deal gone awry. Or has it? Millions in cocaine supposedly have gone up in smoke aboard a merchant ship in San Mateo, Calif. And 27 men, victims of a drug war, lie dead on the dock or in the water. ("Here's looking at you, squid.").

But Kujan smells a rat. However persuasive it may sound, he refuses to believe the version of events delivered by a crippled con artist named Kint (Kevin Spacey). Kint is one of five crack New York criminals who had been involved in the deal, men who threw in together after meeting, in of all places, a police line-up.

One, Keaton (Gabriel Byrne), a former cop who did five years in stir, presumably had been trying to go straight as a legitimate restaurateur, a line his long-time nemesis Kujan believes not at all. In fact, Kujan is convinced that the body identified as Keaton belongs to someone else.

Determined to extract the truth, he takes Kint back six weeks in time, to the origin of the men's partnership. Here we meet the remainder of the quintet - McManus (Stephen Baldwin), Hockney (Kevin Pollak) and Fenster (Benicio Del Toro), a wily lot of rogues unaccustomed to being pawns in another's game.

But Kujan is running out of time. Somebody, somewhere, is pulling strings. Kint is insulated by immunity from prosecution, and refuses to turn state's evidence. He is to be released that day. Impasse.

Lurking in the background is a shadowy and perhaps mythical Turk who may or may not be the puppetmaster. His name, Keyser Soze, is spoken in whispered tones, even by otherwise fearless men who don't believe he exists.

For his part, Kint is terrified.

And we're intrigued.

"The Usual Suspects" benefits hugely from a taut, ingenious script from Christopher McQuarrie, who earlier collaborated with director Singer on the latter's debut film, "Public Access," which captured the Grand Jury Prize at the 1993 Sundance Film Festival.

Spacey, who narrates, steals the picture with a performance as impressive as it is creepy. Remember this one at Oscar time. Byrne, in his best noir-ish fashion, also shines, as do Palminteri, Pollak and Del Toro. The weak link among the main characters is Baldwin, proving once again that four acting Baldwins are three too many.

Gifted Pete Postlethwaite, extraordinary in "In the Name of the Father," here looks 20 years younger, and sounds about as British as Yassir Arafat. His supporting role as Sose's alleged middleman has a gravity and sense of calm menace that only a gifted character actor such as he could provide.

The one real disappointment is the superfluous part given Suzy Amis, one of our finest actresses. She shouldn't have bothered.

But that's a small price to pay for this caliber of film, the best of its kind in years.

....

Film bridges the mediocrity gap
"The Bridges of Madison County"
June 1, 1995

Robert James Waller should thank his lucky stars. Not just the chance arrangement of the heavens that turned his saccharine novel into a publishing phenomenon, but the fortuitous alignment of filmmakers who have fashioned a perceptive, wholly adult love story from the same meager material.

"The Bridges of Madison County" has been made into a picture of great sensitivity, with compelling performances from Meryl Streep and director/co-star Clint Eastwood. Under Eastwood's stewardship, it is also a thoughtful, resonant tale whose emotions are earned.

The film, which opens Friday, need not depend on charitable readers to make it a success. Notwithstanding a glacially slow opening, screenwriter Richard LaGravenese ("The Fisher King," "A Little Princess") has pulled off a commendable feat. He jettisons the worst of Waller's cloyingly sentimental dialogue and "last cowboy" pretensions and turns this simple, unadorned story into a meditation on the nature of love.

At the movie's core are disarmingly rich characterizations by the leads. Eastwood plays Robert Kincaid, a National Geographic photographer who comes to Madison County, Iowa, on assignment in 1965. Seeking directions to the area's picturesque covered bridges, he stops at the farmhouse of Francesca Johnson (Streep), a homemaker whose husband and two children are away at the State Fair.

Haltingly, but with swift assurance of its inevitability, the two begin a four-day affair that will mark them the rest of their lives.

LaGravenese uses the at-first questionable narrative device of telling the story in retrospect, through confessional letters and journals bequeathed by Johnson to her grown children, and by moving back and forth in time. Though shocked to learn of their mother's infidelity, not to mention her unexpected passion, they - and we - soon become absorbed. In the end, LaGravenese's ploy is a convincing one.

Eastwood also takes risks, especially with younger audience members, by infusing his movie with an uncommon stillness. The dramatic silences and naturalistic, pastoral quality of the photography (by Jack Green) are such that the fragility of each moment is keenly felt, as is the sense of bittersweet impermanence. Francesca and Robert cram more fire into four days than many people do in a lifetime. And you believe every minute of it, largely because Eastwood directs with restraint.

LaGravenese also tones down Waller's pulpy sex scenes and affords them genuine eroticism, while lending a sharp edge to the characters' eventual conflict (in a telling breakfast argument) and adding a defining subplot of another adulteress in a nearby town.

As director, Eastwood likewise provides compassionate consideration of lives in isolation and the pangs of unrealized dreams. There is an almost palpable yearning in "Bridges" that speaks volumes about human needs and the repercussions of choices we make.

As actor, Eastwood displays more vulnerability and tenderness than at any time in his career.

Streep's Francesca is everything one expects of the actress at her best: a subtle, nuanced interpretation which avoids the overly studied mannerisms that have occasionally marred her work.

In a remarkable turnabout from her muscular adventuress of "The River Wild," Streep plays the flowering of a frumpy *housefrau* with touching conviction. "Bridges" has ready-made audience

Published three years ago, "The Bridges of Madison County" is one of six books to have remained on bestseller lists right up to their debuts as motion pictures.

The others: Tom Clancy's "Clear and Present Danger" and "The Hunt for Red October," John Grisham's "The Firm," Michael Crichton's "Jurassic Park," and (you guessed it) Erich Segal's "Love Story."

"Bridges" has spent 146 weeks on the New York Times bestseller list, with no sign of faltering.

....

Writer-director's talent no 'Secret'
"The Secret of Roan Inish"
May 4, 1995

In evaluating the work of John Sayles, one quickly exhausts the usual run of superlatives. First, there is admiration for his unique standing among independent filmmakers. There is his integrity and sense of purpose. And there is the consistent excellence of his films.

Few writer-directors own Sayles' ability to make silk-purse pictures out of sow's-ear funding. Fewer still have the uncompromising vision to bring such meaningful material to the screen.

In "The Secret of Roan Inish," a magical mystery tour replete with mythical sea creatures and a captivating young heroine, Styles has rendered a poetic tale of family ties and the power of wishing that is as warming as a cup o'tea when the north wind blows.

The movie is based on "The Secret of Ron More Skerry," a 1957 novella by Rosalie K. Fry which summoned the legend of the Selkie's, supernatural Celtic beings who are half-human and half-seal. The book explores the fate of an infant boy swept out to sea and that of a young girl, enthralled by her grandparents' stories of the event, who leads her kin back to their abandoned home.

Nevermind that Sayles, half-Irish himself, has moved the setting from Scotland to the Emerald Isle. He infuses the language of film with universal metaphors that cast their spell just beneath the level of awareness.

"Roan Inish" ("Seal Island" in Gaelic) is in many respects a return to Old Disney sensibilities, albeit leavened with Styles' trademark "naturalism." It is a children's movie that adults will love. Or perhaps it's the other way around.

Sayles needed a carefully chosen ensemble to work his charms, and he has precisely that. "Roan Inish" introduces winsome 10-year-old Jeni Courtney, a sort of miniature Julie Delpy whose unaffected, matter-of-fact portrayal is as perfect as it had to be.

Courtney has remarkable presence as Fiona, but it would be of little avail without the richly detailed performances of Mick Lally ("Circle of Friends") and Eileen Colgan ("Hear My Song") as her grandparents, and Richard Sheridan and John Lynch as the older cousins she turns to for help.

Whether it's wildflowers dancing in a gentle breeze, seals undulating in a velvet sea, or fog spilling over the lonely land like a dense blue foam, the images conveyed by peerless cinematographer Haskell Wexler are a joy to behold.

The visual complement to Sayles own version of "magical realism," married to a bewitching score, recalls much of the best to have emerged of late from Central and South American literature. It is the resonance of fable which guides people back to their roots, like a divining rod draws us to water. Sayles wants his audience to consider what happens to people when they, like the infant boy, are sent adrift, forced to leave a place and a point of reference that are part of the fiber of their lives, and how they remain tied to a world other than the one to which they have been exiled.

It is a deceptively weighty theme, all together worthy of the filmmakers' talents. And it makes for a lyrical little dream of a movie. Sit back and be beguiled.

....

'Circle of Friends' another winner from Ireland
"Circle of Friends"
April 2, 1995

The Irish, it seems, are either genetically or constitutionally incapable of making a bad film. Based on what has touched our shores of late - and, admittedly, we may get only the best - there's been a steady flotilla of praiseworthy products crossing the Big Pond from old Eire.

Pat O'Connor's "Circle of Friends" is the latest to moor here. Like 1993's "The Playboys," it is a graceful, beguiling little vessel laden with rich characterization, flawless direction and some of the most captivating depictions of the Emerald Isle ever committed to film

Adapting Maeve Binchy's coming-of-age novel for the screen, O'Connor and Emmy Award-winning screenwriter Andrew Davies ("Middlemarch") have fashioned a witty, frequently poignant romance in which comedy and drama are joined as expertly as planks in a hull.

Set in 1957, "Circle of Friends" explores the friendship among three young women at a Dublin college, and the love affair that develops between one of them, a "plain Jane" named Bernadette (Minnie Driver), and handsome upperclassman Jack Foley (Chris O'Donnell), a medical student and star athlete.

Foley could have just about any girl he wants. But he is drawn to Bernadette (a k a, "Benny"), a first-year student who, though something less than conventionally pretty, has an honesty and warmth he finds irresistible.

The feeling is mutual, though at first Benny finds it hard to believe a fellow like Jack would be interested in her. What of Nan (Saffron Burrows), her beautiful, polished friend, or Eve (Geraldine O'Rawe), the trio's rock-steady keel?

Foley convinces her of his sincerity, but there are complications. Benny's parents hope she will marry the oily Sean (Alan Cumming), a sinister sort back home who has insinuated himself into her father's business. Benny abhors the man, and suspects he may be the cause of the haberdashery's troubles.

It turns out that Nan is after older, more prosperous game. Like her chums, she longs to snap the bonds of her small-town upbringing. Each has a strategy for dealing with parental expectations, if not with her hormones. But while Benny and Eve navigate a cautious course, Nan naively uses sex to escape the suffocation of home, learning she is not quite so sophisticated as everyone believed.

Author Binchy's tale is universal on many levels, not least in framing the painful lessons all of us learn regarding trust, betrayal and the necessity of forgiveness. Director O'Connor and the "Circle of Friends" also turn a critical eye on the conflicts between Ireland's people and its institutions; specifically, the Catholic Church. But its subversive undercurrent is subtle, never gratuitous.

The cast is simply wonderful. Driver, making her maiden voyage in a theatrical picture, gives an uncommonly touching performance that will steal your heart. Burrows takes what could have been a two-dimensional character and gives her unexpected shadings. And Cumming is outstanding as the malignant Sean.

For his part, O'Donnell (an American actor) seems altogether at home in the Irish countryside. O'Rawe and Aidan Gillen, who plays Eve's boyfriend, are perfectly matched. And Colin Firth turns in his usual fine job as Simon Westward, the socially prominent catch Nan pursues.

Why do Irish films stand out? One might as well ask how a great ship plows the sea. For all its intricate trappings, a craft under sail is human-scaled. The same may be said of Irish movies. The characters are real people with definable features, not broad parodies or caricatures. There is less reliance on technology and spectacle than on story.

Notwithstanding "Heavenly Creatures," which has yet to dock in Charleston theaters, "Circle of Friends" is an early entry in the running for the year's best picture.

Thus far, it's certainly the most enchanting.

Film is barely sew-sew
"Ready to Wear"
December 25, 1994

Apparently operating under the assumption that something not worth doing is not worth doing well, Robert Altman has delivered in "Ready to Wear" a stillborn travesty of a satire, as threadbare as it is artless.

Altman is defeated before he starts. How does one satirize a world, in this case the fashion industry, that long ago beat you to the punch? How do you needle a class of people who have the pattern on self-satire all sewn up? Worse, how can the esteemed writer-director have spent so many months immersed in the European high fashion swirl and comprehended so little of what went on right before his eyes?

One gets little sense of either what fashion represents — a form of applied commercial art that is increasingly distanced from the consumer and dependent on the media — or the nature of the corporate artists that are the avatars of design: one-man or one-woman conglomerates lodged in an airless world of parasites and toadies.

On top of that, Altman doesn't even communicate the fact that frivolity, dash and circus atmosphere of fashion shows can, in a fleeting sort of way, be fun.

Of *course* fashion is inflated with self-importance and driven by money. It goes without saying that many of those absorbed by it all are shallow and glib. But this is news only to Altman. Most people have known it forever. No wonder the fashion mavens embraced him so eagerly: The man's scalpel has no edge. It's hard to slice and dice things you don't understand in the first place.

At first, you think the movie's tone — pregnant with pretension, the essence of bad Italian cinema of the early '60s — is all together intentional. All too soon you see that it is not.

Altman is the only director in recent memory who manages to make Paris look drab. His characters, who should be flamboyant, for the most part are just as colorless. Apart from Richard E. Grant, the prince of mince as a kind of male Vivian Westwood, and Sally Kellerman, who turns in a zestful performance as a scheming fashion magazine editor, the characters of "Ready to Wear" are nothing more than stick-figured manikins, pouffed into life for instants as transient as the garments with which they adorn themselves.

Kim Basinger, who seems to materialize in just about every scene, is cut from the same cloth. Someone needs to tell the actress she doesn't have to *try* to be bad. Her fawning, drawling "fashion journalist" makes Elsa Klensch seem like Leslie Stahl.

We have to admit, however, that it was a wonderful touch having Sophia Loren and Marcello Mastroianni re-enact their famous striptease scene from "Yesterday, Today and Tomorrow," but this 30-year-old inside joke likely will be lost on most film goers.

At least Altman gets the high-camp, low-content of argot fashion-speak right, complete with all the repetitive, vacuous doggerel that masquerades as commentary.

Speaking of canines, what's with the sophomoric running gag involving dog feces? And does Altman really believe that his climactic emperor's-new-clothes routine hasn't been exploited countless times before? This is what you call out of touch.

The only people in this movie with the right idea are the reporters played by Julia Roberts and Tim Robbins, who, forced into sharing a room, spend the entirety of the film's 130 minutes and their hotel making love.

There is some pleasure to be had in seeing the superb actress Anouk Aimee after so many years, as well as old pros Lauren Bacall, Jean-Pierre Cassell and Jean Rochefort among the usual Altman throng. And no doubt fashion-watchers will be in stitches over the appearance of a gaggle of designers (Jean-Paul Gaultier, Sonia Rykiel, Christian LaCroix, et al) and supermodels (Naomi Campbell, Christy Turlington) who play themselves.

But what little energy is present in "Ready to Wear" derives from runway footage taken from actual shows. Altman's static sequences just can't compete.

Pretending to be satire, "Ready to Wear" is in fact a hymn to gaudiness for its own sake. Altman had the material, only to watch it come apart at the seams.

....

Beautiful 'Nell' overcomes flaws
"Nell"
December 22, 1994

Directed with remarkable sensitivity by Michael Apted, and featuring a mesmerizing performance by Jodie Foster, "Nell" is a motion picture that in many of its particulars is head and shoulders above the rest.

Yet this contemporary illumination on paradise lost and (to some extent) regained is nearly undone by an antiseptic patness that ignores the exacting and often messy business of bridging disparate worlds.

Drawn from the play "Idioglossia" by Mark Handley, "Nell" dramatizes the story of a 29-year-old recluse who has spent her entire life in a remote backwards cabin in the smoky mountains.

When her mother dies, the last layer of insulation protecting Nell is soon peeled away. Fate intervenes in the form of a rural physician Jerome Lovell (Liam Neeson). Profoundly impressed by the native nobility and apparent self-sufficiency of this "wild child," Lovell wants to shield her. Subconsciously, she also represents an unthreatening means by which he can escape his own imposed solitude.

But Lovell errs by making Nell's existence known to a battery of psychologists determined to introduce her to the modern world, albeit it from behind institutional walls. Among them is Paula Olson (Natasha Richardson), who has erected barriers of her own, but will move inexorably through an unexpected rite of passage.

While Lovell erects a tent in the shadow of Nell's cabin, trying to allay her fears and decipher her language, Olson anchors and elaborately equipped houseboat nearby to conduct a surveillance on Nell's activities.

Nell, Olsen soon learns, is not the blank slate she first believed her to be. From here, matters proceed in predictable but involving fashion.

What prevents "Nell" from achieving real distinction is its Hollywoodized script, a weak and largely unconvincing adaptation from the pen of William Nicholson ("Shadowlands").

Too many elements of the story simply are impossible to swallow. Most unrealistic is the relative ease with which these good-hearted souls contrive to merge their world with the Zen-like realm inhabited by Nell. In what seems little more than a handful of days, they have earned her trust, decrypted her speech, and reached an emotional comfort zone. At the same time, Lovell and Olsen find something vital that was missing in their lives — each other.

After an invasive visitation by a Charlotte newspaper reporter and the inevitable helicopter-borne TV crew — a chance for Apted ("Coal Miner's Daughter") to engage in some heavy-handed, if justifiable, demonizing of the media — Nell and her protectors are off to the city.

It is there, in a climactic courtroom scene, that Foster delivers a touching but patently absurd Wisdom from the Waif of the Woods speech, gently expounding on the spiritual emptiness of city dwellers.

This intrusion of artificiality and triteness is an unbelievable blunder in a film whose effects generally are well measured.

Yet, by sheer force of talent, Foster, Neeson, and Richardson bury these contrivances and make "Nell" a film to remember. Though her technique is visible, Foster's Oscar-worthy performance is an emotional tour de force, so exquisitely constructed as to make almost everything else in this mediocre movie year pale by comparison.

The eyes radiate integrity. Her unselfconscious body language communicates Nell's childlike innocence and exuberance as no words ever could. The role also is quite a departure from the purposeful, rigidly controlled characters with which she is identified. An actress of uncommon skill and intelligence, Foster may not be incomparable, but she's damned close.

Neeson and Richardson, real-life husband and wife, turn in subtle, resonant, accomplished performances that perfectly augment Foster's work.

Richard Libertini, here liberated from the broad comedy that has marked his career, lends the role of psychologist Alexander Paley an unexpected gravity. Local filmgoers also will note a solid appearance by Lowcountry-bred actor O'Neal Compton, as Nell's lawyer.

The Charlotte skyline provides the backdrop for all the film's urban sequences. Exteriors were shot in Graham County, N.C. near the Tennessee border. It is no accident that these forested vistas are photographed with painterly feeling bordering on reverence. The cinematographer, Dante Spinotti, also captured the region's pastoral grandeur (as no one ever has) in "The Last of the Mohicans."

But it is both strength and flaw — beautiful, yes, but exposing an excess of pictorial attention at the expense of other virtues.

Still, "Nell" is an auspicious first project for Foster's Egg Productions. Though not as meaningful as it might have been, it is a film rescued by superb acting and an intensely compassionate sensibility.

....

'Pulp' ground into dazzling fiction
"Pulp Fiction"
October 13, 1994

Quentin Tarantino's "Pulp Fiction" is an exhilarating piece of punk delirium, saturated with blood but leavened by the writer-director's biting wit.

It is this blend of extreme violence and sly humor that has become a Tarantino trademark, first with "Reservoir Dogs," his debut as director, and more recently with the script for "True Romance" and the original story for "Natural Born Killers."

"Pulp Fiction" is more measured and less hysterical than "NBK," though every bit as dazzling – and a good deal funnier.

The film is an anthology of three separate but interwoven crime stories that dispense with conventional chronological treatment and borrow from the sort of circular narrative favored by Robert Altman. Characters in one tale interact with those in the next. Some who perish in one timeline are revived in another. But these confluences are utterly unpredictable.

The rogue's gallery of L.A. low-lifes is the product of inspired casting, with the principal roles vividly played by John Travolta, Uma Thurman, Samuel L. Jackson, and Bruce Willis. These are augmented with bristling supporting performances from Ving Rhames, Tim Roth, Amanda Plummer, Maria de Medieros, Eric Stoltz, Roseanne Arquette, Harvey Keitel and, in an especially deadpanned turn, Christopher Walken.

With Jackson and Travolta, terrific as quarreling gunman, Tarantino introduces a new class of thug: the philosopher hitman. The byplay between Jules (Jackson) and Vincent (Travolta), engaged in before, during and after assorted contracts, is consistently uproarious. Jackson has the showiest part in the movie interns *that* up a notch.

To criticize Tarantino's amalgam of styles as being derivative, as some have done, is to miss the point. True, the man is a human movie encyclopedia with celluloid coursing through his veins. And, yes, he can "access" just about any other filmmaker you care to name. Yet the 31-year-old Tarantino, who reserves a cameo role for himself here, employs his various influences in novel, tense, and exciting ways.

His pictures are violent indeed, yet never casually so, even if his characters seem blithely unconcerned with the carnage they inflict. There's a larger strategy at work, apart from providing contrast to or underscoring a scene's inherent humor: Tarantino is an alchemist of chaos.

Ever since winning the Palm d'Or at Cannes, one of the rare American films to accomplish the feat, much has been made of "Pulp Fiction" having resuscitated Travolta's career and given a fresh spin to Willis' tiring schtick, that of the smug wiseacre. Certainly Travolta is in fine form here, not least during his encounters with Thurman (who plays Mia, as in "Missing in Action"), which are wonderfully droll.

And Willis's buzz-cut, major-moxie, prize-fighter-on-the-run is handled with admirable restraint. It's his finest work. Period.

Visually, the film is a smorgasbord of dingy delights, thanks chiefly to production designer David Wasco, director of photography Andrzej Sekula, and Tarantino's bizarre juxtapositions.

On occasion the plot lines sag a bit, though soon regain momentum. While the unrelenting profane language of the screenplay (from a story co-written with Roger Avary) threatens to swap some sequences, Tarantino has an uncanny knack for toeing the line without quite crossing it.

"Pulp Fiction" is a rousing success on all levels, the most audacious film of its year and very possibly the best.

....

Film has charm to burn
"Four Weddings and A Funeral"
April 21, 1994

By now, Mike Newell is so thoroughly associated with the idyllic, frothy romance "Enchanted April" that one may forget the British director made his name with a penetrating drama, "Dance With a Stranger."

Or that he once dismissed the notion of doing light comedy with a tart "I don't do 'happy.'"

The fact is, reluctantly or not, Newell does it about as well as anyone. His latest, "Four Weddings and A Funeral," is a giddy delight with charm to burn. It packs the pews with a clever script, a sublime performance from Hugh Grant, and a winning congregation of "supporting" characters — each of whom gets to take a bow centerstage.

Grant is perfectly cast as Charles, a perpetual guest (if chronically late) at other people's weddings, but a fellow uncertain of his own ability to commit. He's had his chances, heaven knows, with a bevy of ex-ladyfriends constantly on hand to remind him.

Yet Charles is no cad; far from it. He's merely resigned to that species of bachelorhood known as "serial monogamy": one woman after another, but only one at a time.

Until his eyes lock with those of an approachable American beauty, Carrie (Andie MacDowell), a guest at the first nuptial ceremony. He's smitten. She's intrigued. And it seems they were fated to meet.

The picture follows their fleeting, uneasy (and not always convincing) encounters. But it's also about what happens to his friends along the way, among them his effusive female roomie, Scarlett (Charlotte Coleman); the rich and endearingly awkward Tom (James Fleet); Tom's stylish sister Fiona (Kristin Scott Thomas); the gay couple Garrett (Simon Callow) and Matthew (John Hannah); and Charles' deaf brother, David (David Bower).

Thomas and Callow (Mr. Beebe of "A Room With a View") are especially effective. But it's Grant's film to carry. His Charles is stumbling and elegant, rueful and idealistic, but always immensely likable. It is a performance of such finely considered features and momentum that it even manages to lift McDowell — a notoriously limited actress — to an acceptable plateau.

The film's quartet of weddings is choreographed with grace and infused with no small amount of wit, the latter due largely to screenwriter Richard Curtis.

When sadness comes, as it does in the death of a friend, the sudden transition from effervescence to grief seems all together seamless and natural, serving to bring each of the main characters into sharper relief. This is no small accomplishment, but the movie moves so matter-of-factly that you scarcely notice.

Newell might as well get used to it. Audiences love his particular brand of contemporary English frivolity. As well they might.

This one deserves bouquets all around.

....

'Sugar Hill' a glimpse into the world of corruption, drugs
"Sugar Hill"
February 27, 1994

Leon Ichaso's "Sugar Hill" is a kind of "Godfather Goes to Harlem," a contemporary drama of drug lords and shattered lives that manages to climb atop the trash heap of its own cliches and take a broader view.

But in straining to humanize a tribe of contemptible vermin — pushers, mobsters, corrupt cops — the film comes close to dismantling its carefully erected scaffolding of realism.

Wesley Snipes stars as Roemello Skuggs, a man made Rich by the same heroin that killed his mother, destroyed his father, and threatens to reduce him and his older brother Raynathan (Michael Wright) to ruin.

"Consumed by chaos, consumed by guilt," Skuggs is on a spiral staircase to Dante's Inferno, and knows it. He's desperate to escape the villainy of his past and make a fresh start with a wary young woman (Teresa Randle) who's won his heart. But events conspire to keep him at sewer level, fighting turf battles with an erstwhile "mentor" and business associate (Abe Vigoda), and a washed up boxer-turned-thug (Ernie Hudson).

If the story travels a too-familiar back alley to the close, and some of its features are a bit hard to swallow, Ichaso nonetheless handles the scenes with a sure hand. Especially effective is his use, early in the film, of a series of flashbacks shot in black-and-white, which establish a dour and convincing tone.

Ichaso and the movie benefit greatly from the work of cinematographer Bojan Bazelli ("Deep Cover," "China Moon"), a frequent collaborator with Abel Ferrara whose shadowed, atmospheric photography does much to ground the film in the world of the streets.

Snipes is compelling, as usual. He is one of a handful of actors equally adept at action ("Passenger 57"), romance ("Jungle Fever"), comedy ("White Men Can't Jump") and intelligent drama ("The Waterdance").

He can play the lead with breezy aplomb or submerge himself in character parts. In "Sugar Hill" he does a little of both. And Snipes would've walked away with the picture if not for a remarkable performance by Clarence Williams III as Skuggs' his junkie father.

Three most of his career, Williams, late of TVs "The Mod Squad," has been limited to the sort of parts that call less for acting than for voiceless, glowering intimidation, as in "52 Pick Up." Given room to move by Barry Michael Cooper's ("New Jack City") script, he displays unexpected range. In its deftness and intensity, Williams' execution rivals the powerhouse performance given by Samuel L. Jackson as Snipes' crackhead brother in "Jungle Fever." And that's saying something.

Also strong is Wright, who won a Best Actor Award at the Venice Film Festival in 1983 for Robert Altman's "Streamers" but has been underused since.

To some degree, "Sugar Hill" wants to have it both ways. It glamorizes the prosperous pusher's lifestyle (albeit with an edge) even as it deplores it. One would like to believe that this was done mainly for contrast, to bring the violence and horror of it all into bold relief.

On the whole, this is a measured film that's well above average for its type, rewarding the viewer with rich characterization and a stark glimpse into the abyss.

....

Director matures with "Schindler's List"
"Schindler's List"
February 6, 1994

If any skeptics remain as to Steven Spielberg's ability to deal with complex material, let their doubts be put to rest. After an extended, if entertaining, adolescence, the director has come of age with "Schindler's List."

Probing deep within himself to exhume a new emotional vocabulary, Spielberg has dramatically expanded his personal vision without relinquishing the remarkable storytelling gifts that have informed his career.

The key rests with restraint.

No longer is he "referencing" other filmmakers' images and techniques. Gone are the familiar high-gloss sheen and majestic sweep of much of his prior work. They are replaced by a genuinely unalloyed style, brilliantly realized through Janus Kaminski's stark photography.

Based on Thomas Keneally's 1982 novel, "Schindler's List" is the story of industrialist Oskar Schindler's rescue of 1,100 Jewish employees from certain extermination at Auschwitz-Birkenau.

Amid rekindled debate over the Holocaust, some of it sparked by the opening last year of the Holocaust Memorial Museum in Washington, D.C., this parable of conscience confronting evil owns particular poignancy.

A Sudeten-German, the suave, impeccably tailored Oskar Schindler (Liam Neeson) was an inveterate womanizer and hedonist. He was also a resourceful but unprincipled war profiteer, deeply enmeshed in the black market. Although his successful Polish enamelware factory was covertly financed by Jewish money, he had no moral compunction about cozying up to the Nazis when it further and his aims.

Why did such a seemingly shallow and self-absorbed individual perform, incongruously, so risky and endeavor as securing his employees escape? What were his motives in building a new plant in Czechoslovakia and buying the freedom of 1,100? Initially, Schindler used Jewish workers because Polish gentiles had to be paid. Under German occupation, Jews did not. Apart from potential damage to his factory, what could have brought such an altruistic sea-change? Was it the awakening of an essential humanity in the face of horror?

The film implies that Schindler was transformed after witnessing the true extent of German ruthlessness in 1943, during the terrifying liquidation of the Krakow ghetto, and later within the dreaded Plaszow forced labor camp. Yet, in the beginning, he offered sanctuary to Jews with great reluctance.

To their credit, Spielberg and screenwriter Steve Zaillian intentionally keep Schindler at a remove, maintaining the enigma of the man. Wow this distances us somewhat from the central character, the very ambiguity of the portrait strengthens the film.

In the end, Schindler is perhaps too saintly and mythic a figure for any actor to embody as a life-size, flesh-and-blood person. But Neeson does an exemplary job in a difficult role.

The film's truly spellbinding performance is given by Ralph Fiennes, who, as the surpassingly monstrous Plaszow commandant Amon Goeth, mines fresh horrors from the prototypical Nazi sadist. His cruelties are so casual, so offhand, they inhabit a place more nightmarish than even the psychopaths twisted realm.

While negative comment on the film is rare, some have felt that the atrocities so vividly revealed in "Schindler's List" are deprived of their full emotional power by the relative anonymity of the movie's Jews.

It can be argued that Ben Kingsley's character, Itzhak Stern, the Jewish accountant retained by Schindler to run his plant, is a familiar Hollywood "type," and that other major of Jewish characters have the feel of composites. But the profession of faces is eloquent enough, and if Spielberg had drawn more intimate, individual portraits — in the manner of Anne Frank — would this guarantee that more indifferent audiences would flock to the picture? We doubt it.

Nor was it his intention to present too graphic a depiction of Nazi barbarism. What Spielberg suggests is every bit as devastating as what he shows.

That Schindler's list preaches to the converted is understandable. No one criticized "Shoah" or "The Sorrow and the Pity" for failing to galvanize the mall crowds. Its forcefulness lies beyond such concerns.

Diabolical nature of all pogroms, methodical or otherwise, has been well chronicled. But not since "The Killing Fields" (1984) has the perverse psychology of genocide been so wrenchingly conveyed. Once a people has been dehumanized, it is a short step to dispatching them with remorseless impunity.

Spielberg's urgency in putting Keneally's book on screen had much to do with the corollary events — the "ethnic cleansing" in Bosnia. Shooting entirely in Poland, and those very places still haunted by echoes of the past, appears to have added a resonance that even Steven Spielberg could not have predicted.

If the uplifting ending of "Schindler's List" seems rather facile, and the story incomplete, it is well to remember that few films are without flaw, and that no single motion picture could hope to communicate the totality of this singular 20th century event — an abomination greater than even the Stalinist and Maoist purges.

Spielberg plunges us anew into an abyss so dark it beggars the imagination. What is more, "Schindler's List" tears away the invisible barrier that separates the audience from the screen, forces us to look at ourselves in the process of watching.

The view is disturbing.

....

Cryptic musing on an enigmatic pianist
"Thirty-Two Shorts Films About Glenn Gould"
July 14, 1994

Here follow 32 (comparatively) short sentences about "Thirty-Two Short Films About Glenn Gould."

Francois Girard's crypto-biography of the late Canadian classical pianist is as eccentric as its subject. Viewing this arresting series of vignettes is like eavesdropping on an animated coffeehouse conversation. It is intriguing, intellectually. It is often fascinating. But when it's over you wonder just how much you have gleaned.

Glenn Gould was revered as one of the 20th century's greatest musicians. A child prodigy, he could read music before he could read words. He played Bach with unsurpassed artistry.

Yet Gould withdrew from public performance in 1964, at the age of 32. Ostensibly it was to devote his energies to recording and composition. He harbored a certain ambivalence regarding an artist's responsibility to his audience. And he was indifferent to the marketplace.

Girard explores why Gould retreated from the stage. It is suggested that he embraced technology as a means of keeping the world at arm's length. But a final answer is as elusive as the man. He was self-absorbed without being self-important. He preferred the company of ordinary people to that of sophisticates. Apparently, Gould never considered himself a remarkable individual.

The world felt differently. His death in 1982 of a stroke was felt acutely.

Girard, who co-wrote the script, augments his occasionally bizarre narrative with interviews with Gould's colleagues and friends. Meant to enlighten, at times these interludes serve to impede the film's momentum. Otherwise, the construction is relatively seamless. And it is hard to say which is the more expressive, Alain Dostie's camera or the masterly impersonation of Gould by stage actor Colm Feore.

Fere plays it with reined intensity. To some degree, he reveals Gould to be an embodiment of the axion, "Talent does what it can; genius what it must."

Still, for all its originality, doubtless there are those who will find "Thirty-Two Shorts Films" a bore. Some will dismiss the film as having a fine arts sensibility best suited to an airless academic world. But Girard's picture rewards patience and attention.

The themes of solitude and isolation are contrasted with an examination of the public's insatiable – and dogged – curiosity. In the end, we may not know Glenn Gould, but we have some sense of the forces that drove him to brilliance and retreat.

....

Branagh film is really something
"Much Ado About Nothing"
September 26, 1993

Rejoice, good people! We would not regale thee with such glad tidings were not the subject worthy of our manifest enthusiasm.

To be true, "Much Ado About Nothing," as put a'screen by that kindly knave Kenneth Branagh is everything the Bard intended: a spirited, bawdy tale of romance, deception and the eternal battle of the sexes.

Rarely, if ever, has Shakespeare's beloved comedy been presented with such unalloyed exuberance. Branagh's second Shakespearean venture, the first being his acclaimed "Henry V" (1989), is an infectious, superbly acted romp.

Attend:

All is well in the realm of Leonato (Richard Briers), lord of a most stately manor. A rumble of soldiers has returned in triumph, led by the dashing Don Pedro (Denzel Washington). Mirth (and lust) is everywhere apparent. But, lo, treachery is afoot.

Don Pedro has determined to aid his young compatriot, Claudio (Robert Sean Leonard), in winning the hand of Leona's daughter, the lovely Hero (Kate Beckinsale). More, he and members of the household have hatched a benign plot to bring together the committed bachelor Benedict (Branagh) and the sharp-tongued Beatrice (Emma Thompson), a woman who "speaks poniards (daggers) and every word stabs."

Their courtship is a fervent but raucous one, endangered less by their combative ways than by the actions of Don Pedro's sullen and jealous half-brother Don John (Keanu Reeves). Don John has devised a vile fraud, convincing Claudio that his virgin bride has been unfaithful — on the very eve of their wedding.

Enter the grimy, ingratiating constable Dogberry (Michael Keaton), who massacres the language with the same facility used in exposing Don John's villainy.

In the end, the tangle of misunderstandings and hostilities is set aright.

Branagh's direction is inspired. He uses the camera as an active storyteller, linking one exhilarating scene to the next. And his script trims Shakespeare's speeches deftly, losing not one whit of the play's crucial elements, or its enduring accessibility. An earthy rambunctiousness pervades the film beginning to end.

At full gallop, "Much Ado About Nothing" seems more a period Western than a Shakespearean lark. Chronologically, the imaginary world of "Much Ado" could have existed in any several time periods. Ah, but the film's setting is timeless.

Branagh shot on location in the incomparable Italian countryside, between the ancient rival cities of Florence and Sienna. His centerpiece is the 14th century Villa Vignamaggio, overlooking the town of Greve in the heart of the Chianti wine region.

The villa was once the home of the Gheradini family, who sometime around 1503 commissioned one Leonardo Da Vinci to paint a portrait of their daughter, whom the world came to know as Mona Lisa. The portrait was executed on the grounds.

The easy charm and simple life of the area appear to have insinuated their way into the cast, so relaxed and breezy are the performances. Branagh and Thompson are a dream, as usual, and Branagh arrived at the remainder of his Anglo-American cast shrewdly, ensuring the widest possible audience.

Leonard and Beckinsale bring fresh perk and an appealing earnestness to their roles as young lovers, while Washington plays the noble Don Pedro with sophisticated nonchalance. Keaton, meanwhile, reminds us that he should never stray too far from comedy; he almost steals the show from his British mates.

Wonderful in support are Briers and the splendidly Falstaffian Brian Blessed as Leonato's brother Antonio. On the other hand, we can be thankful that Reeves' melancholy character is "not of many words," sparing us an overabundance of this one dimensional actor's presents.

There's expert work from Australian cinematographer Roger Lanser, who worked with Branagh on "Peter's Friends," and composer Patrick Doyle, who contributed a merry score.

But the principal applause must go to Branagh for a deliciously literate adventure at the movies.

....

'Damage' a portrait of compulsion
"Damage"
April 11, 1993

That desire may subvert good judgment, that it may even be greater than the object desired, is by no means a novel theme.

Nor is the recognition that a consuming passion for another defies conscious control. Yet in director Louis Malle's "Damage," the motif is given a powerful emotional charge. As an uncompromising portrait of erotic compulsion, it may be unexcelled, by turns trance-like and melancholy, electric and over the top.

It is not about "reality," at least not in the strict sense. "Damage," based on the book by Josephine Hart, is about a state of mind divorced from reason or consequence.

From the moment their eyes meet at an ambassadorial cocktail party, Dr. Stephen Fleming (Jeremy Irons), an aspiring British Cabinet minister, and the disturbingly beautiful Anna (Juliette Binoche), his son's new girlfriend, are mesmerized.

They explode, almost literally, into each other's arms.

Anna is as inscrutable as the Sphinx, and there's more than a bit of a riddle to her personality and past.

Fleming, a public man, has ambled through a career in Parliament and his quiet, too comfortable marriage to wife Ingrid (Miranda Richardson). Depressed and distant, he is especially vulnerable to temptation.

Fleming's betrayal of his wife, his son, is manifold. Yet guilt only occasionally can insinuate itself through the wall of passion. His intellect demands order, some form of structure for an affair careening out of control.

It is a forlorn wish.

Anna, haunting and haunted, is moved by inexplicable forces. How could she do it? How could she promise to marry young Martin (Rupert Graves) and still sustain an affair with his father?

The film's explanation, rooted in her unusually close relationship with her brother, and his suicide at age 16, is not all together satisfying. And Binoche is perhaps a little too impassive in the role.

Like "Last Tango in Paris" before it, "Damage" explores the landscape of obsession. The titillation factor is there, naturally, but there's more to Malle's vision than that.

Irons and Binoche, clothed, generate 10 times the erotic power most screen lovers do nude. You almost never confront this kind of emotional intensity in an American film.

Some have found David Hare's deliberately far-fetched script to be a trifle pretentious, if not silly. Indeed, you'll either like it immensely or dismiss it out of hand.

But there's no denying the strength of Iron's performance. He plays the sallow-eyed, possessed Stephan with utter conviction. Irons may be a pompous, unmitigated egotist on the set, as has been claimed, but his perfectionism almost always yields dividends, most notably in 1988's "Dead Ringers." Here he is just as persuasive.

Splendidly theatrical, Irons is very possibly the best actor alive.

Richardson, who was nominated for a Best Supporting Actress Oscar, continues to impress with her uncommon range. She makes a rather unshaded, ancillary character crackle with authority. It's hard to imagine anyone negotiating the part more adroitly.

In a welcome return to the screen, Leslie Caron makes the most of her cameo as Anna's frivolous (if highly perceptive) mother.

One must also compliment the expertly composed photography of Peter Biziou, whose contrasting visual styles help underscore the mounting stakes and that lead the characters to tragedy.

Bruno Ganz in "Wings of Desire," courtesy of the Wenders Foundation

International Film Reviews

International Film Reviews

If one envisions foreign language films as a path to discovering other cultures, as well as a means of recognizing the universality of human concerns, the allure is irresistible. Yet many do resist, finding subtitles too disconcerting or bothersome. How unfortunate, for they are denying themselves a window into a larger world and, quite often, superior craftsmanship.

It's hard to name a country that hasn't produced at least one (and generally many more) film classics. Some countries have been especially fertile over the past quarter-century, but every continent has had its share of gems.

Yet for some, foreign is just that – *too* foreign. Perhaps dispensing with the term in favor of something like "international" helps remove the perception of films from other lands as the province of snobbish cinephiles, as obscure and perplexing, intelligible only to connoisseurs.

They are nothing of the kind.

So kindly spare us the carping about subtitles. Unless your vision is poor and the lettering at the bottom of your theater or TV screen is illegible, there's no legitimate excuse to reject seeing non-dubbed foreign language films. It's pure chauvinism. And it doesn't say much for a filmgoer's curiosity about other lands that he or she would refuse to watch a terrific movie just because it's not in English. How lazy can you get? Did audiences whine about subtitles during the silent film era?

When I was in college in the late '60s and early '70s, the multiplex was in its infancy. Steven Spielberg and George Lucas and their legion of imitators had yet to transform the American cinema for the worst – spectacle over content, fantasy over reality, special effects over dialogue.

Students flocked to the single-screen art house cinema in town to experience not only the latest international movies, but the game-changing Italian neo-realist, French New Wave, German Expressionist and Scandinavian films of what was then the recent past. From the mid-'50s to the mid-'60s, we in America saw the emergence of an astonishing array of world-class directors. This in turn heralded the beginning of a Hollywood New Wave that enlivened the late '60s through the mid-'70s. It was heady times at the bijou.

But that local theater also harbored revivals of American classics: the Bogart films, Laurel and Hardy, the Marx Brothers, and the great silent films of Keaton and Chaplin, et al. Few had been watching them since the days of their release, until their re-discovery and renewed popularization during this period.

That's how many of us Baby Boomers were introduced to Hollywood's Golden Age of the 1930s and 1940s, to the immaculate silents (a wholly distinct artform with its own cinematic language) and, coupled with foreign language movies, to the extraordinary possibilities of the film art. It was exhilarating. It was an education. And it left you hungry for more.

As the critic A.O. Scott has pointed out, it was "foreign" movies that taught us Yanks to regard film as an art form in the first place. Surely the early Hollywood moguls never thought of it in this regard. Moviemaking was strictly a matter of commerce. Occasionally brilliant, but commerce nonetheless.

"Each new film was not just a new window on the world but also, at least potentially, a world of style, sensibility and invention unto itself," Scott wrote, "with its own rules, its own language, its own syntax."

Then came home video – the death knell for the true art house. Today, commerce rules again, at least in the U.S. Only more so. And most independent film cinemas have had to go hybrid to survive.

I feel sorry for several generations of young people weaned on the megaplex, on empty blockbusters, witless comedies, films that take their cues from commercials and music videos or, worst of all, movies with little or no interest in telling an actual story. One seldom sees people under 40 in an international film audience (though this is beginning to change). The audience generally trends older, and is often of an international makeup itself.

This is not to say that excellent movies aren't still made, here and abroad. They are, of course. It's just that many international films – those not overly influenced by the more vacuous American sensibilities – seem somehow to have a heightened sense of humanity. Though many are as fanciful as their American counterparts, usually it's fancy with meat on its bones. They give the viewer something to chew on.

Dabbling in such films won't do it. To get up to speed, as it were, you need to immerse yourself. The rewards are boundless. Admittedly, unless one lives in a major city, the number of foreign language films we have the opportunity to see in the theater is but a trickle of the international production. Savor them. Seek out the others on video. Great movies are memorable in any language.

Below are some well worth a look.

....

'Namesake' a warm, generational story of immigrant family
"The Namesake"
April 5, 2007

Like the complex tonal variations in an Indian ballad, Mira Nair's rich, textured, quietly emotional films are long on nuance.

There is also color, warmth and rounded characters drawn in human scale.

"The Namesake," her latest, is a poignant multi-generational, clash-of-cultures saga which telescopes time while alternating between Calcutta and New York City. Once again, ancient traditions and familial longings try to interact with the American Dream of limitless possibility.

The tale opens in 1977 on a train bound for Calcutta. A young man named Ashoke Ganguli (Irfan Khan) is reading a short story by Russian realist Nikolai Gogol when he meets a fellow passenger who encourages him to expand his horizons and see something of the world. This chance meeting, together with the influence of Gogol's writing and a horrific accident, eventually set Ganguli on the path to marriage and immigration to the United States.

The new husband, a chemical engineer, already is acquainted with New York, having studied there for a time, but his new bride, Ashima (Tabu), finds that secular Gotham with its gray, frigid winters and chilly people are too stark a contrast to the familiarity that cocooned them in India. While she will adapt, especially after the family moves to greener environs in the suburbs, her American-born children chafe at the trappings of tradition.

Representing the namesake of the title, their son Gogol (Kal Penn) progresses from wide-eyed little boy (played at age 4 by Soham Chatterjee) to Yale architecture grad, to ardent pursuer of a non-Bengali girlfriend (Jacinda Barrett), a blonde WASP, no less. Although Gogol, who insists on being called Nick, is embraced by his sweetheart's folks, his parents are unsettled by this development. But they hold their peace, partly in hopes that their son will change his mind and their thoroughly Americanized young daughter (Sahira Nair) might yet honor the preferred path. In the end, they are wise enough to realize a new land comes with new permutations, even after a family sojourn introduces the kids to the glories of India.

All this is arresting prelude to the film's second pivotal event, a wrenching but transformational one in a story punctuated by promise, tragedy, acceptance and joy.

In adapting Jhumpa Lahiri's 2003 novel of two generations of an Indian immigrant family, Nair ("Monsoon Wedding") and frequent collaborator Sooni Taraporevala ("Mississippi Masala") have compressed much of the book's involved narrative, generally to good effect, though the transitions in place and time sometimes feel a bit hurried, as if Nair is trying to squeeze too much of moment into scenes that can't accommodate it all.

There's also a rather unnecessary subplot involving the self-absorbed Gogol and his ill-fated marriage to a London-raised Bengali (Zuleikha Robinson) who's moved to Manhattan. Yes, it's in the book, and it's a fairly useful device in amplifying Nair's themes, but that doesn't stop the scenes from feeling tacked on.

Though intelligent, deeply sympathetic and gorgeously filmed, there is a sense of a film that meanders ever so slightly, and may be a shade overlong. Some of this has to do with the film's deliberate pacing. Nair wants us to know these characters, and she takes pains to limn them with identifiable features, especially the father Ashoke (beautifully played by the expressive character actor Khan) and the melancholy mother Ashima (an indelible portrait by the achingly lovely Tabu).

Their son may be the centerpiece of the film, but they are its heart, its spirit and the echo in our thoughts.

....

'Others,' deserving of its Oscar, a film that works on every level
"The Lives of Others"
March 15, 2007

Suspicion is a state of mind - and a habit - that feeds on itself. It is the parent of paranoia

In East Germany, in the all-too-Orwellian year of 1984, obsessive Communist Party loyalist Capt. Gerd Wiesler (Ulrich Muhe) discharges his responsibility to the state by serving as a security (domestic spying) operative. Though his career ambitions pale compared with the opportunism of his immediate superior, smarmy Lt. Col Anton Grubitz (Ulrich Tukur), Wiesler still sees potential in the task of collecting evidence that popular playwright Georg Dreyman (Sebastian Koch) and his girlfriend, celebrated theater actress Christa-Maria Sieland (Martina Gedeck), may in fact be subversives hungry for acclaim in the West.

So he sets about bugging Dreyman's apartment and monitoring the couple's conversations 24/7.

For Wiesler, a buttoned-up, colorless man with no real friends, eavesdropping on others is a substitute for having a life of his own. But in writer-director Florian Henckel von Donnersmarck's brilliantly realized "The Lives of Others," Wiesler soon will come face to face with specters he has never known: conscience and empathy.

"Lives" upset "Pan's Labyrinth" at this year's Academy Awards, winning the Best Foreign Language Film Oscar and triggering much outrage on the part of the "Pan's" faithful. In retrospect, the voters were right.

This is a movie that works on every level: as a gripping story of suspense, as a political statement on a dark time, as a cautionary tale on fear and betrayal, as a study of voyeurism and corruption and as trenchant comment on the danger of taking "homeland security" measures to perilous extremes - all of which can be rationalized.

The goal of the thought police of East Germany is not simply to short-circuit dissent, but to quash that most subversive of all human activities - art - by rigidly controlling its subject matter. The ministry of culture, in the guise of the oily Bruno Hempf (Thomas Thieme), decides who can produce plays, what can be written, who can direct them and who can be in the cast. Despite the fact that his mentor, once-esteemed playwright Albert Jerska (Volkmar Kleinert), has been blacklisted for years, Dreyman has chafed, but seldom pressed the issue.

What he does not know, in the beginning of the film, is that his gifted but insecure lady has been coerced into sexual assignations with Hempt in the hopes that it would guarantee her continued presence on stage. Indeed, the real reason Dreyman is being kept under watch is at the minister's behest, so his romantic rival can be moved out of the way. By contrast, Wiesler really is suspicious of Dreyman.

When Dreyman finally learns of his lover's "affair" - thanks to Wiesler's manipulation of events - she responds that his acquiescence to the state has placed him every bit as much "in bed" with the powers as she is.

If Dreyman wasn't enamored of new horizons before, he is now, especially after the wrenching suicide of his mentor. Unaware that he is under surveillance, Dreyman is willing to risk everything to smuggle an inflammatory article to the Western press.

Cutting back and forth between the couple, Dreyman's interaction with associates, Wiesler's meetings with Grubitz and Wiesler's clandestine listening post, von Donnersmarck's film becomes an examination of the crippling power of terror - taking place just five years before the fall of the Berlin Wall. It will have you looking over your shoulder and checking your light fixtures for microphones.

What an auspicious feature film debut for Von Donnersmarck, who grew up in West Berlin but spent some of his childhood years in East Berlin. His portrait of life in the latter has a palpable feel of dramatic truth. The film is all sterile offices, vacant streets, unadorned apartments and casually superlative acting.

The subtlety of Muhe's performance is remarkable, but the entire cast soon has you forgetting that it is performances one is seeing. It's that good

So is the script, a model of economy and impact, buttressed by a score that manages to induce both squirmy tension and a haunting emotional current

Can art triumph over the authoritarian impulse? "The Lives of Others" believes it can. The world it depicts has vanished. The fear it spawned has not.

....

'Pan's Labyrinth' melds fantasy, action
"Pan's Labyrinth"
January 21, 2007

There is a strange and beautiful alchemy at work in "Pan's Labyrinth," Guillermo del Toro's supremely accomplished fairy tale for adults.

Set in Spain in 1944 against the backdrop of the repressive Francisco Franco regime, it is the tale of a young girl whose innocence wields greater power than the guns and bludgeons of her brutal stepfather, a Francoist military officer whose summary executions of rebels and villagers are as offhand as they are ruthless.

Shortly after the Spanish Civil War, young Ofelia (Ivana Baquero) and her pregnant mother, Carmen (Ariadna Gil), have traveled to a rural area of the north to live with the mother's new husband, Capt. Vidal (Sergi Lopez), a man who takes fascism very much to heart. Ordered to rid the area of its last infestation of guerillas, Vidal sets about the task with a plutocrat's distaste.

With all the grimness around her, the girl understandably prefers to dwell in her own imaginary world, populated by fantastical creatures, whispered destinies and harrowing quests.

But is it imaginary? A short distance from the old mill in which she, her mother and her nanny, Mercedes (Maribel Verdu), live, Ofelia discovers a rocky labyrinth. Deep within the maze she meets its major domo, the mythical faun Pan (Doug Jones), who confides that she is a princess who has lost her memory of her royal standing. She must regain it, and the throne. Using an arcane book of calligraphy and magical images, Pan reveals the challenges she must endure and the feats she must accomplish.

For writer-director del Toro, ably abetted by director of photography Guillermo Navarro, this film is orders of magnitude better than anything he has done before. To mention them in the same sentence with his gaudy horror flick, "Blade 2," is absurd. Even "Cronos" and "Hellboy" only hinted at the wit, style and mastery of form the director could bring to bear.

Del Toro folds fantasy and action into straight drama as seamlessly as could be imagined, then amplifies it with features of a morality play. Has anyone ever fused politics and history with the supernatural so soberly, so beguilingly? "Pan's Labyrinth" is no less than a work of art, meticulously conceived and exceedingly well-played by its stars, not the least of whom is Alex Angulo as the sympathetic and principled Dr. Ferreiro, the physician attending Ofelia's mother.

Chief among the players is the smoothly malevolent Lopez, and Verdu is the grounding glue of the piece as the nanny with a secret life of her own.

In a word, marvelous.

....

Don't look for resolution in Haneke's 'Caché'
"Cache"
April 6, 2006

So taut that it is almost immobile, writer-director Michael Haneke's "Caché" ("Hidden") probably is no one's idea of a thriller, at least those weaned on gripping jolts, cue-the-shrieks music and a pounding sense of foreboding. Conventional entertainment is not the aim.

"Caché" is nothing if not subtle, though it's understated realism and static staging occasionally make a fine film feel airless. That said, it is not long after seeing the picture that plot elements that puzzled begin to coalesce and the first questions start insinuating themselves in your mind. The uncomfortable ones. The kind that make you assay your own attitudes and responses, and find them wanting

It's delayed-reaction cinema. But not simply the liberal guilt trip it appears to be.

United for the first time since their wonderful work in "The Widow of Saint Pierre" (2001), Daniel Auteuil and Juliette Binoche are in excellent form again as a couple who discover they aren't on the most solid of ground. That fact becomes increasingly apparent as the past intrudes on the present, and new stresses worsen already existing fissures of communication and trust.

Georges Laurent (Auteuil), who hosts a popular and influential literary review on French public television, begins receiving strange packages containing videos of himself with his family - shot furtively in their neighborhood - interspersed with unsettling drawings of a crudely sketched figure with blood spurting from its neck. He cannot fathom their meaning. Neither can his wife Anne (Binoche), a book editor, though she soon senses her husband may be holding something back. Is it a bizarre joke, or a sinister portent?

As the tapes become more personal, and the locations change, Laurent confirms he does have a suspicion as to whom the culprit might be. He refuses to divulge it. Instead he barges into the seedy apartment of a man named Majid (Maurice Bénichou) and confronts him. Majid, apparently mystified, denies the accusation. It is clear that he and Georges go back a long way, and that the former might have ample reason to be exacting this curious "revenge." But Majid seems sad and resigned, not malicious

As the days pass, and the police get involved, the Laurents become more vexed at the situation and each other. Though nothing in the tapes is suggestive of violence aimed at them, only a disquieting observation, their anxiety mounts. And it's almost as if Georges is terrorizing himself. Which, of course, may be the plan. The feeling amplifies when Georges grows convinced it may be Majid's son (Walid Afkir) who is behind it all.

"Caché" not only plays off themes of mistrust, ethnicity and the paranoia of the prosperous, but also on the unhappy past shared by France and Algeria. It is foremost an unsparing look at how the fear that threatens a couple challenges the convictions they thought they held dear. In the end, the Laurents are recognizable, yet hardly the most attractive or sympathetic of characters.

Don't expect a pat resolution, or any resolution for that matter. Be patient, too, with the French propensity for scenes that appear to have no connection to anything going on in the film, not even as framing devices. Rather, absorb some highly skilled performances and a script that has more on its mind than its central mystery.

....

Sharp 'Daggers' sheer artistry
"House of Flying Daggers"
January 13, 2005

In the grand, luminous universe imagined by Zhang Yimou, the heart often betrays the self, yet still remains true.

It's only a conundrum to those who enter his realm with a literal mind, for in Zhang's films, the mythic and fanciful dwell side by side with the more earthly realities of treachery, vengeance, deception and sacrifice.

One may regard "House of Flying Daggers" as a companion piece to the director's "Hero," though Zhang engages here in a reversal of form. While both films involve romantic triangles, "Hero" is at base an action epic sprinkled with romantic flourishes. By contrast, "Daggers" is smaller in scale, chiefly concerned with the dramatic arc of its characters' relationships - love at odds with duty - and less with derring-do.

Zhang grounds the story in emotion, toning down (but not eliminating) the familiar fairy-tale business and visual sleight of hand. Not to say the movie lacks finely choreographed (and highly stylized) fight sequences - the battle in a bamboo forest is astonishingly well-staged - but we have become so accustomed to the ingenuity of these lighter-than-air martial ballets that they almost seem beside the point. Perhaps even superfluous.

Zhang follows the symbology of Chinese filmmaking tradition in depicting that duel in the bamboo - Ang Lee did the same in "Crouching Tiger, Hidden Dragon" - but he makes the tradition his own.

Opening with one of the most opulent set pieces in recent memory, "Daggers" relates the tale of three people at the intersection of crossed purposes. The film is set in the year 859 as the once-enlightened Tang Dynasty has begun an inexorable decay. Two crafty police officers hatch a scheme to infiltrate a clandestine army called the House of Flying Daggers, one fervently opposed to the ruling emperor. Leo (Takeshi Kaneshiro), the senior of the two, dispatches friend Jin (Andy Lau) to a brothel to meet and later "rescue" Mei (Zhang Ziyi), a blind courtesan suspected of having ties to the revolutionary faction. She may even be the daughter of its deceased leader. Jin's job: woo her, win her confidence and affections, then strike.

No one counts on the police officers' superiors getting wind of their venture, then taking matters a step further by deploying them as expendable pawns. Least of all, the officers in question.

Meanwhile, Leo has every confidence that Jin will succeed in his mission, for is he not irresistible to women? In classic movie fashion, the conqueror becomes the conquered. Yet in the end, both Jin and Mei are vanquished by love, trapped by fate and destined to deal with one final complication - Zhang's exquisite little plot twist.

Co-written by the director, "Daggers" does have, for all its rapture, a few gaping holes in logic. Why, for example, would government troops bent on finding the faction's stronghold decide to kill the only woman, Mei, who could lead them to it? This, after the mock attacks staged by Leo to convince her of Jin's honesty

Don't examine the course of events too closely. Rather, embrace the sheer artistry of the filmmaking and the spirited performances of the principals. Especially Zhang Ziyi, who rivals Gong Li as something of the Greta Garbo of her era.

The dreamlike sequences Zhang and other Asian filmmakers paint depict human physical prowess as unfettered and unlimited, love in the highest key and, with their rich color palette, a hypnotic natural beauty that borders on surreal. The climactic scene, shot in the Ukraine as the last of fall's chromatic splendor is limned with snow, is a breathtaking masterstroke.

Give the lion's share of credit to Zhang's vision and to the manner in which it is executed by director of photography Zhao Xiaoding. Together with action director/choreographer Tony Ching Siu-Tung ("Hero"), they reveal the exalted ideals of the warrior as inseparable from the techniques of ancient classical music, calligraphy and dance. Ziyi Zhang's traditional sleeve dance, centerpiece of the opening sequence, is as liquid as a brushstroke. And just as captivating.

"Daggers" sings, whether in the air or on the ground.

....

'Motorcycle' an exhilarating ride
"The Motorcycle Diaries"
November 11, 2004

A charismatic film about two charismatic men, Walter Salles' "The Motorcycle Diaries" more than lives up to its rep as one of the year's most accomplished, affecting pictures. It may also be the best.

"Diaries" is a happy synthesis of road movie, travelogue, coming-of-age story and character study, each facet polished to high luster by a pair of wonderful central performances from Gael Garcia Bernal as the 23-year-old Argentine Ernesto Guevara - whom the world later would know as Che - and Rodrigo de la Serna as his resourceful, 29-year-old traveling companion, Alberto Granado.

Salles and screenwriter Jose Rivera base their movie on Guevara's perceptive, posthumously published journal chronicling the 8,000-mile, eight-month trip, with detail also drawn from Granado's "Traveling with Che Guevara: The Making of a Revolutionary."

As fine as the performances are, what helps rivet you to the screen are cinematographer Eric Gautier's breathtaking images of Argentina, Chile, Peru and the Amazon, and Salles' impeccable direction. It is a very different kind of film than his last, the harrowing "City of God," but the director achieves his aim with the same clear-eyed rigor, grasp of nuance and naturalistic drive.

Before settling down to the productive, conventional lives expected of a pair of young, middle-class men, Guevara and biochemist-in-training Granado determine to hit the road for a circuitous adventure from Argentina to Venezuela. The two set out in 1951 (anticipating "Easy Rider") aboard The Mighty One, a sputtering relic of a 1939 motorcycle, which barely makes it out of the Peruvian Andes before wheezing its last. The friends must take to their feet. Hardships? Si.

What began as a frolic, albeit with a planned stopover at a leper colony to serve as volunteer workers, taxes them almost to the limit. But their travails seem mild compared to the misery and inequity they encounter, and often share, among South America's underclass. They also are met with unexpected kindnesses, from the well-to-do as well as the wretched, not to mention people receptive to their transparent little cons. What they witnessed makes an indelible impression, especially on Guevara. By the end, Guevara, a year older, is irrevocably changed. The only question is: What form will that change take?

The more serious elements of "The Motorcycle Diaries," its social criticism particularly, for the most part are presented with a measured touch; very little beating us about the head. And they are leavened with considerable humor. While faintly romanticized, the film's evocation of socialist ideals underscores their appeal (in theory) to those enduring dreadful lives. It is also, of course, highly appropriate. Soon enough, Guevara would become legend for his activities in Cuba. And if one does not agree with his methods in the name of justice, this account, if it is valid, leaves no doubt as to his sincerity.

Among the most vivid scenes, however predictable, are those set in the leper colony, the staff at its hospital and research facility separated by a wide swath of the Amazon River from the lepers they treat. It provides the linchpin of Salles' movie, at once the clearest division and greatest complexity.

Throughout, composer Gustavo Santaolaya's score is a lively accompaniment, seamlessly integrated and never intrusive.

Bernal, whose previous films were the excellent "Amores Perros" (2001) and the amusing if over-praised "Y Tu Mamá También" (2001), is a soulful young actor with gobs of appeal. His portrait of the journey of a bright but impressionable 20-something from idealist to pragmatist to proto-revolutionary is believable every step of the way.

But the principal strength of the film is not so much his or de la Serna's individual performance as it is the way they pull in tandem. Exuberant to exhausted, silly to somber, they make the casts of most "buddy" movies look like candidates for the Hall of Lame. The two are buttressed by a battery of solid supporting players, chief among them Jean Pierre Noher, Mia Maestro, Mercedes Moran and Susana Lanteri.

Salles, a filmmaker almost single-handedly responsible for the resurrection of the Brazilian cinema, was born in Rio de Janeiro, then raised in France and the United States before making Brazil his permanent home in his teens. If "Central Station" (1998) heralded a talent to watch, his latest efforts make him one not to miss.

....

'Osama' bleak, grim chronicle
"Osama"
April 8, 2004

It is tempting to say, rather glibly, that extremists are prisoners of their upbringing. And it is too often true. When one is indoctrinated from childhood, the critical faculties are dulled, submerged. The natural skepticism that is humanity's birthright may never develop.

It is even less likely to emerge when each day is a trial of survival in the face of poverty, starvation and war.

That doesn't not explain why the well-educated and well off are seduced by religious absolutism - the world's chief scourge - as has happened among all too many in the Middle East's erstwhile Cradle of Civilization.

Further north, in the dust bowl of Afghanistan, the roots of this cruel reality are more easily seen. Desperation and fear are a door flung wide to fanaticism. When questions are not even permitted, when any deviation from rigidly applied thought may be punishable by death, the prudent are silent.

"Osama" is an unremittingly grim film about an unremittingly grim time and place, Afghanistan under the Taliban. But writer-director Siddiq Barmak opens the movie with a scene of revolt. A sea of women in blue Burkas pour through a village street, pleading to be allowed to work. Many of their fathers, husbands and brothers have been killed in war. As there is no man to escort them from place to place, and they are prohibited from moving about on their own, they cannot hold jobs. Their families have little to eat. Life is an endlessly bleak prospect.

The women have no choice but to defy the Taliban and risk brutalization at the hands of its patrols, "enforcers" roaming the town in vehicles bristling with automatic weapons. The protest will not last long.

The story centers on a mother and a grandmother who have no living husbands or sons. The only way the mother can keeping working in a crude hospital is if she disguises her daughter as a boy named Osama.

Later, the girl maintains the pose to work in a kindly shopkeeper's store.

But when she is whisked away in a roundup of boys destined for the Taliban's joyless

Islamic "schools," she is in great jeopardy, despite the help of a young boy who tries gamely to hide her identity. The girl's fate is not for the weak of stomach.

It should be kept in mind, however, that this is not only a film that (somewhat one-sidedly) eviscerates a brand of religious extremism. It also exposes the fact that, for some, faith is another kind of veil, behind which men use religion as an excuse to subdue and exploit women in the name of God.

With her haunted eyes and almost palpable misery, Marina Golbahari, is heartbreakingly believable in the title role. Except for some clumsy line readings that remind you this is a movie, she and others in the cast give "Osama" the warp and woof of realism, an almost documentary feel.

There are some similarities to the more artful "Kandahar" (2001), a picture shot on the border of Iran and Afghanistan that dealt with a young female journalist who escaped Afghanistan with her family only to return to rescue her sister. But "Osama" is more bluntly told, unsparing, and so illustrative of the primitiveness of the Taliban that it is difficult to imagine them being a part of the modern world - but a simple matter to see from what they sprang.

Made with fine attention to detail and a sharp, if depressing, sense of place, it is a movie that deserves to be seen. It will not be a "rewarding experience" in the conventional sense, rather, a reminder of a mind-set that shows little sign of diminishing.

....

One 'Barbarian' that's good to see
"The Barbarian Invasions"
March 25, 2004

How refreshing it is, amid all the cinematic detritus floating about, to bump into a movie that is at once intelligent, literate, funny and touching. That "The Barbarian Invasions" achieves this with seeming effortlessness, never seeming to force matters along, makes it stand out like a raft on an empty sea.

It's something to cling to.

French-Canadian director Denys Arcand's follow-up to his 1986 comedy-drama "The Decline of the American Empire" is not a flawless film, but it offers a wealth of themes, excellent ensemble acting and an intensely human panorama.

That, for all its eloquence, the denouement may strike some as rather too perfect, too gauzy, should not inhibit the savoring of its pleasures. For they are many.

Arcand, who also wrote the screenplay, reintroduces us to the principal characters of "Decline," 15 years on. Rémy (Rémy Girard), now in his early 50s and divorced, has had to relinquish his post as a history professor due to illness. We see him first in the hospital.

Dying of inoperable cancer, he is in considerable pain, frightened and angry. His exwife, Louise (Dorothée Berryman), entreats Rémy's estranged son Sébastien (Stéphane Rousseau), an investment banker living in London, to come home to Montreal and be by his father's side.

Sébastien reluctantly flies home, accompanied by his fiancée, but it is for his mother that he has ventured back, still embittered over his lusty father's philandering and the impact it had on his family. Arriving, the son confronts a chaotic scene straight from Paddy Chayefsky's "The Hospital" (1971). It is a place ruled by wretched overcrowding and stifling bureaucracy, all but immobilized by unions and collective exhaustion.

A private room for his suffering father? Out of the question. Ah, but Sébastien knows quite well that money greases the gears, frees the stalled mechanisms. And he uses the lubricant freely, even heeding his mother's plea to usher Rémy's far-flung friends and lovers to his bed. More, he makes a pact with the young daughter (Marie-Josee Croze) of one of his dad's former dalliances to help ease Rémy's suffering. The girl in question, a junkie, brings the father a steady supply of heroin, as the cops and nurses (the only ones whose palms are not lined) look the other way.

In time, the son takes the father and his coterie to a lakeside home for a final few pastoral days. It will be a very different end for Rémy than the one promised in the hospital, complete with rapprochement and gentle euthanasia. Of course, Arcand, while indicting aspects of the Canadian health system, neglects to mention that such niceties are available only to the well-to-do. Not everyone has a wealthy son with a fluid grasp of power.

Still, it is by the lake that we are treated to some of Arcand's best writing, with witty comment on the alternately amused and rueful reflections of aging baby boomers. This, and the unspoken longings of a desperate young woman who, against the odds, is finding purpose after years of drugged stupor.

Though beautifully shot by cinematographer Guy DuFaux, "The Barbarian Invasions" is a movie suffused not by images but by conversation: caustic, vibrant, outrageous, tender. And one could not ask for an abler cast. Girard and Croze are especially fine, though Rousseau, who bears a striking resemblance to American character actor Edward James Olmos, finds ways to make a somewhat stolid character breathe.

The title of the picture refers to invasions of many kinds and on many levels: the literal invasions of history, the sometimes troublesome inflow of immigrants into what were once relatively homogenous cultures, the invasions of other religions into Catholic Quebec, the introduction of alien ideas and mores, the disruption of harmony by adultery, the intrusion of the past into the present, the invasion (disabling or balming) of drugs in the body, the encroachments of disease, and the final invasion, death.

Arcand, you may recall, directed Charleston's own Thomas Gibson in the 1993 drama "Love and Human Remains," from Brad Fraser's adaptation of his own play. The director's new film has some of the same biting humor, as well as some of its sentimentality. Yet it is sentiment that is earned.

A dying man taking stock of his life is nothing new. And neither, for all its virtues, is "The Barbarian Invasions." But the manner and breadth of the telling could scarcely be more accomplished.

....

This Brazilian film is God, Forsaken
"City of God"
April 3, 2003

It is a bit early in the year to refer to a movie as the most disturbing film of 2003. Though it is hard to imagine another picture that will be as unrelievedly grim as Brazilian director Fernando Meirelles' harsh, utterly compelling "City of God."

As gruesome a picture as you are likely to see, all the more so because so many of its subjects are children, this meld of documentary realism and highly cinematic storytelling gets right at the roots of gang culture, casual brutality and the quest to survive in a way not seen since 1993's "Menace II Society."

Tough stuff to sit through at times, and the temptation to avert one's eyes is considerable, but it's the sort of film best seen squarely in the face.

"City of God" is set in the dusty ochre twilight of the slums of Rio de Janeiro, a green-free zone worlds apart from the exotic picture postcards of Ipanema.

It is where Meirelles shot the picture two years ago, and the film's emotionally charged subject matter has become a lightning rod for cultural and political opinion in Brazil, reportedly having been watched by more people in that country than any other film in 30 years.

One suspects this has almost as much to do with the sheer momentum of the thing, its stark intimacy, elliptical narrative and Meirelles' flashy (if not always purposeful) camera tricks, as with its anguished outcry.

He uses the camera in the manner of a Tom Tykwer ("Run Lola Run"), with a flair for depicting gunplay that also suggests Quentin Tarantino. Only there's nothing of Tarantino's playfulness about his lensing.

Meirelles employed unknown actors and denizens of the street for his cast.

How appropriate (and how inescapable) that he should have cast this social indictment in such a way, affording it a vividness and feel of authenticity that it otherwise might not have possessed.

With Lund's assistance, the filmmakers set up an "acting school" in the city, neglecting to tell the residents that they were auditioning for a movie.

"City of God" is drawn from Paulo Lins' best-selling 1997 novel, a massive book of 550 pages and almost 300 characters that related three decades in the history of the barrio.

The author's title derived from an immense housing project erected in Rio in the 1960s now inhabited by some 120,000 people.

Lins, who grew up there, knew the real-life characters thinly disguised in the book and film, not least the marauding drug gangs - manned largely by pistol-brandishing teens - whose reigns of terror are at the core of the movie.

Meirelles distills the story to a single generation and about 10 essential characters, chief among them a would-be photographer named Rocket, who narrates; Knockout Ned, a decent man driven to revenge; a homicidal drug lord-in-the-making called Li'l Dice (later Li'l Ze); and the latter's sidekick, Benny, who's looking for a way out of the killing fields.

But within the bleak inevitability of this universe, few will make it to adulthood.

Most will be slaughtered in pitched battles or blithely swept aside for the most trivial of "affronts," even as some in the police take their cut of drug money and look the other way.

These cops believe private vendettas and mutual annihilation by the gangs and their hangers-on will solve the problem quite neatly, except that the poverty, dehumanization and violence continue to perpetuate themselves across the generations.

This is the first feature for Meirelles, whose background is in television, commercials and, most tellingly, documentaries. While the book and his film are based on a true story, one never is certain where actual events end and embroidery begins, for there are sequences that feel somewhat over the top in terms of human carnage, however astonishingly staged and shot they may be.

But neither does Meirelles let victim or victimizer off the hook. They share complicity in their fates. They have choices. The problem is that many are far too young and impressionable to make those choices.

So much has "City of God" been analyzed and discussed, down to the slightest tilt of the camera, that it even has been given credit in some quarters for inducing Brazil's new president, Luiz Inacio Lula da Silva, to change his policy on public security.

Would that all topical pictures - those of merit, that is - could wield such power. Meirelles and Lund describe the picture as a "wake-up call for Brazilians" loathe to confront the drug crisis. Such movies may leave them little choice.

Again, it's premature to call this the most unsettling movie of the year.

It may not be too soon to call it the best.

....

Almodovar's latest leaves lingering impressions
"Talk to Her"
February 20, 2003

Pedro Almodovar reminds you of no one but himself. So distinctive is the Spanish filmmaker's work that it could not have been done by anyone else. There are few obvious influences or traditions from which his movies emerge, other than that of the more liberated Spanish cinema he helped establish.

His latest, "Talk to Her," is vintage Almodovar: audacious, layered, playful and somber and unconcerned with conventional narrative. It's about life, love, death - the whole thing. But chiefly it asks questions: What is the nature of life? How many ways are there to define what love is? When is an apparent act of perversity also an act of devotion?

Almodovar's wicked sense of humor runs from mordant to racy and back in this touching tragicomedy, whose binding thread is the freeing and constricting powers of need. He has rendered his most mature movie to date.

Once again, his characters (and their relationships) flirt with a sublimely sweet, sublimely dreadful doom. But the director limits his customary slapstick and melodramatic trappings for this story about two comatose women and the men who adore them.

And it is the men who drive the tale. Almodovar's knack for understanding women and working with actresses does not mean his male characters are superfluous. Certainly not in "Live Flesh" and "Law of Desire," earlier films in which men defined the action.

"Talk to Her" pivots on Benigno (Javier Camara), a male nurse who tends to the needs of his unconscious patient, Alicia (Leonor Watling), as one might to a lover. For four years he has talked to her, constantly, softly, his voice and his movements acting as one deliberate, delicate mechanism in the daily routine of her therapy. During this time, he also has cared for his aging mother. These are the lone engagements of a placidly uneventful life, apart from trips to the theater or cinema. His limitations aside, Benigno is a creature of compassion and generosity, though his motivations are at first murky.

Enter a middle-aged writer named Marco (Dario Grandinetti), who keeps silent vigil over the recently institutionalized Lydia (Rosario Flores). She also is deeply embedded in a coma, with scant chance of recovery. These immobilized women both were intensely, expressively physical in life - Alicia as a dancer and Lydia as one of a very few female bullfighters. Soon, the two men are drawn into the each other's sphere, and a friendship begun.

Benigno, we gradually learn, is more than a little obsessive. His actual connection to Alicia is nil, though they had had a casual encounter before her accident. But now, in unconsciousness, she "belongs" to him, and Almodovar unfolds what is at once a tender love story and an (initially) disturbing study of benign violation. Meanwhile, Marco has befriended Benigno, and his loyalty - the linchpin of the story - is soon to be tested by an extraordinary occurrence.

In the end, Almodovar insists that we not only harbor sympathy for a man (Benigno) whose behavior is unpardonable despite its fortuitous outcome, but empathy as well. The director suggests that, like Benigno, we all dwell in prisons of a kind. And it is loyalty that makes them bearable.

The razor-edged frenzy and cruelty of Almodovar's early plots, which were equally jolting and amusing, are absent from this telling. However bizarre, the elements of "Talk to Her" are introduced unhurriedly, and with a kid glove rather than a mailed fist.

Almodovar still can unnerve you, but his shocks now are more measured. As in the silent film ("Shrinking Lover") sequence that seems a diversion from the main action yet proves indispensable to the story. The sequence is, in fact, a front for what's really going on in Alicia's hospital room.

It's Almodovar at the peak of his powers: mysteries and secrets, abandonment and attachment, love and malice, tone upon tone and a rich color palette. Few filmmakers lead us into the lives of intimate strangers quite so provocatively or so deftly, or leave us with so many lingering impressions.

....

'Sex and Lucia' spiced with passion, pain
"Sex and Lucia"
October 24, 2002

Intentionally -- sometimes poetically -- obscure, Spanish writer-director Julio Medem's "Sex and Lucia" is one of the most sensual cinematic puzzles to come along in some time, though its frank sexual content skirts the edge of graphic.

A turnoff to some, an inducement to others. But to view this reality-subverting love story solely in such a light would be to miss Medem's considerable artistry.

His color palette alone is a herald of things to come: cool, subdued hues bathed in sun and moonlight, followed by richer tones, casting images to hypnotic effect.

Wanting to make a more hopeful movie about relationships after his doleful "Lovers of the Artic Circle," Medem has given us a date movie to the 10th power, almost guaranteed to push your buttons (and cross-wire your circuits) even as it confounds with convoluted plot threads.

The film dances around Lucia (Paz Vega), a young waitress in Madrid who seeks refuge on a (curiously) isolated Mediterranean island after the death of her boyfriend, Lorenzo (Tristan Ulloa), a novelist and short-story writer.

Their bond already had begun to unravel before the accident, and now as Lucia absorbs the crystalline skies, brilliant sun and pale blue water, she explores the darker corners of their relationship. It is like finding a manuscript that had been locked away, filled with forbidden passages, that only now can be read and understood.

Not that Medem, or the author that is his stand-in, makes this easy.

On the surface, "Sex and Lucia" is food and sex, life's twin imperatives, spiced with passion and pain.

In varying degrees, it also is concerned with the wellsprings of art, the madness of creation, the elusiveness of love and the basic connections that exist even among strangers.

All very European in sensibility, a shade pretentious and pointedly erotic. Like Lorenzo's story, Medem's film also has a hole it can escape through: audience confusion.

A hit in Spain and on the festival circuit, "Sex and Lucia" betrays some of the hallmarks of the contrived hedonistic romp - sprinklings of irony and misdirection that don't quite divert us from the liberal swaths of skin on display.

Think "Summer Lovers" with a brain and more style. But there are features to commend it.

Vega, who won a Goya Award for her portrait, is as gorgeous as the film, but mysterious as well, with twice the screen presence of a Penelope Cruz.

There are holocausts in those eyes. Ulloa, meanwhile, proves to be a more than adequate sparring partner for her, effortlessly communicating intensity, elation and despondency. It is his narrative, after all, on which the film pivots.

There are solid supporting performances from Najwa Nimri, Daniel Freire and Elena Anaya and a moody score by Alberto Iglesias.

But what will leave the most lasting impression, apart from Vega and the film's dizzying structure, is its photography. More than prettified porn, there are waves of imagery, ethereal and voluptuous that make "Sex and Lucia" a memorable visceral experience.

....

This 'Monsoon' is worth the wait
"Monsoon Wedding"
April 4, 2002

Western pieties about "family values" ring somewhat hollow compared to the reality of the East Indian family depicted in Mira Nair's "Monsoon Wedding."

A film dedicated to her own family, this fine comedy-drama augments the filmmaker's trademark sensuality with a spirited look at the changing face of contemporary Indian life and sexual mores.

It is not, however, a view that Indian traditionalists appear to endorse. As with Nair's previous picture, the erotic feminist fable "Kama Sutra," many in the indigenous motion picture community denounced its modern attitudes while declining to submit it for Best Foreign Language Film consideration. What they failed to discern was the movie's thoughtfully integrated celebration of the ties that bind, the beauties of ritual, and the strength of parental devotion.

Set in New Dehli, "Monsoon" is by far the better movie, and its gently but persuasively argued feminist concerns aren't the least bit incompatible with the fact that the film's most sympathetic character is a man: a loving father compelled to make a painful but courageous gesture to protect his loved ones.

While Lalit Verma (Naseeruddin Shah) is the kind dad we'd all like to have, his character is no mere exercise in wishful thinking. He's a flesh-and-blood fellow with no shortage of foibles.

A classic, harried father of the bride, Verma and his wife Pimmi (Lillete Dubey) have ridden the crests and troughs of their own marriage long enough to have the requisite insight into what awaits their daughter, Aditi (Vasundhara Das). Both feel keenly the bittersweet joy of their eldest child preparing to leave the nest.

"Sometimes when I look at them I feel a love I can almost not bear," Verma tells his wife one evening, as they watch their children sleeping. "When did they grow up so quickly? When did we get so old? If only their lives are happy. For them I am willing to take every trouble, every sorrow in the world."

What neither they nor Aditi's Houston-based husband-to-be Hemant Rai (Parvin Dabas) realize is that Aditi's pre-wedding anxieties aren't simply a case of cold feet; she still hasn't gotten over a love affair with her former boss.

Meanwhile, the bride's unmarried cousin Ria (Shefali Shetty) is emboldened by Aditi's apprehension to be more assertive within the family, ultimately revealing a secret that shocks the family to its core, imperils a long-standing relationship with the family's chief benefactor, and forces Verma's hand on the day of the wedding.

Other subplots involve a budding romance between the excitable wedding caterer P.K. Dube (Vijay Raaz), who is smitten by the Verma family's shy young maid, Alice (Tilotama Shome), and an overtly sexual flirtation between randy teen-ager Ayesha (Neha Dubey) and a college student (Randeep Hooda) who has returned home after years away in Australia.

Although the various story strands may strike one as rather too neatly resolved, it still has the warp and woof of believability, well-acted by all concerned, but especially by Shah. And the joyous, richly realized wedding festivities amid a drenching, cleansing monsoon are not to be missed.

Nair's people come from far and wide, and they are as likely to speak English as Hindi - or, alternately, that curious amalgam called Hinglish. And she has assembled a fine cast of Indian stage and film actors who nimbly sidestep any hint of the maudlin or contrived.

It was a long time between films for the talented Nair, who lives with her family in South Africa. After back-to-back hits with "her debut feature "Salaam Bombay" (1988) and "Mississippi Masala" (1992) it took her a while to regain her direction after the failure of "The Perez Family" (1995) and the blatant tampering by other hands with the final cut of "Kama Sutra."

"Monsoon Wedding," effervescent and humane, is more than worth the wait.

....

Jeunet's feel good French style
"Amelie"
November 22, 2001

"Amelie" is a breath, no, a gust, of fresh air. Frothy, sweet and naughty generally are not words applied to the films of Jean-Pierre Jeunet, whose cannibal comedy, "Delicatessen" (1991), and "Brazil"-ish fantasy, "The City of Lost Children" (1995), tapped into a dark sensibility.

Inventive production design (brilliantly executed) and a pervasive mood are the attributes one most often associates with the director. That, and a genuine love of his craft.

"Amelie" has these qualities, and then some. Technically accomplished, it also is frisky and exuberant, mischievous and poignant. And often quite funny.

This neo-fairy tale has become the French filmmaker's *billet doux* to a troubled time, a charming bit of escapism from the streets of Paris that took Europe by storm and now is capturing hearts in the States.

It's easy to see why. If the film doesn't quite live up to all the attendant hype, which would have us believe Jeunet has reinvented the film medium, that doesn't mean "Amelie" and its elfin star, Audrey Tautou aren't a beguiling whiff of jasmine in a fallow (cinematic) field.

While the 23-year-old Tautou suggests a young Audrey Hepburn or Leslie Caron, there's more of the pixie and less of the ingénue in the character that's made her a sensation. Looking like Juliette Binoche's wide-eyed kid sister, Tautou's Amelie is a shy waitress who lives with her remote (if not unkind) widowed physician father in a Montmartre flat. Her world extending little beyond the cafe where she works, the Metro, a neighborhood produce stand and her apartment, Amelie knows little of human interaction.

Fate takes a hand in transforming her life when Amelie discovers a boy's tin box of mementos secreted behind her kitchen wall. It is a prize she feels she must return to its owner, a former tenant now in middle age, if only she can find him.

She succeeds, anonymously. Suddenly imbued with compassion for the souls around her and a desire to do good, Amelie imagines herself to be "a godmother of outcasts, the Madonna of the unloved." The not-so-random acts of kindness that follow are mixed with impishly diabolical swipes at a cruel grocer.

But it is Amelie's shut-in neighbor, Dufayel (delightfully played by Serge Merlin), an old man fragile of bone but strong of spirit, who convinces her to look inward, fix her own life, and not demure from a chance at love.

The man in question, one Nino Quicampoix, works in a porn store and collects photo fragments from beneath snapshot kiosks. Not exactly the sort of lover a young woman dreams of, but in this universe Nino (Mathieu Kassovitz) is a playful lad with a tender heart.

Pardon us while we climb down from the cloud (in search of a well-traveled gnome).

Shorn of Tautou's presence and performance, "Amelie" would be a shell of the film it is. Hers is more than just a waifish appeal. The camera caresses this latest *comedienne Francaise* with loving fascination; it cannot take its eye off her big brown eyes. And neither can we. Giddy or sad, angry or triumphant, smitten or perplexed, Tautou hits all the right notes. But it's more a matter of charisma than "range."

"Amelie" makes use of some of film's new capabilities with considerable flair. Jeunet's imagery, coupled with flash-pans, computer-generated effects, and other tricks of the trade (shades of Tom Tykwer) are an effective complement to the amusingly droll narration of the early part of the film, which serves to establish lines of "plot." The movie also is disarmingly self-aware, a very modern trait.

Jeunet infuses the picture with the rich, warm color palette beloved of Miramax releases. But he pays fealty to the past as well. Elements of the movie's structure and photographic composition are reminiscent of the silents. The close-up is king. Or in this case, princess. All of Jeunet and co-writer Guillaume Laurant's story threads are neatly knotted in the end, along with the moral that our actions influence our destinies in strange and sundry ways.

One can overlook one or two draggy spots in the middle as Jeunet tries to ride a wisp of whimsy alone. The movie may be a little too pleased with itself at times, but the enthusiasm of the players and the vitality of the filmmaking is infectious.

The humor is both innocent and mordant; the characters at once delicate and indomitable. For many, it will be a film to prize, like a small tin box from childhood.

....

Mexican movie in running for Best Foreign Language Film Oscar
"Amores Perros"
May 10, 2001

One of the most accomplished movies to emerge from Mexico in some time, the Oscar-nominated "Amores Perros" employs the now familiar technique of elliptical structure with interlocking or parallel storylines – an approach revived by Quentin Tarantino.

But this gritty, sometimes shocking film from director Alejandro Gonzalez Inarritu, which stars in the middle and moves fore and aft in time, is more than a derivative bow to one of North America's cinematic bad boys.

While its propulsive soundtrack and fractured visual style suggest "Pulp Fiction," this one is not enthralled with gallows humor or the signposts of pop culture. It has more serious subjects in mind – like the horrors that spring from the gnarled garden of poverty – and the compassion that can mitigate its effects.

The picture opens in Mexico City, albeit like an American action movie – with a car chase and a crash. A bloodied blonde model is wedged inside her crumpled auto, courtesy of two men fleeing for their lives from a band of fellow thugs. In their car is a big black Rottweiler, bleeding from a bullet wound.

This moment of jarring violence swerves into the story's second link, when the dig is rescued by a scruffy, somewhat mysterious homeless man. From that point on, these lives are joined, as the narrative goes from the mean streets and back alleys to opulent high-rise apartments.

"Amores Perros" uses dogs as both characters in and of themselves, and as symbols for human emotions. Some audiences, however, will have a difficult time with the scenes depicting gambling on organized dog fights. It helps to know that these brutally convincing sequences are, for all their gore, the products of crafty filmmaking rather than actual fights.

The first Mexican movie to be in the running for the Best Foreign Language film Oscar in almost 30 years, Inarritu's unexpectedly polished debut feature - which required three years and 36 screenplay drafts - was the toast of the festival circuit.

It has also become an emblem of Mexico's national pride. Inarritu has succeeded in his goal of reminding the country's northern neighbors that his is a diverse and complex culture. He shows that culture shorn of the customary stereotypes and limitations.

Guillermo Arriaga's script gives us a triplicate of tightly would love stories, which Inarritu brings to life in a style that is at once full-throttle (most of the time, anyway) and methodical. Skilled in conveying the urban landscape and the civil war that marks it, Rodrigo Prieto's camera misses little.

Fine performances abound, with particularly string work from Emilio Echevarria, Gael Garcia Bernal, Jorge Salinas, Goya Toledo and Vanessa Bauche. Their characters are wholly alive.

Blending beauty and violence, "Amores Perros" disturbing but hopeful take on love's labor lost has an almost biblical resonance. There is a moment of reckoning in every life, it tells us, yet also the possibility of redemption.

....

Rohmer slowly weaves this 'Autumn Tale'

"Autumn Tale"
October 7, 1999

Most directors adhere to the cardinal rule of cinema, which is to show, not tell; to weave their stories and reveal character through behavior and event rather than extended discourse.

French filmmaker Eric Rohmer, a robust 79 and in the full flower of his powers, could not disagree more. His films are dominated by dialogue, as perceptive as it is true to life. And if there has been a wiser, more revealing picture this year than his "Autumn Tale," we haven't seen it.

The gentle symbolism of harvest time in the vineyards, when the grapes, like people, have matured into full richness and are pregnant with juice, provides a wholly appropriate theme to this completion of the writer-director's "Tales of the Four Seasons" quartet.

Though admittedly "talky" and slow-paced for American audiences, who are inclined to be impatient, "Tale" is a seductively naturalistic exploration of love, the illusion of self-sufficiency, the tension between desire and need, and that subtle minuet of first encounters between the sexes.

Rohmer, together with Godard, Truffaut and Chabrol, helped define the New Wave which transformed French film beginning in the late 1950s. Each of his movies is marked by meticulously composed, character-driven plots. His people are highly expressive and immersed in their own thoughts, but, as is the case in "Tale," too often combine the best of intentions with flawed judgment.

Magali (Beatrice Romand) is a 40-ish widow and winemaker who tends her modest vineyards in the Cote du Rhone region of southern France. Isabelle (Marie Riviere), a book store owner and her confidante, sees through her friend's placid veneer to the yearning beneath. While the happily married Isabelle prepares for her daughter's wedding, Magali's relationships with her children are less sanguine.

Magali buries her loneliness by expending all of her energies in the winery, but Isabelle is determined to help her meet someone worthy. That someone turns out to be Gerard (Alain Libolt), a gentleman of substance whom Isabelle steers her way. Just as eager to help is Rosine (Alexia Portal), a student who is dating Magali's rather less developed son but is far fonder of the boy's mother. Rosine wants Magali to meet her former teacher and lover, Etienne (Didier Sandre), who, despite a penchant for students and an undiminished yen for Rosine, agrees.

Even as they act on Magali's behalf, Isabelle and Rosine do not recognize (at first, anyway) that there are subconscious agendas at work. The inevitable mess ensues.

The story is at once less involved than it sounds and far more complex. Rohmer's understanding of the dynamics between men and women is equaled by his ability to decipher relations between women. But here he adds a new layer.

Although in the past the director's work has focused on the male fascination with younger women, his recent pictures regard the world more from a female perspective. In "Autumn Tale," it's women "of a certain age."

The Rhone Valley is a perfect backdrop, alive with the promise of new and succulent fruit. The performers seem not to be acting at all, so integrated are the characters in their relationships and surroundings. Romand, who appeared in Rohmer's "Claire's Knee" almost 30 years ago, and Libolt are standouts.

This capstone of a film is suffused with generosity of spirit. It may belabor the obvious at times, and its rhythms may slip into sleepiness, but the rewards of "Autumn's Tale" are many and wholly adult. Savor them.

....

Unraveling marriage rings true in film
"The Separation"
January 17, 1999

A father videotapes his 16-month-old son as he sleeps, the child oblivious to his surroundings.

Much the same can be said of Pierre (Daniel Auteuil), the doting parent, who does not see - or refuses to acknowledge - the crisis in his relationship with the boy's mother, Anne (Isabelle Huppert).

Even when he is made to understand the source of her distress, opportunities to resolve differences and repair the damage are allowed to slip away - hurt, pride and an inability to connect subverting the love they still feel.

Director Christian Vincent's achingly true-to-life "The Separation" is French moviemaking at its best. While told largely from the man's point of view, there is admirable balance. Anyone who has lived through the slow disintegration of a marriage or other long-term relationship will identify with the painful progress of their breakup - including that fleeting interlude after the air is finally cleared, the constant bickering stops and intimacy, however briefly, is restored.

Vincent co-wrote the script with writer-actor Dan Franck, on whose justly acclaimed 1991 novel the film is based. It's familiar territory, yes, but handled so expertly and with such depth of emotion and convincing detail that it feels as if one is eavesdropping on a private conversation.

As the film opens, there is a telling moment when Anne pulls her hand away from Pierre's while they sit in a movie theater. She has all but given up trying to get Pierre to talk, really talk, and is growing increasingly sullen. For his part, Pierre knows something is wrong yet can't bring himself to deal with the problem; he's not even sure what it is.

Then comes the bombshell. Anne announces she has fallen in love with another man, someone who does what she says Pierre has ceased to do: "He listens to me. He pays attention to me."

A timeless feminine lament, yet matters are not quite so simple. Moreover, Anne wants her new lover and her life with Pierre - not merely for the sake of their son. She tells him she still loves him and does not want to part. They try it for a time, but Pierre's pain eventually becomes too much. His insecurities and frustration, plus Anne's fits of casual cruelty, propel them to harsh words and domestic violence.

One sympathizes with Pierre, and with Anne, but we see all too readily their failures

- and perhaps our own. Huppert and Auteuil, two shining lights of the French cinema paired here for the first time, appear to have been working together for years. So spontaneous is the acting that they scarcely seem to have a script at all. Few recent films, none of them American, have achieved such naturalism. The collapse of communication, blow-to-the-gut shock, numbing sense of helplessness and grieving for what might have been are conveyed with perfect pitch.

Knowing and nuanced in its story-telling, Vincent's direction is simultaneously detached in tone and compassionate in intent. No artificial reconciliations, no happy endings, no pat summations. This is a film that understands the crucible of love. See it. The relationship it saves could be yours.

....

'Ma Vie en Rose' funny, surprisingly touching film
"Ma Vie En Rose"
April 16, 1998

The setting of "Ma Vie en Rose" ("My Life in Pink"), a wise and affecting first feature from Belgian director Alain Berliner, is a suburban Brussels neighborhood of quiet streets, manicured lawns and hissing sprinklers indistinguishable from its North American counterparts.

The pleasures and problems of middle-class life also are identical, not least the complexity of parenting - and the precariousness of neighborly relations - which lie under the surface.

"Ma Vie En Rose" centers on 7-year-old Ludovic Fabre (Georges du Fresne), a child of saucer-sized brown eyes and longish hair, safe in the bosom of loving parents and three older siblings.

There's just one small complication for Ludo: he's a boy who is convinced he's a girl. And he is confident that God's little mistake - an accidentally discarded X chromosome - eventually will be righted.

Vaguely androgynous, Ludo revels in the feminine, whether being enveloped in the arms of his mother (Michele Laroque) and grandmother (Helene Vincent), wearing a dress and makeup, playing with dolls or surrounding himself with other little-girl accoutrements.

What is at first dismissed as a passing fancy begins to turn serious as Ludo's compunctions go out of control, firing the fear (and enmity) of neighbors, imperiling his father's job and nearly driving his mother out of her mind. Neither his parents, bullying by other boys, or professional counseling can crack the child's resolve, or dissuade him from the idea of one day marrying a sympathetic classmate named Jerome (Julien Riviere). Although he tries dutifully, if reluctantly, to play sports and do other stereotypically male pursuits, his heart isn't in it.

Ultimately the family is ostracized, the father (Jean-Philippe Ecoffey) does lose his job and the Fabres are forced to move to another town. Here, and this really is clever on the writer's part, the first playmate Ludo meets is a girl who prefers the trappings of boyhood. The resolution of this story, however, is anything but pat.

Instead of being fodder for broad comedy, excessive sentiment or some overwrought polemic, Berliner and co-screenwriter Chris vander Stappen treat the subjects of sexual identity and gender confusion in a way that is at once funny, touching and surprisingly revealing.

While the movie's principal messages - the dauntlessness of innocence, the virtue of acceptance - are rather trite, the filmmakers don't leave it at that.

The script recognizes that the child's universe is a realm of dreams, of boundless possibilities where nothing is carved in stone. So utterly unlike the adult world of codified social norms, appearances for their own sake, and certitude over what is and isn't "normal."

Not that the movie harbors a conventional feminist perspective, either. It is entirely understanding of people's discomfiture. It does not take a knee-jerk, disparaging view of the predictable adult male response to Ludo's "threatening" behavior. And it is well aware of the dangers inherent in the development of a child such as Ludo.

Too, the writers make the vital strategic choice of telling the story from a boy's point of view; it is much more acceptable for a girl to be tomboyish, after all. The stakes are much higher, the consequences much more pronounced, for males, despite what we'd like to tell ourselves.

For the most part, the film handles these matters with disarming subtlety, save for some of its too-whimsical dream/fantasy sequences. It deals squarely with the pressures and conflicts parents would face in such a situation, while making pointed comments about the fragility (and hypocrisy) of "perfect" neighborhoods.

The performances are pitch-perfect, especially by Laroque and Ecoffey as the parents who vacillate between loving concern and near-violent anguish, and by Vincent, as the grandmother who gleaned her parental insight somewhat late. And how could you not be impressed by du Fresne in taking on such a role.

Most American films supposedly preoccupied with family concerns don't possess half the clarity of vision demonstrated by "Ma Vie En Rose" — inexplicably given an "R" rating — or half the humor.

....

Visually appealing, yet film is a bore
"The Pillow Book"
August 14, 1997

Skin, paper, celluloid — all surfaces for Peter Greenaway's vision, which largely is about surfaces.

The world's most relentlessly fetishistic filmmaker is at it again, elevating symbol over substance. With "The Pillow Book," the story of a calligrapher who transforms human bodies into tapestries, Greenaway neither shocks nor titillates. He merely bores.

Like a calligrapher, the director blends word and image, color and black and white, past and present, calm and chaos. To this technique he adds multiple representations, scenes within scenes, noir-ish studies in light and shadow, English narration mixed with French and English subtitles, and incessant dissolves — a cinematic navel gazer's box of tricks.

Original, after a fashion, but to what end?

Daring in its own rather limited way, "The Pillow Book" is filled with exquisite images, painterly images. It is less a motion picture than an arresting progression of stills. The film understands that in Japanese writing, to pen a text is also to paint an image. Intriguing, yet after a time these increasingly intrusive visual conjurings do little to further the story, such as it is.

Set in Kyoto and Hong Kong, "The Pillow Book" explores the obsession of Nagiko (Vivian Wu), a contemporary Japanese woman whose life has been shaped by a desire to have her body adorned with calligraphy. As a child, her father (Ken Ogata) would paint characters upon her face and neck in a ritualistic homage, not only to tradition, but in honor of Sei Shonagon, a female courtier of the Imperial house who lived 1,000 years earlier. It was the latter's vivid diary, or pillow book, that inspires Nagiko to produce her own - with her skin as the paper.

As Nagiko becomes a woman, her desire is so compelling that she isn't sure whether she chooses her lovers because they are good lovers, or good calligraphers. With a minimum of emotional involvement, she exchanges sex for calligraphy, until she meets Jerome (Ewan McGregor), an English translator in Hong Kong who convinces the now established high fashion model that she can cease being the paper and become the pen.

Jerome suggests that Nagiko, who aspires to be a poet, write upon his body, which he will promptly present to a publisher (Yoshi Oida) in a genuine attempt to help. Seeing him first as a tool, Nagiko agrees, but the two soon fall in love. But Jerome and the publisher also are lovers, and he betrays Nagiko by allowing his head-to-toe script to be transcribed.

Desperate to reconcile, Jerome tries to fake his own suicide, but dies from a drug overdose. The heartbroken Nagiko paints a lavish love poem on his body just before the burial. In a roaringly melodramatic twist, the publisher has Jerome's body exhumed and the skin surgically removed from the corpse. This bizarre parchment is lovingly "cured," drawn upon and bound.

Using the bodies of other young men to continue her narrative, Nagiko traps the publisher into admitting guilt and planning his own execution. Jerome is avenged. And so is her family, for it was the same homosexual publisher, years before, who had sexually blackmailed her father. A fitting (if creepy) symmetry, one supposes.

For all Greenaway's determination to extend the boundaries of the medium, "The Pillow Book" succumbs to its own illegible scrawl, metaphorically speaking. In the end, the film is a minor revenge fantasy/love story with a hollow core, a film whose actors are reduced to inert canvases. The tale's much-touted eroticism, preoccupied as it is with frontal nudity and the intoxicating scents of paper and skin, eventually becomes labored.

Glacially paced, with a faux-Oriental sensibility, "The Pillow Book" is hands down the most excruciatingly pretentious movie of the year.

There's none of the scathing social commentary of "The Cook, the Thief, His Wife and Her Lover" (1989), though it shares that picture's devotion to kinky sexuality. What's really perverse about "The Pillow Book," however, is Greenaway's characteristic insistence on being obscure, as if the fewer people who understand what he's doing the more rarefied and sophisticated it is. What rubbish.

In the Everything But the Kitchen Sink school of filmmaking, don't expect anything so quaint as a discernible point.

It's hard to imagine a more self-consciously "important" director than Greenaway, a man who wears his iconoclasm on his sleeve, dripping contempt for all those hapless colleagues locked into conventional modes of expression. Greenaway's films, always an acquired taste, seem to be mostly about Greenaway: "LOOK at me!" they say. Or, rather, bellow.

And the noise is getting tiresome.

....

'Red' full of subtle shadings
"Red"
February 16, 1995

The closing act of writer-director Krzysztof Kieslowski's Three Colors trilogy is a melancholy, somewhat enigmatic film which deals with the profound fragility of human experience and the restorative power of human contact.

It is also a fable of chance encounters, how they may represent more than fleeting exchanges and become the blood and sinew of our lives.

Set in Geneva, "Red" concerns the complex relationship between a young Swiss student and part-time model, Valentine (Irene Jacob), and a retired judge (Jean-Louis Trintignant) who has exiled himself from his fellows - notwithstanding a bent for electronic voyeurism.

Valentine meets this dispirited, isolated man after accidentally hitting his dog with her car. At first, she is shocked to discover him eavesdropping on his neighbors' phone calls. But she also finds herself drawn to the elemental sadness in him. Repulsion turns to affection.

Meanwhile, we are provided glimpses of a parallel story, that of Auguste (Jean-Pierre Lorit), a young judge soon to preside over his first case. There are distinct convergences in the lives of the two men, but whereas the older jurist views deciding what is true as an act of purest vanity, the only doubt plaguing Auguste is the suspicion that his lover has betrayed him.

Like its predecessors, "Blue" (Liberty) and "White" (Equality), there's an obscure quality to "Red" (Fraternity), combined with a delicacy of character and observation that makes the smallest gesture or inexplicable event seem pregnant with meaning.

The two previous films were possessed of playfulness and an overtly cinematic approach. "Red" is richer, less ethereal and ironic. This final film - Kieslowski insists that he plans to retire, even at the apex of his powers - is a culmination of a grandly engaging cycle on the unpredictability of fate. In the end, Kieslowski underscores the theme by mingling the destinies of several of the principal characters of all three movies, who take the same ferry crossing the English channel.

While filmgoers would benefit from having seen the first two films, "Red" presents a deeply affecting story that stands on its own.

As a visual and philosophical motif, Kieslowski's use of the hues of the French flag (blue, white, red) is at once simple and inspired. A powerful symbol, red (seen everywhere in the movie) is the color of blood, and of passion. But passion may be expressed in manifest ways. Kieslowski's pensive, low-key delivery serves only to strengthen the inexorable current of feeling that pervades the picture. Its emotional coloration never fades.

Jacob ("The Two Lives of Veronique") is radiant, haunting. Trintignant is masterful. Both performances pulse with subtlety and nuance, in a story that shares these features.

It is unfortunate that "Red" has been disqualified for Oscar consideration as the official Swiss entry in the Best Foreign Film category. But it hardly diminishes the acuity of the director's vision, or our appreciation for him showing us how to perceive the invisible.

....

'Postman' delivers humor, wisdom
"Il Postino" ("The Postman")
July 20, 1995

Poetry is not a thing; it is a way.

This creed is at the very core of "The Postman," a wise, funny, quietly uplifting film about the transforming power of verse.

Like a poem, the success of a film is determined not by how much the creative talent felt in producing the work, but by how much the viewer feels in experiencing it.

By that measure, this sublimely understated picture from British director Michael Radford ("White Mischief") is a considerable achievement. And, wonder of wonders, it just may send you in search of a good book.

Loosely based on a true story, "The Postman" records a brief interlude in the life of the Chilean poet and political activist Pablo Neruda, here played by that masterful French character actor Philippe Noiret. Neruda was forced into exile from his native land in the early 1950s, finding asylum in a small, sparsely populated island off the coast of Naples.

Here, on a bluff above a fishing village, Neruda establishes the beginnings of an unusual friendship with a postman, Mario Ruoppolo, whose only job is to bring the poet his mail.

As embodied by the late Massimo Troisi, one of Italy's most beloved comic actors, Mario hides the soul of a writer behind the appearance and demeanor of a peasant. Acutely shy, this man of dark, sad sack eyes, mumbling intonations, and halting manner enlists Neruda's aid in helping him woo the voluptuous Beatrice (Maria Grazia Cucinotta).

Neruda is taken with Mario's barely literate musings on his work, and soon grows intrigued with the postman's simple yet fresh way of seeing. The poet senses something in Mario struggling to emerge, and decides to help the process along. Mario may want the talisman of language only to gain an intimacy with women, yet Neruda shows him how to find his voice, personally and politically.

In doing so, Mario enters the larger world, albeit a world fraught with as much peril as delight.

If Radford, who co-wrote the screenplay, misses an opportunity for genuine originality (thanks to an overly sentimentalized conclusion), he has at the very least made a film for people who love language - and literature.

In its own gently seductive way, "The Postman" is an ode to life, and to passion, with technical virtues - Franco Di Giacomo's beautifully composed photography among them - that entice the eye as readily as the performances engage the heart.

The film is lent special poignancy by virtue of being Troisi's last appearance on screen. The actor, desperately in need of a heart transplant, risked his life to complete this labor of love, working an hour or two a day. He promptly died, at age 41, one day after his work on the film was finished. So devoted was Troisi that he asked Radford to utilize the actual suffering he was experiencing on film, particularly in closeups, where his gaunt visage and pained expressions reflect a world-weariness mitigated by sensitivity.

His passing was cause for nationwide mourning in Italy.

Troisi had become enamored of making the picture after reading the Chilean novel "Burning Patience" by Antonio Skarmeta, a tale of a postal worker's slow awakening to Neruda's poetry. Radford and his collaborators changed the setting to the isle of Capri, where Neruda had spent his exile.

This film is the capstone to one distinguished career, Troisi's, and evidence of the continued vigor of another. Where Troisi is the spiritual center of "The Postman," Noiret is its sage. Owner of the greatest face and some of the sharpest talent in the cinema, Noiret's Neruda is at once aloof and involved, intimate yet at an intellectual and artistic remove. It's a wonderful juggling act.

Praise also is due Cucinotta, a hybrid of Sophia Loren and Anna Maria Alberghetti, for her delectably earthy portrait of Beatrice, and for the fine comic timing of supporting players Linda Moretti and Anna Bonaiuto.

Few films have this kind of charm. Fewer still ask one to glimpse the world anew.

....

Oscar winner for Best Foreign Language Film entices
"Belle Epoque"
April 24, 1994

"Belle Epoque" works its magic like a long, lazy day in the country, gently but insistently pushing aside all worldly concerns and forcing the body to capitulate to its rhythms.

Surrender, abandon and the rigidity of institutions are the film's most prominent themes, though not the only ones. On one level a breezy sexual escapade, and on another a, ode to life and love unfettered by convention, Spanish writer-director Fernando Trueba's disarming folic impressed enough Academy Awards voters to win the Best Foreign Language Film Oscar last month.

And while it is certainly not the equal of its chief competitor, "Farewell My Concubine," the movie succeeds on all levels that the elaborate tease "Sirens" did not.

The only question is, "Who's seducing who here?"

"Belle Epoque" is set on 1931, and "Age of Beauty" between the collapse of the Spanish monarchy and the outbreak of the Spanish Civil War. But the title refers less to this brief interlude of freedom from the dogmas of church and state, when all things seemed possible, than to the amorous adventures of a young army deserter, Fernando (Jorge Sanz), who seeks sanctuary in the country home of a free-spirited painter (the wonderful Fernando Fernan Gomez).

Establishing himself as a cook and handyman, the handsome lad can't resist the allure of the artist's four beautiful daughters, who have come visiting from the city.

Each of the four owns a different – and very beguiling – disposition: the lush yet manipulative Rocio (Maribel Verdu), the aggressive, vaguely masculine Violeta (Ariadna Gil), the widowed Clara (Miriam Diaz-Aroca), and sprite-like ingénue Luz (Penelope Cruz). Each also has a differing motive for desiring the young soldier, and they are far from modest in expressing it.

In short order, he beds three of them, "saving" the fourth, as it were, for something more permanent.

Superficially, it's the old farmer's daughter gag, in quadruplicate, with a dash of "Tom

Jones" thrown in for spice. Only Sanz is a more diffident suitor than the ever-randy rogue played by Albert Finney.

Contrived? Of course. In the sense that "Tom Jones" was contrived. But the real inspiration for Trueba's take is Jean Renoir's short film "A Day in the Country," based on the short story by Guy de Maupassant – itself influenced by the Impressionist paintings of Renoir's legendary father.

A disciple of the late Billy Wilder, who invigorated sex comedy with such films as "Some Like It Hot," Trueba's movies have been enthusiastically received at home. This is the first of his films to be released in the United States, but audiences may well prefer his approach to the hysterical on-screen antics of countryman Pedro Almodovar, the reigning bad boy of absurdist sex comedy.

Echoing the celebration of the senses of "Like Water for Chocolate," "Belle Epoque" lends food and drink the same reverence it extends to passion, though it concocts a more political dish. Rafael Azcona's screenplay, from a story co-written with Trueba, is as languorous as its sun-drenched setting. It is also pointedly irreverent, blithely zinging church doctrine, religious hypocrisy, and shifting political winds.

Gomez steals the show from his youthful co-stars, playing the old nonconformist painter and father Manolo with warmth, humor and an endearingly off-handed grace. He captured one of the film's nine Goyas (the Spanish Academy Award) as Best Supporting Actor, and it's an absolutely irresistible performance.

Gil earned Best Actress honors for her role as the "conflicted" daughter, a veterinarian with a taste for hunting and other, more predatory diversions. Verdu, Cruz and Diaz-Aroca couldn't be more enticing.

The rest of the cast bring their own ingredients to the pot – Agustín González and Mary Carmen Ramírez are especially fine – but none more effectively than Sanz, whose slightly overwhelmed Fernando can't believe his luck in escaping chaos and falling into paradise. Even if, like the biblical one, it's too good to last.

....

'Concubine' an honest look at China
"Farewell My Concubine"
December 2, 1993

That the makers of "Farewell My Concubine" did not prostitute themselves for the greater glory of Communist China, that they were rigorously, courageously honest, had much to do with the film being banned by the government shortly after its sensational Shanghai premiere last July.

Having shared the coveted Palme d'Or with "The Piano" at Cannes in May, this magnificent collaboration between mainland director Chen Kaige and Hong Kong-based novelist Lilian Lee arrives in America with fanfare befitting a coronation.

And it deserves every blast of the trumpet.

"Concubine" has a history of censorship. Originally written in 1981 as a two-hour movie for Hong Kong TV, it was banned in that city due to the homoerotic thread submerged in the narrative – a component that some viewers here also may find objectionable.

Lee turned it into a novel in 1985, then rewrote the script with Chen, significantly expanding an intimate tale of brutalization, love and betrayal to embrace 50 years of political struggle. The resulting film owns the exquisite delicacy and meticulous detail of Chinese art, underscored by a great theatrical sweep of historical events.

Two boys are initiated into the Peking (Beijing) Opera in 1925, as dusk gathers on the warlord era. One, Shitou, is chosen to play masculine roles. The other, softy featured Douzi, will specialize in female parts, for life.

As the years pass, maturity and stardom dovetail for Shitou and Douzi, now known and revered in the guise of their stage names, Duan Xiaolou and Cheng Dieyl. Above all, they esteemed for their continuing performances of the opera "Farewell My Concubine," a tragedy of a great but doomed king from antiquity and the mistress who takes her life rather than be separated from him.

The classical structure of the opera also informs the movie, which follows the actors' fate through World War II, the fall of the Nationalists, the ascendance of Mao, the fratricidal madness of the Cultural Revolution, and, finally, to a reunion on stage of the two renowned actors in 1977, 22 years after their last performance.

Chiefly, however, "Concubine" explores the jealousies and tests of loyalty that emerge within an uneasy romantic triangle. Xiaolou, whom Dieyi adores, is married to Juxian, a shrewd former whore who manipulated Xiaolou into marriage but comes to love him passionately. Dieyi cannot abide her presence, and retreats into a liaison with a distinguished man of wealth and position.

The communist reordering of society throws their existence not turmoil. Ultimately, and abandoned child, saved by Dieyi years earlier, brings ruin to their lives when he grows into a committed ideologue of the new order. It is deadly irony indeed.

Visually mesmerizing, "Concubine" inevitably will be compared to Bernardo Bertolucci's "The Last Emperor," but it is more involving and less austere. Masterful composition by director of photography Gu Changwei provides not only a breathtaking backdrop and a continuing frame of reference, but an emotional motif.

This, plus first-rate production design, is an admirable setting for a series of flawless, resonant performances. Chen, himself a one-time Red Guard, has assembled a superb cast. Child actors Ma Mingwei and Fei Yang are exceptional in the roles of youthful Douzi and Shitou, respectively.

But the film belongs to Leslie Cheung as Dieyl, Zhang Gengyi as Xiaolou, and the lovely Gong Li ("Ju Dou," "Raise the Red Lantern") as Juxian. They give "Concubine" the one thing so many contemporary movies ack: depth. Depth of characterization, of feeling, of ambition.

While the strains of Chinese opera may sound discordant to Western ears, "Farewell My Concubine" manages to erase all barriers, cultural or otherwise.

It is a memorable achievement that no amount of governmental paranoia can deny, or contain.

....

Argentina's anguish explored
"The Official Story"
February 21, 1986

"No people can survive without a history or without memory," Alicia De Ibanez tells her students on the first day of a new semester.

Here begins a complex mosaic of the ironical and tragic: a professor of history who is out of touch with the true nature of recent events in her native land. Soon she will feel the full weight of the words she has uttered, for she is to learn that just as a nation cannot subsist without identity, neither can an individual, and especially a child.

This is the psychological linchpin of Luis Puenzo's luminous "The Official Story," a political film that possesses not only a conscience but a heart.

Set in Buenos Aires in 1983, in the aftermath of the Falkland Islands War, the film explores the anguish of Argentina, the still-festering wounds of its people, and the as yet unresolved horror of seven years of repressive military rule.

From 1976, when a military junta ousted Eva Peron and first consolidated its power, to 1982, Argentina lived under a continuing state of siege. The army waged wholesale way on guerilla leaders and leftists "subversives," killing thousands, arbitrarily jailing and torturing uncounted others. While a severe worsening in economic conditions placed extreme pressure on the ruling clique, many of its favored grew rich. Though the junta was deposed late in 1982 - President Leopoldo Galtieri resigning three days after the Argentine surrender to Great Britain - some retained their wealth, albeit tenuously, amid widespread calls for reform and retribution.

Ibanez's husband is one such man, an arrogant, aggressively right-wing industrialist who, while lovingly solicitous to his daughter, is indifferent to the pain of the Argentine people as a whole. Fearing he will lose everything he has won to the new democratic order, he ultimately loses far more – his humanity.

Yet Puenzo, who shares screenplay credit with Aida Bortnik, centers his story on Alicia

(Norma Aleandro), a largely sheltered upper-middle class teacher whose naivete is shattered by the knowledge that their adopted daughter, five-year-old Gaby, may in fact be the child of a young couple murdered for their political beliefs.

The seed is planted in the classroom, where students have festooned her blackboard with newspaper clippings prominently picturing the faces of the missing. Reunited with an old friend who, unknown to Alicia, had entered self-imposed exile in Spain only after withstanding 36 days of politically motivated detention and torture, she discovers that her friend's captors had regularly sold off the children of many of the imprisoned women.

Alicia, whose own parents died in a car accident when she was very young, resolves to earn the truth. Met with an antagonistic response from her husband, she turns to official records, combing hospital archives in a frustrating attempt to uncover Gaby's birth certificate.

Eventually, she encounters a woman who may be Gaby's grandmother. The photographic evidence borne by the woman is compelling, and the two establish an immediate if somewhat awkward rapport. But Alicia's husband will have none of it. He rages, first at the woman, whom he dismisses as a worthless "bag lady," and then at Alicia, whom he physically assaults.

Here the film closes, abruptly and without resolution, leaving the viewer in an emotional limbo not unlike that suffered by Argentines themselves.

"The Official Story." – a wry title if ever there was one – is all the more effective because of it. Puenzo gives us the kind of "small story Hollywood seems to have forgotten how to tell. And he presents it in measured movements that, although bitter and urgent, do not subvert balance for the sake of effect.

There are wonderful subtleties throughout, lent force by shrewd use of language. Gaby's favorite word is "divided," which she uses tome and again as an all-purpose verb in conversations with her mother and the family housekeeper. Nothing could be more poignant, and more thematically adhesive. She has been divided from her natural parents, now dead, as have thousands of others; Alicia is divided in her loyalties; her husband is increasingly divided from his own parents and brother, who regard him as soulless.

The performances, all round, are inspired.

As Alicia, Argentine stage actress Aleandro is nothing short of brilliant. Havin suffered a real-life political exile of her own, Aleandro's portrayal gleams with authority and conviction. But it is also rigorously controlled, without melodramatic taint. She is memorably supported by Hector Alterio as the husband and Chunchuna Villafane as Ana. Atilio Stampone's haunting score contributes enormously, and Felix Monti's deft photography, at once economical and cleverly serene, establishes a near-perfect visual tone.

It is not often that one gets a message without the attendant sermon. With even less frequency is one gifted with an altogether flawless film. With "The Official Story," we get both.

— Film Histories —

Film Histories, & The Oscar

"Films are made up of many elements. Literary, theatrical, painterly and musical. But there is something in film that is purely cinematic. When I make films or go to see the films of others, I go in hopes of experiencing this. I'm at a loss to express the quality in words. I hope one day to make a film in which every moment has that power. Until I do, I am still a student." – Akira Kurosawa.

It is the same desire to be transported that I harbor with each visit to the movie theater. To enter another world, even if it has a clear similarity to my own. Movies, like novels, are reality amplified. Sometimes a little, sometimes a lot. But they are always us.

I've enjoyed films from every age, from as many countries as was possible, yet it is the classics of the 1930s and 1940s - the "Golden Age" - that stay with me most vividly over time, and that hold my deepest affections hostage.

Having been born in 1948, I was introduced to them not in the cinema, but on television. Often late at night, in my teens. It is ironic that TV, considered the movies' archenemy at its inception, filled the airwaves in its early days with films made years before I was born.

The stars were imperishable: Bogart and Bacall, Bogart and Bergman, Gable and Colbert, Astaire and Rogers, Hepburn and Tracy, Hepburn and Grant, Olivier and Leigh, Powell and Loy, Gary Cooper, Greta Garbo, Jimmy Stewart, Barbara Stanwick, Henry Fonda, Marlene Dietrich, Ronald Colman, Bette Davis, and some of the greatest character actors who ever graced the screen, like Thomas Mitchell – the list goes on and on.

And the films themselves were immortal: "City Lights," "Top Hat," "It Happened One Night," "All Quiet on the Western Front," "Lost Horizon," "Dracula," "The Thin Man," "Bringing Up Baby," "Stagecoach," "The Adventures of Robin Hood," "His Girl Friday," "The Lost Weekend," "Citizen Kane," "The Big Sleep," "Holiday," "Odd Man Out," "Mr. Smith Goes to Washington," "Gone With the Wind," "The Grapes of Wrath," "Casablanca," "The Philadelphia Story," "A Night at the Opera," "Notorious," "The Wizard of Oz," et al.

These actors and films became so much a part of the fabric of my imagination, so like members of my family, that I became wistful for an era I never knew.

Can any other period in American movies really compare? While I applaud the late '50s, '60s and '70s for their realism and cinematic invention - freed at last from the suffocating strictures of the old studio system - and admire a great many movies from all the years since, it is the '30s and '40s that persist in my imagination.

It was their *ambience*, the world in which they immersed me, as much as any measure of artistic expression they achieved. It was also these films that exposed me to the importance of possessing a social conscience – albeit limited to a populist, man-of-the-people perspective – as well as the fantasy of opulence in the midst of a Great Depression and grasping the horrors of world war.

As many have pointed out, this motion picture era was not without racial and ethnic stereotypes or jingoism in a time of global conflict. With rare exceptions, female characters striving for emancipation were punished in the end if they failed to bow to traditional expectations. African-Americans and other minority groups were treated dismissively if acknowledged at all.

But these movies also helped make me aware of what was happening in the real world. And they led me to some great novels from which many a superlative movie was made.

In this chapter you will see not only retrospectives on the great genres of film, but much celebration of the Oscars (as well as some pointed critiques). Until recently, I always defended the Academy Awards as one of the last bastions of rewarding merit. Yes, the Oscars were no stranger to politics or travesties of judgement, but more often than not, it was about recognizing art and craft, not just record-setting box office.

Sadly, that distinction seems to be waning. We are awash in awards. It may be that the British Academy of Film and Television Arts and its BAFTA awards are the last remaining upholders of standards. I hope this is not the case.

But the truth is, awards are irrelevant to the filmgoer, or should be. They are not the final measure of quality or style or substance. It is the experience of being captivated, in a darkened space, in the company of strangers, that matters.

And endures.

....

The Oscars
'Crazy Heart's' Bridges may become the latest recipient of Payback Oscar
March 7, 2010

Ah, the Oscars. In no other context do we countenance, much less watch with rapt attention, a host of rich and famous folks spending a long, formal evening patting each other on the back for their brilliance.

Do you think investment bankers could get away with such a tableau?

On the other hand, one does enjoy seeing genuine merit rewarded even when it's a makeup call. And anticlimax is something at which the Academy Awards is expert. Many actors have won statuettes for lesser work after great performances have gone begging, and it looks like Jeff Bridges has a better than even chance of becoming the latest top-of-the-line actor to be recognized – well after he should have been, and for a lesser performance.

When co-hosts Steve Martin and Alec Baldwin lift the curtain on the 82nd annual Oscar telecast tonight at 8 at the Kodak Theatre in Hollywood, Bridges will be the sentimental Best Actor favorite for his work in "Crazy Heart."

Not to say he wasn't good. So was co-star and fellow Oscar nominee Maggie Gyllenhaal, although in an unexceptional movie shot through with every boozy-music-star-on-the-skids cliche known to filmdom. After notable performances in worthy pictures such as "Cutter's Way," "American Heart" and "Fearless," a better vehicle would have been preferred for this potential Payback.

The Payback Annals

The Payback has its analog in sports: the blown call and the makeup call, wherein a sheepish referee who realizes he's blundered quietly tries to rectify the mistake on a subsequent play.

Oscar's history is full of Paybacks, which are distinguished from "career-achievement" awards (for actors who never won but should have) masquerading as a given year's "Best of" nominee. The Payback also differs markedly from the Long Overdue Acknowledgment, which dispenses Academy Awards to oft-nominated people who previously had not won - for example, Geraldine Page for "The Trip to Bountiful" (1985) after eight prior nominations; Jack Nicholson for "One Flew Over the Cuckoo's Nest" (1975), after four; Gregory Peck for "To Kill a Mockingbird" after five; or, last year, Al Pacino ("Scent of a Woman"), after six. Heck, Paul Newman had been nominated five times before winning. Several classic examples of the Payback stand out.

Newman had the bad luck to give the finest performance of his career ("The Verdict," 1982) the same year Ben Kingsley was a lock for "Gandhi." When Newman won in 1986 for "The Color of Money," it was plainly a Payback Oscar for an inferior film. The problem is that one injustice creates another; superior work by James Woods ("Salvador") and Bob Hoskins ("Mona Lisa") that same year was penalized by the settling of scores.

Jack Lemmon also is notable for receiving a belated Payback for his Oscar-winning turn in "Save the Tiger" (1973) a pale approximation of his nominated work in "Days of Wine and Roses" (1962).

Most actors accept the Payback graciously, though who can forget Jeremy Irons' pointed comments while retrieving the 1990 Best Actor statuette for "Reversal of Fortune." Two years earlier, to the bafflement of everyone, the Academy overlooked his astounding work in "Dead Ringers," one of the most accomplished performances in memory. Irons made it clear he felt he'd been robbed before and through a rather forced smile made his displeasure plain.

Who else received Oscar makeup calls? Try the late Jack Lemmon, Michael Caine, Elizabeth Taylor and Denzel Washington, just to name a sampling.

To be sure, some actors who have given a host of distinguished performances never win.

Heaven knows, we're still waiting for Peter O'Toole to get his just desserts (it's too late for Richard Burton, sadly).

Oscar's history is full of Paybacks. Yet actresses do not seem to have been accorded them that often, perhaps because fewer good roles are written for them to begin with – since the '50s, anyway. A conspicuous modern exception is Holly Hunter. Fine though she was in "The Piano" (1993), her Oscar should have been earned for a comic tour de force in "Broadcast News" (1987), a victim of fashion and one of the all-time worst miscarriages of Academy justice.

OK, so maybe the Payback is more satisfying than kissing your sister. Yet actors (writers, directors, etc.) will tell you there's something unsettling about having praise heaped upon one's commonplace work while the best stuff is ignored.

On top of that, the Payback isn't always that quick, on the playing field or in the movies. Often, it takes a decade or more to right a wrong. Though on occasion it happens the very next year. For example, Jimmy Stewart winning for "The Philadelphia Story" in 1940 after having lost for "Mr. Smith Goes to Washington" the previous year.

Perhaps you've noticed that Oscar has no eyes. Nor ears, for that matter. And you expect him to judge?

'Ava-tired'

If only James Cameron's "Avatar" had a story as sophisticated as its spectacle. Here is a movie that at times is absolutely magical, even transportive (especially in 3-D), a quantum leap technologically that, if not for its violence, anachronistic military content and hackneyed third act, might have been ranked among the most imaginative children's films ever made. Instead, it's a breathtakingly immersive, if inflated, video game.

Cameron's black-and-white view of life, coupled with grade school-level enviro-moralizing and a cliche-ridden plotline, a Cameron specialty, weakens what otherwise is a truly remarkable movie.

"Avatar" doubtless will sweep most of the technical awards. And therein lies its fundamental hypocrisy. Cameron marries an argument against raping the environment to a more disturbing argument against scientific progress. And what irony! Cameron spent half a billion dollars on the most advanced technology he could find, then argues that the only path to survival is to abandon advanced technology and return to the simple lifestyles of ancient hunter-gatherer people.

Naming it Best Picture in a year of such intelligent, grown-up fare as "The Hurt Locker" would be lamentable.

The nominees are...

Other than Bridges, none of this year's nominees – making up an intriguing cast of household names (Meryl Streep) and the relatively obscure (Christoph Waltz of

"Inglourious Basterds") - fall into the Payback category. What they do offer are some interesting races, especially in the acting, directing and screenwriting arenas. In the latter, former lovebirds Cameron ("Avatar") and Kathryn Bigelow ("The Hurt Locker") go at it hammer and tongs. If they split the vote, and they might, don't be shocked to see Jason Reitman win for "Up in the Air."

With a quartet of deserving Oscar nominees – Reitman for director, George Clooney as Best Actor and Vera Farmiga and Anna Kendrick as Best Supporting Actress – "Up in the Air" may surprise. But the real neck-and-neck race is between Streep for "Julie & Julia" and Sandra Bullock for "The Blind Side." Oscar generally favors youth, remember, so odds favor the Girl Next Door.

One only wishes the customary ranks of the overlooked did not include actresses Emily Blunt and Abbie Cornish, so good this past year in a pair of period pieces ("The Young Victoria," "Bright Star"), and Christian McKay, who gave an extraordinary performance as the rampant auteur of "Me and Orson Welles."

As to that, what we have here is a case of transparent pandering.

In an effort to bolster sagging TV ratings for its telecast – ratings often climb in years when blockbusters are in the running – the Academy reverted to the old practice of nominating 10 films for Best Picture this year as opposed to the usual five.

From 1932 to 1943, there were 10 and sometimes as many as 12 (1934, 1935) nominees for Best Picture at the Oscars. Finding it increasingly difficult to come up with 10 worthy nominees (even in the last years of Hollywood's Golden Age), the Academy dropped the Best Picture field to five in 1944, where it remained until 2010.

All one need do is look at some of those in the running in 2010 to know it's about ticket sales and mass audience popularity rather than excellence, the same problem as pop music's Grammys.

Some will applaud, but this maneuver risks further undermining the Oscars' significance and reputation in an awards-obsessed world.

To be sure, the Academy Awards already is a four-hour commercial for the film industry, and good for business. But a watered-down Oscar that's indistinguishable from a zillion other awards shows? Heaven forfend.

....

Top films of the Decade:
Love, war main themes of the best movies from 2000-2009
December 27, 2009

Back in 2001, after a year and a half of largely desultory films, we asked, "Will the 21st century please stand up?"

It took a while for the new century to shed the '90s and establish its own identity. In the end, and at its best, the decade 2000-09 exceeded expectations. The strongest year overall was 2008, by far, with at least 15 movies worthy of mention as best picture. But only one cracked The Post and Courier's Top 15.

Herewith, our highly personal choices for the Best of the Best. Let the arguments commence.

1. "Faithless" (2001): Liv Ullman directs from a script by Ingmar Bergman. And it's not even close. This is a study of infidelity that is a cut above -- way above -- featuring actress Lena Andre in the kind of mesmerizing turn that Ullman herself used to do. Bergman and Ullman, the team that gave us such extraordinary fare as "Cries and Whispers" (1972), and "Autumn Sonata" (1978), collaborated on yet another triumph -- a film for the ages.

2. "Waltz With Bashir" (2009): Seldom has animation been employed to such sobering ends. "Waltz," with its echoes of an Israeli Army mission in the Lebanon War of 1982, is a rare and riveting motion picture experience, arguably the most haunting movie in recent memory. Brilliant in its innovation, its honesty, its clear-eyed observation and impact. Unforgettable.

3. "You Can Count on Me" (2000): Laura Linney may have given the performance of the decade in writer-director Kenneth Lonergan's superbly realized contemporary comic drama, which captures the essence of sibling amity and discord. Co-starring Mark Ruffalo, this microbudget gem is trenchant, joyous, and melancholy all at once.

4. "Hustle and Flow" (2005): Terrence Howard soared to stardom as a small-time pimp and drug dealer in the slums of Memphis. He is a man treading water, buoyed only by the faint hope, likely futile, that his main chance may come. Brimming with vivid, convincingly realized characters, it is light years removed from the many movies that capitalize on hip-hop culture.

5. "Before Sunset" (2004): Richard Linklater's engrossing "Before Sunset" is a great rarity, not only for its screenplay but for acting so naturalistic and genuine that it gives you the sensation of eavesdropping on a private conversation, one that hits achingly close to home. Through two very human characters (played by Ethan Hawke and Julie Delpy), we meet ourselves in many guises, from hopeless romantic to hopeful cynic.

6. "Capote" (2005): Philip Seymour Hoffman's Oscar-winning performance was not the whole story here. Bennett Miller's direction was first rate, cannily following the pioneering writer as he completed his true-crime history "In Cold Blood." Alloyed to Dan Futterman's screenplay were outstanding supporting performances by Catherine Keener and Clifton Collins Jr.

7. "Pan's Labyrinth" (2006): There is a strange and beautiful alchemy at work in Guillermo del Toro's dazzling fairy tale for adults, set in Spain in 1944 against the backdrop of the repressive Francisco Franco regime. Del Toro folds fantasy and action into straight drama as seamlessly as could be imagined, then amplifies it with features of a morality play: politics and history fused with the supernatural.

8. "The Fellowship of the Ring" (2001): A Herculean task, executed by Peter Jackson & Co. with intelligence and artistry. 'Nuff said.

9. "The Hurt Locker" (2009): Set in Baghdad in the summer of 2004, few movies of any year could match this searing document on the chaos of war. It's tense and believable first scene to last, with a gritty, ground-level approach made frighteningly real with the help of hand-held cameras.

10. "Seabiscuit" (2003): Many will scoff, but Gary Ross' Depression-era tale, based on a true story, was a stirring evocation of Old Hollywood at its best.

11. "Gone Baby Gone" (2007): This adaptation of Dennis Lehane's 1998 crime thriller had enough plot holes to drain the Atlantic, but with dialogue, performances and verisimilitude like this, one makes allowances. The movie's moral ambiguity is matched by deft direction and razor-sharp work from a great ensemble cast.

12. "Once" (2007): A pitch-perfect musical love story. Writer-director John Carney's affecting slice-of-life is so small a picture, it seems almost a vignette. But the characters are so well-delineated, the emotions so rich, and its details so authentic that it generates the kind of intimacy big movies can only dream about.

13. "There Will Be Blood" (2007): Daniel Day-Lewis plays the intense and progressively dark character of Daniel Plainview, a classic early 20th-century mogul in the making: personable and plain speaking on the outside, ruthless within.

14. "Memento" (2001): Writer-director Christopher Nolan won his chops with this cunning bit of "Twilight Zone"-ery. Told backward, the revenge thriller leaves you reeling over what you just saw, or didn't see. Its ingenious narrative approach turned out to be hugely influential.

15. *TIE* "Slumdog Millionaire" (2008): Danny Boyle's refreshing and wildly imaginative film went from obscurity to Oscar shoo-in in the space of a month. Not to everyone's taste, perhaps, but Boyle's storytelling gifts have never been more expressively revealed.

15. *TIE* "The Motorcycle Diaries" (2004): Director Walter Salles is at the peak of his powers in this fascinating story of the young Che Guevara's journey up the spine of South America. Though somewhat romanticized, this ultimate "buddy picture" pulses with humanity and event, showcasing glorious scenery and wonderful performances.

Honorable mention: "An Education," "Bright Star" (2009); "Frost/Nixon," "WALL-E," "Milk," "Man on Wire," "The Curious Case of Benjamin Button," "Rachel Getting Married," "The Diving Bell and the Butterfly," "The Savages," "The Kite Runner," "Elegy," "Mongol," "Crazy," "The Counterfeiters," "Note by Note," "Rescue Dawn," "Starting Out in the Evening" (2008); "No Country for Old Men" (2007); "Little Children," "The Lives of Others," "The Last King of Scotland," "The Queen," "Letters From Iwo Jima," "Why We

Fight," "World Trade Center," "Volver" (2006); "Brokeback Mountain," "Batman Begins," "Good Night, and Good Luck," "Sin City," "Paradise Now" (2005); "Sideways," "Garden State," "My Architect," "Million Dollar Baby," "Hero," "Ray," "Eternal Sunshine of the Spotless Mind," "The Sea Inside," "The Incredibles" (2004); "The Lord of the Rings: The Return of the King," "Master and Commander," "House of Sand and Fog," "Whale Rider," "Mystic River," "City of God," "The Barbarian Invasions," "Dirty Pretty Things," "American Splendor," "Winged Migration" (2003); "Adaptation," "Chicago," "Talk to Her," "The Quiet American" (2002); "Amores Perros," "In the Bedroom," "Black Hawk Down," "The Golden Bowl," "Almost Famous," "Hedwig and the Angry Inch" (2001); "O Brother, Where Art Thou?," "Wonder Boys" and "Requiem for a Dream" (2000).

....

Screen Dream Teams - Chemistry: Major star duos light up the movies
November 16, 2008

Tracy and Hepburn. Bogie and Bacall. Astaire and Rogers. Powell and Loy. Screen immortals, all.

Unforgettable as individual performers, together they were even more than the sum of their parts, a magical alchemy.

They, and the other great couples of Hollywood's Studio Era, defined romantic chemistry for three generations of movie audiences. Their memorable teamwork on screen (and sometimes off) will be celebrated this month in a film festival on the Turner Classic Movies cable network. Running Tuesday and Nov. 25, the festival sports a companion volume in «Leading Couples: The Most Unforgettable Screen Romances of the Studio Era» (Chronicle Books).

The latter, with extensive research and text by Frank Miller, features profiles of couples who performed opposite each other in several films, as well as couples who ignited the screen, or "heated up the negative," in a single, memorable casting coup. Each profile showcases behind-the-scenes stories, biographical overviews, bits of lore and classic quotes, all illustrated with rare stills and poster art.

TCM's voters were hard-pressed to limit their choices, and there was much debate. The Post and Courier's selections expand the field.

The greatest teams
Our Top 12:

1. Katharine Hepburn and Spencer Tracy. What can one say? A shoo-in, a no-brainer, given their incomparable screen chemistry and long off- screen romance. Only the

Fred Astaire-Ginger Rogers musicals are embraced with such perpetual admiration and affection as "Woman of the Year" (1942), "Adam's Rib" (1949) and "Pat and Mike" (1952), to name a few.

Between them, the finest film actor who ever lived and the most iconic female star of all time transformed the battle of the sexes into high comedy. Still, Hepburn's teaming with Cary Grant in equally classic films such as "Bringing Up Baby," "Holiday" and "The Philadelphia Story" could give Tracy-Hepburn a run for its money. Not to mention Hepburn's outstanding one-off with Humphrey Bogart, "The African Queen."

Little-known fact: Curiously, "Woman of the Year" is the only film in which Tracy and Hepburn kiss romantically.

2. Ginger Rogers and Fred Astaire. Theirs was the perfect formula for Depression-era escapism, one that the late critic Pauline Kael called "a great American courtship in dance." The actor with the lighter-than-air constitution joined to a versatile actress who matched him step for step.

Despite the silly plots, their movies (with opulent art-deco sets) still possess an allure all their own. How can you beat "Top Hat" (1935) or "Swing Time" (1936)?

Little-known fact: Because Rogers often was so busy on other movies that she had little time to help craft the dances, choreographer and Astaire "stand-in" Hermes Pan first would work out the dances with the leading man, dancing Rogers' part, then in later rehearsals dance Astaire's part with her.

3. Myrna Loy and William Powell. The essence of the urbane, sophisticated couple, whose wisecracking banter (as a kind of love-play) provided the template for scores of imitators. Powell, the one-time villain of silent Westerns, and Loy, the former femme fatale (who always seemed to be cast as an Oriental), were a matchless pair. As the impeccably attired Nick and Nora Charles in the six "Thin Man" pictures - between quips, insults and dry martinis - they solved the most dastardly crimes with a blithe and off-handed grace.

Of the record 14 films they made together, the most entertaining remain "The Thin Man" (1934), which gave the movies their first modern marriage, and "Libeled Lady" (1936). TV's "MacMillan & Wife" and "Hart to Hart" were affectionate homages to Nick and Nora.

Little-known facts: "The Thin Man" was shot in a scant two weeks. Powell's real lady love in this era was Jean Harlow.

4) Jean Harlow and Clark Gable. What's that, you say? Not Gable and Vivien Leigh in "Gone With the Wind," the ultimate epic? Or Gable and Claudette Colbert in the greatest of all romantic comedies, "It Happened One Night" (1933)? Absolutely. Perhaps no screen team in history brought out the best in each other or fit together so seamlessly as the original blonde bombshell, a gifted comedian, and the soon-to-be King of Hollywood. Playful and immensely fond of each other off screen, on screen in movies like «Red Dust»

(1932), Gable never had to carry Harlow up the stairs.

Little-known fact: The scene in "Saratoga" (1937) called for a discreet peck on the cheek, but when an impish Gable drew Harlow into a passionate embrace, the crew cheered and whistled.

6) Lauren Bacall and Humphrey Bogart. With the tough-talking glamour girl and the gruff cynic, sparks flew early, on set and off. In their movies, they delighted in dishing out loving insults to a partner who could take it, and give it back in spades. Through strength of personality alone, they could take a questionable script and give it punch. In their steamiest movies, "To Have and Have Not" (1944) and "The Big Sleep" (1946), both directed by Howard Hawks, their acting was a sexy game of tennis, with the kind of long verbal volleys that kept audiences rapt.

Little-known fact: The then-19-year-old Bacall was so taken with Hawks' wife, Slim, even dressing and talking like her, that Hawks had Bacall and Bogie's characters in "To Have and Have Not" call each other Slim and Steve (Slim's nickname for Hawks).

7) Ingrid Bergman and Humphrey Bogart. Once was all it took. "Casablanca" (1942). "Of all the gin joints in all the world ..." Immortality. Need we say more?

Little-known fact: Bogart had little to say to Bergman between scenes. She grasped his acting style by watching "The Maltese Falcon" repeatedly.

8) Audrey Hepburn and Gregory Peck. They were magic in one indelible film, 1953's "Roman Holiday," originally planned for Cary Grant and Elizabeth Taylor. Then-unknown Hepburn was third choice to play the fictional Princess Ann. Peck, after a decade of straight drama, wanted to spread his wings in comedy.

Director Frank Capra had walked, opening the door for William Wyler. Of such happy timing are legends made. Hepburn, the wispy gamine, won a Best Actress Oscar and became the toast of the '50s. And in an era mad with royal fascination, the world had a fresh new fairy tale to savor.

Little-known fact: At the height of the Cuban missile crisis, President Kennedy asked to screen "Roman Holiday" to keep himself calm while awaiting the Soviet response to his ultimatum.

9) Judy Garland and Mickey Rooney. Two pint-size dynamos: one a screen and musical legend, the other the most durable star in Hollywood history. Together, in films such as "Babes in Arms" (1939), they were magnetic, bursting with enthusiasm, ready to put on a show at the drop of a hat. Their joyful exuberance as singers-dancers-actors and fresh-faced innocents captured the tone of the times. Problem was, their studio (MGM) never wanted them to grow up. Off-camera, they were pals, not lovebirds, each other's biggest fan.

Little-known fact: They met in the fall of 1933 when both were attending the Lawlor School for Professional Children.

10) Maureen O'Hara and John Wayne. A matched set of equals if ever there was one.

Macho meets tempestuous, and both get swept away, especially in John Ford's romantic fable of a never-never Ireland, "The Quiet Man" (1952). The two were great friends off screen even before they worked together, and amiably competitive as actors on screen.

Little-known fact: Furious over Ford's and Wayne's teasing on "The Quiet Man" set, O'Hara actually threw a real haymaker of a punch at the Duke. He caught it, accidentally breaking her wrist.

11) Vivien Leigh and Clark Gable. They were unforgettable as the irresistible force and (almost) immovable object of "Gone With the Wind" (1939), but finding the right Scarlett and Rhett proved a Herculean task. Gable wasn't all that keen on playing the role, afraid that nothing they could do would satisfy the novel's fans. Leigh, by contrast, burned to play Scarlett, but early in the filming was miserable and thought the whole thing would be a disaster. The stars were not exactly chummy off-camera, but after a rocky start, they did warm to each other in a comradely way.

Little-known fact: It was playwright Sidney Howard who added the word "frankly" to the famous line in the book, "My dear, I don't give a damn," helping Gable to make it the most famous phrase in the movies.

12) Grace Kelly and Cary Grant. Kelly, coolly seductive, aggressively pursuing Grant, the essence of elegance as a retired cat burglar trying to prove his innocence in Alfred Hitchcock's "To Catch a Thief" (1955). The gorgeous backdrop of Monaco seemed perfectly suited to the stars, who made the film one of the most amusing, buoyant romantic thrillers in memory. The two also established a warm friendship that endured until Kelly's accidental death in 1982.

Little-known fact: Grant had announced his (tentative) retirement from the screen in 1953, and was not at all sure he wanted to play opposite a leading lady 25 years younger than he. But Kelly, who quit the movies a year later to marry Prince Rainier, became Grant's favorite of all the female stars with whom he worked.

Who else compares?

--Claudette Colbert and Clark Gable. They set the tone in "It Happened One Night" (1934), the first film to sweep the five major Oscars for picture, actor, actress, director and screenplay.

--Greta Garbo and John Gilbert. Giants of silent film, the first of the great movie pairs, and off- screen lovers as well.

--Jane Russell and Robert Mitchum. Mitchum had a surprising rapport with prim British star Deborah Kerr, and they were superb together in "The Sundowners" and "Heaven Knows, Mr. Allison." But his most natural foil was the buxom, playful Russell, who gave him as good as she got in "His Kind of Woman" (1951).

--Olivia DeHavilland and Errol Flynn. Masculine swagger, feminist pluck and some magnificent costume epics such as "The Adventures of Robin Hood" (1938) and "Captain Blood" (1935).

--Rita Hayworth and Glenn Ford in "Gilda" (1946). Hate, alloyed with lust, was a more powerful emotion than love for their characters.

--Elizabeth Taylor and Richard Burton. Twice married, twice divorced, they were more of a sensation off-camera than on, save for "Who's Afraid of Virginia Woolf" (1966).

--Charles Boyer and Hedy Lamarr. The smoldering "Algiers" (1938) cemented the images of Boyer as the Great Lover and Lamarr as the screen's loveliest female star.

--Elizabeth Taylor and Paul Newman. "Cat on a Hot Tin Roof" (1958) earned both Oscar noms, and triggered sprinkler systems worldwide.

....

Through the Years with Indiana Jones:
Dashing archaeologist dusts off his old fedora
May 18, 2008

Indy was born when Cubby said no.

Still flush from the success of "Jaws," and with "Close Encounters of the Third Kind" soon to debut, Steven Spielberg wanted to make a James Bond movie. But mindful of the personal stamp the director imposed on his films, the man guarding the gates of the 007 franchise, longtime producer Albert "Cubby" Broccoli, turned him down flat.

Not long thereafter, in May 1977, Spielberg and buddy George Lucas were commiserating. It was just days after the premiere of "Star Wars" in a handful of the nation's theaters and Lucas was nervous, fearing his little space opera was going to be an unmitigated disaster. Weeks later, he would be ecstatic, but now, sitting on the beach with Spielberg and listening to his pal's Bondian lament, Lucas had an idea.

"So I said, 'Well, look, Steven, I've got a James Bond film. It's great - just like James Bond but even better," Lucas recalled last year. "I told him the story about this archaeologist and told him it was like this Saturday matinee serial, that he just got into one mess after another.

"And Steven said, 'Fantastic! Let's do this.'"

And it came to pass that this back-burner notion, tucked away in Lucas' voluminous to-do files, would go on to make cinematic history.

Lucas was right; "Raiders of the Lost Ark" (1981) was little more than a gussied-up feature-length version of the 1940s' cliffhanger shorts that had been recycled for young baby boom audiences of the late '50s and early '60s. But what a version. Fast-paced and vivid, "Raiders" crystallized all the great things about those cheesy wartime adventures, with their rambunctious heroes and nefarious Nazis, then infused them with high production values, tongue-in-cheek humor, exotic settings and the inspired casting of Harrison Ford (after Tom Selleck, legend holds, was forced to give it a pass).

On Thursday, after a 19-year absence from the bijou, one of the most popular series ever whipped onto celluloid is back in "Indiana Jones and the Kingdom of the Crystal Skull." Don your dusty jacket, slip on the fedora.

Ford may be 65 now - "It's not the years, it's the mileage," as Indy might say - but the fourth film is no "Indiana Jones and the Placid Pools Retirement Village.» Do you think Spielberg-Lucas-Ford would give us an Indy without all his moxie, all his resourcefulness and resilience, all his dash?

No, "Crystal Skull" will be a rouser, though expect more than a few wry references to age. The movie also offers the welcome return of Karen Allen as Marion Ravenwood ("Raiders"), by far the pluckiest of Indy's heroines, along with four of the finest actors in the business: Cate Blanchett, Jim Broadbent, John Hurt and Ray Winstone, not to mention rising star Shia LaBeouf as Indy's new sidekick.

The screenplay (from a story by Lucas and Jeff Nathanson) is by David Koepp, who has plenty of popcorn movie credits as scripter of "War of the Worlds," "Spider-Man," "Mission Impossible," "The Shadow" and "Jurassic Park."

But he is also the fellow who wrote the sharply satiric "Death Becomes Her" and the tough, gritty "Carlito's Way."

The teaming of Ford and Sean Connery for "Indiana Jones and the Last Crusade" (1989) left a good taste in audiences' collective mouths after the relative debacle of "Indiana Jones and the Temple of Doom" (1984), so expectations are high for the latest and (probably) last installment with Ford in the driver's seat.

"Raiders" chronicled events in 1936. Now it's 1957, with Our Man Jones venturing into the jungles of Peru in a race against Soviet agents (the new bad guys) to find the mystical Crystal Skull of Akator. Blanchett plays Russian agent Irina Spalko, who leads an elite military unit on a quest to harness the skull's unlimited power and set the stage for Soviet world domination.

The skull notion of the movie was inspired by a real-world discovery, of sorts. In 1924, when British banker-turned-adventurer F.A. Mitchell-Hedges was excavating in Belize, he unearthed a strange skull in the ruins of a Mayan temple. Carved out of a single block of quartz, it was said to produce an odd sensation when touched. More, whenever Mitchell-Hedges' daughter, Anna, slept with the skull near her bed, her dreams would be of the Maya and their everyday life, including ritual human sacrifices.

Soon, similar skulls were discovered, some finding their way into private collections, others into museums. But 84 years later, the issue still burns: ancient objects imbued with mysterious powers or elaborate hoax?

Vote for the latter. Mitchell-Hedges was notorious for spinning "colorful" stories. Though he traveled widely, donating important artifacts from his finds to the British Museum, his claims of having "discovered" obscure Indian tribes and lost cities (finding Atlantis was his goal in Belize) actually had been found and documented years, sometimes centuries, before his time.

Few such doubts attend the new movie, which, if it lives up to the "Indy's best ever" claim by Ford, will be a "find" all its own.

QUIZ:

1: How soon before filming began on "Raiders" was Harrison Ford cast as Indy?
2: What is the name of the Shanghai nightclub where Indy and Willie meet in "Temple of Doom"?
3: What is Indy's father's greatest fear?
4: What familiar "hieroglyphics" also adorn the Well of the Souls in "Raiders"?
5: Who plays the flying wing pilot in "Raiders"?
6: At what school is Indy a professor of archaeology?
7: Who, in a cameo role, greets Indy at the airport in "Indiana Jones and the Temple of Doom?"
8: River Phoenix played the young Indy in "The Last Crusade." In what film did he play Harrison Ford's son?

Memorable Indy movie quotes:
--"Snakes. Why'd it have to be snakes?" ("Raiders of the Lost Ark")
--"That's why they call it the jungle, sweetheart." ("Indiana Jones and the Temple of Doom»)
--"We named the dog Indiana!" ("Indiana Jones and the Last Crusade")

'The Crystal Skull': Behind the scenes:
--The film was shot in just 79 days, far less than most major movies, but it's a tradition to shoot the Indiana Jones movies as briskly as possible.
--Harrison Ford had only one day off from shooting.
--Ford spent more than six weeks in "whip training" to get reacquainted with Indy's most iconic prop.
--A total of 36 fedoras were made for the picture by a Mississippi hatmaker.
--The characters of Indiana Jones and Mutt (Shia LaBeouf) needed 30 leather jackets between them.
--There were many different inspirations for the warriors seen in the movie, some inspired by the "Day of the Dead" skull masks used in Latin America, others modeled after ancient Mayan sculptures, still others inspired by shirtless rockers at an outdoor concert.

....

Georgia town to celebrate another fine Laurel and Hardy Fest
October 1, 2006

HARLEM, Ga. -- They were, hands down, the greatest two-man comedy team motion pictures have ever produced. The rotund, long-suffering Oliver Hardy; the meek man-child Stan Laurel. One wide, one narrow. Together, priceless. And without peer.

Hardy (1892-1957) minted his own brand of genteel pomposity, complete with trademark tie twiddle and exasperated looks at the camera. Laurel (1890-1965) devised most of the gags and was a superb physical comedian, but he would have been incomplete without the perfect foil that was Hardy.

Nestled in this small Georgia town just west of Augusta is a treasure trove of memories, courtesy of the Laurel and Hardy Museum. A fitting locale, seeing that it›s Hardy›s birthplace. Curated by Kathy F. Ham and Denise Carter, the museum was born in 1989 when officials and residents of Harlem formed a committee to preserve Hardy's legacy. The Oliver Hardy Festival, held the first Saturday of October each year, was created to help fund a community center.

Over time, word spread and greater numbers of Laurel and Hardy devotees not only started attending the festival, but began contributing memorabilia: photos, correspondence, movies, toys, books, period collectibles, artifacts from the movies, statues, buttons and more. The Laurel and Hardy Museum in Ulverton, England, which would become Harlem's sister city, also donated a variety of items. The growing collection was displayed in the city hall during every festival until it became so extensive that it required its own Main Street building, which opened July 15, 2002.

How big a deal is it? Well, as many as 30,000 people have attended one year's festival, and there is a steady stream of folks who take the seven-mile detour off Interstate 20 to visit the museum.

The 18th annual Oliver Hardy Festival will twiddle to life Saturday at 9 a.m., featuring parades, live entertainment, a dance, raffles, a barbecue lunch, Laurel and Hardy look-alike contest, movies, skits and the participation of members of the Laurel and Hardy International Appreciation Society.

It's fine, but no mess

While Laurel followed his parents into the theater, Hardy took a slightly more circuitous route.

He was born in January 1892 at his mother's parents' home in Harlem. His father, who died when Hardy was only 20 months, owned a hotel in Madison, Ga. His mother, Emily, had to leave the hotel in Madison shortly thereafter and moved her family to Milledgeville, Ga., where she became the manager of the Baldwin Hotel. The young Hardy, then called

Norvell, never knew his dad, but as soon as he turned 18, changed his first name to that of his father.

Years earlier, at age 8, he briefly had run away from home to join a minstrel troupe. By 18, he was even more entranced by the visiting troupes of performers who stayed in the hotel. They doubtless inspired the athletic Hardy's exaggerated antics as an umpire at local baseball games, which invariably provoked onlookers to laughter. He worked as the projectionist and manager of Milledgeville's first movie house, the Electric Theatre, in 1910, then attended Georgia Military College, the Atlanta Conservatory of Music (Hardy had a delightful singing voice) and, for a short time, the University of Georgia.

Hardy left Georgia in 1913 for a newly established film colony in Jacksonville, Fla. In 1918, he ventured to Hollywood, where he worked at various studios as a little-known supporting actor, often as the heavy. That same year he met Laurel on-screen in the independently produced 1918 two-reeler «Lucky Dog.» But their accidental (not to mention providential) teaming did not happen for another eight years.

Inspired comedy

In 1926, Hardy signed with the Hal Roach studios, providing support to such headliners as the Our Gang (Little Rascals) kids. He also appeared in Roach's Comedy All-Stars series, where he frequently was directed by Laurel, who at the time was more interested in writing and directing than acting. Roach knew lightning in a bottle when he saw it and, in short order, this unlikely pair morphed into a single, flawless organism whose comedy was inspired - a reliable constant in an era of unsettling flux.

Laurel and Hardy's voices matched their characters to a T, enabling them to make an easy transition from silent film to sound.

The latter found them developing the verbal catchphrases that, after physicality, became the hallmark of their act. Laurel and Hardy graduated from two-reelers to feature films with 1931's "Pardon Us," though they continued to make features and shorts simultaneously until 1935.

In all, Laurel and Hardy made 107 movies in tandem. Some, such as "Way Out West" and "Sons of the Desert," are immortal, but most of them are hilarious and still easily found on video.

The men remained partners and friends until Hardy's death in Hollywood in 1957. Savor their work anew, or for the first time. And you needn't wait for the festival to pay your respects at the museum.

For more information, go online at www.laurelandhardymuseum.org or call 706-556-0401

....

'A Good Year' as filling as other fine food flicks
November 8, 2006

"No man is lonely while eating spaghetti." -- Robert Morley

A screenplay, like a recipe, is a theme that an imaginative filmmaker can play each time with a variation. And the great food movies are at the epicenter of our epicurean eye.

How many ways can a film celebrate food, drink and the glories of the table? How best to extol the cornucopia for the senses that, in the words of the great chef Brilliat Savarin, is «for every man of every land,» filling our days with fragrance and comforting us when we have outlived all the other earthly pleasures?

Movies cook with bigger budgets, superior art directors and set designers, better actors and more brio than a Food Network program, however seductive, could ever muster.

The key in savoring them is to keep two things foremost in mind: Your mother's admonition that your eyes are bigger than your stomach and never to see any of these films on an empty stomach, especially if you had plans to drop by the supermarket after the show.

Mayle's idyll

Opening Friday, director Ridley Scott's "A Good Year" is the latest exercise in culinary opulence to adorn the bijou. And it looks to be irresistible, with images so delectable you could almost devour them off the screen. Like so many of the finer food flicks - "Babette's Feast," "Like Water for Chocolate," et al. -- it has its roots in literature.

Peter Mayle's mouth-watering novel of Provence, France, has been prepped as a romantic drama for the screen by Scott and his former «Gladiator» star Russell Crowe.

The movie is a lushly photographed *billet doux* to the region and its cuisine, with Crowe starring as a faltering London-based investment guru who moves to France to tend a small vineyard he inherited from his late uncle (Albert Finney). Childhood memories merge with the beauty and pace of the countryside to insinuate themselves into his outlook, and he gradually shucks the last vestiges of his old life for a fuller one.

The film joins a veritable feeding frenzy of tantalizing cinematic treats. To wit:

Bill of Fare: A Top 10 of Great Food Movies Entrees:

1) "Who Is Killing the Great Chefs of Europe?" (1978): Talk about presentation. This delightful mystery-comedy-romance works on every level. With a show-stopping performance by the royally rotund Robert Morley, and succulent support from such players as George Segal, Jacqueline Bisset, Jean-Pierre Cassel, Jean Rochefort and Philippe Noiret, this grand romp flits from London to Paris to Venice and beyond, featuring wonderful forays into kitchens elaborate and small.

2) **"Babette's Feast" (1987):** Isak Dinesen's affecting short story is given Oscar-winning treatment by Gabriel Axel and a superb cast. Two adult sisters of a Protestant minister father live drab lives in an isolated village in 19th-century Denmark. They serve dad and his church well into adulthood, having given up a chance at love. Enter a French refugee, who proceeds to demonstrate how living can be a much broader and enriching experience with a less austere approach to it - and food.

3) **"Eat Drink Man Woman" (1994):** A senior master chef, Chu dwells in a cavernous house in Taipei with three pretty, unmarried daughters: a chemistry teacher converted to Christianity, an airline exec and a student who moonlights in a fast-food restaurant. Life in the house centers on ritual, specifically the ritual of an artful dinner each Sunday. Writer-director Ang Lee›s 1994 Oscar nominee is funny and touching, with a delicacy of approach.

4) **"Big Night" (1996):** Primo (Tony Shalhoub) and Secondo (writer-director-star Stanley Tucci) are two brothers who have emigrated from Italy to open an Italian restaurant in America. But the bistro is getting nowhere, and they must gamble on one memorable night to try to save the business. When the admiring owner (Ian Holm) of a successful neighboring restaurant offers a solution, the brothers think their fortunes will be secured, if they can deliver a feast to end all feasts. Minnie Driver, Isabella Rossellini, Allison Janney and Liev Schreiber also star.

5) **"Like Water for Chocolate" (1993):** Director Alfonso Arau adapted the celebrated novel by his then-wife, Laura Esquivel, crafting a delicious fable about a young woman (Lumi Cavazos) whose life is defined by a domineering mother, but shaped even more by the all-consuming power of cooking. The perfect stew of the exotic and erotic, with excellent performances all around.

6) **"The Scent of Green Papaya" (1994):-** The meld of food and cinema has rarely been as mesmerizing as this story of Mui, who as a child joins a prosperous household as a new servant. Ten years later, she is dispatched to serve a young pianist and his wife, and the musician falls in love with her, teaching the young woman how to read, how to apprehend a larger world. Unhurried, pictorially poetic and exquisitely detailed, this Oscar-nominated French-Vietnamese film is a haunting one.

7) **"Tampopo" (1986):** A witty and affectionate paean to the joys of food, this comedy-satire is the tale of a trucker who rumbles into town to help a young widow named Tampopo (Nobuko Miyamoto) establish the ideal fast-food noodle restaurant. But first he must tell her, gingerly, the unappetizing truth about her wretched cooking. Added ingredients are a number of smaller subplots about the importance of food.

8) **"Mostly Martha" (2002):** German chef Martha Klein is the obsessive, unchallenged potentate of the restaurant's kitchen staff. No one dares critique her cooking, least of all customers. All that collapses like a failed souffle when her sister dies in a car accident, leaving her an 8-year-old daughter to tend. But the pressures of her private and work lives

work a magical change of outlook in a subtle film that›s at least as much about love as food.

9) **"Chocolat" (2001):** A mere bauble thematically, but a luscious one nonetheless. Juliette Binoche stars as a single mother who moves with her 6-year-old daughter to an uptight village in rural France. Opening a chocolate shop directly across the street from the local church is a sinful proposition, thinks the stuffy mayor (Alfred Molina), a situation that only grows worse when Johnny Depp and a band of river gypsies descend on the town. Slight but intoxicating.

10) **"Soul Food" (1997):** A low-budget, haute-payoff gem featuring Vanessa L. Williams, Vivica A. Fox, Nia Long, Michael Beach and Mekhi Phifer. Family matriarch Mama Joe has held her family together for 40 years with the glue of a sumptuous Sunday repast. When diabetes hospitalizes the lady, the dinners stop and sibling tensions start to mount, until Mama Joe›s grandson concocts up a scheme to bring the family back to the table.

Side dishes (an honorable mention):

"Fried Green Tomatoes" (1991, from the book by Fanny Flagg), **"Tortilla Soup"** (2001, a Latin remake of «Eat Drink Man Woman»), **"Vatel"** (2000, based on a true story set in 1671 Holland), **"A Walk in the Clouds"** (1995, for the food, not the mawkish plot) and **"The Wedding Banquet"** (1993, the peerless Ang Lee again).

Bon appetit. (And pass the Pepto.)

....

It's Coming!
Space Invasion - Popular movies give shape to alien visitors
June 26, 2005

They're here! Aliens among us! Ever since pioneering astronomer Percival Lowell trained his telescope on the "canals" of Mars in 1906, imagining their banks to be inhabited, and certainly after Orson Welles' famed 1938 radio broadcast of "War of the Worlds" conned a nation into believing those martians were actually landing, we have been fascinated (or alarmed) by the prospect of interplanetary and interstellar visitors.

Lowell's canals proved to be an optical illusion - he was better at predicting the existence of the planet Pluto - but millions of filmgoers can still enjoy the fantasy of visitations, abductions and interactions with extraterrestrials on the big screen.

Or revisit them on home video.

Of course, daydreams and nightmares of spacefarers come to Earth are as old as antiquity, but let's confine ourselves to the modern age. For starters, Wednesday's opening of "War of the Worlds," Steven Spielberg's remake of the 1953 George Pal version of H.G. Wells' classic.

FRIGHT MAKES RIGHT

Some aliens, like the sweet-natured hero of Spielberg's endearing "E.T." (1982), are cuddly. Others are equally benevolent, like the big brother that descended from the heavens to save us from ourselves in "The Day the Earth Stood Still" (1951) and the well-meaning scientists of "This Island Earth" (1955).

Most, however, run from mysterious to menacing to downright lethal. But these images tend to say more about us and our fears than about any alien intelligence. Since a real alien psychology is just that, and probably inscrutable, we superimpose our motivations on those we imagine.

Movies of the 1950s, in particular, speculated in this fashion. Witness the original "Invasion of the Body Snatchers" (1958), often seen as a commentary on the suffocatingly conformist McCarthy era. Or the long-extinct aliens of "Forbidden Planet" (1956), who lived on through their machines' influence on human foibles.

Apart from its crude special effects, one of the best, tensest science-fiction films ever made was "Them!" (1954), about an onslaught of giant ants made huge by atomic bomb testing in the desert. Aliens of our own creation, they were. By contrast, Earth organisms were turned malevolent in "The Day of the Triffids" (1963).

The original "The Thing From Another World" (1951) may have lacked the claustrophobia and palpable paranoia of its source material, the classic short story "Who Goes There?" by John W. Campbell Jr., but it more than made up for it with its intelligence and overlapping, rapid-fire dialogue in the Howard Hawks style. In fact, Hawks ("Bringing Up Baby," "His Girl Friday"), who produced the picture, is said to have been the real director, not the credited Christian Nyby, a cinematographer and Hawks protege. Orson Welles also was rumored to have had a hand in the film. In any case, it is vastly superior to John Carpenter's gruesome 1982 remake, "The Thing."

Among the most unnerving of films was the original 1960 version of "Village of the Damned," based on the John Wyndham book "The Midwich Cuckoos" about alien children born to human mothers in rural Britain.

YOU OOZE, YOU LOSE

Steve McQueen had his first starring role as a teenager trying to contain the growing, inimical amoeba of "The Blob" (1958). Also fond of gorging on blood was the monster alien of "It: The Terror from Outer Space" (1958).

The spate of goofy, generally forgettable sci-fi comedies that accompanied the good 1950s films like pesky remoras began to fade in the '60s, notwithstanding TV shows like "My Favorite Martian" and "Lost in Space" (later made into dreary features). Still, more than a few were exceptionally odd, such as the spooky "Five Million Years to Earth" (1968), in which an ancient spaceship unearthed in a London subway proves to exert powerful psychic effects on the people in proximity to it, a notion later played with by Stephen

King in his book and miniseries "The Tommyknockers." Eerie, but satisfying, was Nicholas Roeg's "The Man Who Fell to Earth" (1976), an original take on Walter Tevis' fantasy novel that starred David Bowie as a humanoid alien who arrives on Earth to obtain water for his dying planet. He attempts to do so by becoming a high-technology entrepreneur, but fails to comprehend the ruthlessness of indigenous businesspeople.

Goodwill was the impulse behind the aliens of Spielberg's "Close Encounters of the Third Kind" (1977), a film actually completed before George Lucas' "Star Wars," but getting to the bijou a bit later. But with plenty of potency of its own and a lot more seriousness. Never mind that the compassionate folks in the gigantic space ship had been plucking earthlings from their work and homes for decades.

Those films might never have come to be without the seminal success of Stanley Kubrick's "2001: A Space Odyssey" (1968). The majestic alien presences of that movie and its sequel "2010" (1984) were never really seen, but their impact felt omnipotent as well as benign.

Between them, the old '60s TV series "The Twilight Zone" and "The Outer Limits" served up a space ark of alien stories, some of them outstanding, and are widely available in home video collections. Hunt hard, and you may even find episodes of "The Invaders." Need we even mention shows like "The X-Files" or all the various permutations of "Star Trek" on the small and big screen?

Though visually imaginative, the problem with the aliens of the "Star Wars" films is that, other than Yoda and Chewbacca, they were so rarely center stage. Great aliens seldom are supporting players.

STARK TERROR

Much of the power of old movies like "Invasion of the Body Snatchers" stemmed from what they did not show. A great deal was left to that master manipulator, the imagination. This was passe by the 1980s, when gore, titillation and dogfighting in space held sway.

That said, you can argue that the scariest alien ever on screen first stuck out his jaw in 1979. Before it devolved into an old-fashioned bug-eyed monster movie (albeit incredibly tense, and with state-of-the-art effects) Ridley Scott's "Alien" offered the best "hard" science fiction to hit the screen since "2001." The beasties seemed somehow less formidable in the sequel, "Aliens," more an action film (typically) than genuine science fiction.

Their chief competitor: "Predator" (1987), a clever outing from John McTiernan about an extraterrestrial trophy hunter whose prey is our most violent citizens. Save for a couple of ill-placed 007-like puns, it's a nail-bitter throughout.

Speaking of which, for a guilty pleasure, have a look at last year's critically panned but still fun "Alien vs. Predator." It's quite the battle royal, with humans caught in the middle.

Though hardly worth a mention, "Species" (1995) was notable for being full of unintended humor. Not a demerit for Tim Burton's amusing "Mars Attacks!" (1996), a send-up of all the sci-fi movies that had gone before, especially "Earth vs. the Flying Saucers" (1956). Ditto for the spoofy "Men in Black" (1997), which had a fine comic turn by Vincent D'Onofrio as a vicious alien roach, and the affectionate "Star Trek" parody "Galaxy Quest" (1999).

The invaders of "Independence Day" (1997) were a joke. So was the movie. Likewise for "Starship Troopers" (1997).

Undone by a clumsy ending, but solid up till that point, was 1998's moody "Dark City," whose cadaverous aliens looked like they hailed from Planet Nosferatu.

GREETINGS!

Fortunately, another curious (if wary), nice guy alien dropped in on us in "Star Man" (1984), showcasing touching performances by Jeff Bridges and Karen Allen. Same for John Sayles' mute "Brother from Another Planet" (1984, with a fine turn by Joe Morton), the undersea squatters of "The Abyss" (1989) who were already here, and the offworlders with powers of rejuvenation in "Cocoon" (1985), who set up shop near a retirement home. Very thoughtful.

Well-made, but wildly unfaithful to the spirit of its source (the novel by the late Carl Sagan), was "Contact" (1997), a penned-by-committee first-contact story. Like many of its predecessors, aliens in the film eventually take human form to make it easier to communicate with us in a unthreatening manner. The movie has its moments, but the aliens are almost incidental.

The first great alien film of the 21st century has yet to appear. Isn't this when we were supposed to see them all? Maybe it's time to dust off all those star-drive ideas.

For now, the aliens of the galaxy will have to keep coming to us, because we won't be paying them a call any time soon. The swiftest objects devised by humankind (the Voyager probes) plod along at a sluggish 11 miles per second. So even if we did verify life on another a planet of the nearest star, Proxima Centauri, it would take 73,000 years to pass on a few artifacts and mementoes. Barring faster-than-light space drives, folded space, black hole commuting or what have you, all we can do is offer a (landing) cup for their saucers.

The first recorded UFO sighting came on June 24, 1947, by a private pilot in Boise, Idaho. Many more have seen ... something. But before any of us take them to see our leader, perhaps a glass of Romulan ale?

....

Oscars: The Biopic
February 27, 2005

Born in 1928, and not looking a day older, the Oscar depicts a featureless knight holding a crusader's sword and standing atop a reel of film. The five spokes of the reel signify the original branches of the Academy of Motion Picture Arts and Sciences: actors, writers, directors, producers and technicians.

They may need to add a sixth spoke, for publicity and marketing. It is through these categories that many Oscars are at least partially won, with manufactured "buzz" that begins long before critics and other voters actually see the movies and relentless hype that makes the actual statuette itself, at 8.5 pounds and 13.5 inches in height, seem to diminish in stature with each passing year.

Some might argue that ignoring Mel Gibson's "The Passion of the Christ" and Michael Moore's "Fahrenheit 9/11," whatever their merits, makes the Academy Awards even less relevant this year.

Oscar's still head and shoulders over all the other pipsqueak awards shows, at least in terms of cachet, but the golden boy designed by MGM's chief art director Cedric Gibbons in the 1930s has lost some of his luster.

Not that calculation hasn't always been a part of the formula. Ditto for tonight's 77th annual bash.

It's not mere happenstance that actors angle for leading roles in historical biopics, in self-consciously "serious" dramas, or as tragic drunks, warriors, boxers, people dying (courageously) of dread diseases or going not-so-quietly bonkers. Actors aren't dumb; they know what the Academy admires, and they campaign for these roles tenaciously. Four out of the five Best Actor nominees and three of the five Best Actress nominees for 2004 portrayed real-life characters.

From Moses to Mozart, Oscar adores a biopic with gravitas, the more somber the better. The past year offered a bumper crop, at least in terms of numbers, what with films centering on the lives of Howard Hughes, Alfred Kinsey, Che Guevara, Ray Charles, J.M. Barrie, Bobby Darin, Cole Porter and Alexander the Great.

Actors' chief co-conspirators (apart from agents and moguls) are the legions of publicists who nab early magazine covers, plant rapturous quotes about "Oscar-worthy performances," selectively pluck lines from critical reviews, and stage a flurry of talk-show appearances.

So, what else is new, right?

Well, one of the more noticeable things is that there are far fewer stories in the media harping on the ascendance of black actors, a sign that at least some measure of parity is being achieved, and it is no longer so striking a development as to be newsworthy. Despite some glaring omissions (like Kimberly Elise in "Woman Thou Art Loosed"), this Oscar season was the best yet for black stars, who earned five of the 20 acting nominations. And little has been made of it, other than to celebrate the people and their work.

Here's betting that even the usually outrageous Chris Rock, who's hosting this year's ceremony, downplays the milestone.

A LOCK

Jamie Foxx. "Ray." Best Actor. Make book on it.

Some of the other categories aren't quite so solid.

"The Aviator" has everything the Academy usually demands in a Best Picture nominee, including a glaze of pretension and the sweep of spectacle. For one, it's a biopic with a sense of generosity toward its subject. It's also big, brash, star-studded and not so serious in intent that it isn't fun. Add to this the fact that industry lion Martin Scorsese has been nominated for Best Director four previous times and never won - something we're reminded of every 10 minutes - and there's no question that it's the favorite to win Best Picture. It wasn't the best, but that hardly matters.

Still, Scorsese shouldn't count his chickens just yet. If makeup calls held sway, four-time Best Actor loser Jeff Bridges, long overdue, would've been nominated for the John Irving adaptation "The Door in the Floor." Oscar loves fresh blood, too, yet Rodrigo de la Serna ("The Motorcycle Diaries") was ignored for Best Supporting Actor.

If any Best Picture nominee is going to pull a surprise, it will be Clint Eastwood's "Million Dollar Baby," which has something Scorsese seldom manages: streamlined storytelling. It's just possible the Academy will throw Scorsese a bone, naming him Best Director but dissing his movie. If any actor upsets the cart, it likely will be Virginia Madsen, back from obscurity in "Sideways."

Forget the atmospheric box office of "Shrek 2." "The Incredibles" takes Best Animated Feature in a landslide.

American sensibilities probably will prohibit a Best Actress Oscar going to someone who played an abortionist (Imelda Staunton in "Vera Drake"), which leaves that race between Hilary Swank ("Million Dollar Baby") and Annette Bening ("Being Julia"), with Kate Winslet ("Eternal Sunshine of the Spotless Mind") as a dark horse. It's tempting to pick Bening, richly deserving, in a mild upset. But she'll have to overcome recent history. It was Swank (in "Boys Don't Cry") who beat out the heavily favored Bening (in "American Beauty") for the Oscar five years ago. Swank also won the Screen Actors Guild award for best actress at the recent SAG ceremony, and the SAG actor winner has claimed 13 of the past 20 Oscars in the same categories.

AT LAST

Director Sidney Lumet never won an Academy Award despite a resume enriched by such films as "Q&A," "The Verdict," "Prince of the City," "Network," "Dog Day Afternoon," "Serpico," "The Hill," "The Pawnbroker," "Fail-Safe" and "12 Angry Men."

His movies have earned more than 40 Oscar nominations, yet none adorn his mantel.

That the Academy will present Lumet with an honorary award tonight after a lifetime of neglect doubtless will be a bittersweet experience for this longtime purveyor of the socially conscious pictures.

Lumet, like Scorsese, is in esteemed nonwinning company. Oscar has ignored so many film industry legends who never won for directing or acting over the years (honorary Oscars don't count). Apart from Richard Burton, Barbara Stanwyck and Peter O'Toole, other giants who got the shaft include Charles Chaplin, Greta Garbo, Alfred Hitchcock, Howard Hawks, Cary Grant, Preston Sturges, Kirk Douglas, Robert Mitchum, Montgomery Clift, James Mason, Josef von Sternberg, Gloria Swanson, Ernst Lubitsch, Carole Lombard, Charles Boyer, Stanley Kubrick, Deborah Kerr, Trevor Howard, King Vidor and Agnes Moorehead.

....

Isn't It Romantic
February 13, 2005

"Love is an irresistible desire to be irresistibly desired." -- Robert Frost

Ah, amour. Said with a sigh. Can a chuckle be far behind? Perhaps it's our shared recognition of the cosmic joke nature plays on men and women, what with our maddeningly divergent rhythms and cycles. Not to mention ever-fluctuating social expectations.

Thank heaven for comedy. We can laugh at our chemically induced delirium even as we celebrate its glories, especially on the eve of Valentine's Day. It's why we love romantic comedies, maybe even more than unalloyed romantic films that oft take themselves way too seriously.

If "Bringing Up Baby" was the prototype screwball comedy, any list of the great romantic comedies of the American cinema must begin with their tender-hearted template, the Mother of all Romantic Romps, Frank Capra's **"It Happened One Night"** (1934). The astonishing thing is that this 70-year-old movie hasn't aged a day. It's as fresh, as funny, as perceptive a take on the battle of the sexes as ever made it to the screen.

Clark Gable and Claudette Colbert spar and spark in this landmark picture about a runaway heiress (Colbert) soon to be a bride and an opportunistic reporter (Gable) who connect in one of the most memorable road trips in the movies. It was the first film to sweep all four top Academy Awards: Best Picture, Best Actor, Best Actress and Best Director.

Of all the other films of the 1930s, only Ernst Lubitsch's **"Ninotchka"** (1939), with Greta Garbo (laughing!) and Melvyn Douglas (wooing) rivaled it for pizazz.

Make no mistake, we get a kick out of the contemporary stuff. **"Shakespeare in Love"** (1998, John Madden), for example, may be the most perfectly realized romantic comedy of the last 30 years, but the past trumps the present in this category.

CARY ME BACK

Why do so many of the best romantic comedies seem to star either Cary Grant or Kate Hepburn, or both? Especially Grant, what with **"Bringing Up Baby," "The Philadelphia Story," "His Girl Friday," "Indiscreet," "To Catch a Thief," "Father Goose," "Charade"** and **"Houseboat,"** just for starters. Did anyone have better timing, sharper comedic instincts or more style? Nope.

His films with Hepburn were at least as good as the romantic comedies she did with Spencer Tracy.

"Bringing Up Baby" (1938) was the second fortuitous pairing of Grant and Hepburn, this time under the direction of the master of rapid-fire patter, Howard Hawks. With its break-neck pace, off-the-wall shenanigans and impeccable timing, it's considered by many to be the best comedy ever made. Hepburn is a mercurial scatterbrain of an heiress who upends Grant's staid life as a paleontologist, taking him in pursuit of a leopard - two, actually - in the "wilds" of suburban Connecticut. No one ever sang "I Can't Give You Anything But Love" with more hilarity.

It was Cary and Kate again (Tracy was unavailable) in the wittiest comedy yet of the privileged enjoying their privileges, **"The Philadelphia Story"** (1940). Director George Cukor's sophisticated comedy (from Philip Barry's play) earned an Oscar for James Stewart, but was perfectly cast in every way. Hepburn reprised her stage role as a chilly heiress (yes, another one) about to marry a self-made but shallow man. Stewart is covering the society event for a scandal rag, under duress, and escorts her down from her pedestal while ex-husband (Grant) waits for developments.

Hepburn and Tracy had their memorable murmurings as well, with **"Woman of the Year"** (1942, George Stevens) and **"Adam's Rib"** (1949, George Cukor) topping the bill. The one thing all these comedies had in common was great writing, wed to impeccable performances and direction.

Barbra Stanwyck also was a staple of 1940s comedies, chief among her contributions being **"The Lady Eve"** (1941), director Preston Sturges' peerless blend of elegance, wit and nonsense. Stanwyck, as the seductive half of a father-daughter team of con artists, takes bachelor millionaire Henry Fonda for a ride, only to be betrayed by her own heart. Stanwyck also used her feminine savvy to win the affections of bookish scholar Gary Cooper (and all his colleagues) in **"Ball of Fire"** (1941), another gem from Howard Hawks, who was one year removed from having made another priceless film, **"His Girl Friday"** (1942) with Rosalind Russell and Cary Grant.

NEXT GENERATION

More a bittersweet romance with comic flourishes than a straight-out romantic comedy, **"Roman Holiday"** (1953) still makes the list. It remains a captivating fairy tale shot entirely on location in the Eternal City, directed with both brio and sensitivity by William Wyler. It's a Cinderella take in reverse, with runaway princess

Audrey Hepburn (who won an Oscar for her first feature) rebelling against her royal obligations and escaping into the arms of yet another newspaperman (Gregory Peck, in his warmest performance).

Grant returned for a handful of romantic comedies (touched with suspense) in the 1950s and 1960s before his premature retirement, notably in the breezy **"To Catch a Thief"** (1955, Alfred Hitchcock), matching wits with a drop-dead gorgeous Grace Kelly; in **"Charade"** (1963, Stanley Donen) opposite Audrey Hepburn's damsel-in-distress; and, in an uncharacteristically grizzled guise, in **"Father Goose"** (1965, Ralph Nelson), a remake of the immortal romantic adventure "The African Queen," albeit with a greater reliance on humor.

The best of the form in this period was probably Billy Wilder's sparkling office comedy **"The Apartment"** (1960), a film not without its serious points (like "The Philadelphia Story") that was endearingly played by Jack Lemmon and Shirley MacLaine. Wilder also served up **"Some Like It Hot"** (1959, a classic comedy with romantic underpinnings, if not a true romantic comedy.

There are plenty for devotees for the Rock Hudson-Doris Day pairings, chiefly **"Pillow Talk"** (1959, Michael Gordon), but we prefer his delightful duel with Paula Prentiss in **"Man's Favorite Sport?"** (1964, Howard Hawks), a worthy homage to his own "Bringing Up Baby."

THE MODERNS

The mantle of cleverest and most inventive romantic comedies simply has to go to Woody Allen's **"Annie Hall"** (1977), the director-star's finest film. If any movie of the modern era stands up to "Shakespeare in Love" it's this. Allen's masterpiece won a ton of Oscars that year, but he lost out as Best Actor that same year to an extraordinarily accomplished performance by Richard Dreyfus in **"The Goodbye Girl"** (1977). The most romantic kiss of the decade was shared by Dreyfuss and Marsha Mason on a rooftop in the rain, and Neil Simon's dialogue was tops.

On the wilder side was **"Silver Streak"** (1976), director Arthur Hiller's suspenseful strangers-on-a-train romance (rather randy echoes of "North by Northwest") featuring Gene Wilder and Jill Clayburgh, not to forget Richard Pryor.

The 1980ss brought the disarming **"Tootsie"** (1982, and a trio of jewels that holds up to viewing after viewing. **"Moonstruck"** (1987, Norman Jewison) proved Cher could act, and act up a storm, this time opposite an equally impressive Nicolas Cage, while Rom Shelton's **"Bull Durham"** (1988) batted a thousand with co-stars Susan Sarandon, Kevin Costner, Tim Robbins and a crisp, charming script.

But perhaps everyone's favorite of the '80s remains **"When Harry Met Sally"** (1989), Rob Reiner's enduring comedy of platonic regard morphing into something much more. Billy Crystal and Meg Ryan were perfect casting, and Nora Ephron's screenplay was her best.

Let's not forget **"Arthur"** (1981), **"The Princess Bride"** (1987), and **"Working Girl"** (1988).

The 1990s tossed us a bouquet of such fragrant fare as **"Four Weddings and a Funeral"** (1994), **"Sleepless in Seattle"** (1993), **"Groundhog Day"** (1993), **"Much Ado About Nothing"** (1993), **"The American President"** (1995), **"Dave"** (1993, through the lens of politics), **"Shall We Dance"**)1996, the Japanese version, please), **"As Good As It Gets"** (1997), **"Chasing Amy"** (1997), **"Six Days, Seven Nights"** (1998), **"Notting Hill"** (1999) and, of course, **"Shakespeare in Love."**

Like "Pretty Woman" in the 1980s, **"My Big Fat Greek Wedding"** (2002) was amusing enough, but didn't quite live up to its billing as a comedy of wish fulfillment, or mark the new century as a prospective golden age. But the underappreciated **"Serendipity"** (2001), with John Cusack and Kate Beckinsale, did. As did the little-seen **"Bossa Nova"** (2000) with Amy Irving doing her best work since the delightful **"Crossing Delancey"** (1988).

What does the future hold? More of the same, we trust. Because hopefulness and love stroll hand-in-hand and, in the best if all worlds, with a soft smile and a lilting laugh.

....

Can 'Oscar' really pick the best?
February 26, 2004

> *"If you think you're a great actor because you won an Oscar, you're crazy."*
> -- Joe Pesci (who won in 1990 for "GoodFellas")

Poor Marisa Tomei, Mr. Pesci's leading lady in "My Cousin Vinny." Her one great moment besmirched by doubters and naysayers, and even intimations of a substitute envelope. Tomei's Best Supporting Actress Oscar in 1992 continues to be reviled as a sham, somewhat unfairly. Fact is, Oscar has made far more egregious gaffes, dispensing not merely a series of sentimental sops and make-up calls over the years, but flagrant miscarriages of justice. Everyone has his favorite fiascoes.

Here (still scratching our heads that Richard Burton and Barbara Stanwyck never won acting Oscars, but that Angelina Jolie did) are ours.

Of course, different eras, different sensibilities. We have the advantage of perspective. But quality is quality. And could we finally dispense with career-achievement awards (for actors who never won but should have) masquerading as a given year's best work?

For purposes of streamlining, let's begin with 1940 and confine comment to the acting, direction and best-picture categories.

WRATH OF FORD

Alfred Hitchcock's sumptuous "Rebecca" was an admirable choice for Best Picture, until one remembers that it beat out "The Grapes of Wrath," a milestone in motion-picture realism and a pivotal force in American movie history. Ditto for John Ford's "How Green Was My Valley," an excellent film, except that it shared the same year as "Citizen Kane," widely viewed as the cinema's crowning achievement. Ford had won best director the previous year for "The Grapes of Wrath," but the academy gave it to him in back-to-back years because voters didn't much like "Kane's" boy wonder, Orson Welles.

Of course, the years 1939 (with nominees "Gone With the Wind," "Stagecoach," "The Wizard of Oz," "Wuthering Heights," "Mr. Smith Goes to Washington," "Of Mice and Men" and "Goodbye Mr. Chips"); 1940 (with "The Philadelphia Story," "Our Town" and "Foreign Correspondent," as well as "Rebecca" and "The Grapes of Wrath"); and 1941 (sporting "The Maltese Falcon," "Here Comes Mr. Jordan" "Sergeant York" and "Suspicion," in addition to "Valley" and "Kane"), may have been the toughest to pick in academy annals.

By contrast, one of the first certifiable laughers came in 1942, when Greer Garson's portrait of English grace under pressure in the sappy "Mrs. Miniver" capitalized on wartime patriotism to win Best Actress. Nevermind that Katharine Hepburn blew her away in "Woman of the Year," but Kate was not so popular with filmdom in those days. Worse, "Mrs. Miniver" also captured Best Picture over vastly superior films such as "The Magnificent Ambersons" "The Talk of the Town," "Pride of the Yankees" and "Yankee Doodle Dandy."

While 1955's "Marty," drawn from a moving teleplay, boasted a hugely appealing performance from Ernest Borgnine, and a characteristically fine script from Paddy Chayefsky, was Delbert Mann's direction better than Elia Kazan's in "East of Eden"? Hardly.

Another laugher: the 1957 Supporting Actor trophy. Red Buttons' hammy turn in "Sayonara" beating out one of the cinema's most fascinating performances, Sessue Hayakawa's in "Bridge on the River Kwai."

Four words: Elizabeth Taylor, "Butterfield 8." Even she thought the movie stank, until she won a Best Actress Oscar for it in 1960. So much better were Deborah Kerr in Fred Zinnemann's "The Sundowners" and Shirley MacLaine in Billy Wilder's "The Apartment."

"My Fair Lady's" Best Picture Academy Award in 1964 must have been based on costumes and sets, for it certainly didn't lead the field in any other department (Rex Harrison's Best Actor Oscar being questionable at best). "Dr. Strangelove" and "Becket" left it choking in their dust.

Kate Hepburn wasn't always supreme. Anne Bancroft ("The Graduate") and Faye Dunaway ("Bonnie and Clyde") trumped her in 1967. She won Best Actress anyway, in her final pairing with Spencer Tracy for "Guess Who's Coming to Dinner." Wonder why?

Hepburn won the next year, as well (deservedly) for "The Lion in Winter," getting tied by Barbra Streisand ("Funny Girl").

HIGH ANXIETY

Maureen Stapleton was robbed by her fellow supporting cast member Helen Hayes, who won Best Supporting Actress in 1970 for "Airport." Stapleton's real competition was Sally Kellerman in "MASH."

Let this heresy stand. Marlon (Mumblefest) Brando's 1972 Best Actor Oscar for "The Godfather" was ridiculous. Michael Caine ("Sleuth") was robbed. So was Laurence Olivier for the same picture. And what of Peter O'Toole in "The Ruling Class." Brando was a distant fourth.

But turnabout was fair play. A good argument could have been made for Brando as Best Actor the following year in "Last Tango in Paris," or Jack Nicholson in "The Last Detail." But Jack Lemmon got his long-awaited make-up call for the desultory "Save the Tiger."

A bad joke: George Burns in "The Sunshine Boys" was a ludicrous supporting actor pick over Brad Dourif ("One Flew Over the Cuckoo's Nest") and Burgess Meredith ("The Day of the Locust") in 1975. A year later: "Rocky" over "Network"? No way. Sally Field ("Norma Rae"), good as she was, over Jill Clayburgh ("Starting Over") for 1979's Best Actress. Nope.

The plodding feel-good exertions of "Chariots of Fire" (aka, "Rickshaws of Schmaltz") played out like a mediocre TV movie, though it won as Best Picture in 1981 over such superior fare as "Atlantic City," "Reds," and even "Raiders of the Lost Ark."

Paul Newman had the bad luck to give the finest performance of his career ("The Verdict," 1982) the same year Ben Kingsley was a lock for "Gandhi." Which reminds us. A costume design Oscar for "Gandhi"? Are you kidding? For robes? When, in the same year, you had the remarkable creativity exhibited in "Blade Runner"?

Pardon the digression. Newman would get his make-up Oscar for lesser work in 1986 ("The Color of Money"), an Academy Award Oscar that should have been won by James Woods for "Salvador" or Bob Hoskins for "Mona Lisa."

Cher was unexpectedly terrific in "Moonstruck," walking away with Best Actress in 1987. But Holly Hunter gave what was perhaps the best comic performance of the 1980s in "Broadcast News" the same year. She got zilch.

Spike Lee's "Do the Right Thing" was the best movie of 1989. It wasn't nominated. A travesty. Ditto for Jeremy Irons in 1989 for "Dead Ringers." No ticket to the show.

ROBBED & JOBBED

Our admiration for Al Pacino is considerable. Still, Denzel Washington's embodiment of Malcolm X in the film of the same name was beyond compare in 1992. Pacino winning was, arguably, yet another case of the make-up call for past slights. As for Ms. Tomei's Best Supporting Actress Oscar that year, it really should have gone to Judy Davis for "Husbands and Wives" or to Joan Plowright for "Enchanted April." No offense to Anna Paquin ("The

Piano," 1993), but the notion of child actors winning Oscars is patently absurd. No matter how precocious, they simply cannot equal the work of a mature actor or actress.

Tom Hanks won the first of two consecutive Best Actor Oscars in 1993 for "Philadelphia," a rose-tinted cop-out of a film that lacked the courage of its own convictions. He would win again for the clever but overrated "Forrest Gump." Hanks is first and foremost a comic actor, and neither of these rather calculated dramatic performances equaled his great (and largely overlooked) comedic turn in "A League of Their Own" (1992). "Pulp Fiction" was robbed for "Best Picture."

Like so many actors before him in the competition's toughest category, Gary Sinise also deserved a Supporting Actor Oscar for "Gump," but had the bad luck to be competing against Martin Landau's memorable work (as Bela Lugosi) in "Ed Wood."

The entertaining "Braveheart" represented a great deal of work and perseverance on the part of its director and star Mel Gibson. But did this un-historical epic rate as Best Picture in 1995? Not, in our view, against "Sense and Sensibility." Nor should Nicolas Cage, though excellent, have defeated Sean Penn ("Dead Man Walking") for Best Actor.

1996: Best Picture winner "The English Patient" was a solid, well-made romance. The Coen brothers' "Fargo" was better, certainly more original, and even more believable.

SINKING FEELING

1997: "Titanic" over "L.A. Confidential"? Director James Cameron over director Curtis Hanson? Get real. What is this, the Grammys? And where was Kate Winslet's Best Actress nomination for "Jude"? Or Cate Blanchett's for "Oscar and Lucinda"? Unpardonable.

Judi Dench is a delight, time and again. But her 1998 supporting actress Oscar for a bit part in "Shakespeare in Love" could not possibly compare to Kathy Bates' screen-dominating performance in "Primary Colors."

2000: "Gladiator" over "Traffic"? Asinine. Julia Roberts' by-the-numbers performance ("Erin Brockovich") stealing Best Actress from Joan Allen ("The Contender") and Laura Linney ("You Can Count on Me")? Nyet.

2001: Good but not great, "A Beautiful Mind" had no business winning Best Picture over "The Fellowship of the Ring" or "In the Bedroom," despite "Mind's" fine performances. And completely baffling (except for political reasons) was Halle Berry's Best Actress win for the execrable "Monster's Ball," one of the clumsiest and most dishonest movies in recent memory. Berry was merely competent, work not in the same league as that of Judi Dench ("Iris") or Sissy Spacek ("In the Bedroom"). As for play-it-safe Ron Howard as Best Director over Ridley Scott ("Black Hawk Down") and Peter Jackson ("The Fellowship of the Ring")? Balderdash.

We await your outraged e-mails.

Reel Horror: In movies, golden oldies are full of fright
October 26, 2003

Forget ghouls, goblins and creatures of the night.

The most horrifying thing about horror movies is their current, abysmal state. Apart from the occasional nail-biter like "The Sixth Sense" or "The Ring," the genre now is dominated by the slasher film, in which restraint, suggestion and the power of imagination have little emphasis amid bouts of gore - the more gruesome the better.

The fear is that we may never see a great horror movie again.

Now that's scary.

Shock value has a wholly different meaning. We're shocked that people bother to see this stuff. More than ever, if you want to find the best the cinema of horror has to offer, you have to look back, not forward, and on video.

First, a bit of history.

Although Thomas Edison shot a film version of "Frankenstein" as early as 1908, horror as a staple of the screen derives from the early silent films of Germany, among them the 1920 incarnation of "The Golem," a major influence on the Hollywood horror school given momentum by James Whale.

These early efforts often were masterpieces of the macabre: "The Cabinet of Dr. Caligari," Murnau's brilliantly conceived "Nosferatu" (based on Bram Stoker's "Dracula"), "Waxworks," "Vampyr" and "The Hands of Orlac" among them.

Hollywood made some strides with the Man of a Thousand Faces, Lon Chaney, especially in "Phantom of the Opera," but the most frightening films of the '20s and '30s - they retain their power today - were the two versions of "Dr. Jekyll and Mr. Hyde" (the first with John Barrymore, the second with Fredric March), and Tod Browning's milestone filming of the stage version of "Dracula," employing the services of an obscure Hungarian theater actor, Bela Lugosi. There are scenes in this last picture that still give folks the shivers, not to mention nightmares, and there's not a movie made in the last 50 years that can touch it for creepy atmosphere.

The most unsettling film of the '30s was undoubtedly Browning's "Freaks," a film that still fascinates succeeding generations of audiences.

Whale's "Frankenstein" was more elegant and literate than grisly, but this second milestone of '30s horror made a star of Boris Karloff and helped generate a wave of films such as "The Mummy" (again with Karloff), "The Island of Lost Souls" (with Charles Laughton, later remade as "The Island of Dr. Moreau"), and "The Invisible Man" (with Claude Rains).

Soon came the inevitable spoofs. But that's another story.

In 1935 came the seminal "Werewolf of London," followed five years later by "The

Wolf Man" (with Lon Chaney Jr.). There have been countless werewolf movies since, but unlike modern vampire films, which seldom have equaled (much less surpassed) the early works, several contemporary werewolf pictures have, to an extent, trumped their predecessors. John Landis' 1981 hit "An American Werewolf in London" seamlessly mixed full-blooded horror with a sharp sense of humor. Mike Nichols' "Wolf" (1994) had Jack Nicholson getting growly to good effect, while managing to make some subtle but penetrating cultural commentary.

As the '40s dawned, we got "Dr. Cyclops," and with the onset of World War II, good remakes of "The Cat and the Canary" and "The Ghost Breakers." But by far the influential horror films of the '40s were those moody RKO Studio pictures made by Val Lewton between 1942 and 1945, the best being "The Body Snatcher," "I Walked With a Zombie" and the superb "Cat People."

Horror stalled in the '50s, until it was rescued by science fiction. Though not always a happy marriage, some solid films were produced, as well as some inspired ones: "The Thing From Another World," the original "Invasion of the Body Snatchers," "The Fly" and "Them."

We exclude from this list the monster movies "Godzilla," "Rodan," et al, that more properly belong to their own category, and straightforward science fiction.

The '60s were owned by the Hammer Films factory, a small independent studio that made scores of remakes of earlier sagas, but introduced a new style: blood-letting on a grand scale. It is these films, not those from Roger Corman (his stylish Poe adaptations were far more restrained) or Alfred Hitchcock's "Psycho," that really put the modern horror film on the path of gratuitous gruesomeness. But there was also the influence of George Romero's "Night of the Living Dead."

Graveyard horror ruled the early '70s, typified by "Tales From the Crypt" and "The House That Dripped Blood." The late '70s offered Brian De Palma's fine Stephen King adaptation, "Carrie," a surprisingly good remake of "Invasion of the Body Snatchers" from Philip Kaufman, and a hybridized "Alien" from Ridley Scott.

But the horror film entered its most profitable (and lurid) period with the advent of home video in the 1980s. Things just got more and more excessive with such thrillers as "Friday the 13th," "Hell Night," and the execrable "I Spit on Your Grave." Style and imagination were gone, save for the work of a few genuine talents such as David Cronenberg, who would make what was arguably the best horror film of the '80s in "Dead Ringers," and, to a lesser extent, John Carpenter ("Halloween," etc.). De Palma, forever aping Hitchcock, also scored with the slasher flick "Dressed to Kill."

Yet soon enough, special effects supplanted everything, and the interminable series held sway. Still, there were glimmers of quality. Stanley Kubrick made "The Shining," based on King's third novel, and King's British rival, novelist Clive Barker, turned director for the modestly successful "Hellraiser." Meanwhile, Freddy (Robert Englund) became a force to be reckoned with (as did director Wes Craven) in the first "A Nightmare on Elm Street." As usual, a raft of inferior sequels followed in its wake.

By the mid-'90s, some of Hollywood's top directors and actors decided to try their hand. Apart from Nichols and Nicholson, there was Francis Ford Coppola with "Bram Stoker's Dracula," starring Gary Oldman (the best scenery chewing in many years), and Kenneth Branagh with "Mary Shelley's Frankenstein," featuring Robert De Niro.

Vampire and martial arts movies collided for "Blade" (1998), but for the most part the late '90s had little to offer anyone over the age of 12.

Three years into the new century, and we're still waiting for that first great horror film. "Freddy vs. Jason" ain't it. Neither is "Underworld" or the remake of "Texas Chainsaw Massacre." Nor does anything now in the pipeline appear to promise much in the way of originality. Just more special effects, more blood, more one-upmanship.

There's some compensation, however, in the Hughes brothers' "From Hell," and in 2001's "Shadow of the Vampire," but the latter film's power had more to do with its cleverly cheeky approach and Willem Dafoe's uncanny, Oscar-worthy performance than anything else.

No, the best horror films are the oldest ones, and those unacquainted with them should make a dash for the closest video store (avoiding any and all gremlins en route). Many of the greats continue to be available on video as well as being late-night TV standbys.

Spooky you want, spooky they got.

....

They Said It...
The greatest things ever said about Hollywood, the movies and the stars
February 16, 2003

"They can't censor the gleam in my eye." -- Charles Laughton

Caustic, indifferent, catty or snide. Irreverent, clear-eyed, despairing or sentimental. Herein lies one, if not the definitive, collection of the best things anyone ever said about the movies, or about those who make them.

Some are startlingly revealing, others a dash of pure wit. But each is memorable. And they come to you courtesy of a bulging library of books about film, with a special vote of gratitude to "The Filmgoer's Companion," signature work of the late British critic and historian Leslie Halliwell. By category:

THE BUSINESS

-- "Anyone who gets a raw deal in a film studio is no more deserving of pity than someone who gets beaten up in a brothel." - Sir Alexander Korda

-- "Less money, more freedom." - Martin Scorsese, on the world of the '50s B picture
-- "To write a script today means working for a committee of people who know nothing about movies, as opposed, say, to real estate or the higher art of bookkeeping." - Gore Vidal
-- "(Movies) have slipped into the American mind more misinformation in one evening than the Dark Ages could muster in a decade." - Ben Hecht
-- "I felt the urge to direct because I couldn't stomach what was being done with what I wrote." - Joseph L. Mankiewicz
-- "You're only as good as your last picture." - actress Marie Dressler
-- "The son-in-law also rises." - Anonymous, on Hollywood nepotism
-- "There might have been good movies had there been no movie industry." - Producer David O. Selznick
-- "Our town worships success, the bitch goddess whose smile hides a taste for blood." - Hedda Hopper
-- "No one ever went broke underestimating the taste of the American public." - H.L. Mencken
-- "The kind of jackass who likes the movies as they are is the kind that keeps them as they are." - H.L. Mencken
-- "There's no shortage of talent. There's only a shortage of talent that can recognize talent." - producer Jerry Wald
-- "Editing and camerawork can always produce the illusion
that a performance is being given." - George Sanders
-- "Men and women whose names were known throughout the world disappeared as though they had been lost at sea." - Jack Warner, on the demise of silent stars with the coming of sound
-- "If you are in a position to give credit, you don't need it." - producer Irving Thalberg

LEVITY IS BREVITY
-- "This film needs a certain something. Possibly burial."- critic David Lardner, reviewing "Panama Hattie"
-- "There is nothing more old-fashioned than being up to date." - Noel Coward
-- "That's what you think." - critic James Agee, reviewing "You Were Meant for Me"
-- "She ran the gamut of emotions from A to B." - Dorothy Parker, reviewing an early stage performance by Katharine Hepburn
-- "Jack Benny played Mendelssohn last night. Mendelssohn lost." - Anonymous, on Jack Benny's violin playing in a film
-- "Several tons of dynamite are set off in this picture - none of it under the right people." - critic James Agee, reviewing "Tycoon"
-- "The Marx Brothers were comics. Meeting them was a tragedy." - George S. Kaufman

-- "Like writing history with lightning." - President Woodrow Wilson, on seeing "Birth of a Nation"

OFF CAMERA
-- "My difficulty is trying to reconcile my gross habits with my net income." - Errol Flynn
-- "Bogart's a helluva nice guy until 11:30 p.m.. After that he thinks he's Bogart." - Restaurateur David Chase, on Humphrey Bogart
-- "The trouble with the world is that everybody in it is about three drinks behind." - Humphrey Bogart
-- "I ain't really Henry Fonda. No one could have that much integrity." - Henry Fonda, on his image
-- I'm from the let's pretend school, of acting." - Harrison Ford
-- "There but for the grace of God, goes God."- Herman Mankiewicz, observing the young Orson Welles at work
-- "She talks at you as though you were a microphone." - Humphrey Bogart, on Katharine Hepburn
-- "You don't stop being a citizen just because you have a Screen Actors Guild card." – Paul Newman
-- "He looks like a half-melted rubber bulldog." - John Simon on Walter Matthau
-- "The only reason people attended his funeral was to make sure he was dead." - Anonymous, on the death of autocratic mogul Louis B. Mayer
-- "Otto, let my people go." - comic Mort Sahl, to director Otto Preminger at the premiere of "Exodus"
-- "Life is a divine poem, and it is our fault if we recite it badly." - director Gabriel Pascal

AUTHENTICITY
-- "The camera not only picks up shoddiness, but it detects lack of sincerity or shallowness of feeling. This applies ubiquitously to the work of director, performer or designer." - photographer Sir Cecil Beaton ("Gigi"), on what the camera reveals
-- "He's like an old oak tree, or the summer, or the wind. He belongs to an era when men were men." - Katharine Hepburn, on Spencer Tracy
-- "The passion ultimately fizzles out because of the limitations of the goal; because movies are really not that important. We're dealing with a medium which really only wants to involve itself in the superficial manipulation of emotions." - writer-director Bill Forsyth ("Local Hero"), on his waning passion for making movies
-- "Adherence to legend at the expense of facts will ruin America - the work is well under way. And lovers of the movies should consider how far film has helped the undermining." - critic David Thomson, in an essay on the Westerns of John Ford

-- "Acting is the most minor of gifts. After all, Shirley Temple could do it when she was 4." - Katharine Hepburn -- "You see the world much better through a camera." - Louis Malle
-- "Acting is standing up naked and turning around very slowly." - Rosalind Russell
-- "The length of a film should be directly related to the endurance of the human bladder." – Alfred Hitchcock

SELF-AWARENESS

-- "I improve on misquotation." - Cary Grant
-- "Whenever I'm caught between two evils, I take the one I've never tried." - Mae West
-- "I've entered my anecdotage." - Lord Laurence Olivier, on old age
-- "I have played three presidents, three saints and two geniuses. If that doesn't create an ego problem, nothing does." - Charlton Heston
-- "I'm old, I'm young, I'm intelligent, I'm stupid. My tide goes in and out." – Warren Beatty
-- "I don't want to achieve immortality through my work. I want to achieve it through not dying." – Woody Allen
-- "Life is a long rehearsal for a play that is never produced." - actor-writer Michael Mac Liammoir
-- "Everyone denies that I'm a genius, but nobody ever called me one." - Orson Welles
-- "Success is a public affair, failure a private funeral." - Rosalind Russell
-- "I would find it quite embarrassing to get a really good part nowadays, for it would call forth the feeble flames of fires long since banked." - George Sanders, shortly before his death by suicide
-- "Put me in the last 15 minutes of a picture and I don't care what happened before. I don't even care if I was in the rest of the thing. I'll take it in those 15 minutes." - Barbara Stanwyck, on the power of her screen persona

SEX & THE SEXES

-- "An actor is something less than a man, while an actress is something more than a woman." - Richard Burton
-- "Actresses don't have husbands. They have attendants." - Bette Davis
-- "Love is the answer, but while you're waiting for the answer, sex raises some pretty interesting questions." - Woody Allen
-- "What keeps an actress young and beautiful is not repeated surgery but perpetual praise." - writer and critic Quentin Crisp
-- "Women won't let me stay single, and I won't let myself stay married." - Errol Flynn
-- "She gave you the impression that, if your imagination had to sin, it could at least congratulate itself on its impeccable taste." - Alistair Cooke, on Greta Garbo
-- "The girls call me Pilgrim, because every time I dance with one I make a little progress."

- Bob Hope (pre-marriage)

-- "She had curves in places other women don't have places." – Cybill Shepherd on Marilyn Monroe

-- "I've been around so long I can remember Doris Day before she was a virgin." - Groucho Marx

ON BEAUTY

-- "What, when drunk, one sees in other women, one sees in Garbo sober." - critic Kenneth Tynan, on Greta Garbo

-- "The relationship between the makeup man and the film actor is that of accomplices in crime." - Marlene Dietrich

-- "There are two reasons why I'm in show business, and I'm standing on both of them." - Betty Grable, on her legendary legs

-- "I was the first star ever to come out of the water looking wet." - Bette Davis

-- "Sex appeal is 50 percent what you've got and 50 percent what people think you've got." - Sophia Loren

TECHNIQUE

-- "When I played drunks I had to remain sober because I didn't know how to play them when I was drunk." - Richard Burton

-- "My acting technique is to look up at God just before the camera rolls and say, 'Give me a break.'" - James Caan

-- "The best director is the one you don't see." - Billy Wilder

-- "There's not much to say about acting but this: Never settle back on your heels. Never relax. If you relax, the audience relaxes. And always mean everything you say." - James Cagney

-- "He was the first to photograph thought." - Cecil B. DeMille, on film pioneer D.W. Griffith

-- "He articulated the mechanics of cinema and bent them to his flair." - Gene Fowler, on D.W. Griffith

-- "I can't act. I have never acted. And I shall never act. What I can do is suspend my audience's power of judgment until I'm finished." - Sir Cedric Hardwicke

-- "The less you see, the more you believe." - director Jacques Tourneur, on restraint

-- "There is no terror in a bang, only in the anticipation of it." - Alfred Hitchcock

-- "With Charles Laughton, acting was an act of childbirth. What he needed was not so much a director as a midwife." - Sir Alexander Korda

-- "I let the audience use their imaginations. Can I help it if they misconstrue my suggestions?" - director Ernst Lubitsch

-- "A team effort is a lot of people doing what I say." - director Michael Winner

ON STARDOM

-- "I'm afraid you'll never make it as an actor. But as a star, I think you might well hit the jackpot." - Orson Welles, to friend and colleague Joseph Cotten

-- "The only reason they come to see me is that I know life is great - and they know I know it." - Clark Gable

-- "Gable has his enemies all right, but they all like him." - producer David O. Selznick, on Gable

-- "I'm now at an age where I've got to prove that I'm just as good as I never was." - Sir Rex Harrison, in 1980

-- "I'm in the prime of senility." - Lord Laurence Olivier, on his diminishing star

-- "Stardom equals freedom. It's the only equation that matters." - Steve McQueen

BY AND ABOUT CRITICS

-- "A good review from a critic is just another stay of execution." - Dustin Hoffman

-- "The most important critic is time." - director Rouben Mamoulian

-- "A man who knows the way but can't drive the car." - critic Kenneth Tynan, on critics

-- "His charm consists of minor virtues uncorrupted by major pretensions." - critic Andrew Sarris on director Henry Hathaway

-- "Critics only like popular movies after they're 30 years old." - producer Sir David Puttnam

-- "Messages are for Western Union." - Samuel Goldwyn, responding to critical carping about "content"

ON HOLLYWOOD & L.A.

-- "Strip the phony tinsel off Hollywood and you'll find the real tinsel underneath." - Oscar Levant

-- "It's a place where they pay you $50,000 for a kiss and $50 for your soul." – Marilyn Monroe

-- "Seventy-two suburbs in search of a city." - Dorothy Parker, on Los Angeles

-- "God felt sorry for actors. So he gave them a place in the sun and a swimming pool. The price they had to pay was to surrender their talent." - Sir Cedric Hardwicke

-- "A trip through a sewer in a glass-bottom boat." - screenwriter Wilson Mizner

-- "You can't find true affection in Hollywood because everyone does the fake kind so well." - Carrie Fisher

-- "The only place in the world where an amiable divorce means that each gets 50 percent of the publicity." - Lauren Bacall

-- "Paradise with a lobotomy." - Anonymous

-- "The only asylum run by the inmates." - writer-producer Grover Jones

-- "They've great respect for the dead in Hollywood, but none for the living." - Errol Flynn

-- "In Hollywood you can be forgotten while you're out of the room going to the toilet." -

Anonymous
-- "If my books had been any worse I should not have been invited to Hollywood, and if they had been any better I should not have come." - Raymond Chandler
Couldn't have said it better ourselves.

....

Casablanca: Great American Movie Marks 60 Years
December 1, 2002

You must remember this. It was designed as a modest romantic spy thriller, not at all unusual or particularly ambitious. It was set-bound and lacking in movement. But it had a tense and savvy script (Howard Koch and Jean and Julius Epstein), skilled direction (Michael Curtiz) and the happy accident of one of the most impeccably assembled casts that ever graced a motion picture.

"Casablanca" turns 60 this year.

And it has lost nothing at all. Time has eroded none of its appeal, none of its entertainment value, none of its giddy delight. It is the Great American Movie.

"Casablanca" was given a trial release in New York on Thanksgiving Day 1942. Legend has it that that day was chosen to capitalize on the publicity value of U.S. troops' recent landing in North Africa. It also enjoyed a bit of serendipity, coming out shortly before the famed Casablanca conference. But the film competed (in 1944) for the 1943 Oscars, of which it captured three: Best Picture, Best Director and Best Screenplay.

Generally regarded as one of America's three best films, along with "Citizen Kane" and "Gone With the Wind" – a view certainly open to debate – "Casablanca" is the one that may be most deeply enshrined in filmgoer's affections, here and abroad, both as the most memorable love story of the American cinema and as our finest, most durable wartime melodrama.

Have any star-crossed lovers ever gazed into each other's eyes with the same liquid intensity as Rick Blaine (Humphrey Bogart) and Ilsa Lund (Ingrid Bergman)? Did two stars ever have more chemistry?

Like "The Maltese Falcon" or "The Philadelphia Story," a pair of immortal pictures released within a year or two of it, "Casablanca" could not have been more perfectly cast. Forget that old saw about Ronald Reagan and Ann Sheridan first being considered for the roles of Rick and Ilsa, or that George Raft was first in line to play Blaine. Didn't happen. The role was written with Bogart in mind. Reagan, already in the Army, was headed overseas. Hedy Lamarr was the first choice for Lund but was unavailable. Sheridan, a terrific comic actress, did indeed audition, though she lost out to an unforgettably luminous Bergman.

Our gratitude is forever.

ROGUES' GALLERY

The playbill of suave scene-stealer Claude Rains (as Capt. Louis Renault), Dooley Wilson (Sam the pianist), Peter Lorre (the weaselly Ugarte), one-time matinee idol Conrad Veidt (Major Strasser), S.Z. Sakall (Carl the waiter) and Sydney Greenstreet (Senor Ferrari) was inspired, and so, at least, were Rains' and Wilson's performances. Thanks be to the old studio system and its contract players.

A stolid actor on his best days, Paul Henreid turned out to be ideal as the stalwart underground leader Victor Laszlo. The former Paul von Henreid (before the subtle name change) was pursued over a too-young Jean-Pierre Amount (a real-life war hero), a too-inexperienced Joseph Cotten and the too-American Dean Jagger. He was not initially receptive: "I saw the script and I turned it down," Henreid said in 1991. "I thought it was a ridiculous fairy tale."

And so it was. Like most romances. This is not a negative.

In a way, "Casablanca" anticipated the films noir that poured from the cameras of post-war filmmakers. But it also summed up the 1940s in one flawless, indelible package.

MYTH MAKING

The myths Hollywood creates often spawn myths of their own. More than 40 books have been published that center on the film, but few books have plumbed the subject as engagingly as New York Times writer Aldean Harmetz's "Round Up the Usual Suspects: The Making of Casablanca" (Hyperion, 1992), a trove of behind-the-scenes eye-openers.

Here's looking at them, kid. And a few from other sources.

-- The movie was inspired by the play "Everybody Comes to Rick's" (by Murray Burnett and Joan Allison) that critic James Agee called the worst ever written. There was no Ilsa Lund in it, but rather an American woman of easy virtue called Lois Meredith. The manuscript of the play landed at Warner Bros. the day after Pearl Harbor was attacked, and rights were purchased for a then-whopping $20,000, the most ever paid for an unproduced play. Production plans almost were dropped when the playwrights declined to ax the Meredith character from the film.

-- Though shooting commenced without a finished script, "Casablanca" was not shot in sequence, as some believe. Nor was it true that Bergman didn't know until the final day of shooting if her character was going to stay with Victor or run off with Rick.

-- "Bogart was straightforward and devoid of prima donna behavior," Bergman said some years later. "Something that cannot be said about Henreid."

The courtly, aristocratic Henreid certainly was less than enamored of Bogie and his acting: "Before 'Casablanca,' Mr. Bogie was nobody," said Henried, conveniently overlooking "The Maltese Falcon," among other starring roles. "He was the fellow (Edward G.) Robinson or (Jimmy) Cagney would say, 'Get him.'" That may have been true

10 years before "Casablanca's" release – Bogart had endured a long apprenticeship playing cowardly gangsters – but not at the time.

Henreid wasn't finished: "(Director Michael) Curtiz could not tell Bogart that he should not play (the role) like a crybaby. It was embarrassing, I thought."

-- Dooley Wilson was, in fact, a drummer. He didn't know how to play the piano.

-- Warner Bros.' in-house music director, Max Steiner, loathed the tune "As Time Goes By," which was drawn from the 1931 Broadway show "Everybody's Welcome." The song might never have made the cut had not Bergman's post-production entanglements prevented her from re-shooting scenes with new music.

-- The beloved closing line, "Louis, I think this is the beginning of a beautiful friendship," was written by producer Hal Wallis and was recorded by Bogart after production was completed. The second choice was "If you ever die a hero's death, Heaven protect the angels." But it may have been Bogart himself who devised our favorite rejoinder, "Here's looking at you, kid."

-- The plane "warming up" in the background as Bogart and Bergman say their lump-in-the-throat goodbye was a plywood cutout. The fog machine was working overtime, not just to provide atmosphere, but to obscure the plane.

-- There is not now, nor was there ever, such a thing as "letters of transit," exit visas that cannot be canceled.

-- Having seen a preview, Gen. Charles DeGaulle petitioned Warner in December 1942 to open the film in England and in unoccupied France as quickly as possible, to help fan patriotic fervor.

-- "Casablanca" opened to generally strong, if not glowing, reviews and solid but not spectacular box office. The New Yorker opined: "Not quite up to 'Across the Pacific,' Bogart's last spyfest, but it is nevertheless pretty tolerable."

-- Perhaps no German expatriate during the war despised the Nazis more than Conrad Veidt, who nonetheless was obliged to play one with distressing (to him) frequency. Veidt already had made motion picture history in 1919, starring as Cesare in the breakthrough German Expressionist film "The Cabinet of Dr. Caligari."

-- Off camera, the refined, urbane Rains had a Cockney accent so thick it could have been sliced with a rapier.

-- Director Curtiz was notorious for his between-scenes liaisons with young lovelies in his private trailer. "Casablanca" was no different, until infamous practical joker Lorre hid a microphone in the trailer for the delectation of cast and crew.

-- Attempts to adapt the movie for TV were done twice, unsuccessfully.

A live-TV version in 1955 produced eight one-hour episodes, starring several featured members of the original cast (Marcel Dalio, Dan Seymour) upgraded to leading roles. In 1983, NBC premiered a TV series based on "Casablanca," but set at an earlier time. David

Soul, Ray Liotta, Hector Elizondo and Scatman Crothers led the cast. Mercifully, it lasted three weeks.

Harmetz observed, quite rightly, that "Casablanca" was "a unique moment in our cultural history: There are better movies than 'Casablanca,' but no other movie better demonstrates America's mythological vision of itself, tough on the outside and moral within, capable of sacrifice and romance without sacrificing the individualism that conquered a continent, sticking its neck out for everybody when circumstances demand heroism. No other movie has so reflected the moment when it was made, the early days of World War II, and the psychological needs of audiences decades later."

Play it, Sam. And play it again.

....

40 Years of 007: Secret agent lives to save another day
November 10, 2002

He's suave, smooth and eternally 38, the only man alive who wears a dinner jacket under his wet suit.

He has an unearthly mastery of women - until recently, anyway - that makes Valentino look like a piker, along with a pun factory that would try the patience of Monty Python.

And no matter how dire the circumstance, how grave the threat, he never spills a drop of his martini - a commanding confidence that is every man's grail.

James Bond, the not-so-secret agent with the stolid name and lavish tastes, returns for a 20th film (or 21st, counting "Never Say Never Again") in "Die Another Day" (Nov. 22), his franchise looking a trifle frayed around the edges and overwhelmed by all the special effects. But the man himself has no complaints.

Oh, there have been a few cracks in the armor in recent years, some minor identity crises and bowing to contemporary sensibilities. Bond has cut back on the booze, doesn't smoke and treats the ladies with a bit more respect than before (with maybe a touch of trepidation). But if Oddjob couldn't put him out of commission, if Jaws' bite missed the jugular and Blofeld's plots proved futile, do you honestly think fickle filmgoers and a little length of tooth are going to do him in?

Rubbish. We're still stirred, not shaken, as this longest of all movie series celebrates its 40th year.

And now for a little gratuitous sex and violence. Not to mention a juggernaut of gadgets. First and foremost, there's the wheels. It may not be the classic old DB-5 with a catapult passenger seat, but 007 will be back in his trademark Aston Martin (a Bentley in the books) for "Die Another Day," albeit in a six-liter, six-speed, 460-hp V-12 Vanquish. Just the ticket at a mere $230,000.

And there remain plenty of adversaries to test his talents. Who cares if the Cold War is over? Spectre, like diamonds, is forever.

MEN IN BONDAGE

As Mr. Bond looks back on a corpse- and broken heart-strewn career, foiling megalomaniacs, seducing the enemy and dodging doom, he has to be reasonably pleased with the blokes who've brought him to life. Though the big screen 007 isn't quite the chap his creator envisioned.

The current incarnation, Pierce Brosnan, makes an admirable Bond. And would have years earlier, had not his "Remington Steele" TV contract prohibited him from plucking the PPK (as in Walther) from a retiring Roger Moore. Instead, for two films, we got Tim Dalton, the closest to Ian Fleming's literary character as we are ever likely to get, after Sean Connery turned him from a cold-eyed, humorless gent into a debonair master of mayhem. George Lazenby has been reduced to a footnote, but his 007 in "On Her Majesty's Secret Service" looked like a pale imitation only in contrast to Connery's palpable virility.

What Fleming had in mind before "Casino Royale" (his first book) appeared in 1953, however, was a fellow who would possess as anonymous a personality as possible. So the former journalist and real-life intelligence operative appropriated his hero's name from the American ornithologist, James Bond, author of "Birds of the West Indies."

"It struck me," Fleming said years later, "that his name - brief, unromantic and yet very masculine - was just what I needed."

But Fleming wanted David Niven to play the character, despite the fact that the Bond of the books was said to most resemble Hoagy Carmichael. Fleming wanted urbane but dark. What he got was a Scottish actor with a heavy working-class brogue and almost none of the book Bond's refined characteristics, save for that "dangerous look" and Bond's faintly "un-Britishness."

It was up to the team of producers Albert "Cubby" Broccoli and Harry Saltzman to bring the books to the screen. At first, Fleming was aghast at the casting of Connery. So was the United Artists brass when they saw the initial footage. "Try again," read the cable to Broccoli, who ignored it.

But Fleming was in perfect agreement with the producers that the style of the films, and their hero, should draw inspiration from the Alfred Hitchcock classic that became a template for all the Bond movies to come: 1957's "North by Northwest."

FIENDS AND FRIENDS

Who was the deadlier villain, Oddjob ("Goldfinger") or Red Grant ("From Russia With Love")? The most lethal villainess, Xenia Onatop ("Goldeneye"), Fiona Volpe ("Thunderball"), or Fatima Blush ("Never Say Never Again")? The most formidable female partner, Col. Wai-Lin ("Tomorrow Never Dies") or Pam Bouvier ("License to Kill")?

Matters of taste, of course, like bearnaise sauce with tournedos of beef.

Speaking of tasty, now comes Halle Berry as special agent Jinx, fresh from her Oscar bash and figuring on being more in the recent, self-possessed mold of Bond babes than the old, though with a familiar blend of beauty and sexual power. Most of the heroines who've teamed with 007 over the years have been worshipful cyphers (like Tanya Roberts) or willowy, fragile types (such as Maryam D'Abo). Berry, by contrast, will have the moxie of a Maud Adams ("Octopussy"), the toughness of a Carey Lowell ("License to Kill") and the sensual grace of a Claudine Auger ("Thunderball"). Not bad.

Sorry, James, no more pushovers.

Even Miss Moneypenny's not as pliant as she used to be, and 007 still hasn't gotten accustomed to having a female M running the show.

THE FRANCHISE

In 2000, MGM called Brosnan "Our Billion Dollar Bond," the last three films of the current 007 having earned more than $1 billion at the box office. It's also been estimated, by Q no doubt, that the total number of admissions to all the Bond pictures from 1962 to the present is a shade below the 2 billion plateau. That's approximately half of the world's population. But you'd have to be of a certain age to recall how dramatically the first four films riveted the movie-going public. After "Dr. No" countered cantankerous reviews with a surprising box office, mainly on the strength of Connery's magnetism as a rougher, more tongue-in-cheek kind of cinema hero, long lines and splashy ad campaigns were the order of the day. The hubbub for "From Russia with Love" (1963) "Goldfinger" (1964) and "Thunderball" (1965) rivaled The Beatles for global media and fan attention, cresting with the most perfectly realized of all the films, "Goldfinger." The latter also pushed the series into a quasi-science fictional path it continues on today, with greater emphasis on gizmos and spectacle.

Purists, and those who loved the books, generally agree that the best Bond flick was "From Russia with Love," which is as close as the series came to playing it "straight." It may still own the most memorable fight scene in movie history, a claustrophobic train berth tussle pitting Connery's Bond against Robert Shaw's terrifying Grant, who had a sinister detachment even Oddjob couldn't muster.

Big budgets and top-drawer production design have marked all the Bond films, first to last, though few recent movies have managed the remarkably imaginative sets and set pieces designed in the 1960s by Ken Adam, who established the distinctive look of the all the 007 films.

So take your pick, of Bonds or of emblems: amphibious cars, mink gloves, exploding briefcases, poison-tipped shoes, bars of gold bullion, stolen nukes, or femmes fatale with risqué names. It's the same playful, snickering tease:

Bond: "Who would pay a million dollars to kill me?"
M: "Jealous husbands, outraged chefs, humiliated tailors. The list is endless."
So, perhaps, is 007's appeal.

....

Spielberg: Director, Producer, Editor
June 23, 2002

Thirty years. It hardly seems possible.

Could it really have been that long since Steven Spielberg roared down the cinematic on-ramp with "Duel," an unsurpassed emblem for the common man facing a hostile universe? Could it have been more than a quarter-century since he re-imagined the road movie with "Sugarland Express," gave birth to the summer blockbuster with "Jaws," and probed the enigmatic with "Close Encounters of the Third Kind"?

As director, producer, editor and writer, Spielberg has been an impresario for an age of artifice, serving up maniacal truckers and rapacious sharks, alien visitations and religious allegories, old-fashioned cliffhangers and time-tripping hotrods - but also moving evocations of war and conscience.

He has been venerated as an artist and reviled as a purveyor of commercialized pap. Both are true, but the real Spielberg lies somewhere between those poles.

"Minority Report," which opened Friday, marks Steven Allan Spielberg's 30th anniversary in features, following a sturdy apprenticeship in television. ("Duel," originally made for TV in 1971, was released theatrically in 1972.) It seems an opportune time to reflect on an influential career that, it should be noted, is far from over.

Between 1979's farcical "1941" and 1987's pivotal "Empire of the Sun," it was easy to disparage the Cincinnati-born Spielberg's mainly trivial work as director and producer. His films made zillions, but in aid of what? One could acknowledge the delight he brought to millions of general audiences with grand entertainments like "E.T." and "Raiders of the Lost Ark," yet still question the depth of his vision or the seriousness of his intent.

Like his contemporary George Lucas, we wondered if he would ever grow up, or perpetually play Peter Pan. In 1987, he answered the question with "Empire." In 1993, with "Schindler's List," he removed all doubt - at least insofar as his capacity for excellence.

Technically, his craftsmanship as a director has been unassailable, though too often it has relied on a mechanistic approach to character and story. And he has not always known the difference between heart and sentimentality. "Saving Private Ryan" is astonishing in its technical conception and execution ("The Longest Day" made human scale), and finely acted. But on closer inspection, it has a rather simplistic storyline that leaves much to be desired.

If "Jaws" was his "Moby Dick" and "Close Encounters" his "2001" - very much director's pieces with compelling central characters - the "Jurassic Park" series has been strictly a producer's gig, more high-concept marketing than storytelling, a faint echo of Spielberg's earlier concern with the resourcefulness of ordinary people in extraordinary circumstances.

Fantasy and science fiction, of a sort, has been his consistent métier over the years, not to mention his box-office staple, though last year's "A.I." is more properly a page in the Stanley Kubrick canon than in Spielberg's. While it had its flaws, "Close Encounters" is a positively mystical experience compared to his other SF, especially the highly variable material he's shepherded as executive producer: "Poltergeist," "Gremlins," the "Back to the Future" trilogy, "Innerspace," "Men in Black," "Deep Impact" and "Twilight Zone: The Movie," to offer a sampling.

You could make a convincing argument that the vigor and imagination of his early work supersedes the calculation of the middle period and the bravura showmanship of the latter ("Schindler" excepted). Certainly he worked tirelessly at it, and with great commitment, from his high school beginnings with his dad's 8 mm camera to his professional breakthrough in the late '60s.

Like most filmmakers, Spielberg has done some simply awful movies, where his eye for detail bloats (and often devours) character and plot - "Hook" springs immediately to mind. But the best of his diversions exhibit a rare ability as a director: "to deftly organize the elements of a roller-coaster entertainment," as critic David Thomson so aptly put it, "without sacrificing inner meanings."

His handful of serious pictures tone down the excessive "event" quality and the pulsing hyper-reality, and amplify those meanings.

Like him or not, to film, and to film history, Spielberg matters.

....

Sidney Poitier: Charismatic actor dispelled caricatures of blacks in cinema
March 17, 2002

Sidney Poitier was living, vital, undeniable proof of the maxim that an artist is the seismograph of his age.

When, by sheer force of personality and talent, this charismatic actor first superimposed himself on the American consciousness in the late '50s and early '60s, he was the ultimate anomaly: an intelligent, sophisticated black man determined to be depicted as such in a Hollywood system weaned on caricature.

It had been more than 20 years since the powerful black stage and screen performer Paul Robeson had electrified audiences, in part by refusing to have his humanity diminished in the name of entertainment. Now here emerged this similarly tall, handsome young star fairly erupting with intensity, ready to challenge our preconceptions again.

Unlike the ill-fated Robeson, who was ostracized in the States for alleged communist leanings, Poitier became a sometimes reluctant standard bearer for the dawn of a more liberal age, an unapologetic thorn in the side of those who would impede it, and, tellingly, one of the most universally respected and popular actors of his generation.

Perhaps fortuitous timing had as much to do with the acceptance of Poitier's stardom as his considerable gifts, helped by a dignified and well-spoken comportment that, 50 years on, remain signature features. To-day, as the debonair 78-year-old prepares to accept an honorary Academy Award on March 24 for career achievement, and as we assay his legacy, it is useful to remember how potent - and important - a presence he was in the first decade of his motion picture career.

The apex of his influence was in 1967, when Poitier starred in a trio of box office smashes: "Guess Who's Coming to Dinner," "To Sir With Love" and "In the Heat of the Night," each dealing with racial divisions. But he had already made history by this point, becoming the first black male to receive an Oscar nomination for his role in 1958's "The Defiant Ones." This, on the heels of groundbreaking performances in "No Way Out" (1950), "Cry, the Beloved Country" (filmed on location in South Africa in 1951), the prototypical urban youth drama "Blackboard Jungle" (1955) and "Edge of the City" (1957).

Hit followed hit, with "Porgy and Bess" (1959), "All the Young Men" (1960), the memorable "A Raisin in the Sun" (1961), "Pressure Point" (1962) and, lastly, "Lilies of the Field" (1963), a dynamic turn which earned him a Best Actor Oscar.

As he continued to open doors, Poitier became something more than a major box office attraction; he was the entertainment world's epitome of the forceful modern black American, setting the cinematic table for actors of similar gravity: Harry Belafonte, James Earl Jones, Ossie Davis, Cicely Tyson, Brock Peters, Woody Strode, Ruby Dee, Moses Gunn, Paul Winfield, William Marshall, and, by extension, Bill Cosby, whose first shot at TV stardom ("I Spy") owed more than a little to Poitier's film success.

There's a subtle irony here, in that Poitier did not share fully in the black American experience until his mid-teens. Though born in Miami (during a mainland visit by his parents), Poitier was raised on Cat Island in the Bahamas. Despite an impoverished youth and little formal education, he brought back to the States a characteristically Caribbean jauntiness and confidence seldom expressed by black Americans of the time, prominent black writers of the early '50s, by contrast, being more incendiary than blithe.

Coming from a culture dominated by a black majority to one that was quite the reverse, the cultural shock to Poitier was extreme. But he was fated to sink the signposts for the road to Hollywood success for scores of minority - not just black - actors and directors.

That path began at age 18 in New York, where Poitier toiled in menial jobs until serving a brief stint in the Army. Initially rejected for admittance to the American Negro Theatre, he invested six months in eliminating his island accent and learning the fundamentals of the craft. He made the grade on his second try, joining the ANT and soon getting a bit part in a revival of "Lysistrata." Poitier won his first significant role on Broadway in a 1948 production of "Anna Lucasta."

A year later, he had to choose between more leading parts on stage and a seductive movie contract. Producer Darryl F. Zanuck was dangling the offer of a plum role in "No Way Out." Poitier could not resist the opportunity to play a black doctor treating a white bigot (played with customary venom by Richard Widmark).

Poitier never looked back.

If some of the films which seemed so remarkable for their day now feel rather tame, even self-conscious, it had less to do with Poitier or the impulse to make them than with the blandly earnest liberalism of those behind the camera, such as socially conscious producer-director Stanley Kramer, creator of "The Defiant Ones" and "Guess Who's Coming to Dinner."

Social commentary, however needed, does not always make for compelling or enduring cinema, especially when worn on one's sleeve. One suspects that always being asked to heft the banner for racial harmony became wearying to Poitier in time. Although he remained active in the civil rights movement, he appeared to have made a concerted effort to do films that would be judged less on social value than on their entertainment virtues: playing the villainous monarch of "The Long Ships" (1964), a confrontational news reporter in "The Bedford Incident" (1965) (locking horns again with Widmark both times), and supporting Richard Roundtree in "Shaft" (1971).

The latter part of Poitier's career has been a checkered one. He had opened so many doors, in fact, that he had far greater competition for roles that previously were almost automatically his. He tried his hand at directing, turning out a number of popular (and very broad) all-black comedies such as "Uptown Saturday Night" (1974) and "A Piece of the Action" (1977), movies which were not exactly the stuff of legend. He stayed behind the camera for the entirety of the '80s, seeming to abandon acting altogether.

Every so often he would emerge from semiretirement to add weight to such TV biopics as 1991's "Separate But Equal" (playing Justice Thurgood Marshall) or spice to pleasing ensemble baubles like 1992's "Sneakers" (looking 20 years younger than his age). These appearances have been far too few.

Poitier published his autobiography, "This Life," in 1980. An update seems long overdue, something that might capture the conscience and integrity of a man who entertained, unsettled and influenced millions.

In 1967, when he worked alongside a very ill Spencer Tracy in "Guess Who's Coming to Dinner" just before the latter's death, Poitier was awed by Tracy's preparation and energy.

"As sick as he was," Poitier said later, "Spencer was there. And he was there in force." In film after film, decade after decade, the same could be said of Poitier.

....

The Best Films of the 20th Century
December 12, 1999

The American Film Institute has its list. And we have ours.

Last summer's "100 Years, 100 Movies" promotion had a catchy title, but many observers caught a whiff of pandering amid some of the AFI's selections. Not to mention a spasm of parochialism in limiting the list to the domestic cinema. In any case, a mere 100 films hardly are adequate to represent a century of motion pictures.

Your humble reviewer's **200 Movies of the Century** still constitutes only 1 percent of an estimated 20,000 pictures made in the U.S. and other English-speaking countries since 1894. Quite an archive, and quite a chore.

We've supplemented our 200 with separate listings of great silents, foreign language films and documentaries. Together, they are movies we love, movies we admire and, of course, movies we've actually seen. It's a very subjective series of lists, to be sure, one based on my personal experience, not reputation. They're reflective not only of our convictions as to the individual films' quality and enduring power, but also of the reviewer's affections.

Sometimes the films one savors and those one deeply respects are one and the same. Sometimes not. Many of those listed were chosen for their creativity, originality or influence, rather than our entertainment value.

It excludes made-for-television movies, while recognizing such milestones of excellence as "Brian's Song."

All lists are alphabetical. When various versions of the same film have been made, the date is given. We don't [resume to rank them 1 to 200; after the first 100r so picks, they're all of a piece. But if you insist on a selection of the best films of all time, we'll give you two, one for its genius, the other for grand entertainment: "Citizen Kane" and "Casablanca."

Predictable, perhaps, but valid. And sincere apologies to those who were counting on "Galactic Gigolo." (1988)

Let the arguments begin.

200 Great English Language Films

1. Adam's Rib
2. The Adventures of Robin Hood
3. The African Queen
4. After Hours
5. All About Eve
6. All the King's Men
7. All the President's Men
8. All Quiet on the Western Front (1930)
9. An American in Paris
10. Anastasia
11. Anatomy of a Murder
12. Annie Hall
13. The Apartment
14. Arsenic and Old Lace
15. Bambi (yes, Bambi)
16. The Bank Dick, Becket.
17. Ben-Hur
18. The Best Years of Our Lives
19. The Big Sleep
20. The Blackboard Jungle
21. Black Robe
22. Bladerunner
23. Bonnie and Clyde
24. Born Yesterday
25. The Bridge on the River Kwai
26. Brief Encounter
27. Bringing Up Baby
28. Butch Cassidy and the Sundance Kid
29. The Caine Mutiny, Camille (1937)
30. Captains Courageous
31. Casablanca
32. Chinatown
33. A Christmas Carol (1951)
34. Citizen Kane
35. A Clockwork Orange
36. The Conversation
37. The Crimson Pirate
38. Dark Victory
39. David Copperfield
40. The Day the Earth Stood Still
41. Death of a Salesman
42. The Deer Hunter
43. The Defiant Ones
44. Deliverance
45. Destry Rides Again
46. Dinner at Eight
47. Dodsworth
48. Dr. Strangelove
49. Doctor Zhivago
50. Double Indemnity
51. A Double Life
52. Dracula (1931)
53. Duck Soup
54. East of Eden
55. Elmer Gantry
56. The Empire Strikes Back
57. E.T.: The Extraterrestrial
58. A Face in the Crowd
59. Fail Safe
60. Fantasia
61. Fargo
62. Father of the Bride (1950)
63. 42nd Street
64. Frankenstein
65. The French Connection
66. Friendly Persuasion
67. From Here to Eternity
68. Gandhi
69. Gigi
70. The Godfather
71. Goldfinger
72. The Goodbye Girl
73. The Good Earth
74. Gone With the Wind
75. The Graduate
76. Grand Hotel
77. The Grapes of Wrath
78. The Great Escape
79. Great Expectations
80. Henry V (1945)
81. High Noon
82. His Girl Friday
83. The Hospital
84. Howard's End
85. How Green Was My Valley
86. Hud
87. The Hustler
88. In the Heat of the Night
89. In the Name of the Father
90. Inherit the Wind
91. Invasion of the Body Snatchers (1956)
92. In Which We Serve
93. It Happened One Night
94. It's a Wonderful Life

95. The Killers (1946)
96. The Killing Fields
97. King Kong (1933)
98. The King and I
99. King of the Hill
100. Kramer vs. Kramer
101. The Lady Eve
102. The Last Picture Show
103. Lawrence of Arabia
104. The Life of Emile Zola
105. Life With Father
106. The Lion in Winter
107. Little Big Man
108. Little Women (1933)
109. Lone Star
110. The Longest Day
111. Lost Horizon
112. The Lost Weekend
113. Lust for Life
114. The Magnificent Ambersons
115. The Magnificent Seven
116. The Manchurian Candidate
117. The Maltese Falcon
118. A Man for All Seasons
119. The Man Who Came to Dinner
120. Malcolm X
121. Marty
122. MASH
123. Midnight Cowboy
124. Miracle on 34th Street
125. The Miracle Worker
126. Mr. Deeds Goes to Town
127. Mister Roberts
128. Mr. Smith Goes to Washington
129. Monty Python and the Holy Grail
130. Mountains of the Moon
131. Mutiny on the Bounty (1935)
132. My Darling Clementine
133. My Fair Lady
134. Nashville
135. Network
136. North by Northwest
137. Of Mice and Men (1939)
138. On the Waterfront
139. One Flew Over the Cuckoo's Nest
140. The Ox-Bow Incident
141. Paths of Glory
142. Patton
143. The Pawnbroker
144. The Philadelphia Story
145. Platoon
146. The Pride of the Yankees
147. The Prisoner of Zenda (1937)
148. Pulp Fiction
149. The Quiet Man
150. Raging Bull
151. Raiders of the Lost Ark
152. A Raisin in the Sun
153. Rear Window
154. Roman Holiday
155. Room at the Top
156. A Room With a View
157. Saving Private Ryan
158. Schindler's List
159. Séance on a Wet Afternoon
160. The Searchers
161. The Secret of Roan Inish
162. Sense and Sensibility
163. Separate Tables
164. Shakespeare in Love
165. Shane
166. A Shot in the Dark
167. Singin' in the Rain
168. Sleuth
169. Snow White and the Seven Dwarfs
170. Some Like It Hot
171. Sounder
172. The Sound of Music
173. Spartacus
174. Stagecoach (1939)
175. Stage Door
176. Stalag 17
177. A Streetcar Named Desire
178. Sullivan's Travels
179. The Sundowners
180. Sunset Boulevard
181. Teahouse of the August Moon
182. The Ten Commandments
183. The Thin Man
184. The Third Man
185. The Thirty-Nine Steps
186. The Three Musketeers (1973)
187. To Kill a Mockingbird
188. Top Hat

189. Topkapi
190. Touch of Evil
191. The Train
192. The Treasure of the Sierra Madre
193. 2001: A Space Odyssey
194. The Verdict
195. Vertigo
196. Way Out West
197. The Wizard of Oz
198. Woman of the Year
199. Wuthering Heights

50 Great Foreign Language Films

1. Aguirre: The Wrath of God (Germany)
2. Alexander Nevsky (Russia)
3. Au Revoir Les Enfants (France)
4. Babette's Feast (France)
5. Beauty and the Beast (France)
6. Belle du Jour (France)
7. The Bicycle Thief (Italy)
8. Burnt by the Sun (Russia)
9. Children of Paradise (France)
10. Closely Watched Trains (Czechoslovakia)
11. The Conformist (Italy)
12. Contempt (France-Italy)
13. Danton (Poland-France)
14. Da Boot (Germany)
15. Day for Night (France)
16. A Day in the Country (France)
17. Diabolique (France)
18. Eat Drink Man Woman (Taiwan)
19. 8 1/2 (Italy)
20. Entre Nous (France)
21. Fanny and Alexander (Sweden)
22. Farewell My Concubine (China)
23. Fitzcarraldo (Germany)
24. Garden of the Finzi-Continis (Italy)
25. The Golden Age (France)
26. Jules and Jim (France)
27. Knife in the Water (Poland)
28. La Dolce Vita (Italy)
29. La Strada (Italy)
30. The 400 Blows (France)
31. The Leopard (Italy)
32. M (Germany)
33. A Man and a Woman (France)
34. My 20th Century (Hungary)
35. Never on Sunday (Greece)
36. The Nights of Cabiria (Italy)
37. The Official Story (Argentina)
38. Pixote (Brazil)
39. Raise the Red Lantern (China)
40. Ran (Japan)
41. Rashomon (Japan)
42. Seven Beauties (Italy)
43. The Seven Samurai (Japan)
44. The Seventh Seal (Sweden)
45. Strawberry and Chocolate (Cuba)
46. Two Women (Italy)
47. Umberto D (Italy)
48. Women on the Verge of a Nervous Breakdown (Spain)
49. Yojimbo (Japan)

25 Great Silent Films

1. The Battleship Potemkin
2. Beethoven's Great Love
3. The Big Parade
4. The Birth of a Nation
5. The Cabinet of Doctor Caligari
6. Cabiria
7. City Lights
8. Dr. Jekyll and Mr. Hyde (1920)
9. The Four Horsemen of the Apocalypse
10. The General

11. The Golden Age of Comedy (compilation)
12. The Gold Rush
13. Greed
14. Intolerance
15. The Kid Brother
16. Metropolis
17. Nanook of the North
18. Napoleon
19. Nosferatu the Vampire
20. The Passion of Joan of Arc
21. Reaching for the Moon
22. Safety Last
23. Sherlock, Jr.
24. Sunrise
25. When Comedy Was King (compilation)

16. The Thin Blue Line
17. Visions of Light
18. When We Were Kings
19. Woodstock

....

20 Great Documentaries

1. American Dream
2. A Brief History of Time
3. Crumb
4. Down and Out in America
5. Gates of Heaven
6. Hearts and Minds
7. Hearts of Darkness
8. Hoop Dreams
9. The Last Waltz
10. Microcosmos
11. Nanook of the North
12. Roger and Me
13. Sherman's March
14. Shoah
15. The Sorrow and the Pity

FILM NOIR

Movies get their name from shadowy ambience, sinister plots

July 4, 1999

> "Murphy gave her the once-over. She wore a tailored suit and five feet of legs. The eyes glinted like broken glass. Her voice was whiskey and smoke.
>
> "What about it, shamus? Do we make a play?" She gave him a look you could have poured on a waffle.
>
> "Nix, doll. And turn off the baby blues. Time enough for that after we nab the dingus."

By BILL THOMPSON
Post and Courier Film Critic

Film noir is the one American movie genre whose popularity never fades. Musicals are dead. Westerns go in and out of fashion, screwball comedies aren't always in vogue. Even romances and action-adventures are subject to cycles.

But the trenchcoated hero still leans against the shadowed door frame, smoke billowing from his cigarette, a streetlight casting pale illumination across the world-weary face, his thoughts lingering on the femme fatale (or gunsel) who got a little too close.

The enduring works of writers James M. Cain, Dashiell Hammett, Raymond Chandler and their fellows served up a new kind of rough glamour, complete with hard-boiled private eyes, dangerous women and often Byzantine plots.

Movies such as "The Big Sleep," "Night and the City" and "Double Indemnity" have taken on a life of their own, a life Turner Classic Movies celebrates in July and August with its Summer of Darkness, a 94-film festival of film noir. The series, which began Friday, is composed of 18 all-night weekend screenings and will get the goods on such stars as Humphrey Bogart, Barbara Stanwyck and Robert Mitchum, as well as directors such as Robert Wise and Anthony Mann.

Take it and like it

As seductive as these pictures continue to be, even at the surface level, a classic, perhaps defining, element of film noir is the movies' refusal to solve the moral ambiguities they raise. That, and noir's dominant visual storytelling: a near-obsessive attention to lighting, shadow and framing whose signature motif was the Venetian blind.

Above all, the noir pictures were nocturnal films. Combined with the romantic fatalism of many of their endings, they produced one of the most distinctive of all American film styles.

But it was left to French movie critics – well after the fact, it should be noted – to coin the name. And they weren't just referring to the sinister streets and back alleys. The label also described the films' dark moral climate. Quite a few of the directors who made these movies were Europeans whose outlook had been shaped by the destruction and desolation of World War II. Their characters tended to be loners, alienated and obscure.

On the other hand, it's doubtful any director of the '40s or '50s consciously set out to make a film noir. They just thought they were doing atmospheric crime thrillers.

Manufactured genre?

One may argue the whole film noir business is artificial, merely a stylistic protege of the German expressionists of the 1920s, who pioneered the use of light and darkness to convey a movie's mood, and the gangster movies of the '30s. By no means were all of the movies usually lumped into the noir category (see A Film Noir Rogue's Gallery) entirely faithful to its touchstones. Some had happy endings. Bogart's various characters may have been cynical, but they were hardly aimless; they had convictions and took risks not in their best interests.

Bogart summed up all the films noir of the '40s, but it was '50s filmmakers who took the genre a step deeper into cynicism and violence. Not only wasn't evil always vanquished; it sometimes cackled lustily in the wings, enduring its temporary setback and waiting for another chance to bedevil our "hero."

And those protagonists were not sweethearts, pal. Like Chandler's Philip Marlowe, Hammett's Sam Spade, and, to a more brutal extent, Mickey Spillane's Mike Hammer, they may have been shrewd, but they were also tough, unreflective and archetypically masculine. The dames? Save for the rare pure-of-heart damsel (usually a victim), they were sleekly dressed barracuda, smoldering in their allure yet icy and manipulative.

Decadence and decay

Few recall what consternation the '50s cycle of film noir caused with its unapologetic violence - tame by today's standards but considered insidious in its day. Their "bottomless pit of corruption and decay" seems almost quaint now.

Today's filmmakers persist in trying to give the dark sedan of film noir some contemporary, high-octane fuel. With very mixed results. Far and away the most successful attempt at the film noir style over the last 20 years – though purists insist no color film can win admittance to the genre – was "L.A. Confidential" (1997). Three other pictures gave it a run for its money: "Romeo Is Bleeding" (1993), "The Last Seduction" (1994) and "Blood and Wine" (1997). But none fully measured up.

Perhaps it's a mistake to try to recapture a mood so aligned with another era, at least if the intent is to "modernize" it. Noir directors of the '40s knew the prudence of never showing the worst carnage. Like Hitchcock, they recognized the effect was greater if the mayhem took place off camera. Today's audiences, weaned on gore, might find that a cheat.

Which makes the old stuff that much more valuable, and not just to film buffs and historians.

Of course, TCM's repertoire is limited to the movies owned by Ted Turner. You don't have that limitation. A reasonably well-stocked video store should have at least several major film noir classics.

Before you go, check out resources such as "A Girl and a Gun: The Complete Guide to Film Noir on Video" by David N. Meyer (Avon Books), dealing with the films and the filmmaking process.

Then throw on a trenchcoat and turn up the lapels. Add a snap-brim fedora, slight down-angle. Look mysterious. And practice your patter, hawkshaw. Begin Table

A FILM NOIR ROGUE'S GALLERY	"D.O.A." (1950)
"Ace in the Hole" (1951)	"Double Indemnity" (1944)
"The Asphalt Jungle" (1950)	"Follow Me Quietly" (1949)
"Beware, My Lovely" (1952)	"Gilda" (1946)
"The Big Heat" (1953)	"I Died a Thousand Times" (1955)
"The Big Sleep" (1946)	"Johnny Eager" (1941)
"The Blue Dalhia" (1946)	"The Killers" (1946)
"Cape Fear" (1961)	"Kiss Me Deadly" (1955)
"Clash by Night" (1952)	"Laura" (1944)
"Crime of Passion" (1957)	"The Lady from Shanghai" (1948)
"Criss Cross" (1949)	"Lady in the Lake" (1946)
"Crossfire" (1947)	"The Maltese Falcon" (1941)
"Dark Passage" (1947)	"Mildred Pierce" (1945)
"The Devil Thumbs a Ride" (1947)	"Murder, My Sweet" (1944)

"The Naked City" (1948)

"Night and the City" (1950)

"Notorious" (1946)

"On Dangerous Ground" (1951)

"Out of the Past" (1947)

"The Postman Always Rings Twice" (1946)

"Point Blank" (1967)

"Raw Deal" (1948)

"The Third Man" (1948)

"This Gun for Hire" (1942)

"Touch of Evil" (1958)

"While the City Sleeps" (1956)

Near noirs
"Invasion of the Body Snatchers" (1956)

"Key Largo" (1948)

"Sunset Boulevard" (1950)

"Taxi Driver" (1976)

"To Have and Have Not" (1944)

"Vertigo" (1958)

... and some neo-noir mimics

"Bladerunner" (1982)

"Blood and Wine" (1997)

"Blood Simple" (1984)

"Body Heat" (1981)

"China Moon" (1994)

"Chinatown" (1974)

"The Conformist" (1971)

"The Conversation" (1974)

"Cutter's Way" (1981)

"Dead Calm" (1988)

"The French Connection" (1971)

"The Grifters" (1990)

"Homicide" (1990)

"L.A. Confidential" (1997)

"La Femme Nikita" (1990)

"The Last Seduction" (1994)

"Romeo Is Bleeding" (1993)

"To Live and Die in L.A." (1985)

....

A Century of Cinema
January 2, 1994
By Bill Thompson
Post and Courier Film Critic

A silent sneeze. With gale force repercussions.

This week, as filmgoers worldwide celebrate the centennial of the movies, it may behoove us to recall the humble origin of this dazzlingly influential art -- in the laboratory of Thomas Alva Edison.

On Jan. 7, 1893, Edison copyrighted a moving visual image he titled "Fred Ott's Sneeze," thereby introducing a peculiarly powerful new medium. This seminal moment of invention was singularly ignored, even after Edison and W.K.ZL. Dickson completed the first movie studio, the Black Maria, that same year.

In 1895, the Lumiere brothers projected the first motion pictures for paying customers on the wall of a Paris café. Three years later, Edison's assembled scientists began work the Kinetograph and Kinetoscope, forerunners of the modern movie camera and projector. Public curiosity soon mushroomed into mania. The film business had come into being.

And we haven't been the same since.

By the movies' 40th birthday, the great clowns – Chaplin and Keaton, Laurel and Hardy – and the great romantic teams – Astaire and Rogers, Gable and Leigh, Tracy and Hepburn, Bogie and Bergman – were as familiar to us as the couple next door, albeit with a pearly glamor conferred by the silver screen.

An entertainment and art history of film also necessitates a social history of film: its evolution from a rudimentary recording device to a complex global industry that shapes opinion, establishes ideals (and idols), and marks the lives of millions.

For all our sophistication about movies, we tend to take them for granted – their polish, their ingenuity, the refined technologies producing generally flawless sound, image and color. Even modern filmmakers themselves often are unaware of the path motion pictures have traveled, or the pioneering figures – D.W. Griffith, Sergei Eisenstein, the early moguls – who gave the art its fundamental techniques and momentum.

As film historian Gerald Mast has pointed out, the current generation of moviegoers "prefers seeing movies to reading novels, prefers making movies to writing poetry, and has pushed the movies into university curricula, and (yet) is surprisingly ignorant of the cumulative progress of the film art" from an entertainment novelty to a multi-billion dollar commercial and cultural phenomenon.

Silent film was a wholly different art form than the Talkies, and in some ways a more potent one. From the first, those flickering images accompanied by piano evoked a remarkable range of emotions from the audience, who suddenly found their dreams inhabited by wondrous new idylls.

The movies could tell the unvarnished truth or concoct elaborate, fascinating lies. They could idealize or subvert. They could refashion fleeting concepts of beauty or reawaken hope in those who despaired. Most significantly of all, the silents could bridge the chasms of time, geography, culture and language, universalizing the human experience in a way no art form – not even literature – has been able to do.

As a byproduct, they also created a glittering new aristocracy – the movie stars – and a fantasyland for them to dwell in: Hollywood.

The advent of talking pictures destroyed many careers, enhanced others. But one thing had not changed. Commercialism ruled, and film, rather than unsettling audiences, generally reflected their expectations, tastes and prejudices.

There were 20,000 movie theaters in the United States by the mid-1920s, twice the number of a decade before. Business was booming. Technical progress was a constant, yet only when Middle America recoiled from rampant hedonism in the Hollywood community and decried the freewheeling eroticism and violence of its films, did major changes take place.

Hollywood ushered in its first attempt at self-censorship, the Hays Code, which was the industry standard (in theory of not in fact) from 1934 to 1968, when pictures like "The Wild Bunch" shattered it forever.

The problem with the code was that its idealized view of life was distinctly at odds with reality. The arrival of television and the emergence of European films at the end of World War II effectively ended Hollywood's, and to a lesser extent Great Britain's, dominance of the motion picture.

By 1950, TV was luring audiences out of theaters at an alarming rate, forcing studios to counter with ever more preposterous gimmicks. Meanwhile, the first wave of gifted European filmmakers (Bergman, Rossellini, Fellini, De Sica, Godard, Dassin), unencumbered by the code, presented lifelike, provocative fare which undermined Hollywood's smug self-confidence.

Happy endings were no longer a mandate. And a new era of increasing candor, culminating in today's questionable excesses, was given life, complete with every nuance of human light and darkness.

Hollywood fought back with spectacular (in more ways than one) success, concocting an extraordinary universe of special effects and a fresh generation of filmmakers for whom all bets were off. These days, anything goes.

Missteps frequently have been made, and the near total freedom in filmmaking of the '70s, '80s and '90s often has had the ironic effect of repelling audiences rather than expanding film's base. Hollywood would have us believe that, in the middle '90s, the so-called "family films" that marked the '40sand '50s are enjoying a renaissance, but the truth is that quality movies of this type are few and far between.

Because of the average age of filmgoers, and the triumph of the sequel, movies for adolescents hold sway.

The average cost of a film, excluding publicity, today hivers at $20 million. Many A-list productions run well in excess of $100 million, and sink-or-swim pressures are high. In an industry run by agents and marketing gurus, these factors encourage a sort of creative conservatism that the likes of DeMille, Ford, Lean and Lubitsch would have found maddening.

Still, there are signs that the run of sequels may be in eclipse, and that the number of seriously made, thoughtful comedies and dramas is on the rise, at least for now.

Initially, the growth of video over the past 15 years had much the same effect as the introduction of TV, though somewhat less pronounced. Unlike TV, however, it appears that video in many instances has helped increase movie attendance, while generating new technologies that filmmakers quickly adopt.

There has been one other measurable change. Idealization of women fueled the earliest films, an extension of the art world's preoccupation. The '30s and '40s were every bit as noted for their gutsy heroines as their heroes. Women were integral to the movies until the '70s, when good parts for talented actresses fell off dramatically. They remained few until just the last few years. Roles that chart a woman's life from birth to death, not just until age 40, are being written again.

The promise and potential of film today is greater than ever before. Yet, though 100 years of celluloid have run before our gaze, the basic question about the movies has not changed. Should they enlighten or inspire, divert and entertain or both?

In a word, yes. Happy anniversary.

20 Milestone Films

"**The Birth of a Nation**" (1915) – D.W. Griffith writes history with lightning.
"**The Battleship Potemkin**" (1925) – Sergei Eisenstein introduces fascinating new techniques.
"**The General**" (1927) – Buster Keaton directs and stars in the greatest of silent comedies.
"**Napoleon**" (1927) – Abel Gance's immortal epic.
"**The Jazz Singer**" (1927) – An unremarkable film, but the first Talkie.
"**All Quiet on the Western Front**" (1930) – Still the finest anti-war film.
"**Bringing Up Baby**" (1938) – Howard Hawks puts the screws to comedy.
"**Gone With the Wind**" (1939) – A triumph of Technicolor; history as spectacle.
"**Stagecoach**" (1939) – John Ford's archetypical Western.
"**The Grapes of Wrath**" (1940) – Hollywood enters the real world.
"**Citizen Kane**" (1941) – Boy wonder Orson Welles plays with his cinematic box of tricks.
"**The Lost Weekend**" (1945) – The movies take on alcoholism, for real.
"**Lawrence of Arabia**" (1962) – David Lean's all-star paean to the desert.

"8 1/2" (1963) – Fellini's complex film-within-a-film.
"2001: A Space Odyssey" (1968) – Special effects and science fiction on film come of age.
"The Wild Bunch" (1969) – The demons of violence are loosed.
"Annie Hall" (1977) – Woody Allen pours invention into every frame.
"Star Wars" (1977) – The era of space fantasy begins; serious science fiction declines.
"Apocalypse Now" (1979) – Flawed surrealistic masterpiece of Vietnam.
"The Killing Fields" (1984) – A searing document on genocide.

BT in 2001

— Columns & Rants —

Columns, Observations & Assorted Rants

Only a few full-length weekly columns are included in this section. This, of the nearly 1,000 I wrote over 19 years. It might seem a curious omission, but while many column entries celebrated distinctive filmmakers or mourned their passing, mostly they were devoted to news of movies opening, soon to be in release, films in production, and then-current industry developments. A distilled, personalized version of the weekly *Variety* trade paper.

Hardly newsworthy so many years later. It's the ageless stuff that matters.

The lengthier pieces are drawn from column leads showcasing the most significant or interesting subjects of that week. Some are obituaries of a sort, others are retrospectives on ongoing careers.

Otherwise, this final chapter is a bit of a hodge-podge, though hopefully an engaging one, with nuggets mined from the filmic ore: assorted snippets, capsule profiles, industry issues, exultations, lamentations, and sometimes self-indulgent assemblies of pet peeves.

Take them with a grain, or boulder, of salt.

But first, a grouchy opening salvo. It's deplorable that some critics' reviews pander to the lowest common denominator or to the industry publicity apparatus, the latter to curry favor and obtain more invitations to film junkets or interviews with the stars. When a reviewer seems never to have seen a film he or she didn't like, it's called pandering.

But one thing has only gotten worse in the years since I retired from daily film coverage: The nonexistent "critics" invented by the studio publicity machinery to produce fraudulent "blurbs" for advertising purposes. The trade publication *Variety* once put it succinctly with this cheeky headline: "Phantom Crix Are Flogging Flicks."

Or worse still, real critics who supply rapturous blurbs without ever having seen the movie.

Honest critics, in print or online, can only sigh at the black eye this gives all of us.

....

Katharine Hepburn: Unconventional actress could intimidate, charm
July 3, 2003

Good night, Miss Hepburn.

Amid the montage of memories that flickered past the mind's eye upon the news of Katharine Hepburn's death last Sunday, one image stands out, imperishable. It's that of an emancipated young woman, who lived her life as did the men of her era. Self-actualizing, with no apologies.

Even her autobiography, penned many years later, was titled "Me."

She was of durable and forthright New England stock, unconventional in voice (that distinctive, perfectly enunciated Bryn Mawr rattle) and outlook, trained from birth to swim against the current. She could be outspoken (but not by anyone you knew).

As an actress, she had four great partnerships, notwithstanding her long-time associations with the playwright Philip Barry, who wrote "Holiday" and "The Philadelphia Story" with her in mind, or George Cukor, who directed her in some of her finest roles. First and always, there was Spencer Tracy, her onscreen foil and the love of her decidedly independent life. Their nine films together were immaculate. They were THE team.

But as delightful and memorable as movies like "Woman of the Year" and "Adam's Rib" continue to be, Hepburn may have been at her very best opposite Cary Grant, the one actor who might challenge Tracy for the mantle of the cinema's best. Have there ever been two movies one could watch over and over again with undiminished pleasure like "The Philadelphia Story" and "Bringing Up Baby"? Has there ever been another film quite like "Holiday" or "Sylvia Scarlett"?

Not as far as we're concerned.

Equally indelible were her jousts with Humphrey Bogart in "The African Queen," and with Peter O'Toole in "The Lion in Winter," as well as her belated but beautiful performances opposite Laurence Olivier in the teleplay "Love Among the Ruins" and Henry Fonda in the film "On Golden Pond." This last may have been the least worthy of her Oscar-winning roles. It is a film burdened with one too many burnished sunsets and with sentimental writing. But she was there in force. Actors worthy of her, male or female, always brought out the best in Hepburn, although, like Burt Lancaster, her dominant personality could intimidate less-confident co-workers

It would be doing her an injustice, however, to recall Hepburn's career in terms of her leading men, or the other high-powered actresses with whom she crossed swords. You loved her for all kinds of reasons, not least for staying power, for winning two Oscars 30 years after having been declared box office poison.

There was that aggressive intelligence and her adamant insistence on privacy. ("My privacy is my own. I am the one to decide whether it will be invaded.") There was her utter indifference to how she looked (especially as she aged). There was her clarity, her intuitive grasp of just the right gesture or inflection. There was her incomparable diction, her complete understanding of her art (and her blithe dismissal of same). There was her impeccable sense of timing and of movement on stage or on screen.

There was her faintly masculine angularity ("You could throw a hat at her," wrote Robert Hopkins, "and wherever it hit it would stick"). There was, of course, her staunchness of character. And there were her more notable missteps, the foibles that made her seem not quite so Olympian after all.

Numerous biographies of Hepburn have been written, none of which fully capture the flavor of her personality.

The closest may prove to be Pulitzer Prize-winning author A. Scott Berg's "Kate Remembered," based on a 20-year-long series of interviews he conducted with her beginning in 1983, when Hepburn was 75 and Berg, 33. To be published by G.P. Putnam's Sons in hardcover on July 11, the book is described as "a loving tribute and a tender farewell that reveals an unusual relationship in a unique life, one lived large and largely according to Miss Hepburn's own rules."

Not simply a chronicle of her life and work or a recap of her pointed opinions, "Kate Remembered" also contains stories and sentiments she felt should not be made public until her death. It also discusses the actress's final years of failing health (and indomitable spirit).

In her 80s, with customary candor and self-deprecation, she assayed the bedrock of her renown. "I am revered rather like an old building," she said. "Yet, I still seem to be master of my fate. The boat may be only a canoe, but I'm paddling it."

Look elsewhere for a critical study of her plays and films. Berg's biography, like our recollections, is about a love affair.

If she ever had an emblematic line, it was to Bogie, in "The African Queen": "Nature, Mr. Allnut, is what we are put into this world to rise above."

Did she ever.

....

'Children of Men' director denies film's literary lineage
January 4, 2007

They just don't get it.

When novelist (and later filmmaker) Michael Crichton broke through with his 1969 best-seller "The Andromeda Strain," he bridled at the novel being characterized as "science fiction," which, of course, is precisely what it was. An update of the old-fashioned "Hard SF" variety, perhaps, the style popularized by Arthur C. Clarke and Isaac Asimov, but a riveting read and eventually (1971) a fine movie. Crichton rightly feared being consigned to a literary ghetto of scant sales and besmirched reputation.

Many others have followed suit, with far less excuse.

After a brief flirtation with thoughtful SF in "2001: A Space Odyssey," George Lucas and "Star Wars" came along to seduce mass audiences with a throwback to SF's earliest hack-dominated days: broadly entertaining, pulp-style space opera. Its astounding box office success set in motion a wave of "sci-fi" movies and books with all the intelligence and depth of a sleeping Wookie - and set "real" science fiction back 1,000 years. All but forgotten was that extraordinarily fertile New Wave period of genuine literary merit that ran from the early 1960s through the first few years of the '70s. It was dominated by brilliant speculative fiction, penned by gifted artists who cared far more about ideas and character development than gizmos, galactic empires and space battles.

Great SF has always been about ideas - cultural, scientific, social, political -and how they affect people. Real, identifiable people, not cardboard cut-outs. The ones who disparage it most loudly tend to be those who've never read - and seldom seen - the good stuff.

Steven Spielberg notwithstanding, the last time a first-rate filmmaker did not shrink from being identified with science fiction was Michel Gondry, who directed the best pure SF movie of the 21st century (so far) in 2004's excellent "Eternal Sunshine of the Spotless Mind."

Yet now we have Alfonso Cuaron, director of "Children of Men" (which opens here Friday) loudly disclaiming the obvious SF underpinnings of his new movie. "We didn't want to do a science-fiction movie," says the director of "Y Tu Mama Tambien" and "Harry Potter and the Prisoner of Azkaban." "We wanted to do a movie about the state of things." Well, duh, what do you think the best SF does but comment on the present by projecting to the future?

Adapted from her own 1992 book by British novelist P.D. James, this near-future dystopian tale deals with a global infertility crisis that threatens the human race. The setup may be a well-worn SF cliche - it is - but that doesn't prevent it from having the potential for considerable cinematic power.

We understand the risks, especially when many millions of dollars are invested, but we just wish these people cared a little less about marketing and more being honest with themselves.

....

Choleric assent

January 4, 2007

Gabriel Garcia Marquez's great tale of magical realism, "Love in the Time of Cholera," is coming to the screen courtesy of English director Mike Newell, currently shooting the picture amid the stifling tropical heat of Marquez's native Colombia. Surprisingly, it's the first time an English-language adaptation of a novel by the Nobel Prize-winning author has been attempted.

Then again, maybe not so surprising, given how Latin America's chief literary godling, a staunch defender of Castro and the Cuban revolution, has protected his work from Hollywood's clutches. Never mind that his son, Rodrigo Garcia, is a Hollywood-based director (2005's "Nine Lives").

The excellent Spanish character actor Javier Bardem ("The Sea Inside") and Italian actress Giovanna Mezzogiorno play the lead roles of Fermina and Florentino, whose difficult courtship in turn-of-the-century South America was inspired by the experiences of Marquez's own parents. The script was written by Ronald Harwood, who won a Best Adapted Screenplay Oscar for "The Pianist" (2003).

Newell, best known for sprightly comedies made on both sides of the Atlantic – "Enchanted April" and "Four Weddings and a Funeral," among them – reinvented himself to an extent with the tough, convincing mob drama "Donnie Brasco" (1997), and was last seen tackling the Harry Potter franchise in "Harry Potter and the Goblet of Fire" (2005).

It took some persuading on the filmmakers' part to get the 78-year-old Marquez, long a resident of Mexico City, to relent. A $3 million check was some inducement. Yet Marquez, once a film critic and aspiring filmmaker, also recently ceded the rights - for free - to another of his highly cinematic novels, "Of Love and Other Demons," this time to debut feature film director Hilda Hidalgo, a Costa Rican whom he met in Cuba.

Newell promised Marquez that the film, slated for a Christmas 2007 release, would be true to the spirit of the book. But apparently the maestro isn't entirely convinced; he's yet to visit the set.

"I'm sure it causes him (Marquez) some distress that an Englishman would make this film about a very South American subject in what you could regard as the wrong language," Newell remarked. "I'm sure the first thing everyone will focus on is whether he approves or not, and I suspect he's bound to be disappointed."

....

Dole's view of art shortsighted
June 15, 1995

Like all those who were Meese-led about "pornography" during the Reagan Administration, the new conservative element's scattershot condemnation of motion pictures (and music) hits some legitimate targets but is more often way off the mark.

No one should be so naive as to assert that the ceaseless bombardment by tasteless and violent entertainment fare has no effect on audiences. Certainly it does. But censorship isn't the answer. And don't expect Hollywood or the music industry to police themselves, not when there's mega-profits to be had Individual responsibility is our only recourse, though easier said than done.

It's true that scores of phony "mavericks" and greedy, narcissistic types hide behind the First Amendment, obscuring their hunger for fame and profit with a smokescreen of "free expression." On the other hand, many of the same corporate tycoons (such as Rupert Murdoch) who espouse the conservative view also own the companies that rake in billions from the "garbage" they claim to deplore. These are the same people who condemn the "elitist" NEA and praise the "majority tastes" of the marketplace. Someone ought to tell them that majority tastes are precisely what is being reflected in today's mass entertainment, like it or not.

An open society must take the bad with the good, or it is not an open society. And the bad wouldn't draw giant audiences if people didn't lap it up. To a degree, movies and the tabloid media explosion have conditioned us to prefer certain things. But popular entertainment does reflect what's going on in society. "The Basketball Diaries," which opens here Friday, is a case in point: a movie that pushes the envelope but wants to have something significant to say, even if doesn't manage to say it all that well.

A violent society inevitably will have violent diversions, as social critic Katha Pollitt has pointed out.

Or consider this comment from author John Edgar Wideman in Time:

"Which is more threatening to America – the violence, obscenity, sexism and racism of movies and records, or the stark reality these movies and music reflect?"

Sen. Bob Dole made some valid points in his recent tirade. Yet, this outlook simply refuses to recognize that true art, by its very nature, challenges and disrupts the status quo. It is meant to be unsettling, provocative, even incendiary.

....

Hollywood icon Elizabeth Taylor dies
March 24, 2011

She was one of Hollywood's imperishable personalities, a child actress turned adult megastar who was at least as much a legend for her eight marriages, medical travails and philanthropy as she was for her acting.

On Wednesday, the iconic 79-year-old Elizabeth Taylor died of congestive heart failure at Cedars-Sinai Medical Center, where she had been hospitalized for about six weeks.

If Marilyn Monroe was the sex symbol of the '50s, Taylor was its repository of glamour, on and off screen.

And for a fleeting two days in 1985, her film career having wound down, the London-born, three-time Oscar-winning star graced Charleston with her presence.

Cast in the production of the ABC-TV miniseries "North and South," based on the 1982 novel by Hilton Head author John Jakes, Taylor arrived on March 15, 1985, at Charleston International Airport.

Joined by co-star Hal Holbrook and starlet-of-the-moment Morgan Fairchild, Taylor glided out of her private jet into the sort of media clamor she had long been used to. Holbrook and Fairchild were ignored, like attendants at a coronation. But when it came to the business of the set, Taylor was all professionalism, ego checked at the door.

The girl with violet eyes

Taylor served no apprenticeship. She was famous from her first moment on screen at age 12, in the children's classic "National Velvet" (1944). Audience fascination grew exponentially with her young-adult turn opposite Spencer Tracy in "Father of the Bride" (1950), but it wasn't long before her fame rested as much on her not-so-private life as on her movie roles.

Tough and vulnerable, voluptuous and frail, her reputation as a "man-eater" mitigated by a humanitarian impulse, Taylor captivated most of those who worked with her.

"The shock of Elizabeth was not only her beauty," Mike Nichols said in a widely published statement. Nichols, who directed Taylor in her Academy Award-winning role in "Who's Afraid of Virginia Woolf?", was more impressed by her less obvious qualities. "It was her generosity. Her giant laugh. Her vitality, whether tackling a complex scene on film or where we would all have dinner until dawn. She is singular and indelible on film and in our hearts."

Taylor starred in more than 50 feature films, ranging from sentimental family comedy to incendiary melodrama to one of the great filmic boondoggles of all time, "Cleopatra," then the most expensive movie ever made.

Lasting legacy

Taylor received the Legion of Honor, France's most prestigious award, in 1987 for her work in supporting AIDS research. And in May 2000, Queen Elizabeth II made Taylor a dame for her services to the entertainment industry and to charity.

In 1993, the American Film Institute bestowed on her its Lifetime Achievement Award. But her defining role was as "Elizabeth Taylor," marrying and divorcing, gaining and losing weight, going in and out of hospitals – and in and out of the public's affections.

....

Tarsem's film falls flat
July 3, 2008

Before being seduced by the trailer for "The Fall," admittedly a captivating one, remember the film is directed by Tarsem, the singularly named and singularly irksome perpetrator of 2000's "The Cell," as empty an exercise as could be imagined.

For all its arresting visuals and exotic locations, this contemporary fairy tale is little more than a two-hour music video: a pretentious parade of pretty pictures punctuated by sepia-toned grimness. How a movie can be so exceptionally cinematic yet interminably dull is a puzzle. Never mind that it is "presented" by a pair of vastly superior talents in David Fincher and Spike Jonze.

"The Fall" is as incoherent in story as it is pictorially clever, with fantasy sequences lashed by ludicrous dialogue and operatic acting.

Tarsem (real name, Tarsem Singh) obviously possesses an imaginative visual sense. It's substance that eludes -- or doesn't interest -- him. If this is art, as some proclaim, it is art of a very shallow and debased variety.

Filmed, pointlessly, over four years in 18 countries, "The Fall" was a 15-year labor of love for its director. We're told it took years to cast, baffling given the blandness of the performances and the various one-dimensional caricatures.

Doubtless, Tarsem believes his film to be a kind of homage, and some aspects of it genuinely are, like his black-and-white tribute to the great early film stunts of Buster Keaton and Harold Lloyd, et al., framed in the opening and closing credits. Yet in the end, "The Fall" is merely an eye-popping waste of time.

....

Agnes Varna: Filmmaker revisits her life
June 27, 2010

With a twinkle in her eye and the ghost of a smile oft playing on her face, Agnes Varda seems to be as engaging a personality as she is a filmmaker.

Revered by critics and devotees as "the ageless poet-angel of French cinema," Varda may not be terribly well-known in America, though locals who attended the 10th annual French Film Festival last summer at the College of Charleston enjoyed her charming, self-styled retrospective, "The Beaches of Agnes."

The winner of numerous awards such as best documentary, not least the Cesar (French Oscar)and National Society of Film Critics (U.S.) laurels, the movie makes its U.S. broadcast debut at 10 p.m. Tuesday on PBS stations (locally on South Carolina Educational Television). "Beaches" is part of the ongoing series "Point of View," now in its 23rd year as American TV's longest-running independent documentary series.

"Beaches," at once amusing and elegiac, is about a life lived in film. For Varda, whose movies and art installations meld documentary realism and social commentary with a decidedly experimental approach, the intersection between art and memory is the linchpin. While relating the process of making each of her movies, Varda revisits her Belgian youth, her adolescence in occupied Paris, early forays into photography, commitment to social activism and marriage to director Jacques Demy ("The Umbrellas of Cherbourg").

Impish as ever, yet girded by seriousness, she employs all her cinematic tricks in "Beaches" to juxtapose the real and imagined. At the core of it is her concept of the filmmaker's power to mold a vision, much like a potter molds a vase.

Film buffs will recognize fragments of each of her most well-regarded movies, among them "Vagabond," "Cleo From 5 to 7" and "One Sings, the Other Doesn't." And they will be intrigued by the 81-year-old's recollections of her colleagues in the French new wave: Jean-Luc Godard, Francois Truffaut, Claude Chabrol, Alain Resnais and her late husband, Demy.

Interestingly, she was the new wave's only female director. And it was her first film, "La Pointe Courte" (1955), based on a William Faulkner short story, that many consider as having anticipated that pivotal film movement.

One especially playful feature of the picture finds fellow film poet Chris Marker ("The Pier," "Without Sun") appearing intermittently in the form of an animated orange cat that offers pithy comments to all who'll listen.

The title of the film, which also is available on DVD from Cinema Guild Home Video (cinemaguild.com/home video), refers to the actual beaches that have been significant in her life. But even here she can't resist playing with audience expectations and revealing (conspiratorially) just how she did it.

Appearing both as they were in youth and as they are today are members of her family, son Mathieu Demy, an actor, and daughter Rosalie Varda-Demy, an actress and costume designer, and the many "ordinary" folks who found themselves drafted into her films. Also making appearances are Godard; French actors Gerard Depardieu, Catherine Deneuve, Michel Piccoli and Philippe Noiret; British actress-model Jane Birkin; the late rocker Jim Morrison; and American film stalwarts Robert De Niro and Harrison Ford.

Varda is wistful here, but nimbly skirts the divide between sentiment and sentimentality.

"I wanted to be like a bird," Varda told The New York Times recently. "I wanted to be free in my memory, to go from one part to another and see what I would find."

"The Beaches of Agnes" helps her take wing.

....

This 'Book Club' needs better writing
October 4, 2007

There's gobs of sensibility but little sense in "The Jane Austen Book Club." And we are not persuaded. Especially not by an abrupt, highly unlikely sea change on the part of a jock turned Janeite.

Writer-director Robin Swicord's slight but well-acted adaptation of the Karen Joy Fowler novel finds Hugh Dancy once again stealing the show from a flock of talented leading ladies – much as he did earlier this year in "Evening" – and once again it is because he is bequeathed most of the best dialogue in a script not overburdened with tart lines.

Maria Bello, Kathy Baker, Amy Brenneman, Maggie Grace and, in particular, Emily Blunt ("The Devil Wears Prada") all have their moments, as does wild card Jimmy Smits, but Dancy makes the biggest impression as a science-fiction fancier converted to Austen enthusiast. While not exactly the thorn among the roses – some of the oft-disappointed women are considerably more prickly than he – his character vies with Blunt's for command of the screen.

The story: Six contemporary Californians, five comradely women and one man, meet monthly at varied sites to discuss Austen's classic novels. During their months together, marriages are stressed, affairs commence, unsuitable arrangements suddenly become suitable, accommodations are made and love blossoms.

Fowler shadowed the lives of her characters with Austen's candid writing, as the members of the club find their lives and romances reflected in six of the novels. The movie's attempt to employ the same device feels a bit more labored, not to mention lacking in event. It's all gab, gab, gab, whine, whine, whine, with only the most rudimentary of insights into human foibles, insecurities and capacity for independence.

Say what you will about Austen's books as mirrors of relationship issues in any age. It's not that one expects anything altogether new in a film inspired by her works. But a movie still has to engage, to be infused with a modicum of vitality.

Not here, despite the cast's best efforts.

It's the debut feature for the South Carolina-born, Florida-bred Swicord, known chiefly for her screenplay adaptations, not all of which have been well-regarded. Her track record won't be helped much by "The Jane Austen Book Club." The principal problem with the film is that, as a writer, Swicord remains mired in melodramatics. Her last script, for "Memoirs of a Geisha," was roundly panned for its soap-operatic script, and "Practical Magic" also took it on the chin. The one exception to this parade of mediocrity was 1994's remake of "Little Women," for which Swicord's screenplay was unaccountably outstanding. Go figure.

Otherwise, to employ a decidedly un-Austen analogy, Swicord's adaptations tend to creep along the runway, inching their way to takeoff but never quite getting aloft.

But the worst misstep this time out is not pacing. It's the aforementioned depiction of the Blunt character's husband (Marc Blucas), a sports-minded nonreader who is just a little intimidated by his wife's intelligence and passion for literature. Although his desire to be true to himself is believable enough, the man's sudden awakening into a sensitive, sophisticated Austen devotee is not. A feel-good moment that undermines all that has come before, it's wishful thinking of the most feminine kind, and about as plausible as Blunt's willowy Prudie morphing overnight into an aircraft mechanic.

....

Growing up is hard to do – at least for child actors
April 12, 2007

We've said it before and we'll say it again. No matter how precocious or arresting, child actors should not be nominated in the same Oscar category as adults. It's preposterous to choose a child over highly skilled pros who have refined their craft for years - decades in some cases.

It's also unfair to the kids.

Ten-year-old Abigail Breslin ("Little Miss Sunshine") may get lucky like one-time child star Jackie Earle Haley, now 45, who was forgotten until re-emerging 30 years later as an Oscar nominee for "Little Children." She may join contemporary Dakota Fanning, 12, as one of America's most sought-after kid actors, enjoy a few years in the limelight, then disappear after adolescence, like Macaulay Culkin (the "Home Alone" flicks) or Justin Henry (who, at age 8, got an absurd 1979 Oscar nomination for 1979's "Kramer vs. Kramer").

Jodie Foster is the all-time exemplar of a child star who succeeded at both levels. But for every Drew Barrymore, Scarlett Johansson, Christina Ricci, Kirsten Dunst and Natalie Portman, (other than Kurt Russell, where are the boys?) there are scores of child actors who beat a hasty exit (which, sometimes, is a good thing), failed as adult performers, or were harmed by their lost youths before the camera. Where is Tatum O'Neal? The book is still out on current kid rave Dakota Fanning, not to mention ex-child stars Lindsay Lohan and Hilary Duff, who may yet implode.

Daniel Radcliffe, 17, is gamely trying to make the transition from the Harry Potter films. But if history is a guide, the odds are against him. This transition to adult roles is one of the most difficult things to achieve in the entertainment industry, especially when you are identified with a specific character or have made a corner in family comedies. This is partly because audiences who loved child stars as kids or teens won't always accept them as adults — witness Hollywood legends Mary Pickford and Shirley Temple — and partly because most of them never were that talented in the first place. Cute is not talent.

Some child stars are astonishingly good in a given film. Consider Keisha Castle-Hughes in "Whale Rider" or Haley Joel Osment in "The Sixth Sense." But it's deceptive. There's no guarantee of anything when the voice deepens or the figure fills out, particularly when it comes to public tastes. And many have to face the onus of starting over when they're grown. They're beginners again, beginners who were once stars.

....

In appreciation of film shorts
Nov. 10, 2007

Comparing a short film to a feature-length movie is not unlike comparing a short story to a novel. Most of the same criteria for judging them apply, of course, though with a few significant differences. Actually, fewer "rules" attend a short film, which affords the filmmaker greater latitude to experiment.

Do not expect the developed storyline or depth of characterization one may find in a feature film of quality. But do expect clarity and a strong underlying idea. Short films, like short fiction, turn on ideas. These ideas often come to their "authors" of a piece, fully formed, whereas most the themes of full-length films have time to develop gradually and venture off into various subplots.

Short films tend to be either vignettes (with less apparent structure) or capsule narratives. But the best ones are tight, distilled and/or provocative in some way. There need not be a "message" as such, or even a dominant character. Irony can be a potent tool in short films, which can be like aphorisms (a concise statement of a principle or idea). They can also be frolicsome and fun and not take themselves too seriously.

....

The New Dodo: Is it the movies or is it us?
February 2, 2006

Call it the rant of a one-time futurist-turned-budding Luddite.

With disgruntled and overcharged theater audiences gradually disappearing, piracy rampant and the new technologies promising a democratized movie business that puts the consumer in control, it's easy for old fogies to engage in hand-wringing over the future of the traditional motion picture - i.e., the New Dodo.

But some think the situation couldn't be finer. Just listen to the web-gushing of Fast Company journalist Alan Deutschman, on Yahoo Business: "A small cadre of corporate chiefs could control the cinemas, the airwaves and the shelf space in the DVD aisles, but no one can control the Internet. Transmitting video files to consumers over digital broadband connections - whether via cable, phone, satellite or wireless Wi-Max - changes the whole equation."

Sure it does. And very conveniently in some respects. But to what end? To make a nation of couch potatoes ever more prisoners of our media-room sofas? To have the dubious pleasure of watching a movie on one's computer or videophone?

It doesn't matter if your home entertainment center is state-of-the-art, with the biggest flat-screen TV on the market. Nice, but it's just not the same as being in a theater. Do you really prefer to see the sweeping vistas of movies such as "Brokeback Mountain," "The Constant Gardener," "March of the Penguins" or "Pride and Prejudice" on a TV screen (or smaller)?

Admittedly, going to the movies does involve a few hassles, like standing in line (once for tickets, once for snacks), dealing with loutish behavior of some patrons and deafening sound systems, not to mention the occasional parking headaches.

Granted, at home, you can stop the movie to get something to eat or go to the restroom. But that's a double-edged sword. Seeing a movie straight through has its virtues, as does enjoying it without the distractions of ringing phones, doorbells, family tumult or nagging guilt over all that paperwork that needs attending in the next room.

It's great to have choices. But not every technical innovation is an advance. Often, it's just another product someone is trying to sell you. Be careful what you wish for. In the end, you may get less than you think.

....

Cacophony
January 28, 2007

The temptation is to say that "Notes on a Scandal" is the sort of hybridized movie that isn't quite sure what it wants to be. But director Richard Eyre's cat (Judi Dench) and mouse (Cate Blanchett) game is more calculated than that.

What also seems calculated is the score. The music of Philip Glass is once again overbearing and intrusive, written as if the rest of the movie is there merely to provide his compositions a vehicle.

Glass seems to think every movie is "Koyaanisqatsi," the spellbinding non-narrative film he made with Godfrey Reggio in the early 1980s.

....

'Babel' can't find cohesion despite exquisite moments
November 9, 2006

'Babel" is one of those maddening examples of muddled thinking afflicting artistic ambition, a film of exquisite moments and fine performances that isn't quite sure how to unify its elements into a compelling whole.

Though often gripping, and with a touching finale, the movie more often feels unrelievedly portentous, its connections tenuous at best. It's good, but it might have been so much better.

Director Alejandro Gonzalez Inarritu's and screenwriter Guillermo Arriaga's final entry in the trilogy that began with the excellent "Amores Perros" and the disappointing "21 Grams" likewise spins on multiple story strands that are sometimes jarringly intercut. Only this time, instead of a highly localized canvas, the filmmakers divide their story among three continents and varied languages. Languages whose barriers are more than linguistic.

The results are mixed, more depressing in the vein of "21 Grams" than riveting in the manner of "Amores Perros." There's an undercurrent of dread that never subsides until the close, and one can argue that no matter how beautiful the film looks (kudos to "Brokeback Mountain" cinematographer Rodrigo Prieto), or how gifted a director Inarritu undoubtedly is, he (and Arriaga) might benefit from leavening disaster with a touch of serendipity.

....

Medium's impact on the film industry beginning to take hold
April 28, 2005

Will it be the fate of the feature film, shown in the communal experience of the theater, to be little more than a marketing prelude to the extras-encrusted DVD release? An appetizer, as it were?

It could come to that if present trends continue. Or not. Actual box office in 2004 accounted for only 21 percent of feature-film revenues, compared with the 63 percent generated by industry sales of movies to retail stores.

But instead of constricting the variety of movies being made, this direction may well translate into more adventurous filmmaking and fewer mega-blockbusters that fail (often dismally) to win audience or stand the test of time.

Currently, what is most intriguing about the economic impact of the DVD revolution on the motion picture industry are its potential artistic repercussions. The notion of a director seeing the DVD, with all its add-ons, as another creative canvas is a fascinating one, though the companion idea of employing DVDs to rework themes or fine-tune "flaws" in the original theater release does sound uncomfortably like rewriting a novel after the reader verdict is in.

Yet directors who couldn't be troubled to deal with DVDs of their movies just a few years ago are embracing the opportunity to shape and mold them as an aesthetic duty or a kind of redemptive holy grail: just because it bombed at the box office doesn't mean it can't make a pile in home video.

It's led to some overkill, of course. Did anyone really want to sit through all 20-plus hours of the "Alien" series? The good news: DVDs can, and do, offer a vessel for independent-style movies, low-budget features driven by character and story or documentaries on the cutting edge, each at a disadvantage in landing a distribution deal to theaters. Also, DVDs can rescue smaller films that get yanked from theaters before they have a fair chance to build word-of-mouth.

Small art house-like DVD film "salons" also could sprout in small screening rooms in cities where an even wider array of filmmakers could screen their wares, possibly leading to DVD sales; who needs an expensive, over-hyped "film festival" in an already glutted landscape of them?

The bad news: We grow closer by the day to the big screen experience going the way of the kinescope and the bustle. From the beginning of home video, the chief argument against it was that people were not seeing a film as its director intended it be seen. The largest big-screen TV cannot equal the movie screen, even today's shrunken, postage stamp ones.

Also, digital video-making, like digital book publishing, has a not always positive democratizing power. When anyone can make a movie, everyone will. You get saturation, at worst like the scourge of "reality" TV.

But try and stop it.

The looming demise of the VHS videotape and the ascendance of the DVD (at least until the next innovation makes it obsolete) is a profound one for the movie industry's home video "subsidiaries," for they will be moving from a rental-based business model to more of a sales one, especially in outlets like Wal-Mart, Target, and so on. That is, if current consumer patterns hold.

Wall Street certainly has noticed the shift. The DVD as cash cow may unseat many old-school producers and studios determined to churn out $100 million-plus features.

It's not for no reason that legendary nameplate MGM, which (sadly) hardly makes movies anymore, was the subject of a major bidding war. It's the 4,100 feature films in its library that new owner Sony coveted.

....

Promoting a movie to yourself, costly
April 8, 2004

I'm a night owl's night owl. I don't do mornings. Unless, of course, you count the hours between midnight and 4 a.m. Breakfast? What the devil is that? I saw a sunrise once – 1988, I believe.

So imagine my chagrin a few weeks back when I received the latest in a long line of witty (and silly) promotional freebies from the distributors of the Coen brothers' films. Secured inside a heavily fortified box was, of all things, a sleek new waffle iron emblazoned with the title of the movie, "The Ladykillers." Though hardly a top-of-the-line gizmo, it was better than the tin of old-fashioned hair pomade (complete with hair net) I got for the Coens' "O, Brother Where Art Thou." But, as with all such things, it came with an accompanying sense of unease.

For the record, most movie critics automatically give such things away, often hurriedly. If it's a trinket sent out to promote an animated kid's flick, no problem. Zillions of young parents will accept the safer ones post haste. But lots of it are dumped into the circular file (i.e., trash).

If you've ever wondered why your movie ticket costs $7.75, apart from the fallout from $20 million paydays for some high-profile stars, look no further than the costs of marketing and advertising. A percentage of every ticket you buy represents your contribution to selling a movie to yourself.

Of course, the building blocks of ticket costs are more involved than that. But when journalists who cover the movies get bombarded with promotional items and toys over and above the press materials actually needed to do coverage, you have to shake your head in wonderment.

How much did it cost to send this to a couple of thousand newspapers and radio stations? "This" being anything from the Coens' latest gimmick to posters, talking Kleenex boxes, stuffed animals, road-emergency kits, plastic spaghetti-on-a-stick, picnic blankets, lapel pins, coolers, coffee mugs, costume jewelry, baseball caps, large-format books, sunglasses, music CDs, spin-off DVDs and the inevitable T-shirts. All with the movie logo.

Marketing departments are just having a bit of fun, though currying favor is doubtless part of the motivation. And it can get downright absurd at times, not to mention a little insulting. Why, apart from questions of ethics, would I wish to be a walking billboard? However fleetingly amusing these things may be, and regardless of the fact that no professional reviewer is likely to be "influenced" by such largesse, this stuff costs money. Even when a distributor such as Warner Brothers or Universal or Disney has them manufactured by the planeload.

Ninety-five percent of such things usually find their way into a critic's mailbox during summer and just before Christmas. The fraction of it you keep – baubles, mainly – is mostly to remind you just how nuts this business truly is, and perhaps how wasteful Hollywood excesses can be.

....

Test marketing leaves a sullied mark on films
January 9, 1992

Hollywood lately has become more than just enamored of "test marketing," that innocent-sounding practice of gauging viewer reaction to advance screenings of major films.

In the old days, it sometimes helped. One recalls how audience responses to test screenings prompted the filmmakers to make changes that arguably improved, before their general release, such classic movies as "The Big Sleep" and "Lost Horizon" for the better.

This seldom seems the case today.

Those not imbued with the offend-no-one mentality of the corporate mind, those who prefer originality and daring to playing it safe, tend to disparage this trend as part and parcel of "filmmaking by committee." The product of "committee" waffling generally is one of two things: endless sequels or pure pablum.

Most genuinely experimental films are unaffected; they are produced and shot outside the realm of the mainstream. "Other People's Money," a general audience movie adapted from the biting Broadway play, was not so fortunate. After it was test marketed last year, all the subplots – and most of the bite – were edited out, leaving several important scenes in a dramatic vacuum.

Gregory Peck, a principal character in the film, objected to the committee approach in a recent interview with the *Washington Post*: "I can always sort of sense the committee. Very often you get the sense that this was born in the mind of some top agent and concocted as a package and sold to a frightened executive who needs a hit before he gets fired.

"Then there's this awful market testing. It absolutely takes the backbone out of everything because what it amounts to is a picture edited by the ultimate committee, the public. So you get pictures that aren't going to make anybody mad, certainly not challenge anyone's intelligence. Not present them with anything controversial. After a while (watching one) you say, 'What is this *about*?' They've tried to turn motion picture-making into an industry like making shoes or sausages."

To no one's great surprise, neither is Steven Spielberg immune to the power of the exit poll, despite his reputation for creative vision. He admits that viewer comments on advance screenings if "Hook," his $70 million remake of "Peter Pan," went a long way in determining the fate of certain scenes. The result: a cinematic abortion.

It's like a novelist adding, deleting or altering an important chapter to suit the taste of the average Joe Public. In less polite circles, this impulse is called by its proper name – pandering. No amount of "Hey, filmmaking is a business" explanations excuses it.

....

Actor brings film experience to local theater
January 8, 2004

Anyone who covers the arts is accustomed to encountering people of genuine talent who work steadily and creatively, making a significant contribution but seldom winning the wider recognition they deserve. Meanwhile, hordes of mediocrities make tens of millions of dollars dispensing worthless tripe and get lionized for it.

It is one of life's perverse little jests, but it wearies the souls of those who must watch, much less experience, the injustice of it all decade after decade.

By all rights, an actor of the skill of Rodney Lee Rogers should be getting the same sorts of roles in feature films bestowed on that excellent young star Edward Norton, whom he resembles. Not that Rogers hasn't had his successes, as filmmaker and stage and screen performer. He has. But when you see the sort of work he and his co-stars have done in such fare as "Lobby Hero," PURE Theatre's local production of the play by Kenneth Lonergan, you are reminded yet again of that vast pool of American talent that delivers superior product but too often labors for peanuts.

Of course, not everyone aspires to global fame or Bel Air estates. Some simply want to pursue their passions, make a mark wherever they happen to be.

Rogers, a North Carolina native, is back East, having moved to the area from the Pacific Northwest, where his independent film "Steaming Milk" captured best director and best actor awards at the 1997 Seattle International Film Festival. Also screened at the AFI Los Angeles and Cairo International Film festivals, the movie received strong reviews in the trade magazine Variety and other media outlets.

Seattle's loss is our gain. Rogers has teamed with his wife, respected actress and impresario Sharon Graci, to found PURE Theater and introduce edgier theatrical works by playwright-filmmakers like Lonergan, whose film "You Can Count on Me" was one of 2000's best pictures, and Neil LaBute ("The Shape of Things," "In the Company of Men"). This is material that challenges audiences as well as actors and directors.

Currently, the company is in the midst of its run for its third show, the fittingly titled "Fully Committed." That they are.

WORST OF 2003

With the 24th-annual Razzie Award nominations due to be announced Jan. 26, we thought we'd get a jump on them with our own Worst of 2003.

Start with Angelina Jolie's twin killing, the truly wretched "Lara Croft, Tomb Raider: The Cradle of Life" and the well-intentioned but leaden "Beyond Borders." If any actress ever failed to capitalize on an Oscar win to make good movies, Jolie is her.

Then there's the abysmal "Dumb & Dumberer," and the noxious "Cheaper by the Dozen." They deserve each other. Add "Charlie's Angels: Full Throttle," even worse than the first one; "Dreamcatcher," yet another dog based on a Stephen King yarn; the stupider-than-thou "Bad Boys II," the banal waste of talent "Love Actually," the kid-unfriendly "The Cat in the Hat" (the best reason yet to make Dr. Seuss off limits to Hollywood); "The League of Extraordinary Gentlemen," a tedious trifle from a seemingly endless supply of "graphic novels" (i.e., books for those who don't like to read); the witless "Honey"; the chock-full-o'-holes "Bulletproof Monk"; "Le Divorce," which should have filmgoers calling their lawyers; and the asinine "How to Lose a Guy in 10 Days."

Bronx cheers also for "Intolerable Cruelty" (Coens collapse), "Gigli" (Bennifer bombs), "View from the Top" (Gwyneth crashes), "Legally Blonde: Red, White and Blonde" (Reese wrecks), "The Matrix Reloaded" (more like regurgitated) and the laughable "Gothika."

Was there worse? Probably. We just couldn't bear to go see them.

BOOK 'EM

The big screen success of "Seabiscuit," "Master and Commander," and the last of the "The Lord of the Rings" movies, among others, underscores yet again how good books can make for good movies, and how good movies can give their source material a back-end boost on the bookshelves.

Variety reports that 20 books were turned into movies this past year, while noting that several of these adaptations are likely to receive multiple Oscar nominations.

Laura Hillenbrand's best-selling "Seabiscuit: An American Legend" has gotten new life in the book stores, as have J.R.R. Tolkein's "Rings" cycle, the late Patrick O'Brian's Aubrey-Maturin adventure novels, Charles Frazier's "Cold Mountain," Dennis Lehane's "Mystic River" and Frances Mayes' "Under the Tuscan Sun" (OK, so it wasn't such a good movie; at least the scenery was nice).

It's unlikely, however, that Philip Roth's "The Human Stain" was helped by the overly austere and miscast screen adaptation.

AU REVOIR

A fond goodbye to some memorable performers who passed away in 2003, lending their craft to film, stage, and TV. Katharine Hepburn, Bob Hope, and Gregory Peck head the list, of course. But also exceptionally gifted were such people as Donald O'Connor, Art Carney, Gregory Hines, Hume Cronyn, Buddy Ebsen, Richard Crenna, Jack Elam, Charles Bronson, John Ritter and Robert Stack.

It's an especially poignant list for baby boomers, who grew up with the likes of Carney, Crenna, and Ebsen in their best television roles.

....

The Hunger for Renown
February 20, 2003

She's the Material Churl. To be sure, noting the pretenses and absurdities of the career of Madonna, that sardine who would be a salmon, is like shooting big fish in a very small pond.

Witness her latest "achievement": earning richly deserved Worst Actress ("Swept Away"), Worst Supporting Actress ("Die Another Day"), and Worst Song ("Die Another Day," title tune) nominations from the Razzies, an annual spoof of the Academy Awards.

When, oh when, will someone put her out of our misery?

With apologies to her legion of fans, if she is not especially significant for what she has done, she is most certainly notable for what she symbolizes: our era's insatiable hunger for renown. Earlier civilizations believed that fame was the crown of achievement. Now fame is the most baroque form of narcissistic self-regard. This single-minded pursuit of fame – private authenticity (and justification) through public acclaim – appears to be the new version of the pursuit of happiness, with its signposts of ceaseless self-promotion and meaningless commercial "accomplishment."

You could make the same observation about a score of entertainment stars, male and female.

Granted, faux-feminist Madonna is a pop "phenomenon," not a serious artist, and not too many years removed from her origins as an idol of the post-pubescent set. And also granted, she's generated a few memorable tunes and at least two passable film performances ("Evita" and "A League of Their Own"), though more of the latter are not encouraged.

Yet she represents better than anyone the adage that fame creates its own etiquette, allowing the famous to be themselves in a way no one else can afford to be. And we would have no problem with it, if not for her ludicrous proclamations, or the legions of flacks who regard this ultimately trivial talent as a role model, if not the second coming.

You want powerful women? Great. So do we. But how about one of substance?

As Hartford Courant critic Joe Harrington so aptly put it in his riposte to author/Madonna worshipper Gerri Hirshey ("We Gotta Get Out of This Place"), "Hirshey sees Madonna as the ultimate female liberator. As a result, Hirshey subjects us to pronouncements including: 'Let us succinctly regard her as a leather-bustiered Hale-Bopp that hurtled smack into the Information Age at an astrologically and technologically propitious moment and rendered us all slightly awe-struck.' Speak for yourself, Gerri. Hirshey might believe Madonna's media-whore persona was a godsend for women in general, but there are just as many critics who find her facile dalliances with postmodern styles to be posturing of the worst kind. Hirshey perpetually makes the big mistake of a lot of postmodern critics: She fails to realize that when the artist in question is doing what amounts to garbage, his or her so-called 'innovations' don't matter."

Amen.

....

Latest incarnation of 'Rollerball' likely just cheap thrills
February 7, 2002

Few things are more revealing of how Hollywood typically conducts business than a movie "exposé" of a cultural blight that exploits the subject matter instead of holding it up to scrutiny.

Critics cheered when the normally sober director Norman Jewison signed on to direct the original "Rollerball" in 1975, especially since William Harrison was going to adapt his semi-science fictional story, "Roll Ball Murders," for the screen. The picture depicted a 21st-century society in which violence had been outlawed but public hunger for it had not. As if a million years of evolutionary imperatives could be expunged in a generation.

Jewison was highly regarded for taking rather contrived if well-cast hokum ("In the Heat of the Night") and investing it with topical seriousness, as well as for his gentle but funny satires ("The Russians Are Coming, the Russians Are Coming"). Here was a chance to critique American sports culture, a bloated, overhyped elephant even then.

Instead, we got a brutal action movie that gave only lip service to its alleged theme.

Can we expect anything different from the likes of John McTiernan, a prototypical 1980s-'90s action director who was at the helm of the remake? Admittedly, McTiernan made his debut with a flurry of entertaining high-tech films: the relentless "Predator" (a grimly fascinating notion weakened only by some surpassingly silly action movie dialogue), the energetic and influential "Die Hard" (which launched Bruce Willis' big-screen career), and "The Hunt for Red October" (by far the best movie adaptation of the tech-heavy books by Tom Clancy).

What has McTiernan done for us lately? How does "Flight of the Intruder" (bomb), "Last Action Hero" (bomb), "Die Hard With a Vengeance" (dud), and "The 13th Warrior" (megadud) strike you? OK, so 1999's remake of "The Thomas Crown Affair" had some sparkle, but wasn't that due almost exclusively to the chemistry between the leads, Pierce Brosnan and Rene Russo?

Today, with bigger, faster athletes and superior conditioning, modern American sports are even more violent, if perhaps not as dirty, as they were in the mid-'70. And if anything, our collective appetite for the mayhem has grown at the same pace.

Sadly, don't expect much from the new "Rollerball" but cheap thrills and pretense.

....

'America's Sweethearts' slims women down once more
July 19, 2001

Forget *Vogue*. Guys like curves. Not 6-foot, 97-pound near-death experiences with designer bosoms.

It's not that the naturally skinny American female can help being thin. There's beauty in that, too. But here comes Friday's opening of "America's Sweethearts" to hammer home the message once again that the average American woman has got to slim down to willowy spindleness to attain some arbitrary ideal.

Rubbish. It's just more proof of how Madison Avenue and the fashion industry have reinforced the tendency of women to have a distorted body image. If you ask us, women are far more critical of their bodies than are men, most of whom regard the well-upholstered female form with admiration, despite propaganda to the contrary.

....

Declaration of fewer independents
November 30, 2000

The death knell was premature. Less than four years ago, when we were up to our ears in award-winning independent films, some of the more enthusiastic among us were heralding the trend as the end of mainstream movie dominance. Just as the once-mighty studio system had been toppled by ambitious filmmakers with fresh ideas.

As late as last year, *Entertainment Weekly* was, in its characteristically overheated way, declaring 1999 as "The Year That Changed Movies."

But few genuinely independent buyers and distributors even exist today, having been swallowed by corporate whales. For the first time ever, Disney subsidiary Miramax didn't buy a single movie from the Sundance Film Festival, and after the extraordinary flowering of indy films in 1996 and 1997, things have reverted to "normal."

There's plenty of potential product out there, but little of it has proven to be very good. Good or bad, no one's distributing the films to theaters anyway – outside of major metro areas.

What gives? For one thing, art house box office has taken a nosedive. According to Variety, income has fallen from $262 million (on 171 movies) in 1990 to a projected $185 million (on 250 movies) this year. That's a 31-percent decline overall, a whopping 15 percent this year alone.

One root problem is big studio ownership of once small, maneuverable indy distributors, with a boardroom mentality now firmly in place that looks for immediate impact and quick profits – the antithesis of indy construction. Most art house movies need to be moved out gradually, building word-of-mouth and momentum rather than pulled after one week if they don't light up the cash register. The infusion of studio cash also means the intrusion of studio sensibilities.

Another issue is the very definition of the independent film. What is it today? "Billy Elliot" certainly seems to quality. But does "O Brother Where Art Thou?" Many are hybrids of mainstream and "art house" fare. Some have large budgets and mainstream-like advertising resources. Others, made cheaply and hurriedly with the new technologies, reveal a declining level of artistry. Still others are so consumed with ideology that they forget to tell a story.

The long-standing identity of the art house as a place to see revivals, foreign language films, movies with mature and/or eccentric sexual themes, maverick filmmaking and seat-of-the-pants productions is slowly being eclipsed.

What does it say about us as a (pop) culture that our collective interest in foreign language film is at its lowest ebb in years?

Giant megaplexes serve to confuse matters, too, with the doubling of the nation's movie screens meaning that the big theater chains have to find enough product to fill their various cubicles? To do it, they raid the store of newly released art films. Cable venues like the Sundance Channel and the Independent Film Channel sometimes seem to fracture and deplete the audience rather than build it.

The good news, on paper, is that as big studios' specialty divisions continue to act like their parent firms, it opens the door to new small-scale distributors, like the Shooting Gallery. But right now, the mainstream apparatus hoards most of the ammo.

....

The Force compels a new generation (but not me)
January 30, 1997

A great irony attended the original "Star Wars," whose phenomenal 1977 release almost single-handedly breathed life into the moribund universe of science fiction on film – then killed it.

With high-gloss production values, the best special effects since "2001: A Space Odyssey" and an old-fashioned mythic theme, this Galactic Empires throwback to the early pulp days of the genre not only resuscitated SF movie-making, but re-invigorated (in a manner of speaking) fantasy and science fiction publishing. But while the movie's unprecedented box office success expanded the market and gave hundreds of new novelists a shot, it also effectively ended one of the most intelligent and exhilarating periods in SF literature and ensured an unending stream of adolescent comic books on screen, culminating in last year's insufferable "Independence Day.

Frankly, the allegedly revamped "Star Wars" trilogy, the first entry of which opens here Friday, looks like a big con job. For all its new/old footage and spruced-up visuals, it's basically another "director's cut" – a vanity production. George Lucas may trumpet the 20th-anniversary edition of "Star Wars" all he wants, but much of what originally fell to the cutting room floor probably belonged there. Ditto for the two sequels.

Those who've never seen "Star Wars" on the big screen doubtless will get a computer-enhanced kick out of it. The rest of us will wait for "Bladerunner II."

....

Family Films
April 7, 2000

As a group, family films have taken it on the chin from critics in recent years, not to mention legions of bored parents. The culprits: witless plots, stock characters and an undercurrent of contempt for the audience.

The irony is that some of the most intelligent and engaging movies ever made in the genre have appeared in recent years, though they are forced to compete for attention with oceans of inferior films that not only tarnish the whole category but obscure many of the gems of the past.

....

Some alternative Oscars
March 21, 1996

Herewith, our Silver Slug awards for peculiar or otherwise unusual achievements in cinema in 1995:

Best performance by a wigged-out wacko and part-time mastermind who may or may not be the Anti-Christ: Brad Pitt in "12 Monkeys."

Best performance by a Briton playing an American who looked like a Turkish brigand: Anthony Hopkins in "Nixon."

Best performance by a harbor seal touched by magic and transformed into a comely but mute brunette: Susan Lynch in "The Secret of Roan Inish."

Best performance by a certified loon surveying the world from a perch atop a Mississippi tree house: Piper Laurie in "The Grass Harp."

Best imitation of fingernails screeching down a blackboard by a singing raccoon: Jennifer Jason Leigh in "Georgia."

Best multi-threat job by a producer-director-star who lived on coffee and three hours' sleep a day for 18 months: Mel Gibson for "Braveheart."

Give him his due.

....

Some effects *are* special

I've often railed against special effects when they are allowed to dominate a film at the expense of character and story. But let's also have a kind word for special effects wizards, especially those of the pre-computer era, when it required real technical genius to create convincing effects.

Most film buffs are familiar with the master animator, director, and special effects master Ray Harryhausen (1920-2013), but not everyone recalls Linwood G. Dunn (1904-1998), a pioneering Oscar winner most notable for his work on the original "King Kong."

But Dunn worked well into the '90s, developing 3-D TV and digital film-projection techniques that have yet to be surpassed.

....

1999: Odds and Ends

"It never ceases to amaze me how British filmmakers working with such a pittance of a budget can render richly detailed, even opulent, pictures that nonetheless never sacrifice character to spectacle." – from my review of "Topsy Turvy,"

Mistaking beauty or screen presence for 'acting' has been a common failing of many a mainstream movie critic in evaluating the latest 'hot young thing.'" from my review of "Guinevere."

....

Filmmaker Duncan Parker, courtesy of Sebastian Solberg

Documentary Reviews

Documentary Reviews

If history is a guide, few theatrical motion pictures, no matter how well-made or topical, ever really changed anything. They are not designed to do it.

Documentaries offer a very different story. From pioneering filmmaker Robert J. Flaherty's seminal silent film "Nanook of the North" (1922) to such modern classics as Errol Morris's "The Thin Blue Line" (1988), Barbara Kopple's "Harlan County USA," (1976), and Frederick Wiseman's "Titicut Follies" (1967), masters of the form have changed hearts and minds.

Or at least given voice to the voiceless.

Even when a great documentary hasn't managed to bring about lasting change, the impact on our perceptions and the illumination of dark corners often has been profound. Consider Claude Lanzmann's "Shoah" (1985), Fax Bahr and George Hickenlooper's "Hearts of Darkness" (1991), Marcel Ophls's "The Sorrow and the Pity" (1969), or Eugene Jarecki's groundbreaking "Why We Fight" (2005).

Some, like Michael Wadleigh's "Woodstock" (1970), D.A. Pennebaker's "Don't Look Back" (1967), Martin Scorsese's "The Last Waltz" (1978), and Peter Davis's "Hearts and Minds" (1974) helped define an era. Others have aimed to be educational.

For their part, films like Ross McElwee's "Sherman's March" (1985) and Terry Zwigoff's "Crumb" (1994) have registered quirkiness and eccentricity at the most arresting level.

Today we are enjoying a new Golden Age of documentary filmmaking, with more talents giving themselves to the genre than ever before. Though seemingly dominated by the themes of the natural world, war, disasters, architecture and international cuisine, there is still much variety.

As a film critic I was fortunate to see many of these pictures and continue to watch them in the theater and on such platforms as Netflix.

But there's a fly in the ointment for me. I prefer documentaries that are scrupulous and journalistic. And they tend to be a rare breed. A great many documentaries speak only to the choir. Their message may be valid and their points well-taken, but the only people listening already agree.

In much the same way that contemporary talk radio in America is dominated by voices, often strident, of the Right, so too do the ranks of documentary filmmakers – with rare exceptions – appear ruled by the Left. Understandably, since documentaries have always tended to challenge the status quo.

But this is not a dialogue, or even a debate. It's a polarized exercise in rock throwing, a selective presentation of the facts and willful dismissal of those facts that don't buttress one's argument. Unalloyed stupidity also rears its nasty head, as do naivete, short-term thinking, and unabashed propaganda. More's the pity.

I'm all for expressions of righteous anger at tragedy, criminal negligence, and injustice. They serve a purpose. But a film must be truthful if it is to possess enduring power and influence.

....

'Crumb' strips away cartoonishness, reveals art
"Crumb"
September 14, 1995

There is no word in the lexicon of life adequate to describe Robert Crumb, the "underground" artist whose startling, funny, often disturbing images were a touchstone of 1960s' social/sexual satire.

"Eccentric" doesn't begin to say it. Nor does "iconoclastic."

Crumb is a visionary who, by dint of exploitation or simple distaste, enjoys only a small fraction of the dollars generated by his work - a jauntily bizarre meld of comic book grotesqueries and (painfully) honest mining of his private torment.

He is best known for three pieces: the signature "Keep on Truckin' " sketches that seemed to adorn just about everything embraced by the Counterculture; the bawdy "Fritz the Cat" strips, which developed into Ralph Bakshi's X-rated cartoon film; and his cover art for Big Brother and the Holding Company's "Cheap Thrills" record album, which sent the late Janis Joplin's career into orbit.

Crumb detested all three, at least in terms of the hassles it brought him. He was a product of the psychedelic era who considered most of its trappings a bore - especially the music. But he is generally credited with establishing the underground illustration mania inaugurated by first issues of "Zap Comix," for which he created the characters of Fritz and the bearded misanthrope Mr. Natural.

With his work now appearing in prestigious galleries, even so rarefied a critic as Robert Hughes regards Crumb as a major figure in late 20th century art, a man whose drawings reveal "lusting, suffering, crazed humanity ... in all its gargoyle-ish forms."

Director Terry Zwigoff, a collaborator of Crumb's, has produced a fascinating, darkly humorous documentary that, though decidedly weird, never ceases to intrigue. It is no surprise that Zwigoff worked in concert with avant garde filmmaker David Lynch.

Embracing not only Crumb's life, but the stunted existences of his two talented brothers, the movie explores Crumb's preoccupation with the seamy side of America's subconscious. More, it attempts to tap into the forces which shape many of society's splendid misfits.

Chiefly, the film dwells on Crumb's abhorrence of the commercially driven vacuousness of modern American culture, which to him was no culture at all, merely a lobotomized shell.

At the very peak of his fame in the early '70s, Crumb withdrew, his work turning more indulgent and (to some) hostile toward women. Although it appeared that his juvenile streak, never fully submerged, had strongly re-asserted itself, the movie suggests that more complex factors were at work.

And it draws parallels with the condemnation of much contemporary art by those who fail to comprehend the aesthetic experience. This experience requires of the viewer the ability to distinguish fiction from nonfiction, the figurative from the literal, fantasy from reality. Great art is supposed to be unsettling, and one can appreciate a work without subscribing to its ideology. Art is neither identical to reality nor isolated from it, a fact the Jesse Helmses of the world cannot grasp.

Crumb could, and perhaps still can, if he and his second wife's exile to a remote French village has not dulled his sensibilities.

In the end, Zwigoff presents us with an oddly coherent and principled man who knew instinctively that culture is a messy business. Setting the tone with classic jazz, blues and ragtime music from the early part of this century, the director limns the features and contradictions of his knockabout outcast with knowing affection.

"Crumb" uncorks a fellow who'd rather be a brain in a bottle than a person in a body, but who nonetheless took on the dealers of dullness with a vengeance. His muse left him no choice.

....

Iraq documentary a sober analysis
"No End in Sight"
September 6, 2007

The dichotomy could not be more pronounced: right-wing talk radio on one side of the divide, left-wing documentary filmmaking on the other, both competing to see who can be more shrill, more doctrinaire and, ultimately, more irrelevant. When all you do is view the world through the lens of a calcified ideology, preaching to the choir and substituting theatrics for thought, you lose the persuadable middle.

Even those on the conservative side of the battlement likely will acknowledge that "No End in Sight" is a Iraq documentary with a difference. Not to say that writer-director Charles Ferguson's movie is without a slant – the first-time filmmaker, after all, is a one-time member of that left-of-center think tank, the Brookings Institution. But compared with the gale-force windbags one hears hyperventilating on Fox News, or the shameless grandstanding and fact-twisting of a Michael Moore, this long and highly detailed dissection of how we got to where we are today in Iraq is sober, analytical and often trenchant.

Although the film makes some questionable assumptions here and there, it generally avoids guesswork and has little interest in mere provocation.

The crux of the film's argument is that the chief miscalculations of U.S. policy - the use of insufficient troop levels despite repeated warnings from senior military officers, allowing the looting of Baghdad, the crippling purge of professionals from the Iraqi government after the fall of Saddam Hussein and the disbanding of the Iraqi military (which threw 500,000 armed men into permanent unemployment) - largely created "the insurgency and chaos that engulf Iraq today."

Hindsight is impeccable, of course, and some of Ferguson's battery of interviewees clearly have an ax to grind, but if only a third of what "No End in Sight" chronicles is factual - and the evidence appears damning - it represents a breathtaking level of arrogance and naivete on the part of the Bush Administration, and mismanagement of such monumental proportions that it almost defies belief.

Distilled from 200 hours of footage, the film recapitulates events from the fall of Baghdad in 2003 to the end of 2006, featuring extensive interviews with principal actors such as former Deputy Secretary of State Richard Armitage, Gen. Jay Garner (in charge of the occupation in 2003), American soldiers and civilians on the ground, private contractors, Iraqi civilians and an array of analysts.

During World War II, the U.S. government began planning for the occupation of Germany two years in advance. According to "No End in Sight," the Bush Administration commenced discussions 60 days beforehand, often in secret, conducted by a handful of men who had no military experience, no post-war reconstruction experience and no direct expertise on the Middle East. What they did have, Ferguson argues, was ideological purity and an unassailable certitude in the correctness of their views.

During the occupation, key positions in Iraq also have been held by individuals whose lack of background and understanding of the situation are just as appalling.

"No End in Sight" grants that the administration quietly began to try to correct some of its mistakes in 2005, by which time the country was at risk of being dominated by militias, warlords, rogue cops and common criminals. Now, some analysts claim, we are far closer to the possibility of a post-withdrawal Islamo-Fascist regime like that of the Taliban in Afghanistan, but on a much larger, more aggressive scale.

More than 3,000 Americans dead, 20,000 wounded and perhaps as many as 200,000 Iraqis killed. Projections estimate the cost of the war and occupation will top $1.6 trillion. With no end in sight. Are Iraqis better off? Are we safer in the U.S.?

Ferguson, with calm but anguished insistence, utters a resounding "No."

....

Key film: Documentary an ode to craftsmanship
"Note by Note"
April 17, 2008

In art, the technical is a means to locate the human part of the equation. Just as a piano is an instrument that opens doors to the "ideal world" of the composition.

But the making of that piano! An art in itself.

In an age of mass production and often indiscriminate consumption, what is the place of objects crafted by hand? At New York's Steinway & Sons, which is to the piano what Rolls-Royce once was to the automobile, excellence can be achieved no other way.

Director Ben Niles' "Note by Note: The Making of Steinway L1037" is a documentary as harmonious as it is fascinating, an ode to craftsmanship, exacting standards and pride untouched by the impulse toward haste. Simply told, yet edited to quicken the imagination, the film, like its subject, rests at a nexus of hand, heart and mind. It's a gorgeous picture, visually and musically, amplified by comments from some of the most accomplished pianists working today as well as the vital stage-by-stage narration of the workers themselves — cabinetmakers and tuners, et al., who are a perishing breed.

Requiring a full year to make, each piano produced by Steinway is an individual composed of 12,000 parts, with 450 craftsmen and women from around the world contributing the colorations of personal commitment and technique to the Steinway method, and each transmitting hard-won skills to the next generation of artisans. Though the instrument itself, however exquisitely rendered, may be "merely" a conduit — the tool through which the pianist communicates rather than the communication itself — a great instrument enables the artist to "say" so much more.

In this arena, the soullessness of machine tooling and computer design cannot compete. Steinway makes 2,000 pianos a year; some companies in this (declining) industry extrude 100 a day. Not to say the firm does not have some accomplished competitors.

Like a Stradivarius, the Steinway piano is as unique and enriched by personality as the musicians who play them. Niles' camera follows the creation of one, Steinway concert grand, L1037, from the forest floor to the concert hall, chronicling the highly involved process of "manufacture" (which seems an inadequate word) and exploring the complex relationship between musician and instrument.

"Note by Note" was filmed in several Steinway locations: the factory, Steinway's reserved "Bank" and at private auditions wherein world-class musicians toil in the equally exacting process of selecting the piano they will buy.

At only 81 measured minutes, the documentary never ceases to engage on the visceral and intellectual levels. But in the end, the film is only partly a paean to L1037. It is at least as much a celebration of the people who have devoted themselves to the deep and abiding connection of working by hand.

Superb.

....

This 'Pearl' is a real treasure
"A Man Named Pearl"
October 11, 2007

Often used, much abused, "genius" is a word that trips all too lightly off the tongue, appended by the fashionable to the fashionable even when the talents involved are modest, the work of passing fancy. Then there is Pearl Fryar.

It is tempting to call the 67-year-old pride of Bishopville, the Phillip Simmons of topiary — the art of trimming bushes and trees into decorative forms. Like Simmons, Charleston's peerless Picasso of wrought iron, Fryar's greatest genius may reside in the way he lives his life, influencing many, delighting many more.

He is a man of parts, an old soul. Not just gifted, but open and wise. And so fascinating to watch that one almost loses sight of how skillfully made is the movie surrounding him.

"A Man Named Pearl" is a model documentary from producer-directors Scott Galloway and Brent Pierson. Shot in the spring and fall of 2005, and currently being self-distributed in American cities, this story of a North Carolina sharecropper's son who sculpted a positive outlook, as well as astounding garden creations, provides real-world inspiration for young and old. But kids, in particular, can benefit from this genuine, self-taught man's example of energy, passion, commitment and responsibility.

Fryar, who moved to the area in search of work in 1976, has never lost his sense of wonder, a quality reflected in every snip and contour of his primary tool, a gas-powered hedge trimmer.

The film is almost as deft, employing a series of sharply edited interviews with visitors, friends and townspeople that winds up being as much a profile of them as it is of Fryar. More, in a sea of pedantic, heavy-handed political documentaries, "A Man Named Pearl" offers both an effective social statement on race relations and human potential in addition to a generous portrait of Lee County — 46th among 46 S.C. counties in per-capita income — and its people.

Fryar's piece de resistance is his own 3-acre yard, featured in The New York Times, on CBS Sunday Morning and in dozens of national magazines. A (chemical-free) work in progress for 30 years, it is the meticulously tended product of someone with no horticultural training and an uncanny ability to achieve effects with shrubs and trees that the experts insist he should not be able to accomplish. Yet it is not so much a matter of bending nature to his will as it is communing with it, and finding something elegant within. No one could fail to be impressed by this "plant-whisperer's" magical but somehow comforting array of abstract shapes.

Etched in the ground, written in flowers, are his guiding principles: Love, Peace and Goodwill. As Fryar's minister, the Rev. Jerome McCray, says of the garden: "It's the one place in all of South Carolina that people can go, both black and white, and feel love."

For admiring neighbors, keeping up with the Joneses is easy; keeping up with the Fryars is another matter entirely. But they sing his praises. The media interest that Fryar's free-form topiary garden generates has helped channel much-needed tourist dollars into Bishopville and Lee County. His commissioned projects, such as those for the S.C. State Museum, have amplified the community's profile. His impact is more than economic, however. Fryar touches lives. From neighborhood kids to teachers to college students to museum curators and businesspeople, he is rightly regarded as a treasure.

Galloway and Pierson have done an exemplary job, buttressed by fine work from composer Fred Story, whose jazzy score engages throughout; from the careful editing of Greg Grzeszczak; and from J. Steven Anderson's seamless photography.

Don't miss it.

....

Revelations old news in John Lennon film
"The U.S. vs. John Lennon"
January 14, 2007

> *"People want peace so much that governments had better get out of their way and let them have it."* -- President Eisenhower, 1955

All he was saying, was give peace a chance.

And it made some people very nervous.

John Lennon was a born artist, which is to say a born maverick. Yet he did not see himself as a political provocateur, merely a citizen of the Earth who refused to be silent in the face of calamity and suicidal wrong-headedness. That he did not always choose his fellow protesters as carefully as he might meant he and wife Yoko Ono could be manipulated or exploited by extremists whose notion of revolution wasn't quite as benign as theirs.

"The U.S. vs. John Lennon," a documentary time capsule of an era, mines much in the way of fascinating archival footage. Up to a point, it also is a useful riposte to the current conservative climate's dismissive take on the anti-war movement of the late 1960s and early '70s. But writers-directors David Leaf and John Scheinfeld can be just as overzealous, blindly ideological and paranoid as elements of the U.S. government – wary of Lennon's influence on young American voters during the 1972 Nixon re-election campaign – in trying to have him deported as an "undesirable alien."

Look at whom the filmmakers chose to interview. The picture is so weighted to the point of view of aging, unreconstructed ex-radicals and such showboating "journalists" as Geraldo Rivera that the movie depletes its own potency with tired propaganda. Only the presence of moderating voices (Walter Cronkite, Carl Bernstein) keep the movie from going completely off the deep end.

When the only opposing view comes from an extremist of the far Right, G. Gordon Liddy, it is clear the filmmakers have no interest in anything but beating a dead horse. For heaven's sake, we know the Nixon administration's inner circle had an "enemy's list" that featured Lennon's name prominently. We know J. Edgar Hoover's FBI conducted illegal wiretaps and monitored Lennon's movements. We know the U.S. Naturalization and Immigration Service's drive to have Lennon expelled from a nation he had come to love, for all the problems he sang and spoke about.

We also know there is a dark undercurrent of intolerance, chauvinism and arrogance in these United States. Lennon stood up to those forces, but he was intelligent enough to know that no nation has a corner on such "attributes."

These supposed revelations are very old news indeed.

The movie is strongest when it drops its Marxist rhetoric, stops sermonizing to the true believer and renders an elegy for the late Beatle, who, for whatever else one thinks of him, was a man of conviction and principle, as well as an enormous talent.

But the chief aim of the movie is to draw a parallel between the divisive Vietnam experience and the Bush administration's war on terror. There are parallels and significant differences. Yet Leaf and Scheinfeld do not seem to care about subtleties or the complexities of situations. All is drawn in terms of black and white, victim and victimizer. They succumb to exactly the kind of willful naivete of which leaders of the anti-Vietnam War movement so often were accused, and the more thoughtful ones fought to dispel.

Agree with him or not, Lennon was engaged with the world. His chroniclers are engaged with their own ancient feud.

....

Is it a little warm in here to you?
"An Inconvenient Truth"
June 22, 2006

A classic Gahan Wilson cartoon of the late 1960s depicts a senator's aide entering his boss' office with the Washington, D.C., skyline seen through a window. The view is yellowed and hazy, as if a great veil of pollution were washing over the city and the nation it represents. Both men are wearing gas masks.

"Sorry to bother you, Senator," says the aide, gesturing to unseen visitors in the waiting room. "It's some more of those crackpot conservationists to see you."

Funny, yes, and depressing. The exasperating thing is that there are those who still dismiss the possibilities of ecological damage - whether gradual degradation or sudden calamity - and our role in it. Of course, baseless claims of an imminent doomsday by eco-extremists have had something to do with that.

Many ardent, well-meaning environmentalists have been their own worst enemies, making sweeping pronouncements for which there was precious little concrete science. Which just plays into the hands of those who would label them as fringe alarmists or assign them that tart epithet, "tree-huggers." Never mind that in most of humanity's history on the planet, so-called alarmists often have been proven right. Eventually.

There's no mistaking the point of view championed by "An Inconvenient Truth," Davis Guggenheim's documentary on global warming featuring former vice president and Democratic presidential candidate Al Gore. In direct, unhysterical language, the film offers graphic evidence of the effects of global warming, from glacial retreat that will imperil water supplies for an estimated 40 percent of the world's population to the paradox of climate change that simultaneously creates more flooding and increased drought.

Proponents of the theory of global warming insist we should listen to the scientists, not the politicians (notwithstanding their standard-bearer, Gore). Sound advice. But whose scientists? The ones funded by Greenpeace? By Exxon Mobil? By the U.S. government?

That point increasingly seems moot. In his globe-hopping road show, which provided the bulk of footage for the movie, Gore notes that of the 928 peer-reviewed scientific articles published on global warming by the time of the filming, zero percent have disagreed with the consensus conclusion that human activity is accelerating the production of greenhouses gases such as carbon dioxide and that global warming is a fact, not a "liberal hoax." There is also little disagreement that a burgeoning human population will make matters worse if action is not taken.

The film is persuasive in many particulars, but somewhat less successful when it makes (very) long-term extrapolations of the data and presents them as incontrovertible. The further one projects in time, the more murky the conclusions.

Still, whatever happened to the basic concept of erring on the side of caution? Does it matter, in the end, if environmental havoc is strictly a matter of cyclical natural processes or one exacerbated by the consequences of human activity?

Well, yes, if changing our behavior changes the outcome.

The problem with the film is not its information, its warnings or its advice. It's the messenger. That Gore is sincere seems likely, even if the film occasionally plays like a pre-emptive campaign commercial. He is also much less stiff and dour than he was on the campaign trail. But since bedrock opponents of Gore and serious environmental policy change are unlikely to see the film or be swayed, "An Inconvenient Truth" does wind up preaching to the choir. The filmmakers' hope is that many of the members of that choir are young people whose opinions are not yet calcified by self-interest and that some skeptics will give the film the benefit of the doubt and eventually join the chorus.

Is there the political will to intervene, to reverse course? Not as long as short-term economic thinking prevails. And not, suggests Gore, as long as we continue to couch the issue in terms of having to decide between the environment and the economy. Of course, the Clinton-Gore administration's record on the environment wasn't so sterling either. Government's economic mantra of "growth, growth, growth" continues to be at war with reality as expressed by Edward Abbey: "Unrestrained growth is the philosophy of the cancer cell." But powerful forces are arrayed, as always, to defend the status quo.

To its credit, "An Inconvenient Truth" offers more than compelling visuals and empty platitudes; it suggests ways in which we can make a start. But first, the film insists, a "moral majority" must pull its collective head out of the sand.

....

Moore masses assault on the Powers That Be citadel
"Fahrenheit 9/11" and "The Big One"
June 24, 2004

Michael Moore is making an art form of preaching to the choir. But like all art, appreciation is in the eye of the beholder. And not everyone will be receptive to the sermon.

Those predisposed to agree with his point of view on the Bush administration and the war in Iraq undoubtedly will hail "Fahrenheit 9/11" as indisputable proof of, as Al Franken might say, lies and the lying liars who tell them. Those who dismiss the incendiary documentary filmmaker as a self-appointed gadfly and left-wing polemicist probably won't go to see the film in the first place.

So, is it agitprop or a shot of truth serum? Perhaps a bit of both. Moore does detonate a fusillade of seemingly damning data on what he insists is back-room skullduggery and the folly of our campaign in Iraq. He also managed to have shot (or acquired from freelancers) footage of interviews with American soldiers on the ground in Iraq that you probably won't see on the evening news. Their attitudes were, shall we say, less than favorable toward U.S. policy, feelings echoed by some who returned home from a tour disillusioned.

But as usual, Moore undercuts his own arguments with selective references and unsubstantiated allegations. Accusations are not facts. Neither are feelings. He bombards us with so much material that it is hard to process one helping of it before the next one lands at our feet. Moore also spends as much time with emotional appeals – sometimes crossing the line by exploiting one mother's grief – than in methodically assembling his evidence.

That said, some of this evidence is hard to wave away. It is a matter of record. As is the hardline ideology of men such as Secretary of Defense Donald Rumsfeld and his deputy

Paul Wolfowitz. Maybe, as many others have accused, the neo-cons harbored dreams of an Iraqi invasion and Saddam Hussein's overthrow long before the events of 9/11. And maybe the motivations weren't so pure. But where's the proof?

Nor is there any secret about the Bush family's ties to the oil industry, to the Saudi royal family, or to companies like the mega-contractor Halliburton. But it is preposterous to blame decades of frequently errant U.S. policy on one family. And, frankly, there is very little here that even casual readers of a daily newspaper don't already know.

That said, Moore's screed nails its targets here and there, especially as regards political expediency, class schisms, the exercise of power, and the politician's favorite sport: saying one thing and doing another.

There is plenty of blame to go around. But Moore seems to want to absolve the American people of all responsibility, of any culpability in the conduct of the nation's affairs. It's all Big Business and the Administration. Matters aren't quite so simple.

To be sure, some of the information he juxtaposes is very unsettling, and far too detailed to recount here. Some of it is wryly funny. Some makes the blood boil in outrage. Some fires apprehension, not least over the "with-us-or-against-us" ethic of those who decry any dissent as unpatriotic or, worse, traitorous. If soldiers have died for centuries in foreign lands to protect our freedoms, does it not make a mockery of their sacrifice to fail to exercise those freedoms?

Yes, we were attacked. But not, Moore says, by Iraq. It should be added that he does not quibble with the necessity of Afghanistan, but rather points the finger at Saudi Arabia. And Bush. Moore's allusion to Ray Bradbury's "Fahrenheit 451" (the temperature at which paper burns) is witty, if characteristically overheated.

Do we need people like Moore? Absolutely. But his muckraking is questionable, his actual filmmaking techniques no better than second-rate. And he appears to go into every project with his mouth open and his mind closed, wielding a battery of preconceived opinions. Whether or not you agree with him, that's troubling. Then again, Moore doesn't claim even a semblance of journalistic impartiality.

As was the case with his "The Big One," fine points don't appear to interest Moore. In that docu, he is filled with sanctimonious disdain for all corporate creatures above the level of parking lot attendant. In city after city, in between book signings and the dispensing of meaningless generalities to like-thinking audiences (the only folks really worth his time), his impromptu stormings of the walls of Big Business are repelled by those who insulate the management suite.

What kind of reception do you expect when you barge into a company unannounced, camera crew in tow, intent on humiliating the poor sacrificial lambs of the resident security, public relations and human resources departments?

With an arrogance few CEOs could really afford, Moore dismisses such people as unimportant functionaries, easy targets for the (scattershot) public wrath. But they're also human beings caught between. Think Moore cares? Hardly. When he can't get at the big boys and girls who run the show, he takes it out on the small fry. And in mercilessly derisive fashion.

Moore styles himself as the underdog, a guy with whom the workaday American citizen can identify. A lot of people apparently believe it. There's his media guide for the book signing in Milwaukee who says, without a trace of irony, "We're not New York or Los Angeles, so we tend not to get the big celebrities here. It's more people who don't take themselves too seriously, like Michael."

Naturally, this is said into a camera that Moore's standing behind.

Right. Soul of modesty and all that. Isn't he just great.

Where "Roger and Me" was a howl of outrage that succeeded despite its admittedly one-sided muckraking, "The Big One" (whose title refers to the how Moore would rechristen the U.S.) is a misshapen and frequently misleading diatribe which, appallingly, never really explores the problems its director carps about. Its astringency is only skin deep.

Still, it should be said that Moore is at least putting these matters on the table in a public way. If only he had brought some genuine reportage to the fray, and not invested so much footage in the film's least appealing aspect – himself.

Self-involvement, like gluttony, is not a secret vice.

....

'Why We Fight' examines military-industrial complex
"Why We Fight"
April 27, 2006

Are we, as a species, doomed to war?

Don't expect an answer to this larger philosophical question in Eugene Jarecki's trenchant but slanted documentary "Why We Fight." The focus is far more localized, and urgent, with an emphasis on the tug-of-war between America's commitment to democracy and the ways in which capitalism can undermine it.

Namely, a Military-Industrial Complex run amok. Yes, that same conjunction of "unwarranted influence" by the military, industry and Congress that outgoing President Eisenhower cautioned against in his farewell address in 1961. Add to this nexus a fourth player: think tanks and their unelected influence peddlers.

Clearly, says Jarecki, some companies are "making a killing." With a defense budget at three-quarters of a trillion dollars, one observer is heard to remark, "When war is that profitable, you're going to see more of it."

Are we a more militaristic nation than we want to believe? Jarecki clearly draws the line in the sand: The political right views the M-I Complex as a machine necessary for our survival in a changing world; the left believes it's a direct and immediate threat to democracy.

Named after the series of short propaganda films made during World War II by Hollywood director Frank Capra, "Why We Fight" examines a half-century of military conflicts and asks why the complex has, by Jarecki's reckoning, become "the savings and loan of a government system whose survival depends on an Orwellian state of constant war."

Jarecki is keen to demonstrate that our leaders are out of touch with the populace at large. Apart from pundits and policymakers, he interviews the average man and woman in the street about the conflict in Iraq, and gets a more diverse array of answers.

Jarecki makes a persuasive case, for the most part, but his interpretation is unambiguously ideological, weighted very heavily to the left despite nods to an equally ideological conservative point of view on Iraq from such neocons as Richard Perle and William Kristol.

One of the few moderate views comes from Sen. John McCain, who nonetheless believes Ike's fears have come to pass, that too many in Congress are far too beholden to the Military-Industrial Complex. Military contracts are dispersed throughout the 50 states, virtually guaranteeing supportive politicians who are unwilling to upset constituents.

We see American foreign policy evolve from President Kennedy to the second President Bush, and the manner in which militarism has expanded, initially as a response to communism and now due to the war on terror.

Unlike Errol Morris and his considerably more complex "The Fog of War," Jarecki spends much of the film preaching to the choir. And however cogently presented, there is little that is original here.

The director trots out the usual (unsettling) suspects: the history of American interventionism; well-worn critiques of the Vietnam War; the U.S. imposition of the Shah on Iran and the groundwork it laid for unrest; how intelligence is taken out of context to justify questionable decisions; the Paul Wolfowitz-Dick Cheney vision of a transformed Middle East; the U.S. as the New Rome, pursuing an imperial agenda ("The country that must be obeyed ... Spreading democracy at the point of a bayonet"); how various presidential administrations attempt to dupe the press, control the flow of information and dominate the debate; how today's demon (Saddam Hussein) was yesterday's friend; how oil drives the military machine; the basic architecture of how the Pentagon procures weapons; and even George Washington's warning against the concept of keeping standing armies (especially the kind needed to prop up a vast, overextended empire).

Jarecki doesn't help his argument by having Gore Vidal speculate on the "real" reasons we dropped the atomic bombs on Japan (to intimidate Stalin), but he's at his best when channeling comment (not least by Eisenhower) on the ultimate cost of the war machine in draining away immense sums from the nation's more pressing needs.

While Jarecki's assessment of the toll taken on the American political and social landscape seems sound, it's too simplistic to insist that the whole reason we fight is just to sustain the weapons industry and the jobs it creates. Jarecki stitches the film's wide-ranging concerns together with three separate stories: the experiences of two stealth fighter pilots who fired the opening shots of the Iraq war; the anguish of a retired New York City policeman and Vietnam War vet who lost his son in the World Trade Center on 9/11; and a young man joining the Army after the death of his mother.

Thoughtful and depressing, with many of its points underscored by recent revelations, "Why We Fight" would have been stronger still if less uniformly ideological.

....

Enthralling 'Murderball' a life-reaffirming film
"Murderball"
July 28, 2005

It's "Mad Max" in a wheelchair. No helmets, no elbow pads.

Fevered competition and down-to-the-wire suspense melds with laughter, love and camaraderie in "Murderball," a spirited documentary from co-directors Henry-Alex Rubin and Dana Adam Shapiro.

Inspiring and emotionally charged, yet seldom slipping into melodramatics, this chronicle of quadriplegic rugby, its players and their families is a prime example of how the documentary form can take images that are sometimes difficult to watch and make them riveting.

The movie takes us from the gyms of America to the Wheelchair Rugby World Championships in Sweden to the Olympic arena in Athens, Greece, where the Paralympic Games took place side by side with the 2004 Olympic Games.

"You can't really market 'Murderball' to corporate sponsors," says one of the game's chief stars, U.S. team member and committed jock Mark Zupan. "So we changed the name to quad rugby."

Centering on the U.S. team, which had dominated the game for a decade going into 2004's Paralympics, and its Canadian counterparts, when the film is not obliterating stereotypes it is playing as engagingly as any sports documentary. The difference is that when we go on the court or behind the scenes with Zupan & Co. it's quite a different experience from seeing inside the lives of millionaire pro athletes who sit out weeks with a sprained pinky.

These are, if you'll pardon the expression, stand-up guys. Is their sport macho and even a bit reckless? Yeah. What of it?

Based on an original article by Shapiro, "Murderball" is no dippy disease-of-the-week telefilm or plucking at the heartstrings. It's a direct, unflinching picture about family, sex, retribution, honor, skill, and love's victory over loss. More, it treats its subjects as human beings - in full - with all the quirks and foibles (and weird practical jokes) that go with the condition.

We're told how each of these men were hurt, glimpse their passages from anger to reality check to adaptation, see how families and lovers (old and new) have coped, and been enriched.

The strong-willed, intimidating Zupan hovers above the fray. Tough on and off the playing surface (usually, the approximate size of a basketball court), he also reveals another side as U.S. spokesman for his sport, which he shares with the public as well with the newly paralyzed.

The movie won the Documentary Audience Award and a Special Jury Prize for Editing at the 2005 Sundance Film Festival. In some ways, it is the nonfiction equivalent of such memorable feature films as "The Men" (1950) and "The Waterdance" (1992), which plumbed the capabilities of quadriplegics and paraplegics, as well as their limitations.

But it is also about their rousing full-contact sport, no quarter asked, a game played by gladiators in custom-made chariots. Only it's not a battle to the death. It's a chance to reaffirm life.

....

Scaling humanity's summit
"Everest"
July 9, 1998

Breathtaking, magical, spellbinding, moving. Pick your adjective, "Everest" beggars them all.

Documentary filmmaker David Breashears' monument to the daring and madness of the mountain climber's art would be an extraordinary experience on a conventional movie screen. On the six-story-high tableau at the IMAX Discovery Theater in Myrtle Beach, it is astonishing.

To say "It puts you there" is wholly inadequate. You can almost feel the bite of the wind, the cracking of the crevasses, the stark and forbidding beauty of the Himalayas. Yet, amid this profound desolation, human scale is not lost.

Mount Everest, at 29,028 feet the highest peak on earth, represents not only the top of the world, but at least one measure of the apex of human achievement. And endurance.

All but bereft of oxygen, scoured by 80-mph winds and frozen by temperatures that easily exceed 100 below zero, Everest can be a citadel of death for even the most accomplished climber, as events of May 10, 1996, grimly attest.

On that day, more than 23 people from four expeditions left High Camp to ascend the summit. Trapped by a sudden and unexpected storm of fearsome intensity, eight died. This harrowing story, vividly told in Jon Krakauer's best-selling book "Into Thin Air," gains startling immediacy in "Everest," which deals in part with the tragedy (and survivors' muted response) without dwelling on the horror of it.

The documentary almost didn't happen. Breashears and his team of 11 climbers and 16 Sherpas, huddled at Camp II, postponed the final leg of their climb when the storm set in. Krakauer radioed Breashears with the news of those stranded 7,000 feet above, blinded by darkness and whipping snow. Breashears coordinated a rescue attempt with the 10 other teams spread out on the mountain. Without hesitation, oxygen canisters and other supplies destined for the "Everest" team's ascent were turned over to the rescue effort, which could have signaled the end to Breashears' climb and to the most ambitious film of his career.

Most could not be reached in time. But one man earlier given up for dead - Beck Weathers - was saved, albeit at the cost of his hands.

On May 22, exhausted and saddened, the "Everest" expedition summoned the resolve to undertake the final 10-hour, 3,000-foot push to the summit, under clear skies. The team took the South Col route to the crest, the same approach used by Sir Edmund Hillary and Tenzing Norgay in 1953.

Just before 11 a.m., Breashears and Ed Viesturs – the scientist-climber and newlywed on whom the movie largely pivots – took the last, agonizing, triumphant steps to the top, followed shortly by Tenzing's son Jamling Norgay, Spanish climber Araceli Segarra, cinematographer Robert Schauer and five Sherpas. A purist, Viesturs did it sans oxygen bottle.

As he passed them by, Breashears refused to film the bodies of those who perished, so high on the mountain that recovery - even by helicopter - remains impossible. Their deaths would not be exploited.

Breashears shot three minutes of incomparable footage from the summit, a fitting bookend to the ghostly apparition of Katmandu, Tibet's storied capital city, captured in the early scenes.

From a purely logistical standpoint the challenges were daunting. Everest is orders of magnitude more demanding than any other ascent - with a 30-mile hike just to reach Base Camp - and far less forgiving for filmmakers. The team spent five weeks at 22,000 feet simply to acclimatize to the altitude.

Breashears, a skilled climber and winner of four Emmys, had shot the dazzling climbing sequences for the feature films "Cliffhanger" and "Seven Years in Tibet." In 1985, he became the first American to scale Everest twice, and has participated in nine previous filming expeditions on three sides of the mountain - but never with IMAX gear.

Shooting on 65mm large-format film stock in five-pound rolls (which expended themselves in a scant 90 seconds), and with an IMAX camera only slightly less hefty than the customary 70-pound weight, it was a miracle the film was completed. And, perhaps, sheer insanity that it was attempted. Just changing rolls in sub-zero weather was an ordeal.

In climbing, momentum is crucial. Breashears thus risked demoralizing his own team with frequent, and often dangerous, stops to secure the most awe-inducing shots.

The principal narrator of "Everest" is actor Liam Neeson, but voice-overs by Breashears, Viesturs, Segarra and Norgay contribute immensely to our appreciation of the picture while underscoring the personal dimension of the adventure. Their words, and Breashears' images, are augmented by a stirring score.

Made for a modest $6 million, the 44-minute film was produced by Greg MacGillivray, maker of more than 20 IMAX pictures, who first approached Breashears with the idea in 1994. One only wishes it were longer, much longer.

At those times when one despairs of the avarice, cruelty and unfathomable stupidity of the human species, it is gratifying to remember those other things of which we are capable: great courage and sacrifice, even in foolhardy endeavors; astounding perseverance; and a willingness to wager our lives on a grand obsession.

Because it's there? Yes, but also because we're here.

"Everest" is a poem to this spirit, and a film for the ages.

....

'Kurt and Courtney:' Nevermind
"Kurt and Courtney"
June 25, 1998

The drab, banal opening sequences of Nick Broomfield's "Kurt and Courtney" herald a drab, mostly banal documentary, one which spends most of its time trafficking in one-sided innuendo.

If one is not a devotee of the former first couple of alternative rock, the late Nirvana singer Kurt Cobain and his wife, Hole's Courtney Love, the film will hold no more interest than any other tabloid tale of dysfunctional families and a gifted artist whose life is cut short.

Even aficionados may object to the addled assembly of the picture, the sloppy reportage, and the running freak show that accompanies it.

"Sid and Nancy" it ain't. Or "Crumb." Neither, for that matter, is it "Heidi Fleiss: Hollywood Madam," one of the maverick filmmaker's earlier profiles.

Armed with chutzpah and a store of scattershot, half-formed questions, Broomfield set for himself the task of documenting Cobain's legacy, following the singer's apparent suicide in April, 1994. But "Kurt and Courtney" is less about what Cobain and his music meant to rock and to Nirvana's legions of fans than it is a crude dissection of his marriage to Love.

It's also a hatchet job that Love unwittingly participates in by refusing to grant Broomfield an audience, and by her threats, legal and otherwise, to stop the making of the movie, given its less-than-flattering depiction of her. For a time it worked. Last January, "Kurt and Courtney" was pulled, abruptly if not mysteriously, from its slot at the

Sundance Film Festival due chiefly to pressure from Love and her lawyers.

Love comes off as a chronically violent, doped-up groupie who may have exploited Cobain from the start, a would-be Svengali who wooed and married him (in time-tested fashion) to ride his gravy train and/or to kick-start her own career. Hole, which became one of the top bands of the Grunge movement, was strictly small time until Love and Cobain became entwined. Disagreeable maybe, but not sinister.

Love, later reconfigured as a darling of Hollywood and the fashion mags, also is seen as every bit as unstable as her husband, a heroin addict wracked by depression and an inability to support the burdens of fame.

Although many questions remain about Cobain's death – why, for example, was the shotgun with which he presumably took his life devoid of fingerprints? – Broomfield tries but does not succeed in offering hard evidence that Cobain was murdered, and that Love may have had a hand in it.

Broomfield solicits a lot of circumstantial "testimony" that, on the surface, may seem damning, but his sources don't fill the viewer with a great deal of confidence. Save for a loving aunt, and Cobain's supposed "best friend," both of whom discount the possibility of murder, the director either fails or never troubles himself to speak with those who knew Cobain best.

Instead, as the movie drones on and on, we hear repeatedly from Love's estranged father, Hank Harrison, who just happens to have cashed in on the tragedy by writing two books on Kurt and Courtney, and who claims Cobain wanted a divorce; from a detective formerly in Love's employ who believes she is the architect of Cobain's demise; from a one-time nanny who briefly cared for the couple's daughter and recalls Love's preoccupation with Cobain's will shortly before his death; from a certifiable loon called El Duce who blithely insists Love offered him $50,000 to "whack" her husband; and from various other unsavory players with an axe to grind.

Bloomfield also doubts their veracity, and peppers the film with some rather feeble disclaimers. But the show must go on.

What of Love's defenders? We never hear from them. Everybody in the film pretty much agrees she is a manipulative and potentially dangerous witch, now a multi-millionaire, whom one doesn't dare cross.

It's hardly a revelation that Cobain and Love were oil and water together, one seduced by lucre, the other repelled by it. Nor is it news that Love is an exceptionally ambitious woman, perhaps ruthlessly so. But in today's star-driven entertainment culture, this is a badge of honor, not a crime. Shuttled between family, friends and foster parents, much like Cobain, and left to fend for herself, it's small wonder the rebellious Love's personal ethics became, well, elastic.

What is interesting about "Kurt and Courtney" is what the film reveals about the entertainment industry's growing stranglehold on access to its stars, its paranoid control of information, and how entertainment journalists, not just the stalkarazzi, are compelled to greater and more distasteful extremes in an effort to penetrate the fortress and connect with these insulated public figures.

This, and how our collective infatuation with these godlings lifts them to a undeservedly loftier plane, where the rules don't apply.

One of the most telling scenes take place near the close. Love, who has spared no expense to suppress the movie's completion and distribution, is the guest speaker at, of all things, an American Civil Liberties Union dinner extolling free speech. But when Broomfield takes the stage (uninvited) to accuse her of hypocrisy, he is summarily removed by the ACLU's executive director, a Love chum.

It is this otherwise flaccid film's best, most honest moment.

....

'Hoop Dreams' scores slam dunk
"Hoop Dreams"
January 19, 1995

Yesterday's news.

That's what young hopefuls quickly become if they fail to produce in the mechanistic big business of sports, which simultaneously inspires and exploits the athletes on whose fantasies it feeds. This frequently reprehensible but deeply entrenched system is at the core of "Hoop Dreams," a remarkably intimate, honest, revealing documentary from filmmakers Steve James, Peter Gilbert, and Frederick Marx.

It is also an absolutely riveting glimpse into the lives of two black Chicago families whose sons experience a roller coaster ride of triumphs and reversals.

The film is the product of six years' work by director James and his fellow producers, who tracked the odyssey of two young basketball players, Arthur Agee and William Gates, from their street corner heroics through high school and the beginning of college.

As players with potential, Agee and Gates are courted by coaches even in adolescence, which shows just how far the win-or-perish imperative now reaches into the schools.

Yet by now, the meat-market mentality of recruiting and the ready disposability of athletes is well-known, as is the morass of ghetto experience. "Hoop Dreams" also shows the other side: how insufficient motivation, poor judgment and irrevocable decisions (babies having babies, for one) not only can sabotage youngsters at risk but erode the bulwark of family support.

"Hoop Dreams" exposes the raw nerve of painful social realities many prefer to dismiss. On occasion, it is also (unavoidably) invasive. One wonders from time to time how the presence of the camera over so lengthy a period influenced behavior and added to the intense pressure felt by these kids.

But from the point of view of pure storytelling, this true-life chronicle owns all the elements of great fictional drama, with a full complement of joy, tragedy, humor and heartbreak. Not to mention enough twists of fate to keep audiences in suspense until the final minute.

Don't put off by its three-hour length. The film seems half that long, and rarely falters

This is not merely one of the finest documentaries of the year; it is one of the finest ever made, and a worthy Oscar contender.

Acknowlegements

And with profound thanks to...

The Actors
Charlton Heston, Barbra Streisand, Mel Gibson, John Travolta, Jodie Foster, Kevin Costner, Vanessa Redgrave, Tommy Lee Jones, Lily Tomlin, Hal Holbrook, Leslie Caron, Malcolm McDowell, Jeff Daniels, Halle Berry, Martin Landau, William Shatner, Amy Adams, Dennis Hopper, Robert Wagner, Peter Fonda, Kate Nelligan, Tom Wilkinson, Natasha Richardson, Ossie Davis and Ruby Dee, Michael York, Ryan Gosling, Rachel McAdams, Aaron Eckhart, Carl Reiner, Amanda Seyfried, Channing Tatum, Maria Bello, Danny Aiello, Virginia Madsen, Raymond Burr, Ray Liotta, LeVar Burton, Blythe Danner, George Kennedy, Pat Hingle, Kyle MacLachlan, Dennis Haysbert, Linus Roache, Dakota Fanning, Corbin Bernsen, Lynn Redgrave, Tim Conway, Tom Berenger, Kim Delaney, Corin Redgrave, Aidan Quinn, Beth Grant, Thomas Gibson, Campbell Scott, Peter Firth, Sally Pressman, Will Patton, Pat Paulsen, Elsa Raven, Michael Emerson and Carrie Preston, George Takei, Nick Searcy, Robin Curtis, James Doohan, Dreya Webber, Tony LoBianco, Noble Willingham, Mehki Pfeiffer, Rodney Rogers and Sharon Graci, Kimberly Elise, Tom Sullivan, John DeLancie, Anthony James, O'Neal Compton, Sylvia Jefferies, Orlando Jones, Jason Scott Lee, Chris Weatherhead and Clarence Felder, et al.

The Directors
John Sayles, Lasse Hallstrom, Robert Wise, Milos Forman, Anthony Minghella, Oliver Stone, Julie Dash, Ray Harryhausen, Michael Apted, Nick Cassavetes, John Landis, Leon Gast, Irwin Winkler, Héctor Carré, Tim Blake Nelson, Henry Jaglom, Keva Rosenfield, Harry Shearer, Bill Plympton, Chris Munch, Rick Bieber, Ned Fair, Michael Givens, John Reynolds, Brad Jayne, Esther Bell, Josh and Jonas Pate, Martin Bell, Andrew Chiaramonte, Simcha Jacobovici, George Hickenlooper, Charlie Matthau, Will Geiger, Vanessa Middleton, Daniel MacIvor, Elizabeth Janeway, Stephen Sommers, Kevin Meyer, Nick Smith, Peter Care, et al.

The Writers (some of whom also direct and act)
Nicholas Meyer, Victor Nunez, John Sayles, Guillermo Arriaga, Leonard Maltin, Ross McIlwee, Ray McKinnon, Tony Bill, Randall Wallace, Dane Krogman, Michael Guillen, Sharon Jungreis Bowers, Margaret Ford, Marcia Rhea, Greg Pincus, Rose Tomlin, Jackie K. Cooper, Jamie Linden, et al.

... who gave of their time and experiences.

And with a special thanks reserved for two old friends:

Steve Rhea, incomparable location scout and manager who, within the bounds of his responsibilities and contractual agreements, was my ever-reliable "Deep Throat" in providing key information that helped enable my coverage of the Charleston area and state film industry – when everyone else was mum.

Cara White, pivotal film publicist and frequent interview enabler, who singlehandedly disproved the notion beloved of film critics that movie and TV publicists are on hand mainly to keep reporters at arm's length. I was honored to have her write this book's Foreword.

Thanks, too, for the inestimable aid of movie photo maven Jerry Murbach of Doctor Macro fame (www.doctormacro.com).

With kudos to formatter and book designer **Jules Bond** for her skill and artistry, and to stenographer extraordinaire **J.E. Elliott**, whose early transcribing assistance was invaluable.

This is not to forget the former Betsy Moye (who gave me the job), colleagues Fred Smith and the late Frank Jarrell (the duo with whom I shared the movie reviewer post in the beginning); the many layout artists and copy editors for the *Post and Courier* who gave my stories visual pizzaz (and caught my errors); the late, lamented Southeastern Film Critics Circle; local film industry pros Peter and Marjory Wentworth, Ken and Patsy French, Margaret Mullins and Richard Futch, Arthur Howe, Frank Cossa, Monica and Evelyn Brady; art house theater owners Jeff Poole (Stage One Cinema); George and Christine Finnan (The Roxy); Marcie and Mike Marzluff, Mike Furlinger and Paul Brown (The Terrace); Jim Gould (the South Windermere Twin); and a host of equally accommodating multiplex theatre managers, not least the ever-affable Barbara Barnes and Glenn Burns, among the many who let me slip onto the theater late night for previews of the weekend's opening films; film festival mavens Anna Krauth Ballinger, Hunter Todd, Giovanna de Luca, Summer and Brian Peacher, and all those tireless Atlanta-based movie studio PR reps who poured indispensable press kits and screening offers into my lap.

And last, but certainly not least, to booker **Jeff Jacobs**, who ushered so many great independent films into Charleston, and to film producer **Leigh Murray**, with whom I have had so many edifying conversations on movies and the movie business.

Thank you all. *Sine qua non.*

– Bill Thompson

In closing: Author's notes.

It probably goes without saying that if I were compiling my personal all-time best-of list of movies today – my original one was assembled in 1999 – there would be quite a few inclusions and a corresponding number of films regrettably pushed out.

All the reviews I wrote originally were accompanied by bylines and the "star" ratings so common during the time. I have dispensed with the former because authorship is obvious, and with the latter because I always believed that the review itself should be sufficient for readers to grasp the critic's take on a movie's merit, or lack of same. Star ratings are eye-catching and beloved of editors, but superfluous.

From time to time you may note that I employ the old-school editorial "we" in giving my opinion on something. Aside from the Intro to this book (and what you're reading now), I've never liked using the word "I" in my writing. If "we" sounds pompous to some, "I" to me sounds more pretentious, even presumptuous. Anyway, don't let it throw you.

Just one lament: My grand plan to have a montage of great movie stills from the 1930s and 1940s illustrating each chapter fell apart due to copyright issues and the refusal of key studios' licensing departments to respond to my reprint requests, for which I would have happily paid any fees. Ah, well. Such are the travails of small city media members, who grow accustomed to being ignored – except when studios *want* publicity. But it is churlish to go on with this, so I'll just let it rest.

To all of those who read these pieces when originally published, my heartfelt thanks. To all those reading them now, the same.

PHOTO CREDITS

The Interviews: Leslie Caron, courtesy of Plume/Penguin Books
International Film Reviews: Bruno Ganz in "Wings of Desire," courtesy of the Wenders Foundation
Documentaries Reviews: Filmmaker Duncan Parker, courtesy of Sebastian Solberg
Back cover author photo: Courtesy of Jonathan Boncek
Inside author photo: Courtesy of the Charleston Post and Courier and Wade Spees
Terrace Theatre lobby: Photo by Bill Thompson
All photos unless otherwise noted are in the Public Domain

www.ingramcontent.com/pod-product-compliance
Lightning Source LLC
Chambersburg PA
CBHW042123100526
44587CB00026B/4165